The Shake 'n Bake Sergeant

Jerry S. Horton

Order this book at www.amazon.com

or order a signed copy at

www.shakenbakesergeant.com

email: jerryshorton@aol.com

ISBN 10: 1453770275

ISBN 13: 9781453770276

for more information

contact

Jerry S. Horton

email: jerryshorton@aol.com

Edition: September 2018

Preface

The trip was a private getaway. We had been working continuously for fifteen years. I had been running a fifty-person computer company. These years had been tough. At the start I had not realized the immense difficulties I would encounter when I decided to quit my job, mortgage the house and start a business in the basement.

I had struggled to keep the business alive on small cash flows for most of those years. I had been sued three times . . . and survived. I had suffered the tragic loss of our chief software designer and friend, Wai Yu. On a fishing trip to Canada with Terry—my marketing director—and me, Wai drowned. His loss was devastating both personally and to the company. Due to sheer hard work and persistence, the company recovered and was now doing well. It was time to take a break.

As usual, arriving at the airport early and, after check-in, I wandered over to the bookstore to find something to read during our three-hour flight to Ft. Myers. I liked action/adventure and history books, so I perused the shelves to find my kind of book. I bought a book called *The Teams: The Story of the Army Special Forces in Vietnam.*

Once I boarded the plane, I tossed the book onto my seat, taking my time stowing the gear. While the cabin attendants prepared for takeoff, I settled in and started reading. It was interesting reading. Each chapter was written by a different author. Many men's war experiences were described. About three-quarters of the way through the book I came upon a startling passage: *"A Shake 'n Bake sergeant was one of the lesser-known evils to come out of the Vietnam War and infect the Army. These twerps would attend some NCO school for six to eight weeks and come out of it an E-5, buck sergeant. No experience, little skills, but a great big attitude."*

I read this passage again and again. *Damn.* Someone had actually written this for publication—and maybe for millions to read—that *I* was an evil person and a twerp and that the Army had screwed up when it had promoted me to sergeant. I shut the book, closed my eyes, and thought about these stinging words for a moment. I was genuinely embarrassed. Then I got mad. *I had been one of those Shake 'n Bakes.* Was my experience in Vietnam a sham, an illusion? True, I had been a greenhorn to war—as had thousands of officers—but, I had excellent training.

3

I had not thought about my tour in the Nam for thirty years. I had not talked about it with anyone. Now, my past was staring at me and awakening long forgotten and painful memories. At the time, many people had disliked us Shake 'n Bake sergeants. But was I really *that* bad? I read the passage again. "*...a lesser-known evil of the Vietnam War. No experience, little skills, but a great big attitude.*"

As I flew toward our vacation in Florida, I stared out the window and tried to remember what I could of that period of my life. What had happened to me in Vietnam? Was I finally ready to remember? Had I served with honor? Had my Shake 'n Bake cohorts served well? Or . . . did we deserve to be called evil twerps? I groped through my memories.

My vacation vanished from my thoughts and Vietnam emerged. My vacation was over before it started. A new journey had begun . . . a journey halfway around the world, and back in time. Back to the very beginning, it would not end until I had recovered my past as a Shake 'n Bake sergeant in Vietnam.

Acknowledgements

There are too many people to list here that helped me in my journey to the past and so if I miss some please pardon me. The first person I would like to thank is the late Jim Heimstead who, after reading some of my letters home from Vietnam, encouraged me to write the book. Without his encouragement and advice I would have never pursued this quest. I would also like to thank Don Gerrard who as my editor gave me encouragement to write. He is truly a friend and great advisor.

Most of all I would like to thank all the men of the A-1-8, Company A 1st Battalion 8th Infantry, with whom I connected with from over 30 years ago. Their memories of those past events provide a major contribution to this story. The story is written in the first and third person as I remember it and as they have relayed to me. Most of the pictures in the text were contributed by them.

I tried my best to say it just like it was, both with the high and lows, the good and bad. What I have concluded is that no words can really describe the reality of it all. Jerry Loucks, who saved my life in Vietnam, once told me, "Say it straight and it will come out that way." So here's to you Jerry, I tried my best.

Infantry

Infantry has been the decisive force on every battlefield throughout history.

"I am the Infantry

I am the Infantry

I am the Infantry – Follow me!"

The words dominated the Vietnam War and dominated me once upon a time. Infantry in Vietnam was often carried into battle by helicopter. The infantry's mission was the same as it had been for centuries – close with the enemy by means of fire and maneuver in order to destroy or capture him or to repel his assault by fire, close combat, and counterattack.

Most believed the war was fought by guerrillas using hit-and-run tactics. The reality was that most battles were fought from entrenched fortified positions. Enemy forces assaulted U.S. fire bases and when U.S. forces assaulted enemy positions, the fighting was intense. The statistics for U.S. combat divisions indicate that casualties were as high as or higher than those in the Korean War or in World War II. This was my reality.

The most prized award in Vietnam for U.S. military personnel was the Combat Infantry Badge. Only relatively few of us who served in Vietnam received this medal, most were infantrymen. We fought the enemy face to face.

This is a true story about an infantry sergeant in Vietnam, a Shake 'n Bake sergeant who fought the enemy face to face and whose sole purpose was to lead infantrymen into battle.

Chapter 1

Polei Kleng Field Hospital, Vietnam

Wednesday, 12 March 1969

THE HELICOPTER SHOOK as though it would shatter into a thousand pieces. "Hold on. We're gonna make it!" screamed the pilot. We flew through the smoke, loaded down with nine wounded men, and I was lying on the bottom of a pile of bodies. I was unable to move, but I thought, "I can make it, too. Just a little while longer, I wasn't meant to die like this."

I couldn't see much, but I heard the moans of the wounded each time the damaged chopper shook. "There it is!" someone yelled. "There's Polei Kleng. Damn, we're going to make it." As the chopper banked I stretched my leg out from under Flea and turned. Smoke and fire covered the field. Polei Kleng had just been mortared.

Airfield at Polei Kleng

The pilot took the chopper down hard and fast but at the last minute pulled the nose up and made a soft landing. I saw the field hospital tent to the left of the runway. "At least we made it to the hospital," I mumbled.

We landed, then all hell broke lose. Soldiers yanked seriously wounded men off the chopper as fast as they could. Someone yelled, "Get off before it blows!" Bodies littered the metal runway. I wondered if this was what hell was like. I had always heard that war is hell, and now I knew it was true. I lay there in the middle of chaos, wounded and unable to move.

A dark-skinned medic ran up to me. He was wiry, focused, and had a small black mustache. His piercing eyes stared into mine. "You all right, sarge?" he asked in a raspy southern accent. "We're gonna take care of you, buddy. Just relax." He and another medic placed me on a stretcher.

I saw another medic about ten yards away. He was near panic. He was trying to save Revis, one of the men on my chopper and even though he had been shot three times. The Flea, another one of my men, stood next to the medic. Flea's eyes filled with tears.

"Somebody get the sand out of his eyes!" the medic yelled. *"It's a sucking chest wound. Keep the bandage tight or he'll die."*

Everyone focused on Revis. The medic worked frantically, but finally stepped back and turned his face. Another medic quietly pulled a sheet over the body.

"Damn the war, anyway," the pilot said.

Revis was my comrade. He was at the end of his tour and should have gone home. Yet, here he lay on the dirty metal tarmac in a hellhole called Polei Kleng. And not a damn thing anyone could do to save him.

Another chopper arrived, I saw men scrambling, then voices. "Here comes the sergeant major," a voice from behind bellowed. "He's wounded. Make room. He's the sergeant major."

The medic turned. "Who gives a damn about rank? Just get him in the goddamn tent. We got our hands full."

Pain washed over me again. Nothing seemed real, nothing seemed right. Sticky blood covered me, my own special blanket of life. As long as I hurt, I knew I was alive.

"Okay, Sarge," a voice said as my gurney lifted. "We're taking you to the doctor. Hang in there."

Within seconds I was inside a dark tent with bare light bulbs dangling from long cords. The musty hospital smell overpowered the odor of my own sweat and blood. A couple of doctors and a few medics moved back and forth among the rows of cots, some with I.V. bottles hanging over them. Moans and groans came from each row. At least I wasn't getting shot at any more.

I tried to think about something besides the war. I tried to do my out of mind and body thing just to get away. But vivid images of the firefight I had just been through haunted me. I couldn't prevent myself from reliving that firefight, and everything else that had happened since. I had to beat those violent images out of my mind. *If only I could sleep.*

But each time I closed my eyes, I reawakened a few minutes later, right back in the thick of things. My mind raced, my heart pounded, I relived the battle, our assault on that bunker, then the explosion and our retreat. And what about my men still in the Plei Trap? Were they okay? What was happening there now?

"Where you hit, Sarge?"

I looked at the medic, mumbled, "I'm not sure. Maybe in the leg, maybe in the shoulder. And my hand. I know my hand is messed up." I didn't have the energy to also tell him about the shrapnel stuck in the side of my head, but from the amount of blood oozing from my face and head, I knew he'd figure it out.

A doctor appeared next to the medic. "Check his head. Wipe it down and see how bad he is. See if his eyes are dilated."

The medic checked me over. "It's okay now. We can give him morphine."

I felt the shot enter my arm and blessed relief coursed through my veins. But I was still conscious. Unlike my luckier comrades who slept, I still knew what had happened. I had sustained extensive damage to my shoulder, arm, and leg during a firestorm battle with the North Vietnamese Army (NVA). The NVA had us surrounded almost all day. They cut our company in half, and then attacked us. There must have been a thousand of them.

After spending hours on the ground wounded, with nothing but determination to survive, I was ready for whatever release from agony that the drug could provide. For the first time since battle, I started to relax. But even with the drug, it was difficult. Even with the drug, it was all I could do to push it out of my mind.

I thought about it over and over, trying to make sense of it. "I can't believe it happened. They were all over us. We were surrounded. How did we get out?" Then I wondered about my men. "What about Shea,

3

Pappy, Sam? Where are they? Did they die? Will they be okay? I am their sergeant; I am supposed to be there. Maybe they'll send me back." All of them could have been wiped out by now. I remembered the yelling. There was fire all over the place. It was chaotic. "Damn, I must go to sleep to rest, to heal. But I can't, I am supposed to be there. I am their sergeant." I lay there for what seemed forever, guilt dripping over me but finally the morphine did its job and my mind and body floated away to another place.

The medics at Polei Kleng cleaned my wounds as well as they could and made sure that I was stable enough to transfer to the next hospital. I was shipped out on the next Dustoff (air ambulance helicopter) that day and flown to the 71st Evacuation Hospital at Pleiku.

A beautiful lady dressed in a light green outfit hovered near me. "Are you an angel?" I asked. "I'm not dead, am I?"

"No," she said with a smile and squeezed my hand. "We're gonna fix you right up."

She and another nurse cut away my clothes with scissors. One of the nurses brought a large needle and asked me to roll over.

I felt a warm glow all over my body.

"Hope this will make you feel better," she said. It was a shot of Demerol. I floated on a cloud somewhere. I was in the place I needed to be for what was about to happen next.

They wheeled me immediately into the operating room for surgery. A bunch of people huddled around me. I became very thirsty; I thought of watermelon for some reason. I don't know why. "I'm gonna get some watermelon when I get home, " I blurted out.

The doctors and nurses laughed. "Hey, where're you from?" one of the doctors said. "You've got quite an accent."

"Are you okay? Can you feel that?" another asked.

"You just relax," another voice said from the distance. "You'll be getting your watermelon. Just wait."

I worked in synch with them. We were a team working to fix my body. I cooperated anyway I could as they opened all my wounds and removed the shrapnel.

The next thing I knew I lay in a hospital recovery ward. I must have dozed off during the operation. The only thing I remembered was watermelon. I felt an ache in my leg, shoulder and hand. The pain grew until it became unbearable. I looked back at my shoulder. There was a big hole in it – no skin, no tissue, just a raw hole. What the hell had they done to me? I panicked. I looked at my hand and it was the same. I couldn't see my leg but figured it was the same. Then a terrible thought occurred to me. They weren't finished. I must have still been in surgery and just woke up too soon. I thought if I didn't move that maybe everything would be all right.

But they were done for now. Where my shoulder had been peppered with dozens of small holes, it was now sliced open like a side of beef. My arm and my leg were given the same treatment.

For the first time, I felt alone. Completely alone, fighting shock and the unending pain from my wounds.

The Army had kept us searching for the enemy for days on end, we were sent on the most difficult and dangerous missions. I remember Pappy grumbling, "They don't care about us. We're grunts. No one gives a damn." Flea said again, "We gotta stick together. But why can't they give us some goddamn food?" We were exhausted and filthy. Shea complained, "How can we fight without socks and water?" My men didn't want to fight any more; they just wanted to survive and go home. They wished they could be sent to the rear, at least for a couple weeks to rest. But there was nothing we could do about it. We were the U.S. Army grunts . . . some of the few thousand soldiers who did the actual fighting.

The Army treated us like a pack of wild dogs, good for sniffing out the enemy and chasing the NVA all over the Plei Trap. We had humped all day for weeks, with nothing but cold c-rations and rationed water. We dug in after dark every night, and then mounted constant ambushes until daybreak. I remembered looking at Jerry Loucks and saying, "I wish we would just get it over with. Why can't we just shoot it out and be done? That would be better than hunting them every day and getting shot at every day." Jerry with a haggard look replied, "I know. I'm tired of this shit too. I want to find them, kill them, and get it over with."

My mind, my body, and my spirit were exhausted. It was no different for any of my men. How could I—how could my men—fight in this condition?

As I lay there I thought about life and death. Especially death. Until then, I had not been certain I would survive and return to the World. Now, I knew I would return but I would never be the same. "Why wasn't I happy?" I thought. "I hope they know that I wasn't an animal living in the jungle in dirt, hunting the enemy relentlessly to kill them." I had lost my youth to the hellish experience of war. As I laid there I realized my only bonds to reality were my letters from home.

And now my letters were gone. I moved on my hospital cot. "Where are my letters?" I asked.

"What letters?" the medic asked.

"They were in my fatigues."

The medic just looked at me and walked away. No one could do anything about it; they were gone. Fighting another wave of shock and pain, and stifling the long moan that hovered at the back of my throat, I thought about my family.

Visions of my family and friends came and went with increasing frequency between the doses of pain medicine. I lay as still as possible on my cot, wondering if I would live until morning and I couldn't stop worrying over not being able to fulfill my life's dream. I was in Vietnam because of that dream. That's why I had volunteered and chosen to stay in the infantry. I wanted to return to college. I wanted to become an engineer. I needed tuition money. The GI Bill would pay for it . . . *if I lived.*

I forced myself to ignore my pain and the sounds of suffering coming from all the wounded and dying around me. I wanted to focus on my life at this point in time. I needed to remember every moment, both good and bad. Funny thing. Although I hadn't completely relished my role as a Shake 'n Bake sergeant in the Vietnam War, I knew I had prepared to be a leader all my life. Someday …

But I wouldn't think of the future yet. Not until I had remembered the past.

Chapter 2

My journeys over the last years began when after graduating from Stonewall Jackson high school in 1965, I had no plan for the future and very little money. All of my buddies were struggling in the same predicament. None of them could afford to go to college. Many took local jobs there in Charleston, West Virginia. To get a good job in those days, you had to know the right people. It was especially difficult to get a start in one of the trades and it was impossible to get hired at the chemical plants in Kanawha Valley, the biggest employers in our area. There were no new openings.

Then one day I heard that the steel mills in Chicago were hiring. It was my way out. I reluctantly told my mom I was leaving for Chicago. Funny, she knew I had to go, she knew that I was contributing nothing but worry to the household, and it was time for me to find my place in the world. I remember the night before I left, she helped me pack my things. It took us the longest time. We both moved in slow motion. I put the essentials into an old suitcase. She treated me so lovingly, so gently, so knowingly. It was painful to think of leaving her.

We both knew our relationship would never be the same. I would probably never come home to live again. Her little boy, the one she had cared for so well, was leaving her. When I left the house, she was crying. She told me, years later, that she was remembering the time she had left Pt. Pleasant to start her new life in Charleston. She was remembering her own loneliness, and her determination to succeed. It had been difficult. A struggle like none she had ever imagined. I was about to experience a similar transformation. She hoped it would be a happier one.

Dad drove me to the bus station, he had been divorced from mom for four years but was still around and he was worried for me. Chicago was a rough and dangerous place. There were lots of ways to get in trouble there. Serious trouble. I was headed for an unknown land, which neither of us knew much about. Dad was confident that I would find my place in the world and deep inside he knew I was smart enough to make it on my own. As we walked to the bus, he told me he wished he could go with me.

At eighteen years of age, I was bound for Indiana Harbor, a suburb of Chicago, carrying most of my belongings with me. I was ready to face the world on a rainy cold winter's day in January of 1966. My goal was to get a job in a steel mill.

Twenty hours after leaving, my bus rolled into Indiana Harbor. It was one of the filthiest places I had ever seen. Black soot from the steel mill hung in the air and the streets and buildings looked like they had survived centuries of rough times. Charleston was an old city, with several parts that were dirty and rundown, but, for the most part, it was well-preserved and had charm. Indiana Harbor was another world. It was nasty, and populated with restaurants, businesses, pawn shops and taverns that all looked like jails; heavy steel bars covered their windows. Trash laid everywhere—in the gutters and on the sidewalks.

When I looked out of the bus window, my heart sank. This awful place was going to be my home! I made a decision right there, while standing in the terminal that I had to have the courage to make it. I had to harden myself mentally and rise to the challenge. I had to call on every ounce of my inner strength. I didn't want to be this far from home, but it's just that the steel mills hired hillbillies, and I was a hillbilly who needed a job. I was lucky they hired me right away.

The plant complex was huge and covered about five square miles. There were so many buildings in the complex that I had to ride a bus to reach my job in the shipping department. On the way, we passed huge open-hearth furnaces and even from inside the bus, I felt their intense heat. I saw red-hot steel ingots that were twenty feet high being removed from the furnaces. It was a vision of Hell.

Our bus, the air, and the ground around us—everything at the plant—was covered with black soot, and the place smelled like rotten eggs. It took some getting used to. Many days I could actually see the soot particles floating through the air, as thick as rain.

My job was to prepare the sheets and rolls of steel for shipping. This entailed banding them, then moving them into railroad cars. The work was monotonous. The idea was just to get through the day. My boss was a flat-topped foreman, who acted like a prison guard. He watched us like a hawk. Sometimes he would take out his stopwatch and time us, while we banded the steel. We were his inmates, shut up in a dangerous warehouse, living only to make the day's quota. Make up the order, ship the steel, get the quota. Over and over again. I hated it. All day long, I'd think negative thoughts. I can't do this for the rest of my life. My mind will die here . . . and my heart will die with it.

At eighteen years of age, working my first real job, I was experiencing Hell. In Hell, people moved slowly and were expressionless, caught in perpetual boredom, living mindlessly, doing meaningless work. They were blasted with unbearable heat, and then with intense coldness. The devil watched them intently, to make sure that these "damned" were truly miserable and never stopped their toiling. Yes, I was having my first taste of Hell . . . and already wishing I had an easy out.

During this period, I wrote home regularly and sent my mother money. I always told her that I was doing well and was very happy. I didn't want her to worry. I did not feel homesick, however, because after Dad had left my mother, the house I lived in never seemed like a home again. I had a mother and a dad and a brother and a sister, whom I cared about, but if "home" is a place where you feel secure and welcome forever, then I did not have a home.

I had an empty space in that place where "home" was supposed to reside. I had only myself. My home would have to be in my mind and heart, and wherever I was living at the time.

In September of 1966, I packed my belongings and flew to Louisiana. I felt like I had just escaped from hell and was returning to the world. I had saved close to two thousand dollars . . . enough for one year of college. I was ready to return to a learning environment. My goal was to become a college graduate. It was more than a goal; it was a burning desire. I was hungry for the education.

I completed my first semester with a very satisfying 3.87 grade point average.

My Christmas was depressing. I went home to visit my mother. She was having a hard time making ends meet. This knowledge made me more determined than ever to succeed. I owed it to them, and to myself. Education was my only way out of a similar existence.

Life was difficult on my own, since there was no one to give me moral support from day to day. In time, I learned to deal with my loneliness, and to become mentally tough. My fear of failure soon disappeared. I learned the meaning of taking responsibility for myself , to be careful in my decision-making and to live with the consequences . . . good or bad. But there was always one nagging concern that haunted me night and day. Money.

I mailed work applications to many local oil companies, hoping for a summer job that would provide funding for the following school year. I received no responses. I applied for a scholarship from the school and for a loan, but I received neither. None of my relatives could help me financially. After posting a 3.87 grade average the first semester and a perfect 4.0 the second semester, I had to leave school flat broke. I had no choice. I took the bus to New Orleans and shipped most of my belongings to my mother.

That was May of 1967. I was nineteen years old. All my worldly possessions were packed into a duffel bag and suitcase that had brought me to Louisiana from Chicago. I had no real plan in mind, just an aching hope that something would turn up in New Orleans. I felt no fear, just disappointment for having to leave college. It wasn't fair. I had aced every class. I was so hungry to learn more. For the first time, I felt despair and defeat. I knew my life's calling was to be an engineer but did not know how to get there.

In New Orleans, I took a job as a busboy at Jimmy Moran's famous restaurant, in the French Quarter. I met many famous people, but the pay and the tips were not enough to encourage my return to college. Then I found a job on an offshore oilrig, sandblasting the bottom of the rig. The job paid $2.25 per hour and I worked twelve hours a day. I worked fourteen straight days, during which time I lived on a tugboat tied beside the rig in the Gulf of Mexico. After two weeks on the job, I would get seven days off. Then fourteen days back on again.

This job was far more dangerous than the one at the steel mill. I was required to hang upside-down—beneath the rig—while suspended by ropes and boards and, in this position, to handle the high-powered hose that performed the sandblasting. I dangled there, forty to fifty feet above the water line and over a maze of rusting pipes. When I was not operating a hose, I worked in the tugboat's hold, feeding seventy-pound bags of sand into the sandblasting hopper. I lasted only one fourteen-day shift and quit.

After leaving the oilrig job, my goals disintegrated. I did not know what to do next. I gave up the idea of working to save money for college. I could get a job, but not one that produced enough money to make a difference. College was out of my reach. It was a dream that only rich people could pursue.

Without a plan for my future, I put the future out of my mind and became intoxicated with the present. I felt consumed by a desire to experience my life only from day to day. I saw other young people living without worry, and felt open to such a "free" lifestyle. I attached myself to the hippie dream and became one of them.

I embraced the philosophy that I could do anything I wanted to, as long as it didn't hurt anyone else. I could live for today. Tomorrow would come, so why worry about it? At nineteen, life as a hippie was fun, and I was hooked. I became a believer. For the time being, my past didn't exist. I didn't play basketball. I forgot about old friends. I wrote my mom once or twice, but lost contact with all relatives. I was embarking on a journey to escape from reality.

Many hippies talked continually about California. It was the land of milk and honey. It was the hippies Mecca. Many thought that the hippie movement would change the world. It would create a New World and California would be at the center of it.

As time went by and I heard more and more about California, I knew that I had to go there. Could I live off the land? Would I find something or someone special there? I had to know. I had already put my future on hold. The future could wait some more. California would be my next adventure. I had an uncontrollable desire to experience this new world. In my mind, I had already become a vagabond, a gypsy, an explorer. A journey to California was the only way to realize my fate.

With what little money I had left, I bought a nice rucksack and a good sleeping bag. Then, with my remaining savings in my pocket—about one hundred dollars—I left New Orleans for San Francisco. I hitchhiked Route 66, across the middle of Texas, through New Mexico, and up the valley through Arizona, then over to Southern California. From there I worked my way up the coast. I really didn't care how long my journey took. If I had to make a few detours along the way, what the hell? I had the rest of my life to get there!

I finally reached San Francisco, I found a city like no place I had ever been, nor imagined. The entire city seemed to be misplaced in time. The houses were narrow, friendly and quaint. The streets dipped and soared across rolling hills. On every street corner hippies were congregating. It was a city full of hippies! The climate was refreshing - the air was damp

11

and cool and there was always a breeze. This place energized me. I could travel everywhere on foot, and move throughout the city easily to see everything I wanted.

In those days, thousands of young kids just like me were migrating into San Francisco's Haight-Ashbury district from all over the United States. Haight-Ashbury, a small area that bordered on Golden Gate Park, had become the Mecca of the hippie movement, and everyone wanted to be there. This was where it was "happening," whatever "happening" meant. I had journeyed from Louisiana to visit the Haight and I didn't even know what it was! I hadn't watched a TV in over two years, so I wasn't responding to some media event. I was simply going there because I had heard so much about it, and to have a good time and live life as a hippie. Life was simple then and I had no worries - I was just looking to have fun.

There was absolutely no end to the variety of clothes and hats that hippies wore. My impression was the same as if I had fallen into a hole and emerged in an Alice-in-Wonderland play. I was amazed at how well these people had discarded rules of society. They seemed to rely on a different set of rules, the rules for just being human. I was witnessing the birth of "free love," that philosophy which caused the sexual revolution in our county during the 1970s and 1980s. I was totally carried away with it all.

After spending a month in San Francisco, I made the decision to move on. Although I was having fun and had made many new friends, I was restless. I simply could not spend the rest of my life hanging around parks, accomplishing nothing.

I traveled into the mountains of California and spent a few days contemplating my future. After the weeks spent in the Haight-Ashbury, I saw problems in the hippie movement. The Haight was populated with many rip-off artists, con men and women, crooks, vagrants, runaways, weekend hippies, and all kinds of scheming people, not unlike in the "real" world. I did not like dealing with them. For every one of these people, however, there were at least two like me, simply someone eager to experience a new way of life.

It was worth the experience because I had learned a huge lesson - that the new life we all sought, the great hippie experience, the wonderful adventure, it was always within - it was me and was within my own mind.

The experience was happening within me. It was just getting high on life, my own life.

I decided to head back east. I hitched rides from Yosemite National Park to San Diego, to Phoenix, and then to Flagstaff. From Flagstaff I hitched straight across the middle of the United States and then up north to Chicago. When I arrived in Indiana Harbor, I checked into another "fleabag" hotel and headed for the employment office of the nearest steel mill. They gave me a job as a day laborer, and I started to work immediately. My job was cleaning tar off the concrete floor in a very large room. It was a filthy job, I was sure they couldn't get anyone else to do. I got tar all over my shoes and clothes, it was impossible to clean it all off. I hated it immediately. Later on I found out that there was no possibility of working overtime at that plant. I concluded that I would not be able to save enough money fast enough to get back into college.

One day covered in tar, I stood there in the middle of that room staring into space. I asked myself," How can things get any worse?" Then I screamed at the top of my lungs, "I give up, they can have me, take me." I made a desperate decision.

I wanted to go back to college at all costs. I knew it was my destiny. I saw it clearly now. Let them draft me. That's the way. I'll go to college on the GI bill when I get out. I reasoned," It would take only two years, and then I would be back in college. It was simple but it was desperate. It beat cleaning tar off of concrete for laborer's wages. I decided that to join the Army, it would be better in West Virginia, so I quit my job, gathered up all my stuff again and headed back to Charleston. I was hitchhiking, of course, my preferred and only means of travel.

13

Chapter 3

It took me more than thirty hours to reach my hometown. I had long hair, I smelled, and my clothes were dirty. I looked exactly like the hippie I had been. It had been a long hard trip and I was excited to see my old stomping grounds again. Everything looked different. The streets were narrower and smaller than I had remembered. Everything that was familiar looked old and tired. The Lincoln School playground was the same, but I didn't recognize anyone, and the kids who were there seemed very young. It was hard to imagine that I had been one of them only a few short years before. Much had happened to me. I guess I was a changed man.

I didn't know where my Mom and Dad were. I hadn't seen or talked to either of them in a long time. I had simply lost track so I headed for Aunt Polly's house. I knew she would greet me with open arms.

I walked with my rucksack past the Valley Bell store where I had spent so many nights with the guys, hanging out and ogling girls. *God, I have come a long way.* Then I walked four blocks to five corners, from where it was only two more blocks to Polly's. *Take a deep breath, Jerry. It won't be long now. I wonder what people will think? God, I have come a long way. I'm not the same person as when I lived here.* Past five corners, then by the A&W root beer stand. Man, we used to have so much fun here. The A&W stand had the only quart root beers with slush on top. Turn the corner, okay, there it was - Polly's house, hope they're home. I was at the front door. I felt excited but my body ached all over from the trip. *Here goes nothing.* I banged on the metal clanker and waited. A few minutes passed. I was exhausted.

Finally the door opened and there stood Polly. She stared and stared at me for a long time. I spoke. "Polly, it's me. Jerry. I'm home."

She smiled, her eyes filled with tears, and she pulled me in and hugged me for a long time. She said, " I am so glad you're home. We missed you."

As Smitty was coming down the stairs Polly yelled, "It's Jerry!"

Boy, did I get a big bear hug. Polly and Smitty didn't see me as I was; they saw me as I had always been. They saw that chubby little dark complexioned boy who was always quiet, who hung on every word his favorite Aunt Polly and Uncle Smitty said. I was still special in their hearts. They were very special people.

Once I rested up, and after Polly fed me, I decided to tell them my plan. I didn't know how else to say it so I just blurted out "I'm joining the Army."

I waited for a reaction. At first there was just silence. Then Uncle Smitty said, "Could you say that again?"

I repeated. "I'm joining the Army."

After a few moments, Smitty looked at me and said, "I'm proud of you Jerry. If that's what you want to do, then do it."

And Polly added, "Jack's joining the Air Force. You can both stay here and have a good time until you leave." Jack, their son, was out of town, but would return in several days. That was all there was to it. It was done. Polly and Smitty had accepted and supported me, without hesitation.

Jack returned and we waited together for our enlistment dates, we spent time chasing any girl we could get our hands on, drinking, and just hanging out. Basically we raised as much hell as we could before we had to leave. We haunted every pool hall, bar, drive-in, and nightclub in Charleston. We sought out—and found—every type of sinful activity we could find. We didn't care; we just wanted to have fun and we did. Hanging over our heads were the never-discussed perils of war.

I met my old buddies, Johnny and Smoky, at one of the local pool halls, where they were permanent fixtures. Both had become first-class pool players. They made their money from gambling and pool hustling. When I told them that I was going into the Army, they both said the same thing: "You could get killed!" Then they wrote it off as another crazy thing "the Big H" would do; however, the thought of *dying* on the battlefield was the farthest thing from my mind. I figured I was smart enough to find a way out of Vietnam. Besides, I had plans for my future.

Wednesday, 18 October 1967

I was inducted into the United States Army at the Armed Forces Examining and Entrance Station in Beckley, West Virginia. I was given the grade of Private (E-1) for an active duty commitment of twenty-four

15

months. A week later, the Army tested me. My AFQT score was 62. That made me average according to Army Test Standards.

Jack was inducted into the United States Air Force a few days later.

I traveled by bus to Fort Benning, Georgia. It was a long trip from West Virginia, time passing slowly. I was glued to the window, looking out at nothing in particular. My mind was in a fog. I was not in a hurry.

The bus was packed with soldiers and civilians. About ten or fifteen of the other recruits aboard were headed for Fort Benning as well. I overheard what they were saying, but I kept to myself. I had no idea what was about to happen to me at the base. I decided that no matter what happened I would let my body take care of it. I made my mind go somewhere else. My mind would not know the terrible pain my body would have to endure. Luckily I already knew this trick would work. I had discovered this at an early age as my "out of mind and body thing." Let your mind go somewhere else and your body could take anything.

The army post was located deep in the heart of Georgia, near the city of Columbus. The Army was the town's only industry. On the December day we arrived the weather was sunny and bright.

As my bus approached the post, I thought Fort Benning looked like a prison. It had uniformed armed guards, a high fence topped with barbed wire, and identical buildings, row after row of them. Everything was neat, clean, and orderly, and almost new. It was a soldier factory, and I was one of the raw materials to be processed.

The bus drove through most of the post before we reached the receiving station. It was early—about seven in the morning. The bus

16

stopped with a whooshing of the brakes, the door swung open, nobody moved. To a man, we were frozen in our seats. Pretty soon, a huge, lean black man wearing a Smokey the Bear hat—the meanest looking black guy I had ever seen—stepped onto the bus. His loud unpleasant voice reverberated in the quiet. "Get the fuck off this bus, you bunch of pussies, or I'm gonna kick each and every one of your asses! *Now*! Go! Go! *Go!*"

I jumped up, hitting my head on the bottom of the overhead luggage carrier, and grabbed my bag. With each step toward the door of the bus, I heard the terrifying voice. *"Fuck, shit, pussy!"* As I gathered with the others into a tight group, he bellowed, *"Get in a fucking line!"*

I had never heard the f-word used so much in such a short time. I was impressed.

At this moment, standing more or less at attention in the early Georgia sunlight, I learned the most valuable lesson the Army ever taught me. I learned how to blend into the crowd—to become invisible. I made no movement. None. Not even to smile or scowl. I tried to move into my out-of-mind-and-body thing, but instead I stopped thinking. I stopped breathing.

The "going invisible" technique didn't work this particular day. Unfortunately, my hair was longer than most of the others in the line. The big black guy—whom I would later come to know as my Drill Sergeant, Sergeant Garrett—took an extra few moments to place his big nose about two centimeters from my face while calling me a lowlife pussy who wasn't worth the ground I walked on. He swore that he was going to personally cut off all my fucking hair. Since I had gotten the sergeant's wrath right away—and survived—I was actually relieved. And, in some weird sense, I felt honored.

Quickly we lined up, with our gear beside us. I will have to admit we did look like a pitiful bunch of pussies. Garrett had his work cut out for him. It was difficult to follow his simplest orders like walking down the street in a straight line. Most of us shuffled, and Garrett hollered and harassed us all the way to the supply building, where we received our first Army haircuts and gear.

We were like wild horses and Garrett had to break our spirits so that we would follow orders on command. It was the Army's way. If we didn't learn fast, we would have a heavy price to pay. Those who learned would become more confident and self-assured. The system was simple:

17

the Army broke us down and then built us up again. The result of the training was crucial. We would become a *soldier* . . . a man who could stand on his own, while at the same time knowing how important it is to follow orders and be a team player. In the future, our lives and the lives of many other men would depend on these abilities.

The first step in Army indoctrination is humiliation, and it is accomplished through the uncomplicated procedure of cutting off hair— *all of it.* Shorn of our locks, we were just a pathetic collection of kids. We had been stripped of our dignity.

Feeling naked and self-conscious, we went through a series of long lines at the supply factory to receive our uniforms, boots, and bedding. The Army was very well organized. In a short time we had our gear and in the right size. We were issued green fatigues which were surprisingly comfortable and tough. We were even issued green underwear, which used to ride up my ass. We were instructed to pack our street clothes. From that moment on, we would wear the required regulation attire.

The first few weeks of Basic Training were pure hell. After my body was "cleansed," I started to feel pretty good. My class arose every morning by four thirty a.m. and almost immediately started to exercise. I remember singing at the top of my lungs while I jogged through the woods.

I wanna be an Airborne Ranger!
I wanna go to Vietnam!
I wanna live a life of Danger!
I wanna kill a Charlie Cong!
Sound off. One Two!
Sound off. Three Four!
Sound off. One,Two,Three, Four, One-Two . . . Three- Four!

The Army was engaged in the serious business of trying to make men out of us . . . in weeks, not years. We had to forget about home and Momma. Fort Benning was our home now, and Garrett was our Momma. If we got out of line, he would rather kick our asses than look at us. Many recruits had a tough time of it since they really were pussies. For the most part, these were young men who had never played team sports, never gotten into fights, and had never ever raised any hell.

18

Garrett had an uncanny ability to ferret out pussies in order to give them a special dose of Garrett Hell. I never—I mean *never*—smiled or even inwardly chuckled when he did this because I was scared to death he would see me. If I cracked one semblance of a grin, the inevitable would happen. Garrett would bark, "*Horton*, what the fuck is so funny? Drop down and give me fifty pushups. Get your ass down, *now!*" It took few bouts of pushups for me to learn how to become invisible.

An important part of our training was a competition . . . to see who could avoid Garrett's wrath by becoming the most invisible. Everyone wanted to be a ghost when Garrett was around, but *someone* had to be *visible*. If we so much as glanced at him, he bellowed, "Are you eyeing me? Get down and give me thirty, *now!*" By learning to become invisible, we were playing right into the Army's plans, of course. Mastering this skill meant we were learning to follow orders, keep our mouths shut, and do things the Army's way.

Another Garrett lesson was teaching us to be team players, no matter what personalities, intelligence, race, or personal beliefs we had, or how much we might dislike each other. We quickly learned we had to respect and help each other to get a job done. If *one* of us failed . . . we *all* failed. Sergeant Garrett would not punish just one individual, he would punish all of us . . . the entire class. Sarge taught us that everyone must take the responsibility to see that everyone else was doing his job, or that person could get all of us killed. This was a sobering thought, one we did not take lightly.

Although the consequences in the Army were more extreme, this idea—the importance of teamwork—was not new to me. I had already experienced being a team member, fighting for a common goal. This is what I already learned growing up on the street playing basketball at the playground court with my buddies. I had the advantage of being schooled in the streets growing up in West Virginia.

Our training schedule never changed and was organized like this:

0430—Wake Up
0530—Physical Training
0630—Personal Hygiene/Breakfast
0730—Move to Training
0800—Training
1200—Lunch

19

1245—Training
1630—Return to Barracks
1700—Dinner
1800—Preparation for Next Day/Counseling/Extra Training
2000—Soldier Preparation Time
2100—Lights Out

Every morning at four-thirty Garrett arrived at our barracks, banging a garbage can lid and yelling at us to get our sorry asses out of bed. It amazed me that I could respond so quickly. I could shit, shower, shave, dress, and be outside—lined up and ready to go—in less than ten minutes. It was always dark when Garrett would announce that we were going on a little run. The route never took place on flat ground, but rather through the woods and along the power lines, where the ground was uneven and the footing slippery.

At first I thought I would die from the rigors of these runs, but after a while my legs got used to them and then, when we did run on flat ground, it was a piece of cake. Flat ground is rarely an option in war zones, especially in some areas of Vietnam, where we were headed. Garrett knew this. We were the only platoon to run the power lines, and soon we were in the best shape.

Sometimes Sergeant Garrett had us run the power lines while carrying our rifles. We sang: "This is my rifle; this is my gun. This is for shooting; this is for fun." When we sang "This is for shooting..." we lifted our rifles high into the air. When we sang "...this is for fun" we had to grab our nuts with our other hand. This particular exercise only occurred when someone inadvertently referred to his weapon as a "gun." We learned to watch our vocabulary quickly.

Once we had completed our morning run, Garrett allowed us to low-crawl under his barracks for twenty or thirty minutes as he put it. We were filthy before we had chow. The barracks were twenty meters wide by forty meters long. Underneath them, the hard rocky ground was barren of grass and the floorboards above us were covered in spider webs. While crawling, we inevitably ate the dirt from another guy's boots. Soldiers must go anywhere, without question and without fear. But to endure the low-crawl, I always had to use my out-of-mind-and-body technique.

20

If we were lucky, Garrett allowed us to low-crawl in the standard exercise area which, although muddy, was preferred to the under-the-barracks crawl. If we low-crawled the exercise area, we had to finish by going hand over hand down the monkey bars. I struggled a long time to master them. During these exercises, Garrett would cuss and chew our asses out more than anyone I had ever known.

After low-crawl, it was chow time, an event that used to be known as breakfast. I never experienced anything remotely like a breakfast in the Army; somebody always put a lot of effort into making food as tasteless as flour. It was cooked in bulk . . . big bulk. Most of the so-called chefs were recruits in training. They were the unlucky ones—the ones who were assigned to KP (kitchen police) duty. KP was the hardest, most unrewarding lowlife job anyone could be assigned.

The worst food served at Fort Benning was called "shit on a shingle." This was white gravy laced with a few bacon bits and served with heavy, gummy biscuits. The combination tasted like plaster. Talk about sticking to your ribs . . . we needed a rest period before we could start running again.

The rest of each day consisted of various training courses, drills, and more PT (physical training). At the end of the day, we returned to the barracks to clean up our lockers before bedtime. Then we collapsed into bed, exhausted.

After the first few weeks we were taught the specifics of how to be soldiers. We learned about Army organization and personnel. The various ranks in the Army were either commissioned (officers, who had graduated from an officers' school or who were professionals, like doctors) or noncommissioned officers or enlisted. As a recruit, I was an enlisted soldier.

In Basic Training we received careful and extensive instruction in how to fire our weapons, how to take them apart, clean them, and fight with them. I had neither hunted nor been around guns as a kid so I didn't know what to expect the first time I had to fire a rifle. At first I was scared. The weapon definitely controlled me. But once I had fired my M-14 rifle and felt its recoil and heard the loud popping sound, I wanted to become its master.

Later, I would learn to love my weapon—the heft of it, the feel, the sounds it made, and the way it smelled. My M-14 became my best friend . . . my mistress. I knew she could save my life one day. In the future I

21

would sleep with her and kept her close by at all times. I took care of her and she took care of me. In time I earned my Sharpshooter badge.

Private Horton in Training

During bayonet training we were informed by our instructors—who were great psychologists—that we must accept the fact that we would either have to kill enemy soldiers or be killed by them. Each time we exercised, each time we lunged with our bayonets, each time we addressed Sergeant Garrett, we had to act with intensity, competence, and strength. We had to demonstrate that we were formidable. War was serious business. We believed the message and took our lessons seriously.

There were always a few recruits who, for one reason or another, couldn't make it. Most of the time they were either overweight or underweight, but some they had health problems or were just hard cases. If they couldn't make it through Basic Training, they had to endure a special type of hell. They would be placed into a *recycle troop*, which meant they had to repeat the entire Basic Training program. The Army rarely gave up on anyone. Recycling through Basic Training was the biggest nightmare ever conceived by the Army, and the thought of having to endure such an ordeal made us all work like hell to avoid it. Sergeant Garrett reminded us daily that recycling could happen to any of us at any time.

Basic Training, a nine-week program, was designed to transform boys—like me—into soldiers, ready for combat with the enemy. The training was both psychological and physical.

After learning the basics of being a soldier and how to use our equipment, we learned the Army's code of conduct, and how to carry out

23

overnight maneuvers and long field marches. Most of us graduated to Advanced Individual Training for Infantry, where we learned more about combat. Soldiers who were destined to be clerks, truck drivers, and personnel with similar duties did not receive additional combat training. The troops of every nation including the Viet Cong and the NVA, had to learn the same basic skills of combat that we did . . . if they wanted to survive.

Several recruits who went through training with me did become clerks in the rear units or were sent to safe assignments in Germany. I had heard rumors that in Vietnam there were over 400,000 troops in the rear units supporting the 70,000 men who were fighting in the jungles. Someone said that *only one in thirty* was placed in a position of being shot at regularly in Vietnam.

When I heard these statistics, I thought I had a good chance of missing Vietnam altogether and a ninety-five percent chance of missing combat. I felt lucky and wasn't at all worried about my future as a soldier. That other five percent barely entered my mind.

At Fort Benning almost all of our training occurred outdoors. We sat on cold bleachers for hours, listening to instructors. In December and January it could get pretty cold. Sometimes large groups of us would doze off while leaning against each other. Of course, Sergeant Garrett or our instructor of the moment would jolt us awake. If too many of us dozed, we were given a little PT until we were wide awake again.

Sergeant Garrett was the epitome of self-confidence. He wasn't afraid of anything on earth. He treated us like men after first relieving us of our pride and prejudices and showing us how weak we were. He convinced us that we could achieve anything if we put our minds to it. He made us stand tall. When we performed well, he would say, "Good job. " And we knew he meant it. We worked our hearts out for him . . . and we matured and became confident of our prowess.

Strong as an ox, Garrett was only thirty-one and a Vietnam infantry combat veteran. He taught us about our enemies—the Viet Cong and the North Vietnamese Army (NVA). He taught us that we "gotta be ready to kick Charlie's ass, or he'll kick yours." He'd say, "Show me that you are tough. Show me that you mean it. *Growl!*" And we would growl.

And so, within just a few months, I had become another soldier for the United States Army. I had received their best training. Nevertheless, I for some reason I knew that my chances were good, I believed my experience growing up gave me an edge. I had confidence; I had already gone one-on-one with myself and won, time after time. The confidence I gained during those important years would be needed now . . . to go one-on-one with a deadly new enemy one day. I felt ready.

During the ceremony at the end of my training, I marched proudly across the parade grounds with the others. I was assigned as an 11B, which meant that my Military Occupational Specialty was to be the infantry. Someone handed me a job description of my future duties, and I learned that I had been assigned to fight in a war. I was to be a foot soldier in Vietnam. I hadn't expected this. The odds were against me. *I was part of the five percent.*

Job Title: Infantryman (MOS 11B)

Job Description: The infantryman supervises, leads, or serves as a member of an infantry activity that employs individual or crew-served weapons, in support of offensive and defensive combat operations. Assists in the performance of reconnaissance operations. Employs, fires, and recovers anti-personnel and anti-tank mines. Locates and neutralizes mines. Operates and maintains communications equipment and operates in a radio net. Constructs field expedient firing aids for infantry weapons. Performs as a member of a fire team during a movement to contact, reconnaissance, and security, an attack, defense, situational training exercises and all infantry dismounted battle drills. Processes prisoners of war and captured documents.

Chapter 4

At the end of Basic Training I was assigned to Advanced Individual Training (AIT) for Infantry at Fort McClellan, near Anniston, Alabama. Most of my unit was assigned to AIT in Fort Polk, Louisiana. Once we shipped out, I never saw them again. Those who were not assigned to AIT were destined to be clerks and never see combat. Needless to say, these trainees jumped for joy.

I never saw Sergeant Garrett again. But later I found out that at the age of thirty-one, Alfred Douglas Garrett, Sergeant First Class, was killed in action on October 27, 1968, during his second tour of duty in South Vietnam. He was in Lam Dong at the time of his death, serving as a U.S. Army advisor to the South Vietnamese Army.

SSG Alfred D. Garrett
Drill Sergeant

I graduated from Basic Training December 22, 1967. It was three days before Christmas when everyone was going home for the holidays before reporting to the next assignment. I had no plans. My family situation was bleak. My mother had moved to Seattle to live with my uncle, and I didn't know a soul there except for the two of them. My dad and my brother were still in West Virginia, but they had started a new family with Dad's new wife, Peg. My sister had married and she and her new husband had moved to Cleveland. My Aunt Polly and Uncle Smitty were the only ones in Charleston. There was no longer a place I could call *home.*

The Army rules would not allow me to stay on the base once I had graduated from Basic. It was too early to report to Fort McClellan. I stayed in a local hotel for my first Christmas alone.

My room was very clean and neat, as you would expect in a small southern town. Since there were no troops on base, I had the hotel to myself. I made plans to have Christmas dinner at a restaurant three doors from the hotel. I passed the time in my room reading and sleeping.

Since it was Christmas, I also thought about the birth of Jesus and about what Christmas meant to me. I wondered about my fate. I thought about my family, whom I missed. I remembered the old days at Grandma Horton's house on Christmas Eve—those cold, clear winter nights in West Virginia, where the air was crisp and clean and the ground was covered with new snow. Jack and I would walk over to Grandma's, very excited about the upcoming Christmas party. Forty or fifty people would pack the house. Everyone would be full of holiday spirit, laughing and singing. How good it would have been to be with them. But time brings changes. That family, as such, no longer existed as a unit. Those had been special days. Life had been good then. Now I was alone, spending Christmas in a town full of strangers.

I slept right through Christmas Eve and into Christmas Day. I went for a walk and then enjoyed a surprisingly good dinner of turkey, dressing, and cranberry sauce, almost as good as the dinner Mom used to make. The restaurant was filled to capacity that day. Evidently there were many in town who were alone and wanted the company of others. They talked to each other the way good friends do. Someone mentioned that a local church sponsored a live nativity scene and carol singing. Since the church was only a couple blocks away. Later that evening I walked over to take a look.

When I arrived at the church I found a beautiful nativity scene, with both people and animals, and a group of carolers singing familiar Christmas hymns. The church had provided chairs and benches for people to sit on while listening to the music. I perched on a picnic table nearby and when I knew the words sang along with the others. Pretty soon the spirit of Christmas filled me. Here I was, in Columbus, Georgia, a thousand miles away singing carols with strangers. Although I was away from my family and friends, I felt content. Maybe, because I was alone on this special day, I could better understand the real meaning of Christmas. I also realized that no matter where I was or what I was about to face, I would never truly be alone. That was the Christmas message. I received the spirit and the blessing. I enjoyed the experience. It was one of the few times I went to church. I always felt that it was important to believe in God, but church was a formality. However, it certainly made me feel a lot better that day.

On the seventh of January, I took the bus to Anniston, Alabama, to begin the next phase of my military training. Fort McClellan was very different from Fort Benning. The weather was colder and damper. During the next nine weeks of training, I never saw the sun shine. Fort McClellan was also smaller than Benning, more heavily wooded and very hilly. It was the headquarters for the Army's Women's Army Corps (WACs) units and also for the chemical warfare training program.

I asked the Military Police (MP) at the gate for the location of my training company. Within the next hour or two, I had received my bedding and gear and found a vacant bunk in the barracks. I just followed the program, which was organized to a fault. The Army made it easy. Wait for an order to be issued and obey it. There were mothers all over America who wished their sons had been as obedient. Yes, sir. Yes, ma'am. Do the deed. A mother's dream.

I hung around the barracks the rest of the day . . . waiting. In the late afternoon, a sergeant informed us that we would attend a compass course that evening. A night compass course was a military training exercise in which three-man teams travel from point A to point B, navigating with the aid of a compass. Each team has a different route to follow. Typically, the course will wander over four to five miles, through a woods or other rough terrain. The purpose of this exercise was to learn survival, without the aid of the sun as a guide, in unknown territory and with limited visibility, without getting lost or freaked out. It was an extremely important exercise and taught soldiers to have confidence in their ability to deal with night situations.

We assembled at dusk on the exercise field, where our instructors gave us the basics on using a compass and some instructions on survival. It was nearly dark when the lecture was completed. The sergeants in charge organized a hundred of us into small teams. Each team was instructed to follow a pre-marked compass course which would return us to our base.

28

The instructors then walked away. I had already made it my policy to take the lead in team exercises, because I wanted to control my destiny as well as be able to offer assistance to the other guys with me. I took the leadership role when I could.

Everything went by the book until it was dark and we unexpectedly walked into a swamp. It didn't take a genius to know we were in trouble. Our instructors hadn't mentioned such an obstacle. We must have been lost! During a hurried discussion, my team members and I mentally retraced our course. We appeared to be where we were supposed to be. We had to choose between our training, which said we were in the right place, and our instincts, which told us we were lost. We chose to trust our training.

The swamp was like those in horror movies, with snakes, hanging moss, fallen trees and stumps of others hidden under the water, and ice cold water to slosh through. I suppose there were a few dry places in that swamp, but we never found them. We couldn't see ten feet in front of us. We groped our way through the maze, hour after hour. Without the compass to guide us, we would have been completely lost.

As I led the men through the water, I had to constantly break a layer of ice with my legs.

We quickly became numb from the waist down. It was pitch black and silent. The only sound was the three of us grunting and talking about our progress. We became disoriented a couple of times, but we finally made it out of the swamp. A few other teams remained lost the entire night. The NCO instructors had to search for them with flashlights.

When the exercise was over, there were a few sprained ankles, a few cases of hypothermia, and a few cases of mental fatigue. It is not an easy experience to be lost and alone at night under difficult circumstances. Some people simply cannot deal with experiences needing mental discipline. We learned that the Army had designed every team's course to eventually include the swamp. It was an important measurement of competency, and the kind of training we needed for active duty in Vietnam.

In Basic Training at Fort Benning, the emphasis had been on learning the Army's expectations, on physical training, on learning to follow orders, and on practicing the basics of combat training. In Advanced Training, the emphasis was on learning how to survive in Vietnam. This

29

was not a continuation of child's play. It was real and we had better pay attention.

As the training became more personal and weighty, so did the weaponry. We learned how to fire, maintain, and fight with the M-16, the M-79, the M-60, and grenades. We were told that the M-16 was the basic automatic weapon used by the U.S. infantry in Vietnam. It could fire in both automatic and semi-automatic modes. It was lighter than the M-14 we had used in Basic Training. The lighter weight was important in Vietnam, because of the weight of the equipment infantryman had to carried through the jungle.

The M-79 was a grenade launcher. Many soldiers in Vietnam were assigned to carry and use them. It allowed a soldier to fire grenades at an enemy as far away as 200 meters. The M-60 machine gun was an awesome weapon, critical in combat situations, because it was capable of emitting automatic and heavy rapid fire. One man could fire the weapon continuously, through the use of belt-fed ammunition, thus wreaking havoc on enemy positions. There was no comparison between the plastic water guns or dime-store rifles used in my childhood games and these real weapons of real war. I did not assume I knew anything about them and took my training seriously.

For the first time we were trained on combat conditions in Vietnam. We were taught how to recognize, locate, defuse, and use booby traps. We were taught the combat habits of the Viet Cong and the North Vietnamese Army soldiers, the NVA. We were taught how to use quick-fire techniques in which we walked through a course, picked up our weapons on a moment's notice, and fired them without aiming. We were taught how to arm and throw live grenades. Our instructions were more detailed. The Army was preparing us for war.

Training in the Field

Combat was now our profession, we actually got paid every month for it. There were other valuable lessons to learn, some were about our own self. I remember a tall 6'3" kid in the barracks who was a really gung-ho kind of guy. He was big and beefy and looked like a football tackle with blonde hair and blue eyes, an All-American boy and football jock. He talked about how he was going to be an airborne ranger, and how he couldn't wait to get to Vietnam. I think he volunteered for Vietnam. He let everyone know that he had been a real bad ass in high school. When he would start that bullshit in a group of guys, I would just walk away.

He must have heard me talk to some of the guys about my adventures as a hippie in California, and about the kind of music I liked. Pretty soon Mr. All-American made it known that he didn't like my friends or me. He took to harassing us, needling us in front of the other guys. He was always taunting me; it was clear that he wanted to fight.

But I didn't want anything to do with him, first because he was twice as big as I was, and second because I knew it was important to stay out of trouble that was my style. One day our entire class was hanging around in the barracks. I was lying in my bunk not doing anything at all and Mr. All-American was lying on the next bunk over. Out of the blue he said a few smart-ass things to me that I just shrugged off. Then he got up and walked around in front of my bunk and stood right in front of me. He said something I cannot repeat about my mother.

This was a direct insult that I couldn't ignore. He said it in front of most of the guys in the barracks. At point he crossed the line, and

31

without me really knowing it, my mind snapped. Rage boiled over and exploded in me. I leapt from my bunk and pounced on top of him. In seconds, he was down on the floor and I was on top of him, digging my hands into his eyes. He was screaming bloody murder, telling the other guys to get me off of him, but I wouldn't let go. I forced my fingers into his eyeballs with the intention of ripping them out. Soon he had blood pouring from his eyes! I had completely lost control. I was shaking with anger; my rage was in full force. While attacking him, I was making a shrill, blood-curdling animal sound. It was frightening even to me.

When the guys finally got me off of him, I was so full of rage that I shook like a leaf. It took me a long time to calm down. Once they had pulled me off, several of the guys were attending to him, while about six more surrounded me to prevent me from doing anything else to him. Their concern was first to get him to the infirmary and second to make sure that the NCO wouldn't find out about our fight.

Luckily I didn't do any permanent damage to the guy, but my ferocity shocked everyone. No one in the barracks talked to me for a few days after that. Either they were afraid of me or they thought I was crazy. They all stayed out of my way. That day I established a new meaning for the term "bad ass" in my barracks. It was the meaning the Army had been teaching us - "kill or be killed."

My childhood games of taunting friends and foes to see who was the toughest were over. I was not playing games anymore. I was in training to become a real warrior. If necessary, I knew I would respond with deadly force. War was now my profession.

The material used for Advanced Individual Training consisted of many courses from Geneva Convention rules to drill and ceremony, map reading, first aid, grenade training, and survival skills.

We learned about chemical weapons and how to move through a building filled with smoke and gas. One day we had to enter a building filled with tear gas, remove our gas masks, and find our way out while holding our breath.

We learned to go on patrol and we spent many days in the field. We also attended courses about various aspects of life and combat in Vietnam.

Even though I had never fired a weapon before joining the Army, I enjoyed weapon practice. I learned to zero my rifle by carefully adjusting the sights to guarantee my hitting the bull's-eye when the center of the target was in my crosshairs. I learned how to field-strip the rifle, to keep it clean and ready for use at all times. Dirt causes the M-16 to jam. There was plenty of dirt in Vietnam. I got to be pretty efficient at field-stripping and could break down my weapon in two or three minutes.

The Geneva Conventions enumerated the rules of war and how to conduct ourselves in a war zone. A number of our instructors were Vietnam veterans. They taught us the specifics of how to get through our twelve-month tour alive and how to deal with "Charlie," the enemy.

The WACs (Women's Army Corps) were stationed across the base from us. We could sometimes see them, but they rarely looked our way. Most of the guys would have made a move on them, but no one I knew ever got a response, much less a date. Maybe they knew where we were headed and didn't want an emotional connection.

Toward the end of this intensive training program, a sergeant came to me with a surprising offer. He asked if I would be interested in attending Noncommissioned Officer School (NCO School) to become an infantry sergeant. I was more than surprised at this offer, but I immediately accepted it. I figured that as long as I was in school, I was not in Vietnam and if I had to go there, it might be better to go as a sergeant than as a buck private. Besides that, I liked the idea I had some control of my own destiny and I supposed that meant I like being in charge. Better to become a sergeant.

Most of the soldiers in my barracks were being shipped directly from Fort McClellan to Vietnam. Four of them were assigned to units in Germany. I believed in simple logic when making difficult decisions. *Simple logic has gotta work 95% of the time. What the hell have I got to lose? I can only get in trouble 5% of the time.* By going to NCO school, I felt I had bought myself a little more time and stayed on the 95% end of things, before the 5% caught up with me . . . again.

Chapter 5

Monday, 1 April 1968 Becoming a Shake 'n Bake

It felt good to be returning to a place I already knew and where I felt comfortable. My training was to take place at the NCO Academy at Fort Benning, Georgia. Only three months had passed since I had become a buck private. The forest of pine trees and the sandy soil and scrub grass looked good to me. I got a kick out of seeing the new class of raw recruits on the post. I felt different. I believed that I was already a soldier. I headed for special training with a sense of eagerness. I was already "somebody," and when I graduated this time I would have earned the rank of E-5, known to everyone in the military as an instant NCO. An instant sergeant. A *Shake 'n Bake sergeant.*

Most noncommissioned officers rise through the ranks in the Army after years of service. When I—and others like me—will go from an E-1 to an E-5 in only six months, I will become a *Shake 'n Bake.* This nickname was taken from the Betty Crocker quick-mix product for baking chicken and had become very popular during the sixties. Chicken pieces were placed into a bag containing Betty Crocker's mix. The cook would shake it and then bake it. In a very short time, she had delicious chicken. In three short months, the Army produced instant sergeants *Shake 'n Bakes.*

My initial pride in being chosen for NCO training was soon blunted because I couldn't find anyone on the post who liked us NCOCs. The name simply meant a noncommissioned officer *candidate . . .* a sergeant *in training.* We would not be promoted to the position of a noncommissioned officer until we had completed a twelve-week training period followed by 9 week on-the-job training at an existing military base located stateside.

The older NCOs resented us because we would receive our stripes in school, and not in long-term service or combat. The enlisted men, whom we would command, resented us because we were inexperienced and we might have taken their opportunity for field promotion from them or get them killed while we matured on the job in combat. We were often treated with the same disdain by commissioned officers, although their training had been very similar to ours.

The essence of the problem was based on gut feelings. No one believed the Army could train a sergeant through schooling alone. A squad leader in Vietnam had to have real combat experience. Period. Shake 'n Bake sergeants would have rank and responsibility, but they would be absolutely useless . . . or so it was believed. But that wasn't the belief of the Army; Sergeant Major Wooldridge had different views on the subject (see Exhibit 1.0)

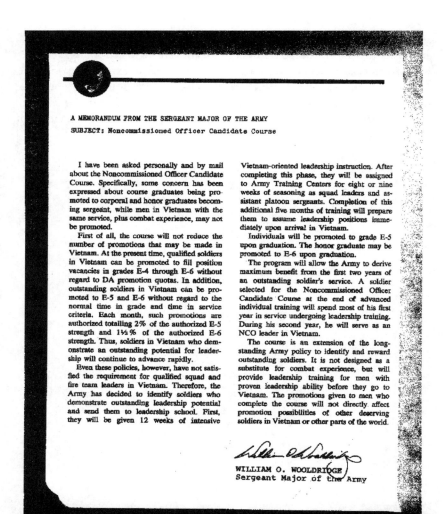

I have been asked personally and by mail about the Noncommissioned Officer Candidate Course. Specifically, some concern has been expressed about course graduates being promoted to corporal and honor graduates becoming sergeant, while men in Vietnam with the same service, plus combat experience, may not be promoted.

First of all, the course will not reduce the number of promotions that may be made in Vietnam. At the present time, qualified soldiers in Vietnam can be promoted to fill position vacancies in grades E-4 through E-6 without regard to DA promotion quotas. In addition, outstanding soldiers in Vietnam can be promoted to E-5 and E-6 without regard to the normal time in grade and time in service criteria. Each month, such promotions are authorized totalling 2% of the authorized E-5 strength and 1½% of the authorized E-6 strength. Thus, soldiers in Vietnam who demonstrate an outstanding potential for leadership will continue to advance rapidly.

Even these policies, however, have not satisfied the requirement for qualified squad and fire team leaders in Vietnam. Therefore, the Army has decided to identify soldiers who demonstrate outstanding leadership potential and send them to leadership school. First, they will be given 12 weeks of intensive Vietnam-oriented leadership instruction. After completing this phase, they will be assigned to Army Training Centers for eight or nine weeks of seasoning as squad leaders and assistant platoon sergeants. Completion of this additional five months of training will prepare them to assume leadership positions immediately upon arrival in Vietnam.

Individuals will be promoted to grade E-5 upon graduation. The honor graduate may be promoted to E-6 upon graduation.

The program will allow the Army to derive maximum benefit from the first two years of an outstanding soldier's service. A soldier selected for the Noncommissioned Officer Candidate Course at the end of advanced individual training will spend most of his first year in service undergoing leadership training. During his second year, he will serve as an NCO leader in Vietnam.

The course is an extension of the long-standing Army policy to identify and reward outstanding soldiers. It is not designed as a substitute for combat experience, but will provide leadership training for men with proven leadership ability before they go to Vietnam. The promotions given to men who complete the course will not directly affect promotion possibilities of other deserving soldiers in Vietnam or other parts of the world.

WILLIAM O. WOOLDRIDGE
Sergeant Major of the Army

Exhibit 1.0 Memorandum from Sergeant Major of the Army

I worried about these negative things at first, but I soon learned that being an infantry squad leader is the Army's toughest job. First of all, I would be solely responsible for my squad of seven to ten men. On a daily

36

basis I would motivate them, help them do their jobs correctly and efficiently, direct them under fire and assure they accomplished their mission, and insist upon the completion of routine activities that they might consider unnecessary. I would have to do this while working *beside* my men, and not leading them from a distance. My men and I would be in the dirt *together*. I would do everything they did, but I alone would take the heat from above if any of my squad members screwed up.

The men in my squad would become my family. As an infantry squad leader, I would look out for their welfare. I would encourage them to come to me with their concerns, problems, or needs as the first link in the chain of command. I would take whatever steps were necessary to get the issues solved. I would set the example and not shirk my own responsibilities. I would be tough. In reality, I would work for my squad, as well as for my superiors. This was my duty.

My job was considered by some the toughest and most important job in the Army. Without sergeants there is no structure for combat. I was determined to perform all my duties to the very best of my ability.

At the time I volunteered for NCO school, there were a hell of a lot of disadvantages and few advantages. But, as I reflect on this period of my life, attending this school was one of the best decisions I ever made. I learned the value of good training, of acquiring and maintaining personal discipline, and of working cooperatively with others to get a job done. I also learned how to effectively command others while earning and keeping their respect. These were some of life's most valuable lessons.

For the first few weeks at the academy, my classmates and I were subjected to the same harassment we had experienced in Basic Training. This harassment was both physical and mental. We had to continue with push-ups, the low crawl, and running everywhere throughout the post, but being young and in good physical shape made these tasks bearable. The mental harassment was more difficult. It consisted of incessant pressure to perform at our absolute peaks. The TAC NCOs, our training sergeants, yelled, cursed, and intimidated in an effort to break our spirits. They exerted pressure to keep our uniforms and personal effects neat, clean, spit-polished, and in excellent working order. This was to ensure that we understood the importance of paying attention to details even under extreme conditions. We would set the example for our men to follow when engaged in combat.

Orderliness is a habit. The Army knew, through years of experience, that soldiers need this discipline. Most of the world doesn't understand this concept and our educational system doesn't teach it. In striving to be consistently neat and clean and to have our personal effects in order, we learn the importance of paying attention to details. In any of life's situations, but especially in combat, such attention to detail can make the difference between success and failure . . . or life and death.

As our structured harassment continued into the second week, I recognized that something important was occurring. We were acquiring new attitudes and beliefs, which would have a profound effect on our future judgments, behavior, and characters. We were taking control of our destinies and conquering our demons. We were learning to stay focused. We were learning that, in Vietnam, if we didn't stay focused we would either die or cause someone else to die. That was the bottom line.

By the third week at the Academy, I began to feel like an NCO. Our training had become intense as we earnestly focused on the business of soldiering. We worked with the Rangers, who had prepared a three-week course especially for us. The Rangers were a group of highly trained soldiers who were graduates of the Army's special Ranger School in northern Georgia. They were trained to penetrate behind enemy lines and perform dangerous missions under harsh weather conditions. They were analogous to the Navy Seals, but Ranger activity was land-based. Many of our Ranger instructors were Vietnam veterans. They carefully instructed us in the combat situations we would face. We were beginning to feel like first-class soldiers. We were being set apart and prepared for something special . . . to lead others in combat, a formidable responsibility and not to be taken lightly.

In the last two months my training was identical to that given officer candidates. Our classes took place in the same classrooms of the Infantry School. During this period, harassment and discipline continued, but the Army's goal was not to attempt to break us (to weed out those who were unable to become leaders) but to have us finish the program. They needed us in Vietnam.

Our classrooms and our training were the finest the Army had to offer. The instructors were first-rate and, as Vietnam combat veterans, each man had extensive experience with the subject matter he taught. The classrooms themselves were state-of-the-art, with a variety of audiovisual

38

aids and video and projection systems. The Army spared no expense to teach us about the war in Vietnam. The classes were so instructive that officers from other countries were also in attendance.

The NCO candidate course consisted of many subjects. It included cross-training in leadership, communications, survival techniques, weapons, and infantry combat leadership. The course also included extensive conditioning exercises: physical training (PT), squad drilling, and bayonet fighting. Every candidate received the same training.

I learned that leadership is not the same thing as management. Leadership goes beyond the basic motivational concepts that are taught in management schools. Leadership includes trust and mutual respect. No one will follow a leader who does not practice and encourage confidence, integrity, honesty, competence, and justice. Each of these is an essential ingredient for any team effort to accomplish a worthy—and in combat situations, dangerous—goal.

In NCO school we learned how to accomplish the mission and to provide for the welfare of the men. We learned that we could not do the first if we didn't do the second.

Leadership ought to be a required course in every grade school, high school, and college throughout our country. We should not leave the learning of these valuable lessons to chance.

History shows that the Shake 'n Bake sergeants performed well in combat. They served with distinction as leaders in our infantry units. They suffered high casualty rates in combat because they were assigned to units that experienced heavy fighting. There were 1,003 Shake 'n Bakes killed in combat out of 20,068 men trained. This casualty rate, at five percent, was considered to be extremely high. I had no idea that I was pursuing one of the Army's most dangerous careers.

Horton in NCO School Friday, 7 June 68

I was a graduate of the twenty-fifth class of that year of NCOC training. I was promoted to Sergeant E-5 as an 11B20 Light Weapons Infantryman. Of the 133 graduates in my class, eight became combat casualties in Vietnam. There were three Medal of Honor recipients among the 20,068 graduates of NCOC Infantry.

Shake N' Bake Casualties: Killed in Action in Vietnam

Year	Class	Graduates	Casualties
1968	41 Classes	5,640 Graduates	453 KIA
1969	49 Classes	6,572 Graduates	343 KIA
1970	30 Classes	4,150 Graduates	192 KIA
1971	17 Classes	2,595 Graduates	14 KIA
1972	7 Classes	1,111 Graduates	1 KIA
TOTAL	120 Classes	20,068 Graduates	1,003 KIA

Chapter 6

After graduating from NCO School, I was assigned to on-the-job training (OJT) training at Fort Ord, California. Fort Ord was located near Monterey on the Pacific Ocean, only one hundred miles from San Francisco.

I traveled to California by first hitching a ride with a buddy as far as the Denver area, where I spent a couple of days, and then I caught a Greyhound bus the rest of the way into San Francisco. When I arrived there, I stored my Army stuff in a locker at the bus station and proceeded, for the next few days to become a hippie again. My hair had grown out beyond regulation length, so I didn't look too military. Anyway, the other hippies I met in San Francisco were friendly and welcoming, just as they had been before. I told a number of them that I was going to Vietnam; they had no problem with that. They knew the war was not my fault. They still accepted me as a person. I met no soldier haters among them.

As soon as I reached San Francisco, I decided that I was going to have a hell of a good time for a few days before checking in at Ft. Ord. I had some leave, a little Army pay in my pocket, and no serious concerns. Having fun was the ticket!

I partied for two days and nights straight. During this time, I wandered on foot all over the City. Just being there refreshed me. I was tireless. It felt great to be in San Francisco again and I had no problems there; thanks to the Army, I was in excellent physical condition, and took those steep hills in stride.

I may have caught a little shuteye in Golden Gate park, but, for the first few days, I didn't sleep at any crash houses. I was dressed in jeans, a sweatshirt, an Army fatigue jacket and, of course, tennis shoes. This outfit probably constituted most of the civilian clothes I owned at that time.

One night I went to the Avalon Ballroom to see the rock band Big Brother and the Holding Company. The Avalon, located near downtown in the Mission district, had replaced the famous Fillmore Auditorium as the place to give rock concerts. The Avalon was just a large white stucco auditorium with a stage in the center. There were no chairs in it; it was just a large dance floor with a stage.

That night Janis Joplin sang the songs from her album, *Cheap Thrills*, the very first time she had ever sung them in concert. Her performance was absolutely amazing to hear. And all the while I was listening to her, anything and everything was going on around me – people were eating, drinking, dancing, sleeping, doing drugs, making love, whatever they wanted. There must have been at least a thousand hippies in that place "rocking out" to this great music, which was played full blast from huge speakers, and with so much heart.

That night I became a hippie again. Janis connected with each of us; we were one with her and with her music. That sexy low voice, and her ability to sing and really feel the blues, was the greatest music I had ever heard.

Pretty soon I started dancing with a tall blonde girl who was quite beautiful. I didn't really know how to dance anything but the jitterbug very well. What we did together could not really be called dancing either; there were no steps to follow. It was more like feeling the music with our bodies, and swaying to the vibrations as though we were filled with the music. Everyone was dancing that way. I must have done a good job at it, because that girl danced with me until four o'clock in the morning.

About halfway through Janice's performance, her band took an intermission break. While the music was silent, somebody turned out all the lights. There we were, in this massive ballroom filled with hippies, milling around in total darkness. I will never forget my beautiful blonde friend, and how we held each other very close there in the darkness. Words didn't matter. We were young. We just held each other, enjoying the vibrations we felt.

Then someone focused a small spotlight near one end of the stage. By straining we could see that a white-haired old black guy was being assisted onto it. As he slowly walked over to a chair and sat down, the spotlight followed him. Then someone handed him a trumpet. He started playing Dixieland - real slow, real sweet. That huge ballroom fell completely silent. We could only see that one spotlight on that old musician in a corner of the stage. Otherwise there was total darkness. Everyone was mesmerized. What was this? Except for the music, you could hear a pin drop.

Then, in a minute, another spotlight switched on and another old guy was helped onto the stage. Pretty soon he too was playing his music. Now there were two instruments, two sounds weaving their sweet notes together. This same process - new spotlight, new musician, new sweet notes - continued, one old guy at a time, until the stage was filled with a dozen musicians. All of them were black, all of them were over sixty-five, and all of them were blasting Dixieland into our souls like you never heard it before.

The Avalon rocked and rocked and rocked. An electric connection flowed between those old musicians, their music, and that crowd of hippies. It was as though everything in the room blended together and carried us to some place or some level that none of us will ever forget. At that moment, the Avalon rocked with perfection; this was how life was supposed to be! Those old men, whose names will remain forever unknown since they were never introduced, had showed us the true power of music. I wished that experience could have lasted forever. I forgot that I was even in the Army.

All good things must come to an end, so after a wonderful visit to San Francisco it was time for me to report to Ft. Ord. I retrieved my Army stuff from the downtown Greyhound bus station locker and hitchhiked down to Monterey. I had completely lost track of time and much to my surprise, I arrived a couple of days late. When I arrived at Ft. Ord, the 1st Sergeant just looked at me and grunted. "Well, Sarge, did you have a good time?"

At least, when I reported for duty, I had my uniform on.

OJT (On the Job Training) is designed to give us an opportunity to gain experience leading troops in the field before Vietnam. My troops would be men who had completed Basic Training and were in Advanced Training for Infantry . . . men like me, just seven months ago. Now they would take orders from me, their drill sergeant. I was the Sergeant Garrett for these men. I hoped I could be half as effective and worthy a leader as he had been.

I was assigned to a barracks next to the mess hall. I shared a room with Karl Parish, which was convenient, since we were both assigned to the same platoon. Karl was a Specialist 4 and had just completed his tour in Vietnam as a soldier in the 101st Airborne Infantry. We soon became close friends. Karl was assigned to Fort Ord to serve out his time in the service. I was surprised to learn that he was adamantly opposed to the

43

Vietnam War. Every time we talked about Vietnam, he urged me to get out of going any way I could. His experience there had been completely negative. Karl had contracted malaria and had been stationed in the Central Highlands, near a town called Kontum, and in the Plei Trap Valley.

I performed the drill instructor's job, just as my drill sergeants had done during my tutelage in Basic Training. I led the marching and the drills. I participated in PT and helped the students work their weapons on the rifle ranges. I made sure they stayed awake during class, and supervised them in the barracks. Sometimes they came to me with their problems. We frequently held overnight field maneuvers. I worked side by side with my men. I enjoyed being a leader and found it easy to bond with those in my charge.

Ft. Ord was located near one of the most beautiful beaches in the world, close to a small town called Carmel-by-the-Sea. From that beach you could see some of the prettiest sunsets visible anywhere on this earth. Frequently Karl and I would take our leave from the post at the end of the day, camp out on Carmel beach, party with the hippies all night, and just make it back to the post before reveille the next morning.

Each night, we would collect huge logs beside the road, haul them to the beach, and build a bonfire. Once we had a fire started, hippies would start to show up. The crowd would grow from five or six people to sometimes fifteen or twenty. Invariably during the night, as the music got louder and the fun continued, joints were passed around. The cool fresh air blowing in from the Pacific, the night, our hippie friends, and the fire, were captivating.

Since Karl and I lived in the barracks with the company cooks, we became their good buddies and would be given cases of C-rations to bring to the beach. We shared our rations with the hippies we met there. There always seemed to be at least one good musician around our campfire, and if we were not listening to their music, we would have Cream with Ginger Baker or Eric Clapton blasting away from Karl's portable tape deck. On the weekends Karl and I traveled up to Haight-Ashbury and hung out. I worried sometimes that we were having too much fun!

It was like Karl and I weren't really in the Army, and the Vietnam War was not really there facing me. While on the beach with my hippie friends, I would forget about the war entirely. It was a strange world -

44

here I was partying with hippies on one of the most beautiful beaches in the world all night, and preparing myself for war all day. But somehow my mind was at peace with these two contradictory realities. I just focused where I needed to from moment to moment, enjoying each event as best I could. How sweet life was, those nights on Carmel beach!

One weekend on leave I drove down to Los Angeles with Willy McClean, one of the guys in my platoon. He was a young kid, only seventeen, who had gotten in trouble with the law and agreed to join the Army rather than go to jail. Willy had invited me to visit his parents house in L.A. His parents had a nice Southern California house with a pool. Very middle class. We were hardly settled in when Willy told me we were going to meet his cousin, Tiny Tim of the Hell's Angels. I said, "Cool, let's go."

So we drove across L.A. to his Aunt's house.

Tiny Tim lived in the garage next to the house. He was a massive guy - at least 300 pounds worth. He sported a kung fu mustache and was dressed in the standard Hell's Angels leather attire. Tiny Tim looked mean as hell, but everything was cool because I was the kid's sergeant, as well as his friend.

Tiny Tim's room was indescribable. He had hung German silver helmets, knives, guns, bandoleers of ammo, posters, maps, newspaper headlines, pictures of women, everything you can imagine, all over his walls. It's like his life was displayed there on those walls. I guessed the room looked just like you would think a Hell's Angel's room should look, a sort of den of sex, threats and violence. Soon the kid, Tiny Tim and I all set off together to see what kind of action we could stir up in Los Angeles.

First we went to a park, bought some cheap wine, and hung out with hippies, listening to a band play. Then sometime during the day, we heard about a Hell's Angels party that night. Of course we had to go!

The Angels' house was located in an older residential section not too far from the park. Originally it had been white, but now it badly needed new paint. We walked through a front yard, which was covered in Harleys and dead grass. The Harleys were left completely unprotected. *That's far out*, I thought.

Tiny reassured us that nobody but nobody would steal an Angel bike. Angel bikes had Satan's protection. If any bike was ever stolen, all the

Angel groups in the country would be notified. "Would you want every Angel in the U.S. looking for you?"

We walked into the main living room, which was full of bikers and their women, all hanging out, smoking cigarettes or pot, drinking beer and other things, and talking. Tim was eager to introduce me to everyone. They all thought it was really cool that I was the kid's sergeant. The bond between these gang members was so tight, the mere fact I was there - through my connection to the kid and Tiny Tim - meant that I was welcome. Otherwise, I would not have made it through the door.

By that time, due to the wine we had been drinking all day, I was pretty wasted. I remember that someone announced my name, Sgt, Horton, and said that I was headed to Vietnam. Everyone cheered. In that moment I realized that the Hell's Angels had accepted me as one of their own that day. I was given a pass to be one of them and as the Angels did, I too lived on the edge. They respected me for that.

As the afternoon wore into night, the music grew louder. There were biker women all over the house, but most of them were clearly attached to tough-looking Angels. These women all looked as wild as I could imagine. I thought they would probably try anything. Most of them had dark hair and wore jeans, dark sweaters or vests, and plenty of tattoos, some made of words and some just designs leading down into their clothes. In the dim light they all seemed very sexy to me, even the plain-looking ones, probably because of their tight-fitting clothes and the wine I had been drinking. I wanted to make a move on one or two of them but I couldn't tell for sure who was attached to whom. At first I was afraid even to talk to them, for fear of getting some Angel ticked off.

When Tiny Tim, Willy and I left about noon, most of the house was still asleep. Willie told me later, back at the post, that the party had continued for another day and a night. I just remember that, once outside, the fresh air felt good on my face. I took a deep breath and thought, *I've been to a Hell's Angel's party and I've survived!*

Pretty damn good. Once we got back to the post, it took me a couple of days to fully recover.

Life at the post meant the boredom of continued drilling until, several weeks later, Karl and I attended a two-day rock concert in Big Sur, California. Big Sur is actually a forest more than a town, right on the Pacific Ocean, about 100 miles south of Monterey. It was a magical place, completely filled with trees that were thousands of years old. These forests covered dramatic mountains that in places literally fell straight down to the sea. Big Sur appeared to be a location frozen in time.

The concert was held on a cliff near the Pacific where multiple shades of green, turquoise, and blue ocean blended together to form a natural, unforgettable stage-setting for a unique gathering of hippies and folk singers. Joan Baez, Judy Collins, The Mamas and the Papas, and the Green River Mountain Boys were just a few of the artists scheduled to perform the weekend we were there. The artists and the hippies mixed easily, and the concert was more like a community get-together than a formal performance.

At first, the organizers tried to charge people for attending the event, but there were so many hippies - they were just all over the place – that they gave up. Anyone who was in Big Sur was automatically a part of what was happening.

Judy Collins' voice, mixed with the sounds of the ocean, and held the crowd, mesmerized. As she sang, we were surrounded by the ocean, the breezes and the sounds of the Big Sur forests. There was so much pot and incense floating in the air; it finally overcame the strong sweet smell of the forest. People wore beautiful multi-colored clothes, and somehow flowers seemed to be everywhere. Soon a lot of people were dancing around stark naked. I was reminded of my early hippie days in New Orleans.

The concert lasted all day, into the night and through the following day. People crashed everywhere. We had gathered to enjoy the music, the location, this unique time in history, and our friends without worrying about tomorrow, or what was happening in the rest of the world. We lived for the moment. Who knew how long it would last? After the weekend was over, I found it difficult to make my way back to Ft. Ord. Why couldn't I be a hippie for the next year, instead of going to Vietnam? When my thoughts turned black like this, I would comfort myself by recalling the statistics that promised I had only a one in thirty chance of ever getting in harm's way in that country. And, as usual, I felt lucky.

Sometime during my twelve weeks at Fort Ord I learned that the Army was looking for helicopter pilots. They would be willing to send me to flight school where, after twelve more weeks, I would graduate a warrant officer. I signed up. Learning new skills and acquiring knowledge about anything was like being in college. I knew the benefits would become increasingly more valuable with time.

So instead of going from Fort Ord to Vietnam, I was accepted into Flight School in September of 1968. I received my orders to report to Fort Wolters near Fort Worth, Texas.

~~

I was given a week's leave before flight school training. I decided to visit family members in West Virginia because I had learned that soldiers could fly standby for a reduced airfare.

Karl Parish drove me to the San Francisco airport. I said my good-byes to Karl, knowing that I would probably never see him again. My Army uniform had new sergeant's stripes sewn on the sleeves. I observed the bewilderment in the faces of several people in the airport when they saw a young man, with a youthful virtuous face, wearing a uniform with three sergeant's stripes. I knew they were thinking I looked like a kid playing soldier.

Chapter 7

Sunday, 1 September 68   Mineral Wells Texas

After a few days leave in West Virginia I hitchhiked to Texas. Later in a letter home I wrote.

I'm here in the Army again. I had a good time hitchhiking down from Charleston, and made it to Dallas about six p.m. Friday. I then commenced to party and have a good time until midnight, then hitchhiked over to Fort Worth (30 miles away) and continued to party at an all-night place I found there, something like the Checkmate but better. The next morning I hitchhiked on into Mineral Wells, accompanied by a hangover. To my surprise, when I arrived, my uniform was not at the bus station.

After my night of partying, I had decided to check into a hotel and think about what to do now that my uniform had not arrived. I had shipped my bags separately from West Virginia and they were lost by the bus company. Plus I decided to catch up on some much needed sleep. By this time, I calculated that, between the hitchhiking and the partying, I had been awake about four days straight.

Mineral Wells was a very small town located just outside of Ft. Worth, Texas. It had one hotel, one restaurant and a few stores. The town seemed to exist to meet the military's needs. My hotel room was old but very clean and cheap. It would do. I had been partying hard and I was exhausted.

The Fort Worth bus station was within walking distance of my hotel. Several times during the day, I checked on the arrival status of my bags. Each time, I was told they had not yet arrived. They must have been transferred to another bus. They would show up. I'd have to be patient. They were doing everything they could to locate them. Other than worrying, I spent all of Saturday and Sunday resting at my hotel. What in the world would I tell my superiors when I showed up at flight school wearing jeans and a sweater, with only an Army jacket for a uniform? Monday arrived. No uniform. As the time passed, I was sure I would be kicked out of flight school before I had spent a day on the premises.

My bags arrived on Tuesday. The damage was done. I was now in a hell of a situation. So I decided to report to the Fort Wolters in my civilian clothes, even though I now had my uniform. It might show that I was concerned about reporting for duty immediately upon receiving it.

Unfortunately, not only was I reporting late, I looked more like a hippie than a sergeant.

Reporting to Fort Wolters in civilian clothes and two days late was quite a surprise to the officers of the 4th Warrant Officer Company. They had expected me on Saturday. This was Warrant Officer Flight School, the training and discipline was rigorous. Too late, I realized I should have reported in my civvies and not waited the three days for my gear and uniform.

Within seconds I had a Major, two Captains, two Lieutenants, and a Warrant Officer watching me do pushups on the floor of the orderly room while they shouted a stream of degradations. The room overflowed with officers and NCOs, all of whom seemed to be yelling too. Everyone who wasn't yelling was watching—and enjoying—the show. I had become quite a spectacle.

Fifty pushups later I was fading. They wanted more. They told me in great detail what a lowlife I was, how I didn't deserve to be in flight school, and that an officer would know better than to go AWOL over lack of a uniform. They assigned me to a holding company until they could decide what to do with me. Memories of my humiliation in the office of my school principal when I was a kid returned. Being late does have consequences.

Later that day, I talked with others in the flight school training program. They were unanimous in suggesting that my superiors would make me sign up for an additional two years of active service before they would let me continue flight school. Flight training was expensive. The Army could not afford to lose pilots so soon after training them. They would use my slip-up as a means to tighten the noose.

I was concerned about this new revelation. What if I signed up, then discovered that I didn't like flying? Was I willing to wait three years before returning to college?

I decided to forgo flight school. Better to go to Vietnam and get it over with than commit to another two years in the Army. I told the officer in charge that I wanted out of the program. He immediately sent me to the post commander. The commander was a lieutenant colonel.

He listened to my decision in a very civil manner. He said that he wanted me to continue with flight school and explained his reasons in detail. Although he didn't change my mind, I appreciated his honesty and his willingness to treat me with respect.

50

I told the colonel of my goal. "I want to become an engineer, sir. I've wanted to be one since I was a boy. I believe it is my calling in life. I finished one year at Louisiana Tech with almost straight A's. I joined the Army because I didn't have the tuition money to finish the last three years. College and then engineering are my passions. I'm hoping to finish on the GI Bill."

As I talked, the colonel listened intently; he knew I was serious. After I finished, he spoke in a quiet voice. "This means you will go to Vietnam right away, Sergeant."

"Yes, sir, I know. I might as well get it over with. I'll just have to fight my way to college, that's all. I'm willing to risk my life in Vietnam for the opportunity to earn my degree."

"Jerry, I think you would have made a good pilot, but I admire your determination to make your life count for something. I hope some day you will become an engineer. I know you'll make a good one. Keep your head down in Vietnam."

By the time I left the colonel's office, I knew I had made the right decision. The colonel had treated me as well as he would have treated his own son. He had listened. He hadn't used his position of authority to talk me out of my decision. He had encouraged me to hold fast to my dream.

The next day I was assigned to another holding company. While awaiting my new orders they put me in charge of the post's burial detail. The Army provides a full military funeral for all veterans whose family requests one. I was put in charge of the pallbearers for these events. Before the burial itself, I was to remove the flag from the casket, carefully fold it, and present it to either the widow or mother of the deceased. Another group of soldiers fired the rifle salute. The mission of the burial detail was to honor the deceased.

One day a young black soldier who had recently returned from his tour in Vietnam was killed in a senseless fight in downtown Dallas. His funeral was held in a white clapboard, one-room church. When I arrived with my burial detail, the church was completely filled with family and friends. I sat in the front of the church with five other young soldiers— all of us Caucasians—facing the black congregation. Below us, the open casket rested on the floor in front of the pulpit. We could see the young man lying in the casket as though he were sleeping. It was hot that

51

particular October day, and the air was stale. The heat was soon forgotten, because the service was electrifying.

At least five preachers conducted the funeral. One, who wore a long black trench coat, reminded me of Reverend Leroy on the Flip Wilson television show. As he was preaching, he would suddenly break into song, then return to his sermon, then break into song again, and so on. Every few minutes, he would stop to exclaim, "Strange things do happen." After each pause, the choir sang a few words.

The mourners were mesmerized. They experienced tension, sorrow, and hope at the same time. At one point I glanced at the young soldier to my left. Tears ran down the cheeks of his baby face. He was so young it looked like he didn't even shave. Soon we all were carried away in the emotion of the moment. We were part of the family that day, and we grieved with them. The service was a powerful event for me. I saw humanity at its very best that day. By our presence, we six soldiers honored both the deceased and his family. We stood tall, clean, and proud. Through us, they saw their young man at his best. I will never forget it.

I served on the burial detail for a month or more before my orders for Vietnam arrived. My departure date would be the fifteenth of December. Just like that, my leaf was headed into new, more turbulent waters, towards who knows what dangers?

I took my leave of Ft. Worth, Texas on November 10th, on a chilly winter's day, and headed back to West Virginia. The Army had given me a thirty-day leave and then Vietnam. As I stepped out onto the highway to hitchhike home, I had the orders stuck in my back pocket.

With only thirty days of freedom left, why did I waste my time hitchhiking? I could easily afford a plane or bus ticket, and I needed to be with my family. But I also needed time to think about my life. Out on the road I could think. Out on the road I felt free. In the wide open spaces I was my own man.

When I reached Charleston, it was two in the morning. As I walked through the silent streets, I felt alone. Each time I hitchhiked into this town, I had the same experience. The old familiar neighborhood lay before me - Lincoln School, the playground, the Valley Bell. They were all the same, but I was different somehow. Even though the streets were quiet and my mind was at peace when I neared home again, I knew that events were about to hurl me into rapid and uncontrolled currents. This

52

made me wonder whether I was the same old Jerry. I had traveled so far in such a short time. And now like a time traveler, I was returning from a distant adventure and I saw my homeland through new eyes. It looked more like my past than my future.

I was not a particularly religious person, but before I went to Vietnam I made my amends to God. One day my Aunt Polly told Jack, who was also home on leave before Vietnam, and me that Grandma Horton wanted us to take her to church. She wanted us to dress up in our best military uniforms. Grandma was proud of us and she wanted to show the whole church what fine young grandsons she had.

Grady Horton, my grandmother, was my father's mother. She had lived in Charleston all her life. She was the kindest and most gentle person I have ever known, and she treated all of her grandchildren real special. She was always happy to see me and told me how proud of me she was when I enrolled in college. Grandma was an intelligent and dignified lady, and her life had been tough. She had raised six kids in rough times.

Grandma went to a Methodist church called Humphrey's that was right across the street from Lincoln Playground. From early childhood it had looked like a castle to me, with its brooding dark brown exterior and two steeples, one at each end of the building. Inside a magnificent pipe organ reached up the back wall and beautiful stained glass windows filtered holy light all around. This church was one of the oldest traditional churches in Charleston. Grandma had been attending since it started. So she was known to the whole community.

The day we went to church, Jack Smith was in his blue uniform and I was in my green. As we walked up the steps of the church, Jack was holding one of Grandma's arms and I was holding the other. She was beaming from ear to ear. This was her day. I knew that everyone who saw us thought, *what a fine family, that Horton family.*

I felt proud that day. Everyone was watching us. The church was packed and most of the congregation was Grandma's friends and neighbors. The preacher acknowledged us as guests and had us stand before the congregation to be seen. When Jack and I stood up, we lifted Grandma up with us. Everyone smiled and there was loud applause. I stood tall and straight. I could feel Grandma beaming. I was smiling myself, inside and out, and I wanted everyone to see me with my Grandma and Jack, and understand what we represented – honor, duty, and pride. I wanted everyone to see that we were set apart, that we were chosen to represent them in our duty to our country. This was our sacrifice which we would make for them, for those people watching us in the congregation. They needed to see us. They needed to know that we were there to serve them. Grandma wanted them to know that her children were the men who were going to defend our country. It was for her, and for them, that we would put our lives on the line.

This was a proud moment, and it was also a profound moment for me. But today I know that Grandma had another reason for inviting Jack and I to church. She knew that we were soon to be in harm's way, and she knew how important it was to hold our hands together in prayer. She wanted God to look out for us. She prayed for us and so did the congregation. She knew more wisely than we what we were headed for. She knew that we had to be prepared to die - by making our amends to God. Thank you, Grandma.

Chapter 8

Sunday, 15 December 68

December 15th arrived too soon. My family all stood on the runway at Charleston Airport as I walked up the steps to that Eastern Airlines plane. I turned to say goodbye one more time. They smiled and waved. I was heartsick. I felt like a condemned prisoner that day, a guy facing his last days on earth. I didn't want to get on that airplane. I tried to stretch time, to make it go slower. I was leaving for the unknown.

Leaving for the Unknown

Finally, it was time to leave. I couldn't avoid it. Damn, time had gone by too fast. Life was so good. Why did I have to go?

I boarded the plane and looked around. I was the only military guy on that airplane. Nobody else was going where I was going. Nobody else felt what I felt. I found my seat and looked out the window. I saw them standing there. I cried like a baby.

Later I thought about the war I was headed into. I wondered if I had been destined somehow to be a soldier. Why did I play those war games I played as a kid? Why was I headed to fight in Vietnam for my country? Was it fate that drove me there? There weren't plastic green soldiers there, but real bullets, real people, and the game was for real.

In Seattle, I took a bus to the army post at Fort Lewis, Washington, an embarkation point for those assigned to duty in Vietnam. Ft. Lewis was actually covered in pine trees – it was very pretty. The facilities were Spartan but comfortable. The post was full of young men all going to Vietnam. Troops seemed to be constantly moving in all directions. I saw chaos everywhere I looked. Even though the post was large, I felt like I had no private space to myself.

I had never seen so many troops in one place. Thousands of us milled around in our drab green fatigues, waiting for our departure dates. The sky was as gloomy as our spirits, and it rained every day. I got reacquainted with Army chow and slept on the standard Army bunks. I had the same quiet, desperate look about me as the other soldiers. We went about our business slowly, just passing the time. We didn't initiate poker games or drinking parties. We didn't drill; we didn't practice anything. We just sat around and waited.

I called home twice a day. Phoning was expensive, but it didn't matter. There was a row of pay phones near the PX where I stood in line to make a call, often in the rain. I paid cash if I had it, or I called collect. I talked for five or ten minutes, until the soldier behind me complained.

Every single day a list was posted. I lined up with a thousand other guys to check the numbers and one day my number was finally listed. I would be leaving the following Wednesday morning at seven. I had to rise early enough to turn in my baggage by three in the morning, and then catch the bus to the Sea-Tac airport at five o'clock. My plane would fly to either Da Nang or Cam Ranh Bay. Da Nang was located in the northern part of South Vietnam and Cam Ranh Bay was in the central part. When I arrived, I would probably be sent to the 90th Replacement Battalion, where I would be assigned to a unit— either the 1st Air Cavalry or the 25th Infantry Division.

I left Sea-Tac air base near Fort Lewis on a large jet full of young soldiers. The plane carried 220 troops. Stewardesses served food and beverages, just like on a commercial flight. But this plane was different. Everyone was dressed in olive drab and everyone was uncharacteristically quiet. I slept a lot. When awake, I spent my time daydreaming of home. Once again I did my out-of-mind-and-body thing. I went somewhere else in my mind and traveled beyond the limits of my body. It was a way to cope with the unknown.

I wondered if I would be a good sergeant. Could I lead other men in battle? Would I be brave enough, strong enough, and knowledgeable enough to keep them out of danger while we fulfilled our missions? Would they follow my directions and trust me?

We flew for thirty hours, stopping twice to refuel. The first stop was at Honolulu Airport. The weather was balmy and warm. I remember the terminal had an enormous pond filled with exotic fish. Palm trees and mountains created a beautiful vista, one that was totally new to me. I wished I had time to explore the entire island of Oahu. After refueling, though, we flew on to Guam.

What a contrast! As soon as we landed, a blast of intense heat hit us. The island looked flat and barren . . . and unwelcoming. We had no interest in debarking. Our last stop was in Cam Ranh Bay, Vietnam.

Finally Vietnam. My new home. I deplaned, with the other soldiers, and my first impression was negative. The heat was intense. Sweat rolled off my face and soaked my fatigues. The signs of war—trucks, tanks, planes, and people—filled this vista. This was my new reality. I had entered the war zone.

Even though I was here it all seemed surreal. How could I have gotten here? Am I ready for this?

Chapter 9

Thursday, 19 December 68

Within a few minutes after our debarkation, buses appeared to take us to our barracks.

As we drove through the base, we saw that Cam Ranh was like an armed compound, with barracks, supply buildings, and hangars organized around the airfield, only it was more primitive than I had expected. Our barracks—permanent structures with thick walls of sandbags around the bases—were similar to the ones we had occupied at Fort Lewis. Behind the barracks, in the near distance, I saw tree-covered mountains. Jeeps and trucks sped across every open space.

After I pulled my gear off the bus and ate some army chow, I was assigned to the barracks. I was told that I would be shipped to another location, either that night or first thing in the morning. I didn't know anyone, but I recognized a few soldiers from the plane. No one tried to make friends, since we would be assigned to different locations. None of us were in the mood for small talk.

I thought many of my compatriots were scared, but I didn't judge them for feeling that way. I had butterflies myself; none of us knew what to expect. At Fort Lewis, we had heard plenty of wild stories about Cam Ranh being the object of attacks by sappers who were skilled VC or NVA infiltrators sent to damage fixed defenses , and about the fighting that raged in the mountains surrounding the base. As far as we knew, we could have been under attack at any moment, and we hadn't received our weapons yet.

I wrote in my first letter to home:

I am in Vietnam now and at Cam Ranh Bay waiting for further shipping. I do not have an address yet and I will not have one until I am assigned to a regular unit. I do not know how long that will take. I arrived at 5:00 in the morning and was processing until about an hour ago. It is now 11:00. Our flight took 30 hours and we stopped in

Hawaii , Guam and here. The plane was very big — carried 220 troops. I am now assigned to a barracks and will probably ship to another shipping point tonight or in the morning. I found out that the next shipping point is Ben Hoa . I'm going ahead and say that I'm probably not going up in the highlands like I said.Ben Hoa is a little east of east of Saigon. When I get to Ben Hoa I'll spend a little time there and be assigned to a permanent unit which will be close by.I think I'll be doing what I was trained for and that's a squad leader in infantry. This will probably be better than sticking me in mortars. At least I'll be doing a little of what I was trained to do .Right now it is not that hot cause we are close to the ocean but when I ship out it will be hot. It also does not seem like Vietnam right now except seeing these funny little Vietnamese running around. Boy, they are really weird looking. It all seems strange to me right now. It feels like you ought to jump out and hit one but they mind their own business and get along. Well I'll find out after a little while anyway.

I think this is the first time in my life that it really hurt to leave home.

I mailed it through the standard army system. No stamp was needed. I merely added a code to the envelope, designating that I was in a war zone. I learned, later, that my letters took approximately one or two weeks to reach West Virginia.

I remained at Cam Ranh Bay for two days. I could not get used to being around the Vietnamese people. They were surprisingly small and appeared quite fragile. They moved freely about the base, communicating in a few words of broken English. It was my understanding that they lived in a nearby village and worked at Cam Ranh. The military police carefully checked their paperwork before allowing them onto the base. Because these Vietnamese were about the same height and dressed similarly, they looked the same to me. They rarely looked directly into anyone's eyes, so my initial reaction was not to trust any of them. I remembered what Sergeant Garrett had said, "Don't trust the Vietnamese. They are the enemy. They will kill you if they have a chance."

Chapter 10

Friday, 20 December 68

It is 4:00 in the morning and I'm at the airport in Cam Ranh Bay waiting to go to my next station. I am not going to Ben Hoa close to Saigon like I thought. I am going to the 4th infantry replacement at Pleiku which is in the north and about 20 miles from the Cambodian border. I will be in the 4th infantry division and will be operating in the North near the Cambodian border. I no doubt will be a squad leader too. Pleiku is right at the end of the Ho Chi Min trail you also hear about. I really don't know what to say about getting assigned up in that vicinity – only I don't like being that close to the Cambodian border. I no doubt will be at the replacement station at Pleiku for about 7 to 10 days and then will be assigned to a unit around that area. I am going to sign off now and I will continue writing when I get to Pleiku. Well, I am in Pleiku now and it is 3:00. I will find out my permanent address next Tuesday or Wednesday for sure. I will also find out exactly where I will be in the area. I will not get paid until next Tuesday or Wednesday. I will be in training Monday, Tuesday or Wednesday here and will be going to my unit Friday which is Christmas. It is hot here and they say it is very cold at night. Pleiku base camp is about 14 miles out of the city of Pleiku. We drove though the city on the way out here and it was something else. I never saw such a dirty place in my life . People live like rats and the whole city can be best described as a giant penny arcade. There are a lot of Vietnamese who work here on the base camp and they seem friendly but I wonder why the Army allows it cause it would be so easy for VC to sneak in and blow up something. It is really a weird feeling. I found out that the Cambodian border was just 28 miles from here. The 4th division is all up and down the Cambodian border.

I was told that I would be going to an area near the Cambodian border where there was a mixture of South Vietnamese people and tribesmen. These tribesmen were Montagnards. They lived in the surrounding mountains and jungle in a few villages and were friendly toward Americans. I was told that if I encountered anyone in the jungle I could safely assume that they were the enemy. If they were not Americans and they carried weapons, I was instructed to shoot first and ask questions later. That is, if I wanted to live.

The Ho Chi Minh trail was the Communists' main supply route from the north. The enemy moved both men and supplies down this trail on a daily basis. In our area of operations, the trail split into many small arteries on the Cambodian border. The U.S. Army was never allowed to invade North Vietnam, or to follow the enemy into Northern Cambodia, to cut this enemy supply route. As a result, the enemy built a huge transportation system that was just out of our reach. They supplied the war, at will, with millions of tons of supplies and thousands of soldiers. Our operations could consist only of attacking enemy units that had infiltrated South Vietnam, or that were based near the border, next to the Ho Chi Minh trail.

American soldiers in Vietnam called home "the World," because Vietnam was not considered part of the real world. The World was where I would return when I left Vietnam. Until then, I was not part of any civilized society. I was in the Nam. The Nam was a unique society . . . a society of war. It was not of our world. I would soon find that the rules for operating in this society were different from any I had ever known.

At last they let us board the plane which was a large C-130 cargo plane. We marched up the wide ramp into the tail of the plane. After more delays, we rolled down the runway. It took forever to get that flying warehouse off the ground. There were no seats on this transport, merely a few straps that folded out from the walls. I sat on my haunches, as did the other soldiers. I held onto a strap so tightly my hands ached. Like the hundred others around me, I hoped that the noisy and cumbersome airplane would stay in the air.

An hour or so later, I felt the wheels touching down. As he walked to the rear of the plane to release the tail ramp, one of the pilots yelled at us. "Okay, guys. Here we are. Welcome to Vie-et Naaaam!"

As the ramp powered open, bright sunlight poured through the aircraft and with it a stifling, blistering heat. I grabbed my gear and headed down the ramp with the others. As I stepped out of the plane, I was hit with the overpowering stench of burning fuel. The air smelled hot, and when it hit my lungs, it was still scorching. The sights around me were completely foreign. I was on another planet, not another country in my world. In reality, I stood on a metal PSP (pierced steel planking) runway, in the middle of a huge military complex named Camp Holloway. I consoled myself with the thought that thousands of men had made this trip and had seen the same strange sights I was seeing now.

61

When I reached the terminal, I was happy to find it was air-conditioned. This was where I wanted to be. There was a snack bar, but I wasn't hungry. I asked a clerk what to do next, and he said I should relax and wait for someone to get to me. I found a place on the floor and waited.

Camp Holloway consisted of rows of hangars and barracks to house the people who worked there. The barracks had steel roofs, thick walls, and protective window screens. They were sandbagged on every side. I didn't need to read a manual to learn the significance of that silent message.

A half hour later, the clerk yelled that my ride was outside. I scrambled to my feet and swung my duffle bag onto my shoulder. Outside, I found a filthy ten-wheeled truck and a PFC soldier-driver who was every bit as dirty as the truck. He informed several of us that he would be driving us to the Replacement Center at Camp Enari. The route would take us through Pleiku City and then south on a decent blacktop road. The distance was fourteen miles. Most of the time this trip was made by bus, that had windows covered with wire mesh to guard against the enemy tossing grenades into them. We were getting special treatment . . . an open truck.

The 4th Division used several types of vehicles, including a three-quarter-ton pickup, military jeeps, and this huge truck known as a deuce-and-a-half. It was the Army's basic delivery truck. The deuce-and-a-half was a six-wheel drive, ten-wheel vehicle, with olive drab camouflage and an overhead rack for carrying things. They hauled troops one day, chow the next, then supplies, whenever necessary. They were the Army's workhorses.

After we were seated in the truck, a soldier with a rifle climbed aboard. He was our protection for the trip. The driver also had a rifle. After we left Camp Holloway, we saw places where fields of fire had been cut back about thirty meters on either side of the road. It was strange to see South Vietnamese peasants walking the road, trying to sell watches and cigarettes to the GIs driving by. They also tried to sell boom boom, which was slang for sex.

As we rode along, the rifleman educated us about the area. He pointed out Dragon Mountain, the major geological feature. We passed through several small villages that seemed to be primarily whorehouses and bars.

Most of the houses were made of mud and elephant grass. They smelled of rotten food, incense, spices, and ginger.

We noticed numerous Army trucks parked among these houses. South Vietnamese soldiers, who treated the trucks as their personal transportation, drove most of the vehicles. I wondered why the ARVN, Army of the Republic of Viet Nam or the South Vietnamese Army, had so much U.S. military equipment.

Pleiku, a city inhabited mostly by South Vietnamese and located at the foot of mountainous jungles, was at the end of the Ho Chi Minh trail, and was about three hundred miles due west of Cam Ranh Bay. It was a major staging area for North Vietnamese Army units (NVA), which invaded South Vietnam by traveling down the Ho Chi Minh trail.

While driving through downtown Pleiku City, which was mostly a mixture of old French colonial buildings and tin huts, I saw the hustle and bustle of a Vietnamese city up close. Pleiku was a one-and-two-story city filled with wide streets which streamed with people of all ages and little shops along the sidewalks. The shops lacked front doors, and customers bustled in and out at will, like we would an outdoor market. The store's names were displayed on banners above the openings. The whole city looked like one giant penny arcade. Little three-wheeled trucks and bicycles were the prominent means of transportation. I was struck by the attitude of normalcy. The Pleiku citizens moved about, seemingly without regard for the war.

I saw bands of Vietnamese girls with umbrellas standing beside the road, four to seven per group, selling cold beer and souvenirs. I found out later that the ice looked like Swiss cheese because it had been buried in the ground to keep it from melting. They carried the beer and ice in plastic vinyl carriers with little insulation. The carriers had straps which they hung over their shoulders. The women always banded together to sell the beer, and there were almost always boom boom girls among them. They had beer and boom boom for sale.

Never, in all my travels throughout the United States, had I seen such a dirty place. People lived like rats. The houses were literally shacks stacked next to each other without any apparent plan or organization. Fine red dust from the pulverized soil covered everything. The scene was like a movie of some faraway planet, but I wasn't watching it. I was in it!

We passed several Army truckloads of American soldiers, crammed full with gear, rifles, and ammunition. The men were all a dirty-brown color and they had a wild look I will never forget. They looked paranoid, wild, dirty, and dangerous, like people you would not want to mess with. I was amazed to see American soldiers looking like this. I could not believe American troops could be wild animals. As we passed they just stared directly at me, as though I were nothing but a piece of meat.

Later I wondered what they were thinking – here I was, the new troop, in a clean uniform, on my way to Enari. They had been green like me not so long ago, and in a short time had received a lifetime's worth of experiences, and now they were hardened by war. I felt their stares. It was as though they stared through me. They must have thought," He'll be with us soon; he'll be one of us, or he'll be dead. We looked like you once." They said, "Just you wait, sergeant." I knew I would never forget those faces.

Their faces represented the reality of war.

Chapter 11

Friday, 20 December 68

The perimeter of Enari was heavily fortified, complete with towers and armed guards. As we approached the gate, several Military Police (MPs) stopped our truck to check us out. At Enari, only the MPs and the soldiers on perimeter guard duty were armed. Sometimes new recruits would be issued weapons, but that was for limited training purposes only. Everyone returning from the field to Enari had to lock their weapons in rifle racks when they arrived. Then every man was re-issued his weapon upon leaving the camp.

Entrance to Enari

Enari seemed smaller than Cam Ranh Bay, but it had a large combat perimeter reinforced with a heavily-fortified bunker system, with concertina wire and minefields. Vietnamese entered and left Enari all day long. It was the job of the MPs to check them out as they entered, and to keep an eye on everyone and everything leaving the camp. The Vietnamese lived in villages outside the wire perimeter or in Pleiku.

At the time I arrived, Enari housed five thousand troops in almost nine hundred buildings. The camp covered an area of twenty square miles. Its original name had been Dragon Mountain Base Camp, but it was renamed in December of 1966 to honor the young First Lieutenant Mark N. Enari, the first officer killed at this location. Lieutenant Enari had been a platoon leader with A Company, 1st Battalion, 12th Infantry, and was killed while providing cover for wounded members of his platoon while they were being pulled back to positions of relative safety. Lieutenant Enari was the first 4th Division soldier to earn the Silver Star posthumously.

Even though Camp Enari was a large, well-protected base, it was dangerous to be there. We never knew when a mortar or small arms attack would occur. It was quite common for the camp to have incoming mortar rounds. By design, bunkers were located near the barracks. We could easily take cover in the bunker, which was a very large hollow pipe covered with sandbags. Over the years of the war, many soldiers lost their lives in and near Enari.

Camp Enari was like a small town. It had no main street, but many smaller roads and walkways. It provided various amenities: an NCO club, a quartermaster area with a commissary, a big PX with a snack bar, a laundry, and an outdoor movie theater. It also had a post office, a hospital, a big motor pool, and at least two helicopter landing pads.

One pad supported the Medevac helicopters, called Dustoffs, which were used by the medical center at Enari. The Dustoff compound was about 400 yards west of the end of the Air Force base runway, near the Pleiku-Kontum highway. Our guard told us to remember those Dustoffs sitting on the runway. These pilots were highly skilled and regularly saved the lives of wounded soldiers by rescuing them while under fire and flying them to safety and the hospital.

The clerks assigned me to A Company, 1st Battalion and 8th Infantry, called A-1-8. In the company's assigned area there was an aid station, a baggage building, several boardwalks (like sidewalks between the buildings) lined with artillery canisters painted blue and white, and a "piss tube," right out in the open. It was an efficient but totally public latrine. Some of the buildings were sandbagged including the barracks where we lived. I was told the boardwalks and trenches were used mostly during the monsoon season, when the ground turned to seas of mud.

The camp was organized by battalion and each battalion had its own set of barracks, called "hooches" organized by platoon. The basic hooch structure consisted of wooden walls framed around a wood floor and topped with a half-tent. The barracks hooches were lined with army cots. Senior officers were housed in trailers and the headquarters staff were housed in bunkers and in Quonset huts.

After I was processed into the replacement center, the sergeant told me to find the A-1-8 barracks that would be my new home for the next few days. So I headed toward the barracks and when I entered, I saw dim lights on a group of guys who were smoking and playing cards. They were tough-looking and dirty as hell. The barracks had shit all over the place. Nobody looked up as I entered to put my gear away. I found a cot without stuff on it and lay down. I was tired as hell.

I just wanted to relax. My mind was whirling. I had seen a lot of new things that day. I was beginning to realize that it would take a lot to become as tough as these guys, let alone be their sergeant. I was now entering a world in which there was absolutely no bullshit. I would have to be one tough SOB to survive. And there wasn't a damn thing I could do here but survive or die.

After a few minutes I heard heavy artillery firing outside, not too far away. I thought they must be shelling the NVA somewhere beyond the perimeter. The thunderous sound was deafening. For a moment I wondered if I should do something. *Were we under attack?* But then I noticed that the guys across the hooch never stopped playing cards, so I lay back down again. It sounded like a war movie with the constant firing of big guns.

Two bunks away from me there was a guy with a tape recorder. He was recording the sounds of the artillery firing, and he was talking into the tape recorder at the same time. When I listened carefully, his words made it seem as though he was in a real battle. He would say, "Yeah, we got another incoming round."

Then he would add something like, "They are shooting at us again."

Next I heard, "It's really heating up all along our sector."

And "Now the enemy is scrambling about, massing for a direct charge up the hill. Unless we're lucky, we might get overrun."

This guy was acting out a full battle fantasy, using Enari's big guns to provide authenticity. I wondered if he was going to send that tape home.

I looked over at the guy and said, "What the fuck are you doing that for?"

The guy just stared at me and kept on recording his battle. I thought to myself, *Nobody who hears this is going to take us seriously, not with that kind of shit going on.*

Later, after eating a hot meal in the mess tent, I joined the others in rinsing our steel trays in fifty-gallon drums of hot water which had been heated with diesel-fired burners. At Camp Enari, the smell of diesel fuel permeated the air.

The changes in weather bothered me. I had gotten a cold, even though the daytime temperature reached 110 degrees. When the sun set, the thermometer fell to 50 degrees.

Sunday, 22 December 68 A Letter Home

It is Sunday now and I am still in division base camp. I won't be able to send my address to mail my letters until Tues, Dec. 24. I will be going out in the boon docks Thursday morning. It is pretty boring right now cause all we are doing is waiting for our training that will be Monday-Tues — Wed so we leave Thursday. Last night I went to a Christmas program and sung Christmas carols all night. A little after I went to a small club they have for replacements and they had a Vietnamese band there. I swear they had as good equipment as bands back home and they sang all rock and roll. It was interesting. Everyone enjoyed it cause it sounded so much like back home in the states. This morning the commanding general gave us a speech. He told us that the fourth infantry division covers 200 miles along the Cambodian border and on the average of 40 miles wide. He said that in the past this division fought all the real big battles with only the regulars from the North and it was conventional fighting. He went on to say that he thought we would enter a new phase of war where we would only look for smaller units of VC that live here and the NVA regulars would stay over the Cambodian border until the Paris peace talks are over. Anyway I think for a little while the firefights will be small and not like the past. For a little while only. I don't guess I'll see Bob Hope. You know I still got a cold and it gets up to 110 during the day and you freeze your rear off at night here. I really cannot understand this stupid weather. All I need is the monsoons to start up here.. for a little while only.

68

The other new arrivals and I began our training on a Monday. We received information about the 4th Division operational procedures and objectives and about the activities of the enemy in recent weeks. Then we were introduced to our responsibilities in the field, with some general rules about how to conduct ourselves while in Vietnam. It was valuable information.

Tuesday, 24 December 68 Letter Home

I want to tell you that I am going to the 1st of the 8th infantry in Dak To north of here. I am kind of high cause I have been drinking a little but my mind is spurting out everything that I believe without any blocks or inhibitions. Tonight I went over to my Battalion's headquarters at division headquarters to get my M16 rifle and the first thing they did was thrust a beer in my hand cause it is Christmas eve and by the way I want to wish you a merry, merry merry,merry Christmas even though I am far away there is reason to rejoice cause it is the birth of our Lord. Over where I was picking up my rifle the battalion commander and all the officers and NCOs got me drunk cause it was Christmas eve and they wanted to cheer me up.

I completed my training on Wednesday, which covered details about the Central Highlands, our operation area, things to watch out for, and my duties as a soldier. The instructors emphasized how we were expected to treat the South Vietnamese people. There were some final checks regarding our knowledge of weapons and how to maintain them. We received a brief lecture on the insects and animals that lived in the bush.

Then our instructor talked about leeches. From the back of the room I could barely hear the sergeant's voice. He pointed at a picture of a leech and announced, "Leech is the name for a carnivorous or blood-sucking worm. Here in Vietnam, they are flat-ringed worms, ranging in size from one-half to eighteen inches long. Gentlemen, they consume three times their weight in one feeding of your blood and then subsist for months on the stored food. They will attach themselves to your young asses in an instant. You will have to deal with them for most of your tour in Vietnam. They are all over the place."

For some reason, everyone chuckled. The sergeant went on. "With proper care, men, leeches won't hurt you. They have a large round mouth that functions as a sucker. Jaws around the mouth opening hold many fine, conical teeth. Wounds produced by the leech's bite will bleed for a

69

while after the leech is removed, because they secrete an enzyme that keeps the blood from coagulating as it feeds. With proper care, these bites will heal."

I sat there and thought about this for a while. *My pecker, oh my precious pecker! What if I got one of those leeches attached to my pecker?*

I fell into a cold sweat just sitting there thinking about it. Then, just as I snapped out of it, the sergeant blurted out, "Now I know you guys are sitting there wondering 'What if I get one of these things attached to my pecker?'

"First of all, I can tell you that it will not happen and secondly, if it does happen, I am glad I am not you. For God's sake men, don't get a leech on your pecker. It will be a bitch to get the damn thing off."

Nobody laughed.

Friday, 27 December 68 Letter Home

I am not out in the boondocks yet cause they were expecting an assault on the division base camp here at Pleiku. In fact we drew weapons and ammo and we were on standby but the enemy did not show. I did stand guard last night. I about froze to death – it's gets very cold at night. I think tomorrow I will go up to the front. I'll probably ride on a convoy 65 miles up to Dak To – it's about a three hour trip. I have been talking to a lot of guys about Dak To and they said it was very hard living and very hard work but they have little contact with the enemy. When I get up there I will be going on a lot of four man short range recon missions but after a while I'll be a squad leader and then a platoon sergeant.

On Saturday, I was told I would not be leaving to join my squad yet because they were expecting an assault on Camp Enari. I drew a weapon and ammo and was put on standby alert. The company clerk handed me an M-16 and a bandoleer, which is a wide belt worn over one shoulder and across the chest, with pockets to carry the ammunition. He instructed me not to load my weapon until I was actually on duty.

There were a number of reasons rifles were not normally issued at base camp. The most important was to avoid accidents or incidents involving weapons. When you have five thousand soldiers working in a confined area, anything can happen. A story circulated among the new replacements that a soldier in Dak To had blown away a lieutenant paymaster because the lieutenant didn't have his paycheck ready.

That night a deuce-and-a-half picked me up at my barracks for guard duty. I hopped aboard the back end of the truck, with several others, and was driven to the perimeter of the base. Two of us were dropped off at a heavily sandbagged bunker, and the two who had been on duty took our places on the truck. Since the camp was on alert, there were guards in every bunker continually.

From the observation post, I saw the razor-sharp concertina wire encircling the base. I knew that a mine field lay beyond it. Right now it was quiet, but from the security of the bunker I felt that anything could take place outside that wire. The enemy must be out there somewhere. Although I had heard the phrase "outside the wire" many times, standing in the bunker brought the reality of its meaning home to me.

My partner and I took turns standing watch. He told me that, a few weeks before, he had been on tower duty when a little skirmish had broken out with Charlie. The next day the men discovered they had killed their barber! The Vietnamese man who cut hair at Enari by day was a VC by night.

Guard duty in the Nam was critically important. Each soldier depended on the other to stay alert. If a soldier got caught sleeping, he was automatically court-martialed. This was a challenge in the middle of the night, when it was cold. Each soldier scans the darkness for movement, at first with their eyes and then through a starlight scope. A starlight scope is similar to binoculars, but shaped like a large telescopic sight for seeing in the dark. It magnifies the available light 10,000 times to produce clear green images not visible in the darkness. I was told that I could see lit cigarette 200 yards in the distance. After using the scope for a while, I imagined that everything I saw was moving. Then I tried to go somewhere else in my mind for a couple minutes, to seek relief from the tension and the boredom, but not for too long, as I might fall asleep. I dared not do my out-of-mind-and-body thing; I would fall asleep for sure. Constant vigilance was needed with Charlie in the area. I was lucky that night. The VC didn't attack.

My partner and I were relieved at dawn and we returned to our barracks to get a few hours sleep. I told myself to enjoy the experience. Tomorrow night I would be in the field in a foxhole. Except for a few short breaks in the months to come, this would be the last time I'd have the luxury of a cot, a pillow, and blankets, the last time I would have the warmth and safety of an enclosed structure …. the last time I'd have a hot meal, with a selection of choices and time to enjoy the coffee.

Rest, Jerry, you're on your way, bud, it's happening tomorrow. You will need to have your energy, and you must be able to focus. This is some serious shit out here.

Chapter 12

Monday Morning, 30 December 68 Trip to Dak To

This was the big day. I was to join my unit. For weeks I had thought long and hard about this day, and now it was here. I was going to the real war zone. From my brief training at Enari, I had learned a few more things about being a squad leader in Vietnam and about the specific role I would be playing in my company. Shake 'n Bake sergeants were welcomed with open arms because they were needed so badly. Most companies were critically understaffed. All I had to do was live up to their expectations.

I was feeling better now because I had just gotten over the worst case of diarrhea I ever had in my whole life. Diarrhea was never pretty in the World but to have it in Nam was really the pits. I had spent the whole weekend running outside the barracks and squatting in the bushes, or searching for a john.

My diarrhea was so bad that, even on guard duty, I had to sneak away to the bushes, squat and do my thing. It would come on me suddenly and violently; I couldn't ignore it. My education in learning how to suffer in the field was off to a good start.

Once I got off duty, I didn't eat anything for a day and my diarrhea went away. What a relief! It had overwhelmed me for two whole days. Since there was no privacy in Vietnam, most of the guys with me got a pretty good show a few times, but I am sure it was one they could have done without.

But it turned out that I wasn't alone. Many guys new to Vietnam suffered from severe short-term diarrhea. It certainly wasn't the food; I was eating the same Army chow I had grown to know and hate stateside. I guess leaving the World and entering the Nam took its toll on everyone. I found out later it might have been the malaria pills I had taken.

Now with my diarrhea behind me, so to speak, I walked down to the A-1-8 Company HQ about 0700 on Monday and found the truck, and a few of the guys who would be making the trip with me to Dak To. We were to ride a convoy up to Dak To, which was about sixty-five miles and would take about three hours.

When I reported to the officer in charge, he told me to find one of the clerks and draw my weapon for the trip. I received an M-16 , I would soon realize that it would be my lover, my protector, and my honey for the next ten months in the Nam. I would hold it closely, sleep with it; I gave it respect. Just by carrying it, I felt better. The clerk issued me a magazine of ammo, but it felt light and I soon discovered that it was only half full. "Hey, I need more ammo! This isn't enough to shoot shit with."

"Easy, Sarge. That's all you get."

"How do I fight the war with half a magazine?"

"Sorry, Sarge, orders is orders."

As I climbed into the truck, I noticed that both the cab and the truck's floorboards were sandbagged. As we drove away, a few other trucks queued up to form the convoy. A jeep and an APC (armored personnel carrier) were waiting at the gate to provide protection for the long trip north. Apparently sudden attacks were common along Highway 14. The NVA regularly tried to blow up that road. We were instructed to stay alert.

There were four trucks, one APC, and a jeep in our convoy, with maybe seven or eight replacements on board. Most of the trucks were hauling supplies. Two soldiers were returning to the field after their week of R&R leave (Rest and Recuperation) in Hong Kong, Taipei, Bangkok, or some similar place.

The convoy got underway. We drove through downtown Pleiku again. The city appeared quiet, but this concept was deceiving. Enemy troops were just a few miles away, maybe even watching us at that moment. In Vietnam, we were never completely safe.

I saw a lot of South Vietnamese soldiers in Pleiku, strutting around like they owned the place. They acted like conquerors not soldiers defending their country. Here I was, on my way to the field. I was going to be doing their fighting for them, and they were walking around town as though they had nothing better to do. I wondered how many of them were really "barbers."

Along the way we passed hundreds of Vietnamese often, entire families, walking beside the road. Where were they going? I wondered. We drove through Kontum, a city smaller than Pleiku, and located halfway between there and Dak To. It was cleaner and it didn't smell bad. As we drove through Kontum we saw Montagnard tribesmen. They were small mountain people who looked like Native American Indians. There

74

were eight different tribes of Montagnards lived in Vietnam but here in the Kontum area, they were mainly the Banhar tribe. They were good soldiers, they liked Americans, and they fought by our side against the NVA.

Kontum is the site of a famous 120-year-old French cathedral, and a Montagnard church, built in 1913. I learned later that the city had many jewelry shops, a Montagnard orphanage, and a large market, with several decent restaurants. One interesting landmark, smack in the middle of town, was a whorehouse, located in a building that looked like an old western bordello. It was also rumored that Kontum was a GI's No Man's Land. It was a hot hang-out for the NVA. Our men were commanded to avoid the city since the VC hung out there and would go there to have fun so it was a very dangerous spot to visit.

A seasoned soldier traveled in the back of the deuce with us three replacements. His name tag said Jones, and he had jumped on as we left the gate at Enari. Jones tried to sell us some GI Insurance. We looked at each other in consternation. *Was this guy for real, or not?* Then Jones burst out laughing, and we knew he was joking. Some joke. We were trying to take it all in but really we felt overwhelmed. Then Jones told us that if there was an ambush we should bail out of the truck on the opposite side from the ambush and take cover. *More bullshit,* I thought. In a few minutes Jones went to sleep.

About thirty minutes out of Kontum, just as I was feeling a little more relaxed, I heard a big explosion. The truck came to a screeching halt. I latched onto my rifle and thought I was ready for anything. Jones grabbed his weapon and jumped over the back of the truck without saying a word. Seeing this, we new guys looked at each other with scared faces. What should we do? Nobody knew. Finally, I scrambled back to the tailgate and tumbled out onto the road. Jones yelled at me. "Get the fuck over in the ditch, Sergeant!"

The other guys followed me into a drainage ditch. We heard the ratta-tat-tat from M-16's, and then a metallic sound of clack, clack, clack. We lay there, not moving. I realized that I was clutching the M-16 in my left hand, and the magazine the clerk had given me in my right. In the excitement, I had failed to insert the magazine. Now, listening to the sounds of firing, this half-filled magazine looked pitifully inadequate.

A lieutenant suddenly appeared in a crouching position and said there were ARVNs just ahead of the convoy and they were in a firefight with

NVA. We had taken a few stray rounds, so he had stopped the convoy until the road was clear. "They will probably call in air strikes," he said. "Stay where you are."

A short time later, I saw what looked like Korean War vintage A-1 Skyraiders circling overhead. Then they started to dive, laying heavy fire into the woods about a hundred meters from the road. As they climbed back up into the sky, they performed somersaults and other fancy stunts, like they were in an air show! There were three of them, and they wreaked holy hell in that wood line.

While we were lying in the ditch, I asked Jones about the planes and their pilots. He said they were members of the South Vietnamese Air Force, and that they were damn good with those old planes and would do a job on the enemy. I found myself cheering them on. I wanted them to utterly destroy the enemy. By the time the planes flew off, we heard no more shooting. Everyone climbed back into the trucks and the convoy continued down the road.

Tan Canh and Dak To were our next stops. Dak To was a Battalion Headquarters. Dak To was only thirty miles from the Laotian border. Ben Het was nearby Dak To nearer to the border and was at one time a Special Forces Camp. Our base camp was called Charlie Base and the landing strip that supported it was known as Eagle Airport.

Charlie Base was two and a half miles wide with an airstrip right down the middle. A tent city grew on each side of the runway. The villages of Dak To and Tan Canh were each less than a mile down the road. The 4th Division kept several companies at Dak To, at least one battalion headquarters, and several artillery batteries supporting both 105 and 155 millimeter artillery.

Dak To was hot and dry between the months of November and May, then it rained non-stop until late October. The temperature was always over ninety-five degrees during the day and only dropped to eighty at night. In the mountains, it fell into the fifties. Neither climate was ideal.

Dak To was a filthy hole with only one redeeming asset. When you came in from a mission in the field, you could always get hot chow and a real shower. These simple things became luxuries and meant a lot to the infantryman.

The geography around Dak To was very mountainous. These mountains were almost vertical, with triple-canopy jungle growing right up their sides. The jungle was so thick it was impossible to walk through

76

without a machete. Dak To was nestled in a valley beside a river, and hemmed in by Rocket Ridge on the far side. Rocket Ridge was completely bare of jungle and cratered from the effects of bombing. Heavy fighting had occurred there during several big battles. The NVA had used the ridge's higher elevation to rain rockets on Dak To, because of its strategic crossroads and the airstrip. The Dak To area was a good place to get killed. The enemy was always close by. As a result, American and ARVN troops were always patrolling in and out of the base.

Dak To carried the scars of most of the history of American fighting in Vietnam. During the Tet offensive in 1968, our men fought hand-to-hand around the perimeter of Dak To and up on Rocket Ridge itself. The base was also the site of the famous Battle of Dak To, in 1967, in which the Army inflicted the greatest defeat on the enemy of any battle in the entire Vietnam war. The statistics tell the story: 1,644 enemy were killed and 289 U.S. servicemen lost their lives. In that battle, our men had to call napalm bombs on their own positions because they were outnumbered and becoming overrun by the enemy.

The bases at Dak To and Ben Het were originally set up by the Special Forces to keep the enemy from infiltrating into Vietnam from the Ho Chi Minh Trail and to give early warning of enemy infiltration so that we could launch counterattacks. The Special Forces, with the aid of Montagnard soldiers and various mercenaries, originally manned these bases. Later, the Army took them over and established forward firebases that were closer to the Laotian and Cambodian borders. When I arrived in late December, a few Special Forces squads were still stationed at Dak To.

Army firebases were always built on mountain tops. First, all the timber and vegetation were blown up to make a circular field of fire that would allow a clear range of vision. It was important to see the enemy coming and be able to shoot directly at him. The firebase was designed with a perimeter of bunkers surrounding the command bunker, which was in the center. If possible, a landing zone (LZ) for choppers was constructed within the perimeter. If that were not possible, then the LZ would be placed just outside the perimeter. Firebases were always hot and dry and dusty except during the aforementioned monsoon season, when they were in deep mud.

When our convoy arrived in Dak To, I noticed that the airstrip and the base were completely rimmed with concertina wire and bunkers. There was only one way into the firebase, which appeared to be about two or three times larger than a company-sized firebase located out in the field. Everything seemed to be crammed together, and everything was filthy and smelled like fertilizer. Every soldier I saw carried his weapon and a loaded bandoleer. It was obvious to me that the clerks weren't playing ammo games in this town. Filthy grunts moved every which way carrying rucksacks, M-16's, machine guns, and ammo belts.

When I got off the deuce at Dak To, a clerk told me to get more ammo, some grenades, and my rations, and be prepared to fly out to join my unit on Hill 1049, a firebase located fourteen kilometers south of Dak To.

From this point on, everything happened real fast. It was a little unsettling to realize that, after loading up with ammo, I would take my first chopper ride . . . *within an hour.* No more waiting around for hours or days for the next order.

I couldn't believe how heavy my rucksack was. With a bandoleer of clips containing my M-16 ammo, the grenades, the C-rations, a poncho liner, poncho and assorted other gear, I found myself staggering to the helicopter pad.

A Huey helicopter waited for me with its rotor turning. The pilot stared straight at me. The doors were open on both sides and the interior was piled with supplies. Three other soldiers awaited instructions. The pilot motioned for us to climb aboard but, for a moment, I hesitated. I thought the damn rotor blade would take my head off. When I saw that the others had cleared the blade, I picked up my rucksack and started running. I tried to climb aboard with the others, but the pilot motioned me away. He shouted over the engine noise that I would have to sit by the door and let my legs hang over the side. There wasn't room for me inside the chopper. I hoped he was kidding. He wasn't.

The Huey lifted into the air and I watched as the ground moved further away. Only centrifugal force kept me from falling out. Talk about thrilling! I was practically sitting on air. Just then the pilot performed a steep bank to fly over the base. Suddenly I was staring straight down at the ground! I thought, *Naw, I can't die like this . . . falling out of a chopper.*

Mountains Southwest of Dak To

After a few seconds that seemed like minutes of hanging upside down, the helicopter and I both recovered. Now I got to see the real Vietnam. These big mountains—thick with vegetation—were uncompromising and dangerous. The enemy could hide for a thousand years and remain undetected. I compared these mountains to those in West Virginia and California. I was in awe. For a moment, I thought, *How beautiful!* Then . . . *how deadly!*

Chapter 13

While the chopper was touching down on Hill 1049, the pilot shouted at me over the whump-whump of his motor. "Run like hell! We might be under fire! I may have to take off!" I had heard that chopper pilots were skittish on the front lines. They made a good target for the VC. I was not about to be the cause of an avoidable problem. The second we touched down, I jumped out the door, running full tilt with my heavy rucksack and rifle.

When I was safely away from the helicopter, I turned to watch it take off. The chopper still sat on the ground. Its rotors whipped red dust and yellow smoke into a fantastic cloud, creating an indescribably beautiful picture of particles in perpetual motion. The dust and smoke were pushed down and away from the bird, swirling out from its blades into billows of color, before they were forced back into the air, only to be sucked back again. The branches of trees in the background swayed like the skirts of hula dancers.

I watched the barely visible silhouette of the helicopter pad man as he continued to signal the chopper. I wiped the dust from my eyes, adjusted my rucksack, and spent another couple minutes examining my new location. I was standing atop a bald hill located at the end of a long ridge. A steep set of jagged mountains surrounded me. Down one side of the ridge, elephant grass reached six feet towards the sky. Although I had spent my life in the beautiful hills of West Virginia, I had never seen anything like this. The firebase was tucked right into the midst of jungle vegetation. The name for Hill 1049 represented the hill's elevation above sea level.

I noticed several soldiers relaxing under some nearby trees. With arms crossed over their chests, they examined me . . . their new and very green sergeant. Obviously nobody was shooting at anyone. There was no imminent danger to me or to the helicopter. In fact, the chopper was shutting down its motor! The pilot had enjoyed a little joke at my expense. I was a jackrabbit being chased by an imaginary fox. My dash to safety had made a great first impression. I couldn't tell if my audience laughed or not and I didn't want to find out.

The firebase was dirty and foul-smelling . . . a mixture of burnt diesel fuel and gunpowder. Debris littered the area. I walked past scraps of paper, plastic wrappers, empty C-ration boxes, and empty cans. The soldiers' uniforms—if you could call them that—were ragged and filthy. At that moment, I wished I were anywhere but on Hill 1049. I had a job to do with total strangers. I had no knowledge of what was going to happen. Somehow I had to appear confident and . . . macho. I was an optimist. In any situation, I could tell myself that things could be worse. Now was the time to relax. Suddenly it was quiet. The chopper motor had shut down. I heard the sounds of the jungle.

One of the soldiers called out to me. "Hey Sarge. How's it going?" His cigarette perched precariously at the edge of his mouth. The smoker, whom I came to know as The Flea, sauntered toward me on the LZ (helicopter landing zone) with a couple of his pals, Pappy and The Spider. While he was checking me out, Pappy said, "Do you think this one's got anything, Flea? I heard he's one of them NCO school boys."

Carey Pearce ("The Flea")

The Flea blew the smoke from his cigarette into the air while slowly circling around me. "Take a bag, drop in one green soldier, a copy of the UCMJ (Uniform Code of Military Justice), and a few ideas from some big-assed Brass in Washington who thinks he knows what Viet-Nam is all about. Shake 'em up. Bake 'em up. Thirty days later, yuh've got it . . . an instant sergeant. And here he is, men. Our very own FNG (Fucking New Guy)!"

I had a lot to learn about living and surviving in the field. Number One: it was important to find humor in every situation. It took the place of an aspirin or a beer . . . or having your wife or girlfriend for comfort. Chopper pilots enjoyed telling a green soldier he was landing under fire, just to scare the heck out of him and get a laugh from the guys on the ground. Those on the ground enjoyed seeing the soldier in his regulation-clean uniform running with a full rucksack, like the enemy was hot on his heels. They'd say, "Here comes another FNG!" Another new guy they'd have to break in. Another burden for the squad. Another question mark in everyone's mind. Will this FNG be stupid enough to get himself killed before we can train him?

I muttered a vague hello and kept walking. Pappy, Spider and The Flea ignored my gesture and just nodded their heads. I noticed eight or ten other dirty-faced guys sprawled on the ground by their foxholes silently watching my progress. I nodded at them. I was surprised to see that most of them were reading *Playboy* magazines. (I learned that when Pappy had returned to the field from his R & R a few days before, he had brought them with him. They aren't available at base camp, and he had made a special attempt to find several old issues. He had simply laid the magazines on his ruck, without saying a word. They had disappeared in a finger-snap.)

I marched past my spectators to the camp's headquarters in my clean uniform feeling totally inadequate and self-conscious. Although I tried to convey the appearance of being older and wiser, I was a twenty-one year old kid who looked eighteen.

I found my platoon leader, Lieutenant LePeilbet, and the leader of 3rd Squad, Sergeant Donald Lestock, working at headquarters. Headquarters was simply a cluster of foxholes in the center of the perimeter. When I introduced myself, the lieutenant shook my hand and said he was glad to see me. He needed squad leaders. I would be assigned to a squad in his platoon immediately. Sergeant Lestock would help me learn the ropes. I would replace a David Fawcett, who was going to the rear.

82

Sergeant Lestock

When my instructions had been delivered, I turned to Lestock. "Sarge, may I ask you something?"

"Anytime, Sergeant Horton!"

"What's the problem with those guys over there . . . especially the ones they call The Flea and Pappy? They seemed a little . . . hostile."

Lestock squared his shoulders and examined me for what seemed like eons. "Those two? You have to prove something to them. You'll figure it out."

"Prove what, exactly?"

Lestock chuckled. "Relax, Sergeant. It involves a little common sense and intuition. Maybe they've forgotten what it's like to be the new guy around here. Maybe they're not sure they want to make a friend out of you, just to see you die or leave the squad, for one reason or other. Maybe they don't want to let it show that, when the shit hits the fan, they're going to be just as scared as you are. You haven't done anything wrong, Sergeant. You're replacing a man they've trusted with their lives. Here in the Nam, you have to earn respect. That's something that doesn't come with stripes. I'm sure you will. Welcome to the 4th Platoon, Sergeant Horton."

Lestock and LePeilbet knew I was a Shake 'n Bake and they slotted me to replace a seasoned veteran named Fawcett anyway. As a squad leader in the 4th Platoon, Fawcett was at the end of his tour of duty. He had earned the respect of his squad and was headed for home. He had been a department store manager in the World, before being drafted into the service, and he hoped to take up his civilian life where it had left off.

Lestock walked me over to meet Fawcett. He was a thin and wiry guy with red hair. He was very happy to see me. Of course, he should be. I was his ticket home. He shook my hand and said he would introduce me to my squad. He was leaving that same day so I would be taking over his duties immediately. As he introduced me to each of the men, he went out of his way to explain who would show me the ropes. He made me feel there was no big deal about being a squad leader. In particular, he said that I had a great bunch of guys to work with.

Regardless of what Fawcett told me, I knew I would have to win the confidence of each squad member on my own. In order to trust me, they would have to feel sure of my abilities and know that I had their safety in mind. I would have to listen to them . . . carefully. At that time I didn't know that, although many in the squad had been in the field for some time, none had actually been in combat. All of us would experience our first action as greenhorns. With the training I had been given, I felt competent in the mechanics of war. My challenges would lie in learning to understand and support the men.

As Fawcett boarded the chopper and lifted off, I watched with the men of 2nd Squad . . . my men. Everyone waved. When we returned to our foxholes, I heard, "Sit down, Sergeant Horton. Make yourself at home." The speaker was Joe Shea. "Sergeant Horton." Just hearing that title gave me a little more confidence. I sat in the dirt across from Shea, and my initiation as squad leader began. We talked. Then a soldier who introduced himself as John Wayne joined us. He was a skinny, blonde headed kid who volunteered for everything but had a hard time getting things done, always had a tired look and said he was in the Special Forces so everyone called him John Wayne. Joe and a few of the others continued to talk never paying much attention to John Wayne. The squad had dealt with FNG's before, but never a green sergeant so I was unique. But they gave me the treatment to size me up. They hoped to learn what their FNG was made of.

Their assessment went like this:

- Was he going to be a prick?
- Was he going to get me killed?
- Was he gung ho?

84

- What did he think of the war?
- Was he a pussy or what?

Instantly I knew what was going on. It was the same stuff I heard growing up on the street. They learned that I was a hillbilly and so were The Flea and Pappy. That helped. They saw that I was easy-going, and learned that I wanted to get through my tour and return in one piece. That put us on the same page.

I asked a few questions of my own and listened carefully to the answers. I learned that this platoon had been on the firebase a long time, but in the past six months had experienced little contact with the enemy. Many of the soldiers in the platoon were new to the field like me. I asked about Lieutenant LePeilbet and was told that he was an all-right guy and fairly fresh to the Nam himself. We talked a long time about the World. I learned where each man was from and what his life had been like before the war.

As the days passed, I worked hard to take care of squad details, to deal with the lieutenant, and to show my concern for each man's state of mind. That meant my men didn't have to expend effort on mundane things. Their only problem was whether or not their FNG sergeant would do something stupid and get one of them killed. I got this message loud and clear that first day, but I never said a word about it. I would simply have to prove myself in time. My men were just going to have to wait and see.

Chapter 14

The Squad

"Sometimes," I thought, "sometimes I think I've been here before. I've done this before. It seems so strange; this is war." Maybe, "those days growing up on the playground it was the same. We were a team banded together just like here in the Nam. That's what gave us strength. Here I am again. Only the names have changed, but it's the same. I have been here before."

My world in the bush revolved around my squad. We had become an away-from-home family. We ate, slept, and worked together. We experienced the same fears and frustrations, and we shared the same desire—to do our best for our country and the Army, and to go home alive after our term of duty. Everyone was homesick at one time or the other, and home was the topic of the day whenever we had a moment to think about it.

There were no expressions of jealousy among the squad members. No petty bickering. No groundless arguments. We looked out for each other and followed orders. A few of the men in my squad were seasoned veterans as far as conducting SRPs (short range reconnaissance) and ambushes were concerned. None of them, however, had experienced direct contact with the enemy. None had been in a firefight. We shared our concerns and whatever knowledge we had of survival techniques.

A squad was supposed to have ten men. But, there was constant movement of men as they were either wounded, or finished their term of combat duty, or transferred in or out from other squads. There were a few soldiers from neighboring squads who hung around with us so much that I considered them to be my men. My squad, which was officially 2nd Squad in 4th Platoon, consisted of the following troops, over time:

Private Edwin Weaver was a baby-faced kid with a Ph.D. in sociology. He arrived soon after I took over my squad and served as our platoon's medic because he was a conscientious objector. When drafted, he elected to serve the war effort, but refused to carry arms against the enemy. He, and other soldiers like him, were people who by reason of religious, ethical or moral belief were conscientiously opposed to killing in war in any form, but who did not object to performing noncombatant duties (such as being a medic) in the armed forces.

It is often easier to make such a decision than it is to stick to it. Even though Ed arrived in Nam as a noncombatant medic, once he found himself in combat situations he started carrying a weapon. It is very difficult to remain steadfast to an ideal when your life is at stake and you're in your early twenties.

Private Paul Summerlin was a street-toughened, athletic black kid from New York City. Immediately after graduating from high school he had received a letter to report for the draft. He ignored the summons. He received a second letter. He ignored it. A registered letter arrived from the draft board. Paul answered the summons on the twenty-second of May, 1968, and on that very same day he was inducted immediately into the Army. He completed his basic training, AIT for Infantry, and went on to become a paratrooper. He was sent to Vietnam with the 82nd Airborne Division and, a short time later, became a member of the 4th Infantry Division. Paul volunteered to go out on patrols and often walked point. Airborne, as he was called, had a can-do attitude. He would volunteer for anything and showed no fear. When he was given orders, he usually replied "Airborne!" to indicate his acceptance. Airborne and I became friends right away. We had been schooled on the street and spoke the same language. Airborne was one of only two black soldiers in the platoon.

Paul Summerlin ("Airborne") and Roman Rostinoff ("Socks")

Private Joseph Shea was an Irishman from Connecticut. He was energetic and a big talker . . . but he was not gung-ho. Back in the World, he had been a gardener for a golf course. He thoroughly enjoyed that job and talked frequently about going back to it. Shea was unusually friendly. He talked to everyone and took a genuine interest in whatever they had to say. Very patient, he could listen to people's ideas and complaints for hours. Consequently, everyone liked him. But . . . "never volunteer for anything."

That reminds me about the time we were on patrol, Shea slipped and fell. His M-16 went off. Everyone hit the ground on both sides of the trail. Shea was in front of me, he looked around with a sheepish smile, "I guess my rifle went off by accident." Lieutenant LePeilbet showed up, "what the fuck is going on." Shea told him," I tripped and my rifle went off. Sorry." LePeilbet lectured both Shea and me how this was a major violation of infantry protocol. He looked straight at us to say," every man is responsible for his weapon and that it is on safety at all times while we are traveling." Shea swore up and down that his safety had been on, but Lieutenant LePeilbet pointed out that it would take extraordinary skill to fall and hit the safety switch on the weapon at the same time. "That's almost impossible," and that was LePeilbet's final word. Of course, Shea knew he fucked up. The shot could have given our position away or he could have shot the man in front of him. It was a lesson for all of us.

Private Carey Pearce ("The Flea"), a hillbilly from Arkansas, was one of those gutsy guys who had the ear of other men. Although he had strong opinions about everything, and a cocky attitude to boot, he was well-liked. A cigarette dangled from his mouth whenever smoking was allowed, and his nervous energy kept him in constant motion. He was fearless and tireless. Everyone called him The Flea because, whenever he talked, he became so animated he literally hopped around like a flea.

The Flea was small and skinny and well-adapted to living in the dirt. He, too, had graduated from airborne school and talked constantly about how difficult and rigorous the training had been. Whenever Airborne (Summerlin) visited our squad, the two of them would sing in harmony the airborne training songs. They became obnoxious in their braggadocio, but we enjoyed being entertained by them. The days and nights were endless and tedious and dangerous. Any diversion was welcomed.

At first, The Flea didn't like me and he frequently gave me a hard time. After he saw that I was a sergeant who didn't mind walking point and that I thoroughly supported my men, he accepted me. When he discovered that we were both hillbillies, he was ready to become my close friend. The Flea carried more than his weight as a soldier and was cool under fire.

Shortly after I met The Flea, I asked him why everyone called him The Flea. Even though he was in my squad, I had a hard time remembering his real name. Nobody ever called him anything else.

Without saying a word, The Flea whistled for his puppy, a dog he had found in the wild one day and befriended. "Come here, Charlie!" he called. The pup jumped into his arms and started licking his face. Flea was obviously delighted. "Charlie's got fleas, of course. Let's see yuh catch one."

The Flea and his Pup

That reminds me of a few days after I took over 2nd Squad, Lieutenant LePeilbet noticed that The Flea's puppy, Charlie (named in honor of the NVA), was foaming at the mouth. He showed the dog to Sergeant White, our platoon sergeant, and they both agreed this was a bad sign. The dog might have rabies. The rabies virus is present in the saliva of an infected animal. It can be transmitted through even a lick from the animal's tongue. Several soldiers had played with the puppy. The lieutenant immediately shot the dog and had it sent to Pleiku for testing. The brain tissue of the affected animal had to be examined.

The Flea and several others had become very attached to it, something you're not supposed to do in Vietnam. Flea stared at Lieutenant Lepeilbet, "Why did you have to shoot it first, sir? Maybe it had a curable disease. Maybe he would have been well by tomorrow with some simple medication." The Flea smoked and hopped from one foot to the other, trying to work off his nervous energy and agitation. He was always like that.

The results, however, came back positive. Every soldier who had played with the puppy was ordered to the medic's hooch to begin a series of rabies vaccine injections. They are applied in the stomach area and are very painful, especially for those who were as skinny as The Flea. I thought most of the men in my squad were going to have to take the series of injections.

Since our company was going to be moving out on patrol, it turned out that only The Flea, Country, and Mike Hughes received the shots. Others began but never finished the series. Sometimes war takes precedence over such things.

Private Sam Seldon hated military life and made no bones about it. Physical demands took their toll on him. A college graduate, being an infantryman in Vietnam was as far from his career goals as he was from his home state. He made it a point to play devil's advocate and challenged my authority or decisions whenever he could. He saw me as the voice of the military establishment and behind my back, he called me The Sergeant from Haight Ashbury. Later, this was shortened to Hashbury.

John Campbell and Sam Seldon

Sam had to analyze every situation and every order and figure out the results before he would take action. Lieutenant LePeilbet advised him to rely more on his instincts. "To survive in the Nam, a man has to have the instincts of a hunter," he'd tell him. The coaching helped, because Sam ended up a damn good soldier. I was glad he was in our squad.

91

Private John Campbell, our machine gunner, was a big and tough country boy. Everyone called him Rick, for reasons that escape me. One of the tallest and broadest men in the squad, he was stuck carrying the M-60 machine gun for us. The entire squad looked out for him and made sure he had whatever he needed. An M-60 gunner was very important in a firefight, and Rick performed well under fire. He saved us from possible disasters many times.

Private Don Cheek, our M-79 grenade launcher, was from Arizona. When I arrived, he was already a squad member. He loved to play the guitar back in the world; many heard him play at Firebase 25.

Private Don Cheek

Although Private Robert Rawls (Pappy) was in my platoon, he was in my squad for only part of my tour. Like The Flea, he came from Arkansas and, at twenty-four, was one of the oldest in the company. He liked to give us fatherly (or, as he phrased it, uncle-ly) advice on any subject. Pappy was as skinny as a flagpole, but had the energy of several of us. He was always there for us when the chips were down.

Pappy Rawls with the M79   *Pappy Rawls taking a break*

Pappy did not like Shake 'n Bakes and he let me know it. With a Shake 'n Bake in the squad, there was less opportunity for the rest of the grunts to advance. I didn't argue with him, because it was true. After a while, my quiet style apparently won him over.

Roman Rostinoff was very short and slight of build and quiet in demeanor. He was an accountant in the World and I felt sorry for him, because life in the Nam was particularly hard for him. The long jungle humps exhausted him, and he found it difficult to carry his loaded ruck. It was continuously bouncing off his back or getting caught in the bushes. He became a toughened soldier, and one we could depend on. Everyone called him Socks, I never knew why.

Private Gary Feldman was a farm boy from Illinois and we called him Country. Country was quiet and waited to hear everyone's input before offering his own opinions. He was extremely intelligent and a practical thinker. He liked to talk about his farm and about going into the hog-raising business. Even though he was a workhorse, he was very easygoing in nature.

Private Richard Meli was street-wise and had made good money running numbers as he grew up. By the time he was drafted into the Army, he had already saved enough money to buy a pleasure boat in New Jersey, where he ran charters off the coast of New Jersey, his home state. During this period, he acquired the nickname Spider. He was a good soldier and had seen enough action to be experienced in the field.

Spider was our jack-of-all-trades and handled any assignment given him with ease. When we were stationed in one location for a couple of weeks, he built a complete bamboo hut into the side of the hill. When we were on patrol, he would tell us stories about his adventures on the high seas. He could make his voice sound like Long John Silver's. He was an unforgettable character, come to think of it; he walked and talked like a pirate all the time. He told so many pirate stories over and over again, I'll be damned, he was becoming one.

Spider sharpening a machete

It's funny how life often repeats itself. These were my troops now, we were a team. It just happens. I realized it and so did they. I was their leader, their Shake 'n Bake sergeant whether they liked it or not. It was up to me to ensure that we would make it. My responsibility was to make sure we played as a team. The only problem was this was not the playground anymore. This time we were playing against hard-core NVA infantry that pound for pound were the toughest jungle fighters on earth.

Chapter 15

Sergeant Donald White—Platoon Sergeant

I will never forget the first time I met Sergeant White. As I approached him, wearing my brand new, ridiculously clean Army fatigues, he quickly sized me up and then made contact with my eyes, staring into them. He looked as tough as a wild boar. I stared back at him and waited for him to speak. "Welcome to Vietnam, Sarge," he said. "I'm your platoon sergeant. We are a top-notch outfit and now you're part of it. I fully expect that you'll do all right, since you had all that Shake 'n Bake training." He was only partly teasing me. He knew what I'd be up against in the Nam, and he honestly hoped my training was adequate for the task ahead.

Sergeant White was only thirty-four years old and already an E-7. He was a tough old coot and had no problem keeping up with the younger troops. A career man, he did everything by the book. Everything.

Sergeant White had a powerful influence on me. He showed me how to become a combat soldier in the best traditions of the Army, by being one himself. There was never a man I talked with who did not respect Don

White's toughness and knowledge. He made sure each and every man in our outfit knew his job and excelled in it. He prepared us well for what was coming.

The platoon sergeant carries out the orders of the lieutenant and ensures that the platoon's squad leaders and their men follow those orders. Sergeant White was LePeilbet's right-hand man, the two men worked to carry out the missions assigned to them by the company commander. Since Sergeant White was experienced and in his second tour in Nam, and LePeilbet was a cautious and conscientious leader in his first tour, they made a good team. As a result, we were considered one of the best platoons in the company and, some would say, in the division.

Sergeant White paid great attention to detail. Frequently he would appear unannounced at our positions, after we were set up on patrols, to inspect our foxholes and to advise each man on his fields of fire. He seemed to anticipate our problems and our needs. We could show no weakness, however, because he would immediately call any of us out, in front of God and everybody else, and he knew how to do it!

He stressed that we were in a war. Although we were not in a firestorm at that very minute, we could be . . . soon. We had better be ready for it. One day he took my squad with him to inspect two dead NVA—enemy soldiers—who had been killed not far from our Company's position. They were killed the night before by an LRRP (long range reconnaissance patrol) team. Sergeant White wanted us to see what a dead enemy looked like so that we wouldn't freak out when we had to kill one. When we arrived at the site, both bodies were lying there in the dirt with their eyes wide open. The NVA were much larger and heavier than I had expected, much bigger that the typical South Vietnamese.

Randy Chrietzburg and a couple of his men from the Tracers (a specially-trained team of the LRRPs who sometimes worked with our company) had been on an ambush mission near a trail. In the middle of the night, Randy woke up to find two NVA standing over him. He had his M-16 in his hands and he opened up on full automatic and killed both soldiers instantly. One of the dead men was an NVA officer who carried a pearl-handled Swedish pistol; the other was a regular NVA soldier.

Sergeant White touched the dead officer with his toe and slightly pushed his body. He ordered each of us to do the same thing. Everyone had to push on the corpse with his foot. The regular NVA had five holes across his chest. They were small holes. When Sergeant White turned the corpse over, we saw that the entire back was missing. Next, Sergeant White searched each body for anything that might yield useful military information. By providing us with this experience, Sergeant White taught us to respect the reality of the Nam in a hurry. This was what happened in a war. Men died in war. If it hadn't been these two NVA, it would have been Randy and his men.

When we walked away from those dead NVA, no one said a word. I wondered if my men were thinking what I was thinking. *Either kill or be killed. Either kill or be killed.* As leader of my squad, I was deeply affected by the experience. I was responsible for the lives of the men by my side. It was one thing to see pictures or videos of war situations, it was quite another to see the enemy in person. *Either kill or be killed.* It was a sobering thought.

Chapter 16

Monday, 30 December 68

I was in the jungle, sitting in a foxhole, in a strange country with a squad I didn't really know but was going to live with in the coming months. I arrived by helicopter yesterday. I was hot and filthy dirty from digging my first foxhole in the Nam and I was likely to stay that way. Water was in short supply.

Our location, Hill 1049, was fourteen klicks (kilometers or 1,000 meters, or about two-thirds of a mile) directly south of Dak To. It was high on a ridge near the end of a string of steep mountains. We were positioned on top of that ridge. Off to the northwest, we could see the rest of the mountain chain. It was covered in dense triple canopy jungle.

I remember writing a quick note.

I'm way up in the hills, about 10,000 meters from Dak To. Dak To is nothing but a hole in the ground. I wish you could see how dirty I am right now. There is no way to get clean because water is rationed.

The hardwood forest in Southeast Asia was so old and had grown so high—about sixty to ninety feet—that the upper limbs had grown together two or three times. It was known as a triple canopy jungle, which meant that it effectively shut out the light. It was also very dense with as many as twelve thousand species of plants. Our aerial reconnaissance found it next to impossible to see beneath this natural canopy, which meant the jungle was a perfect hiding place for the NVA.

I can still remember the cacophony of sounds that first night as the sun set. The jungle became a living entity. Big cats yowled, monkeys screeched and chattered, birds tweeted, and insects chirped. It was noisy and unnerving . . . and endless.

On the other side of Hill 1049, to the south and east, fields of elephant grass led into a valley. Because of its height and density, the elephant grass was dangerous to walk through. An enemy could hide until it was too late to react.

Closer in, over on the east side of the hill, was the helicopter pad on which I had landed yesterday. It had been cut into the ridge when this firebase was built. One of the men told me that, earlier this month, an

FNG had arrived at this very same pad but had jumped off of his helicopter on the wrong side, and was hit by the rotor. His body was instantly cut to pieces. The men in his company, and the pilot, had simply collected his body parts into a poncho, put him back on the chopper, and sent his body home. This was that FNG's first and last day in the field. What a useless waste; all because no one told him to get off the chopper on the downward side of the mountain. He jumped off on the uphill side into the whirling blade.

I also learned that two men had jumped off of that ill-fated chopper that day. The other guy was Christian (Chris) Krukow (pronounced Kru-ko) from 3rd Platoon, whom I had met just this morning. Chris was tall, definitely over six feet, but he only weighed one hundred-forty to one hundred-fifty pounds. He was skinny, wiry, and strong. He carried a machine gun for 3rd squad (in 3rd Platoon). Chris was a friendly but quiet Minnesota country boy with blondish hair. He was also a serious soldier. I liked him right away. I later learned that, beneath his quiet exterior, Chris was the consummate practical joker.

When that chopper landed, Chris ran out on the low side and the FNG ran out on the high side, heading up the mountain. The rest was history. Chris told me that he had been given instructions on how to get off a chopper but apparently no one had told the FNG which side to jump off on. I wondered how that chopper pilot felt.

After Chris and I were introduced, he asked me if I had heard the phuck-you lizard yet. When I said no, he proceeded to tell me that they looked like an ugly iguana and that their mating call sounded just like their name. He told me to listen for them after dark. I smiled but I thought Chris was feeding me some good old country boy bullshit.

Approximately eighty men from A Company were dug in with me on Hill 1049. We had plenty of firepower with us. I wasn't worried about the enemy getting to us. My foxhole was directly below the mortar bunker.

Our foxholes were close to the jungle. I sat quietly by my foxhole looking at the jungle as though I had been a soldier all my life. I heard artillery fire somewhere in the distance. It sounded like our 105mm howitzers. These cannons were our artillery. Most were 105mm (diameter) howitzers, and the really big guns, the 155mm howitzers.

The largest firebases, like Firebase 25—where A-1-8 had been stationed before my arrival—had a battery of 105s attached to them. These were usually delivered to or retrieved from a firebase by huge Chinook CH-47 helicopters. The smaller and more temporary outposts—like Hill 1049—were without artillery.

I was accustomed to wearing Army fatigues, but I had been issued my first pair of jungle boots in Enari. After wearing them for a few days, I really appreciated them. The sides were a heavy green canvas and the soles were tough black rubber glued over a thin steel plate to protect against punji stakes. The boots laced up the front. They were as comfortable as tennis shoes and dried out quickly after fording a stream.

Huey helicopters, called "slicks", delivered our supplies. In less isolated locations, truck convoys delivered them. Regardless of the means of transportation, our water arrived in plastic bottles, our ammo in cans, our weapons in wooden containers, our food in cardboard cases, and our mail in bags. If a slick were in danger of coming under fire, it would hover—while someone on board threw our supplies off the cargo hold—and then leave posthaste. Sometimes the water bottles broke on impact.

Bringing Supplies up to the Pad

C-rations were issued to us whenever possible. I had difficulty learning to eat and appreciate them. C-rations were known affectionately as *C-rats*. Unless my family sent me food, C-rats were all I had to eat in the Nam. One box of C-rats equaled a meal. The cardboard container was only three-by-six inches. It typically held a couple cookies, a slice of bread in a can, a can of fruit, and the main course, which was usually beef stew, beans and franks, beef or ham slices, or, sometimes, eggs. The eggs

100

were usually thrown out by everyone. Each box also contained salt, pepper, chewing gum, instant coffee, matches, toilet paper, cigarettes, and a plastic spoon. Needless to say, the proportions were miniscule for soldiers who normally had hungry appetites.

We were each delivered a case of C-rats at a time . . . twelve meals. I was told that we were supposed to be eating LRRP (Long Range Reconnaissance Patrol) rations—the same food given to the Long Range Patrol soldiers. These were dehydrated meals, and they tasted much better than C-rats. We rarely got our hands on them. It was rumored that the men at Camp Enari routinely stole them from our supplies for snacks. Although LRRP rations were gourmet fare compared to C-rats, they weren't the food of choice for long patrols; they took too much water.

When our C-rats came in by chopper, we spent a few minutes separating the "keepers" from the others and carefully packed them into our rucks. We threw the others into either the fire or the latrine area. There were no sit-down dinners. Each man ate whenever and as often as he wanted food. One reason was that someone had to stand guard while the others ate. Sometimes, just to be sociable, two or three men would eat their C-rats together.

In addition to having enough food and water, a regular concern for each of us was catching malaria, which was a common scourge in jungle areas. To resist it, we took a daily dose of Dapson, which came in pill form. Every Monday, we also took *Chloroquine Primaquine*. We called this one the Monday Pill or the Shit Pill, because it gave us loose bowels. Since one day was like another, we could keep track of the passage of a week through this pill. It was always distributed on a Monday.

These malaria pills were a constant point of friction between the medics and the grunts. The grunts blamed every malady on them. Couldn't sleep? Couldn't eat? Diarrhea? It had to be the malaria pills. Bad news from home? Grouchy? Plain fed up with the Army? Malaria pills. A few of the men told me they refused to take them, hoping they'd catch malaria. Then they would be sent to the rear for treatment. A few in our company did get sick. Given this situation, the medics would hand out the pills in person and watch us swallow them. Even though we took these precautions, a relatively large number of the infantrymen got malaria in Vietnam.

Water was a problem. We couldn't drink the water from the many streams around us without treating it for bacteria first. Once it was treated, it tasted weird. We relied on water brought in by resupply. I was informed that, even when we were not under fire, water deliveries were irregular and I should learn to ration it.

A jungle is not the same thing as woods. The very first night on Hill 1049 I thought I could hear every sort of animal lurking in the jungle surrounding us. According to others there were supposedly more than two hundred species of mammals prowling around in it. The trick for us was not to attempt to eliminate them—it was impossible—but to keep them in the jungle and away from us. That sounded more reasonable than it proved to be. A few soldiers had heard of occasional patrols being threatened by tigers, but so far none had been attacked. The message to me was plain: *Keep your weapon handy, Jerry!*

Insects were another matter. Everybody was bothered by insects, especially mosquitoes, which in the Nam carried malaria. We kept Army-issue plastic bottles of repellent tied to our helmet straps. This kept ninety percent of the mosquitoes away from our faces and necks. After a few days, my nose got used to the smell.

There were ticks and leeches, snakes and rats . . . in abundance. Leeches attached to every part of our bodies when we had to cross a stream . . . which was too often. We spread repellent over our boots and lower pant legs in the hopes of preventing their attachment. *Sometimes* it worked. No one ever reported being attacked by a snake. That was amazing, considering how many poisonous varieties inhabited the jungles. We were on constant alert for them. Now rats . . . they were another story altogether. Rats lived in the bunkers on every firebase. As soon as we dug a bunker, it would fill up with rats. Gerry Richardson of 1st platoon recalled having a rat run up his leg one evening half way to his crotch and then reversing himself to continue running in the trenches. How did these disgusting vermin find our bunkers so quickly? It was and remains a mystery.

In Vietnam, everything was different from the World. I could no longer rely on my old ways to guide and protect me. My old rules no longer applied. *Simple logic did not work 95% of the time and thinking that I could get in trouble only 5% of the time.* I was permanently on the five percent side of things, I could not make mistakes. My out-of-mind-and-body technique for coping was downright dangerous. I couldn't afford to lose my attention for a second for my sake and most importantly, for the sake of my squad members. Events were not under my control. None of us could hide from Sergeant Garrett's kill-or-be-killed rule.

David Fawcett, the sergeant I replaced as squad leader, had given good advice. While learning the ropes, I should let the old-timers look out for me. Above all, I should not do anything stupid. I should just take care of business and keep everyone alive. The men didn't want to be heroes. They just wanted to get back home. I understood this line of reasoning.

Beyond that, the golden rules were simple: Don't ask anyone to do something I wouldn't do. Always put the welfare of my men first.

The men in my squad did not have to like me, but they had to follow me without question. During our initial meeting, they seemed friendly enough, and I quickly decided I fit in with them. However, most of them ignored me immediately after the introduction. Before we could become friends, they wanted to see me in action . . . and reaction.

Tuesday, 31 December 68

On New Year's Eve, 1968, it was hard to be in a holiday mood. I spent it working on my foxhole. My platoon was the only one in the company to pull duty on New Year's Eve. Lieutenant LePeilbet was taking no chances. If the NVA appeared, we would be ready.

Later that night, Spider visited each of our squad's foxholes and gave us a drink of whiskey from a fifth of Jack Daniel's that he had received in the mail that day. I heard that Spider received booze regularly, but nobody ever figured out where it came from. Spider toasted each of us with a drink in the dark of the night, and then wished us a Happy New Year. What he didn't tell us was that he was under Lieutenant LePeilbet's orders not to let any man have more than one drink. In case of attack, he did not want Charlie to catch us drunk.

And neither did I.

Wednesday, 1 January 69

That next morning, the Air Cavalry flew us out of the firebase in a fleet of helicopters to LZ Tinglebells. Once we left the choppers, the company took four hours to walk about three kilometers. We had difficulty humping though the dense jungle with our heavy eighty-pound rucksacks. We had to make our way through thick underbrush, foot by foot by foot and ended up in a creek bed and lost for a while. Everyone was tired, hungry and thirsty. Once we reached our destination we set up in a large flat area and were ordered to rest. We remained in our location for the rest of the day and passed the time sleeping, cleaning our weapons, writing letters, playing cards, or preparing for the night's operation.

The NVA liked to attack during the night when the rest of the world was sleeping. That's when they invaded villages, intimidated or killed the residents and stole their food and supplies. They disappeared into their jungle hideaways before daylight. We received orders to get ready for an operation which involved setting up an ambush in the dark and catching the enemy as they left a particular Vietnamese village in the early morning hours.

This was my first actual wartime operation. I felt excited. It was to be the first real likelihood of contact with the enemy for the entire squad. Surprisingly, I did not feel afraid, and I sensed that my men didn't either. For one thing, there were a lot of us—an entire company, and, for another, we were armed to the hilt.

Thursday, 2 January 69

My first firefight mission sent us a few klicks away from the LZ Tinglbells to search a Vietnamese village for NVA soldiers. We moved out at midnight. We humped through the jungle and arrived at our destination in the wee hours of the morning and silently surrounded the village. Everyone moved into ambush position in the darkness and lay there, waiting for daybreak. Any NVA in the village would be trapped there. My squad was lying out in the open on a rocky flat area. A stench was coming from somewhere, we did not know where, but it stunk to high heaven. I thought, *so this is the real native Vietnam… It smells like shit.*

Joe Shea and Don Cheek had taken up positions in the bushes not far from me. Just before dawn, an old Mama San walked out of the village and headed directly toward Joe and Don's position. They didn't know what to do and quickly looked over at me for suggestions. I told them, with hand signals, to stay put because if she saw them she would give away our ambush. They crouched in the bushes like stone statues and let her continue her approach. None of us knew what to expect. Was this a

104

grandmother who had a grenade? The Mama San got within ten meters of Joe, then wheeled around and dropped her drawers. She squatted and took a crap right there in front of him!

Joe managed to keep from making a sound but for a while, he thought he was going to die laughing. Later he told me that he had been wondering what the white stuff was all over the field behind him, now he knew - it was toilet paper!

All of a sudden, before we had time to think to think, the shooting started. The entire company began firing and bullets were flying over our heads. We did not know what was happening. We saw streams of light from tracer bullets flying over our heads. Without warning, we were in a fierce firefight - my first one.

Once the shooting stopped, it seemed that we had to lie in our positions for an eternity waiting for the all-clear signal. Finally Sergeant White came around and gave it. He instructed us to rest as much as was possible because we would move out within the hour. Since we had been up all night, making the trek through the jungle and enduring the tension before the melee, my men were absolutely exhausted. So was I. White told us that four soldiers had been moving down a road into the village. Lieutenant LePeilbet had spotted them. He yelled in Vietnamese for them to stop. Instead of stopping, they opened fire. Since local officials had reported a platoon of NVA in the village, Lieutenant LePeilbet returned fire and the war began.

It was not until Sergeant White noticed that one of the men from the village was shooting an M-79 grenade launcher directly at him that he realized something was amiss. He immediately called for a cease-fire. The four soldiers firing at us were not the enemy! They were South Vietnamese soldiers (known to us as ARVNs, which stood for Army of the Republic of Vietnam). Why had they attacked us, rather than answering Lieutenant LePeilbet's challenge?

Two of the South Vietnamese soldiers were killed in the melee and the other two were wounded. The ARVNs had opened fire on us because they thought *we* were the enemy. Since we had been informed that the enemy was encamped in the village, we thought *they* were the enemy. What a confused mess!

An hour passed. We received no orders to move out. The word came down that our battalion commander had flown in to review the situation. We had accidentally killed some allies. He, Captain Hockett, and

Lieutenant LePeilbet met with the village chief, talked things over, and concluded that the ARVNs were not supposed to be in the village and they had opened fire on us first. The problem was tragic, but not our fault.

The village chief, by telling us that NVA were occupying his village, had provided the wrong information. Actually, there was a mechanized unit of South Vietnamese soldiers stationed there. Had the chief deliberately set us against the South Vietnamese? It was anyone's guess. I made another mental note to add to my growing checklist. Make sure the enemy is really the enemy before firing. It turned out that this was the only time we really had to worry about this; our company was headed back to the direction of the Cambodian border where there were only NVA.

With daybreak, I discovered that part of my squad had been set up for our ambush in the village outhouse, which happened to be the open field around and behind us. My men had lain in shit all night long. Many of the men got it all over the front of their fatigues and on their shoes. Ed Weaver and Joe Shea were literally covered in it.

John Gray and one of the village huts

Even though we had this miserable stench on us, we slept like babies after the firefight. My squad had no choice but to endure the foul smell.

106

Water was rationed again. Washing our clothes was impossible and cleaning them up with rags a useless gesture.

Because of the South Vietnamese causalities, Lieutenant LePeilbet felt miserable all day. Sergeant White suggested that at least our men had performed well under combat conditions, despite the jamming of several weapons. He thought the reason for that problem was twofold: the magazines had been loaded too full, and some of the weapons had become dirty while soldiers were maneuvering into position. As a result of this report, the lieutenant ordered everyone in my platoon to load the magazines with only eighteen rounds, rather than the normal twenty, and to work harder at keeping the rifles clean.

I took the message to heart and ordered my men to spend extra time on this important daily chore.

We were awakened with news that the Brass had ordered us to move out of the village and continue to our next mission. This time we would have to hump the entire way. No helicopter rides. As I heaved my ruck onto my back, I began to realize that humping was to be my normal means of travel here in Vietnam.

We left the village and headed straight upward, into the hills. Third Platoon took the lead, with an Italian Lieutenant directing them and Jerry Loucks walking point. His friend, Chris Kruckow, walked behind him, covering his tracks with his M-60. Our platoon was next in line, followed by 1st Platoon. Headquarters followed them and 2nd Platoon followed in the rear. Each soldier kept ten to fifteen meters between himself and the next man while walking, then came closer when stopping or resting. We worked like a giant accordion, fanning out and squeezing together as we traversed a narrow pathway or forded a stream.

We worked our way through some heavy jungle brush, then immediately ran into tall elephant grass, which was worse, because now we couldn't see five feet ahead of us. The men on point had to hack their way through the grass with machetes to cut a path for us. I worried that the NVA would hear us and that we would get lost in the maze. I kept my eye on my squad members as we humped endlessly, realizing they were as tired as I was. We had no choice other than to endure the ordeal.

In training, we never wore a rucksack. I went through Basic, AIT, OJT and NCO schools without ever hearing the word rucksack. Of course, in training I never had to carry three days' worth of supplies. Only in the

Central Highlands did this become a necessity. Now, my men and I wore a rucksack crammed full of supplies. Mine flopped all over the place, made too much noise and rubbed my body raw. I felt like a pack animal. I knew I had to come to terms with the weight of this monstrosity, and soon.

(One of the theories for success in the Central Highlands was that the American soldier should carry enough food and ammo to move and fight independently for several days. We would typically pack four to five hundred rounds of M-16 ammo, while the enemy might only have one hundred-fifty to three hundred rounds. They would be lighter and more mobile, but we would have the firepower . . . and the advantage. I never heard a single man complain about carrying heavy ammunition.)

I knew that the key to humping success was conserving energy. This meant stopping and moving only when necessary, and sitting only when there was a definite timeout period. It took enormous effort to merely stand in place with a ruck on our backs. It took even more effort to constantly replace the ruck. Most of the time, we sat with it on our backs. Then all we had to do was roll sideways to get to our feet.

We humped for several hours after leaving the village of our fateful firefight. The terrain changed with every kilometer we traversed. Soon I had no idea where we were. We were on constant lookout for punji sticks—sharp bamboo sticks carved by the enemy and placed in hidden positions in the bush with their points protruding. None of us wanted to trip and fall on them. They could be anywhere, in mountainous areas, in the valleys, in the jungles, or even in the tall grass. There was no way to know where we might find them.

We emerged from the bush at the base of a mountain which had streams flowing from it. It was beautiful, and any other time we would have enjoyed it. Because of the firefight at the village, we were in no mood to enjoy scenery. Our bodies were completely exhausted. And . . . some of the men still smelled like the dung field.

We had been humping for eight hours, and it was late afternoon. Everyone was complaining wondering where we were headed. I had to tell them I did not know. The men wanted to settle in for the night before dark. They would have to dig foxholes, no matter what time we halted. There would be no rest until that standard operating procedure (SOP) had been completed.

We arrived at a deep gorge with very steep banks which made walking extremely difficult. As the company halted I noticed there was a commotion up front. Then the word made its way back that we were lost. One of the Lieutenants, an Italian guy, got us lost and kind of broke down that he did not know how to get us out. We were lost. This happened in a creek bed that led up to a swift river. Time passed, we were in limbo. After a while, Sergeant White was called to the front of the column with his map. White took over as the leader, and he and Jerry Loucks soon figured out the best direction for us to take. It was decided the Sergeant White would take the lead from there.

The river, far below, was swift and would be difficult to cross. Our path lay across that river and straight up the steepest bank we had ever seen!

The entire company slowly snaked its way down the gorge and into the river. It didn't take but two minutes for someone to fall into the swiftly moving current. He had eighty pounds on his back and a rifle in his hands, while wearing his fatigues and boots and a helmet. He completely disappeared, except for his legs, which were sticking straight up out of the water! This happened directly in front of me, and I couldn't believe my eyes. One second the soldier was crossing the river and the next he was out of sight. He had evidently stepped off a rock and into a hole and turned completely upside down. The weight of his rucksack took him straight to the bottom, headfirst.

At the time, Sergeant White and Jerry Loucks guided each man across. They had sent Chris Kruckow ahead, to take the point-and-hold position, until the men could reassemble on the far bank. When the soldier first fell in, they gazed at each other with stunned faces, and then burst out laughing. They watched him disappear, thinking he was going to pop up at any second, but when he didn't, they immediately dropped their rucks, dove into the river, and pulled him out by his feet.

It was Sergeant Dave Muck of 3rd Platoon. If they hadn't pulled him out, he would have drowned. When he was able to talk, Muck told us that his ruck was so heavy he couldn't move. He had lay on the bottom of the river for what seemed like hours and he was very grateful for his buddy's quick actions.

Dave Muck in underwear and Greg Rollinger in front

We decided to string a rope across the river to use as a guide and stabilizer. Each man walked slowly, while tightly grasping the rope and slipping and sliding on the slippery river rocks. The bank on the other side was a sixty-degree incline. Once across the river, we needed more ropes to pull ourselves and our heavy rucks to the top of the gorge again. Never, during this agonizing ordeal, was the enemy off our minds. They would have had a field day. We were seventy-five sitting ducks.

Later, Chris Kruckow learned that Sergeant Muck, who was also a Shake 'n Bake had been a lifeguard in the World. When this news got around, he was immediately nicknamed "Flipper" for his underwater skills.

Once we had all successfully crossed the river and started our hike up the embankment, we came face to face with another Vietnam endurance test. We called it the Wait-a-Minute Bush. The plant was actually a vine, with devilish thorns that lay backwards on the branches. If we brushed against one small branch, the thorn would stick into our fatigues. Then the entire vine would attach itself to us. The more we struggled to free ourselves, the more we suffered from increasingly more thorns. To get free of the thing, we had to carefully pull the entire vine free with one tug. Inevitably, someone else had to help us get loose . . . *very carefully*, or they, too, would become entangled. That's why we called this demon the *wait-a-minute* bush!

Unfortunately, there was a mess of wait-a-minute bushes waiting at the top of the riverbank. As each soldier ascended its steep sides, he got entangled in the thorns. Sergeant White was struck in the eye by one of the branches and had to have medical attention from Doc Driver. White couldn't see well for the rest of the day, but he continued to lead our company out of its predicament.

We humped until dark and were soon navigating by moonlight. We knew that the enemy moved during the night and we were in no mood or condition to tangle with him. It was ten or eleven in the evening before we reached a safe location. No one knew if this was our correct location, but at least it was safe and provided good cover. As always, we had to dig in. We worked until midnight preparing our foxholes just in case of attack. As we settled in for the night, I saw my men plucking wait-a-minute thorns from their uniforms. Even after this long, exhausting, dangerous day in Vietnam came to a close, we had to take turns standing guard duty for the rest of the night . . . Sergeant Muck included.

Chapter 17

The equipment my men and I carried in Vietnam was for all practicable purposes our homes. We lived *in* it and *with* it . . . and *because* of it. Every man in my squad carried, in addition to his own weapon and its ammo, the following equipment:

three belts of ammo for the M-60 machine gun	a helmet
six hand grenades	a poncho liner and a poncho
one or more white phosphorus grenades	the rucksack to hold all this equipment
one or more smoke grenades	towels for the rucksack straps
a rifle cleaning kit	maps and a compass
two claymore mines	several days' supply of C-rations
M72 LAW rocket launcher for tanks	one or two canteens with water
5 plastic bags for making sandbags	a belt to hold the canteen
30 magazines of M-16 ammo	water purification pills
(540 rounds plus a magazine in the rifle)	extra water, at times
Jungle boots	C-4 and matches for cooking
a pencil and paper for writing home	cigarettes
Letters from home and letters in progress	a gas mask

Later, I also carried a Bowie knife strapped to my right leg.

The most critical part of this equipment was our M-16 rifle and its ammunition. For other men, their critical equipment was either the M-79 grenade launcher or the M-60 machine gun. These were the three main weapons used in our company.

I took excellent care of my weapon. I cleaned it, slept with it, and kept it within reach at all times. It was there when I ate and when I went to the bathroom. I never let it out of my sight. My weapon was the difference between life and death. The Army had taught me well.

The M-16 was the standard weapon issued to most of the men, and it was a classic. Eugene Stoner had designed it in the 1950s to be lightweight but very efficient. Made of pressed steel and plastic, it weighed only six-and-a-half pounds. It fired a high velocity 5.56mm round that was small and powerful, so that each man could carry more ammunition into combat. Each of us carried magazines—containing twenty rounds apiece—in bandoleers, which either hung around our necks or wrapped around our waists. We usually loaded only eighteen rounds at a time; this seemed to prevent jamming, a chronic problem with this weapon.

The M-16 could fire in either semi-automatic or automatic mode at a rate of seven hundred rounds per minute. In semi-automatic mode, it fired one round each time the trigger was pulled. In automatic mode, it fired indefinitely—until it got too hot or jammed. When using the M-16, we were usually better off not setting it to full automatic, because we could then squeeze the trigger several times, quickly, and produce a better grouping and accuracy of bullets. The rifle had an effective range of four hundred meters but, since most firefights occurred within fifty to one-hundred meters of the enemy, it became a perfect weapon.

We were told that if we kept our M-16s clean they would not jam so we cleaned them daily. However, it was difficult to keep the ammo clean. We traveled through acres of dirt and mud. Dirty ammo caused jamming, too.

One M-60 was assigned to each squad. Each M-60 had a machine gunner and an assistant machine gunner who helped feed the ammunition. In my squad, Rick Campbell carried the M-60 and was our machine gunner. At twenty-four and one-half pounds, it was much heavier than the M-16 and it took our biggest and strongest soldier to do the toting. Because it was so heavy, some guys lovingly called it "the Pig."

113

We treasured this weapon. With its high rate of automatic fire, it could wreak havoc on the enemy, thus making us feel eminently safer.

With belt-feed ammo, the M-60 could fire five hundred rounds per minute continuously. It also fired a much larger projectile (7.62mm), so the ammo was too heavy for one man to carry. It had to be divided among all of us with one or more belts being carried by each man in the squad. Every belt held one hundred rounds, and every fifth round was a tracer. Everyone looked out for our machine gunner because we knew that, in a firefight, Private Rick Campbell could save our skins.

The M-79 grenade launcher was a single shot, breech-loading weapon, developed by the Army in the 1950s. It was affectionately called the "bloop gun" because of the sound it made when it was fired. In the hands of someone who knew how to use it, the M-79 was capable of great accuracy. It was also a very effective anti-ambush weapon, since grenades could be fired very rapidly at the enemy, overpowering their attack and forcing a retreat. This weapon had an effective range of one hundred fifty meters for individual targets and three hundred fifty meters for area ones. It opened at the breech and loaded like a short, stubby shotgun. It fired more than twenty types of grenades, including the standard 40mm ones which created explosions of shrapnel. The weapon could also fire white phosphorus grenades, flechettes or beehive rounds, and illuminator, smoke, or CS (tear gas) rounds.

The flechette or beehive round was composed of thousands of tiny darts which were fired like buckshot does from a shotgun. It was developed for use in ambushes. Beehives were devastating and would wipe out anything in their path.

White phosphorous rounds, known as Willie Peter, were deadly and dangerous to handle. If it got on your skin, the phosphorus could burn right through your body. White phosphorus was a chemical that burned at high temperature on exposure to air. I carried a white phosphorus grenade and was always apprehensive that it would get caught on a bush or tree and go off.

Carrying ammunition through the jungle was very difficult, to say the least. We carried more ammo in the Highlands than we would have elsewhere because we were out in the bush and could not count on regular resupply. Our operation was different from that of the 1st Cavalry, who were on air missions or short patrols. We were always humping the ground, moving closer and closer to the enemy. For that

114

reason, we had to be prepared for long stays and fights. Even carrying an enormous supply of ammo, it was amazing how quickly it was used up. It was too quickly.

Being a good soldier took more than training in the use of weapons. Mastering the art of daily living in the bush made our lives tolerable. It took me some time to learn how to pack my rucksack the right way so everything would fit. If I didn't pack it right it would literally kick my ass. When packed correctly, the rucksack rested high on my back, so that my legs supported it. Otherwise, the weight of the pack would cut deep sore spots in my shoulders and the front of my chest. We often wedged towels under the rucksack's straps, to keep them from causing damage.

Packing the rucksack to walk with ease through the jungle with its weight balanced on my back, was critical to my performance as a soldier. I also had to lead by example and help others so I had to master this skill soon after I arrived in the field. It was the first big hurdle I—and all FNGs—faced, and once I learned how to deal with it, life became more bearable.

There were other important skills necessary for my living comfortably in the bush. One was using the poncho and poncho liner to build a temporary shelter with sticks. I had to set up a shelter for sleeping every night after I dug a foxhole. The poncho liner was pulled over my head while sleeping. I breathed through it and so it was great for warding off mosquitoes and other varmints. The poncho liner made a small tent for privacy and protection against the rain, or as a ground cover, or to keep the dew off at night. It took me several weeks to adapt to these less than perfect sleeping conditions. Soon, I could sleep in any situation, on any terrain, and at any time. Maybe my travels as a hippie helped me in this regard too.

Learning how to pick the best possible place to sleep was another skill. I became an expert at looking for and choosing soft ground. Soft ground was treasured because it was genuinely restful. As a grunt I quickly learned how important the smaller things in life were. It was the basic elements that counted the most. Personal survival, caring comrades, good health, and hope for the future were the things that kept us going, but a little soft ground once in a while made our lives bearable. Our bodies were pushed to their limits and those few hours rest was a small treasured reward.

Chapter 18

The Platoon Leader and Platoon Sergeant

My company, commanded by Captain David Hockett, consisted of four rifle platoons and a team of reconnaissance soldiers, called Tracers. I was one of three squad leaders in the 4th Platoon, which was commanded by 1st Lieutenant Andrew LePeilbet. In addition, we had a scout dog and his trainer. Ordinarily, each platoon would have had four squads, with as many as ten men each. At full strength, a company with four platoons would number between 110 to 140 men. We were rarely at full strength. We had about 75 men.

Captain Hockett in jeep and Ken McCormick with curly hair in back

The chain of command worked like this; I communicated with Sergeant White and Lieutenant LePeilbet. I communicated the orders they gave me to my men and made sure they understood them. I listened to the men's bitches and to their legitimate problems. I went to bat for them with White or LePeilbet. I broke in the new privates and taught them how to keep their weapons clean and in good working order. I taught them how to pack a ruck and how to hump. I distributed the M-60 ammo to everyone and one of my most important jobs was to make sure our M-60 gunner was happy.

My platoon leader, Lieutenant Andrew R. LePeilbet, made quite an impression on me. He was a no-nonsense, straightforward guy. He gave me the responsibility of 2nd Squad. I had been trained to handle the duties of a squad sergeant, and LePeilbet accepted that at face value.

Lieutenant LePeilbet was as new to Vietnam as I was. He was in the early part of his first tour, and he was a dedicated leader. While he was learning the ropes, he relied heavily on Sergeant White's advice because White was a career man on his second tour in Nam.

The lieutenant emphasized the importance of strictly following the rules regarding the flow of orders through the chain of command. He wanted me to call my superiors by their rank and last name and to emphasize this code of respect to my squad members as well. In this regard, he said, I should set myself apart from the men I led. I should set the example, take total responsibility for the behavior of my men and, when they screwed up, take the heat. These rules provided an orderly structure within which 4th Platoon and its three squads could operate efficiently as a unit.

Lieutenant LePeilbet talked to me about trust. "Here in the Nam, Sergeant Horton, trust means everything. If you conduct yourself like a professional, if you are calm and never panic under fire, then you will have the trust of your men. They will look to you as an example for their own behavior. If they like what they see, they'll have confidence in your leadership."

Lieutenant LePeilbet worked directly with the company commander, Captain Hockett, who was responsible for the company's overall strategy. He planned platoon ambushes and made certain our platoon fulfilled its part of the overall company operations. Both the lieutenant and Sergeant White worked closely with the three squad leaders to ensure that we knew how to carry out our missions. Teamwork was the key to our success and good communication throughout the chain of command was paramount.

When a mission was in the works, the lieutenant called his three squad leaders together and issued a SMEAC. This acronym stood for Situation, Mission, Execution, Administration and Command. It encompassed the elements needed to convey the details of the mission to everyone involved.

118

- *The Situation included an assessment of the mission:* how many friendlies would we encounter; how many enemy were involved; was shooting expected?
- *The Mission defined our goal:* was it an ambush; a recon; a rerun of a previous mission
- *The Execution explained how we would accomplish the goal:* when would we leave; how many men would be involved; when would we would return?
- *The Administration and Logistics information consisted of practical statistics:* what should each man carry in the way of ammo, rations, grenades, and so forth?
- *The Command and Control details focused on:* who was in command; what radio call signs would be used; who would take over if the leaders were wounded; what firepower support—artillery, mortars, or aircraft—would be available for the mission?

Andy LePeilbet looked very young, even though he was actually a twenty-four- year- old college graduate from Sacramento, California. He was fresh out of Officers Candidate School and definitely very smart. He had a lighthearted but business-like personality and he smiled continually. He liked his job and definitely projected a positive image as a leader. We wanted to follow him.

LePeilbet was athletically built. Before joining the Army, he had been a rodeo bull rider, which may have led to his nickname—Bronco. Of course, the men never called him that to his face.

Lieutenant LePeilbet was conscientious and cautious when he assigned missions to us and he treated each man respectfully. Before we departed on a mission, he made sure we were well prepared. After giving a SMEAC, he asked for our questions or comments, and he listened carefully to our concerns.

Later in the month of January our platoon went out on its first mission by itself since I had joined the company. It was sort of a test run cruise for us to discover what worked and where our weaknesses were. We were three days from the company perimeter, en route to an ambush site. It had been tough humping through the thick jungle all day, and now

119

everyone was tired. We were just sitting, resting in a small clearing, taking a break.

Some of the guys were lying down on the ground while others were working on their gear, eating or doing minor chores. If men were talking, they did so very quietly. Even though we were resting, we had to be careful not to give our position away.

Sergeant White was quietly going over a map of the terrain with Lieutenant LePeilbet's radio telephone operator (RTO) Mike Hughes, who was up on one knee, leaning on his radio. I was standing behind them, eavesdropping. The lieutenant was sprawled on the ground nearby, head against a tree, listening to White.

All a sudden, Lt. LePeilbet jumped up and pulled his shirt open. He looked at his chest, but he didn't see anything. Sergeant White looked up at him, "What happened, Lieutenant?"

The lieutenant replied, "Something stung me on the chest!"

He examined his shirt carefully, but nothing was there, so he re-buttoned it. "I guess it's gone," he said and he sat back down.

He leaned against the tree again but then he jumped up once more and, grasping at his shirt, tried to reach around his back. "Damn, what is that?" he yelled in a loud voice.

LePeilbet started hopping around while he was tugging at his shirt. Then he ripped his shirt completely off. RTO Hughes looked at his back. There were at least three scorpions clinging to it, stinging him like hell. Hughes quickly stood up and knocked them off with his hand.

Lieutenant LePeilbet was now yelling, "Damn! That really hurts! Oh shit! Oh fuck!"

He was hopping around like a Mexican jumping bean. None of us had ever seen the lieutenant act like that before. At first we couldn't tell whether he was serious or what. I thought, *Maybe he sat down on some fire ants.*

I had never seen anyone move in such jerky motions before, especially a big guy like the lieutenant. He acted like a man possessed.

After a few minutes, when the yelling and hopping continued, some of us realized that the lieutenant was in serious pain. Sergeant White, Mike Hughes and I rushed over to him, but the lieutenant hurt so bad he couldn't stop moving, and he couldn't stop yelling. He couldn't even tell us what was wrong. It took the three of us to keep him from jumping around. Glancing at his back, we could see multiple wounds; each sting was now a large red welt. Obviously they were so painful the man couldn't control himself. We knew he was really hurting bad to yell like that, given that he was compromising the platoon's position. When the lieutenant finally quieted down, we laid him on the ground to examine his stings.

Lieutenant LePeilbet was now sweating profusely. Through chattering teeth he told us that he was getting numb all over. His body was shaking fiercely and he was grimacing to keep from yelling again. I began to wonder if the man was going into shock.

Doc Driver, our platoon medic, was a very laid-back kind of guy. He enjoyed a special status in the company, because he wore hippie tie-die shirts with fringe on them and other hippie clothes adorned with peace symbols in place of the regulation fatigues. When he was in base camp, he usually had beads around his neck. Today he was in Army fatigues but he still had his beads on.

Driver frequently used hippie phrases like "Far out!" and "That's heavy, man" in his conversations and nobody seemed to worry about it. He was one the few men in the company to have lived through the May 1968 firefight when the company got overrun on Firebase 29 near Ben Het. Because of that experience, Doc Driver and Jerry Loucks were the only two men in our company who had real combat experience.

Nothing ever fazed the good doctor. He was always laid-back, composed and cool. He had seen it all in Vietnam, and he let everyone know it. Nobody fucked with him. Sometimes I worried that Driver might not be able to get it together in an emergency, but on the other hand his calm reactions were reassuring.

But when Driver came forward to examine the lieutenant, and saw his condition, he completely freaked. He stated unequivocally in a loud, shaky voice that if we didn't get LePeilbet to a hospital within forty-five minutes, he would die. It turned out that Driver had recently received some G2 sheets about scorpions which said that they were dangerous as hell, and could kill a grown man in a short time.

When we heard this pronouncement, we all looked at each other like, *What the fuck, Doc. Are you sure?*

Driver's eyes were bugged out. He looked really scared. He practically shouted, "Hell, yes!"

Poor Lieutenant LePeilbet was lying there taking all this in. Doc Driver kept hollering at RTO Hughes, "Get the fucking chopper, man, or the lieutenant's gonna die!"

We didn't know it at the time, but Driver was scared shitless of scorpions, spiders and snakes. He must have run into one on a bad trip. Who knows?

Hell, medics were supposed to exert a calming influence, but this one was making us all freaked out. Looking at him, at that moment I thought Doc Driver was the most uptight hippie I had ever seen. Within a few minutes of hearing this report from the platoon medic, everyone in the clearing except the lieutenant was upset. Now he remained calm.

"You gotta get him out of here. I don't care what it takes; you have to get him out of here right now - no matter what. Do it now! I don't have any medicines! Somebody do something!"

I could see that Driver was working himself up into a frenzy. Hughes, the lieutenant's RTO, had already called for a Dustoff, but, due to other battalion activity no choppers were available. There was nothing we could do but wait, and hope that all the noise we made had not given away our position to the NVA.

Seeing Doc Driver's rising hysteria, Sergeant White took charge of the situation. The lieutenant had made one hell of a ruckus, and the Medic's distress had spread to us all. Now order must be restored.

First, Sergeant White ordered the men to take up positions in a loose circle, and he briefly showed them their fields of fire. He told everyone to stay in position, and to remain quiet and watchful. He did not want the NVA surprising the platoon while we were trying to get the lieutenant evacuated. Then he ordered Pappy and The Flea, who were busy trying to find the scorpions in the thick underbrush, to locate a clearing nearby where we could carry the lieutenant.

White's coolness and discipline helped to relieve the congestion around the lieutenant and it calmed the men down. It also helped the platoon to defend itself. The leader had gone down and the next in command had taken charge - just as the Army manual had stated he should. I saw what Sergeant White was doing, and I took mental notes.

Doc Driver did not carry any medicines for scorpion bites with him, so there was very little he could do to help the lieutenant. We had tried to make him comfortable on the ground and beyond that, there was not much anyone could do. Hell, there aren't any medications for scorpion

122

stings anyway, but at the time, we didn't know that. Driver just stood around, repeating to anyone who would listen that Lieutenant LePeilbet was going to die within forty-five minutes. The lieutenant just looked at him; he didn't say anything.

Finally, Sergeant White took Driver by the shoulders and gently but forcefully led him across the clearing, out of the lieutenant's earshot. Then he looked Doc Driver right in the eye and said, "Shut the fuck up! You're gonna give someone a fucking heart attack, and it might be Lieutenant LePeilbet."

After that, Doc Driver calmed down.

It was distressing for us to see the lieutenant going pale and limp and realize that there was nothing we could do. Hell, he was our leader. Luckily we had Sergeant White with us. Otherwise the whole platoon might have panicked. By now Hughes was yelling at somebody over his radio, trying to locate anything that flew. But by the time a chopper arrived at our location, two hours had passed. The lieutenant was completely limp, numb and unable to walk.

When the Dustoff finally arrived, we carried the lieutenant carefully into a clearing and lifted him into the cargo hold. We kind of crammed his body into the back of the helicopter because he could not move his arms and legs very well. The chopper was called a Loach (light observation helicopter) and it immediately took him to a field hospital.

When Lieutenant LePeilbet arrived at the hospital he had to be carried to the entrance. The doctors examined him but it turned out that there wasn't really any antidote for scorpion stings. So they just cleaned the wounds with soap and water and kept them covered in cold compresses while they healed.

Because there were so many of them, the lieutenant's stings were considered pretty serious. But since he was a large and muscular guy, he was in no real danger of death. Scorpion stings are poisonous but not typically lethal to humans unless they have an allergic reaction.

A medic stopped by the lieutenant's bed the next day and stared at the patient. Seeing that he was on the mend, he said, "Lieutenant, how are you feeling today?"

Lieutenant LePeilbet had his face in the pillow, and he answered a muffled, "I'm better."

Then the medic said, "That's good, sir. By the way, would you like to know about scorpions?"

123

The lieutenant was groggy but he turned over to face the medic. "Yeah, Doc. Tell me" he said, looking up.

The medic told him that a scorpion's stinger was called a telson, and that it was located at the very tip of the abdomen. The telson is where it injects the venom. He added, "Although the scorpion can regulate the amount of venom it injects, this is not typically enough to cause death in humans. Of the over 1050 species of scorpions found around the world, only a small number are dangerous to humans."

He told the lieutenant that he studied scorpions as a hobby. "You probably got bit by the west Asian scorpion, called Hemiscorpius lepturus."

He added, "The thing about it is, its venom has not been documented, but it does cause inflammation and loss of feeling at the wound site, followed by a deadening and shedding of the skin around the wound."

He rolled the lieutenant over and examined his back. He commented, "You must have gotten large blisters. Didn't you? This reaction is similar to that caused by the bite of the American brown recluse spider."

The lieutenant nodded. Then the medic said, "As many times as you got stung, you got lucky. It could have been worse. In rare cases, some people have died from multiple stings."

The lieutenant suddenly laughed, and said, "Yeah, my platoon medic, Driver, told me all about that. Thanks for the info, Doc."

"You be well, lieutenant."

Later Lieutenant LePeilbet told me that immediately after he was stung he had experienced surprisingly intense pain. It radiated all across his body and was especially bad at the armpits and groin. At first he was mystified by this, and he thought he might die. He also had agitation and anxiety, along with increased body temperature, sweating, chills and a general feeling of numbness. In other words, after receiving all those stings, he was in a world of hurt.

With bed rest, it took several more days for the lieutenant to recover. When he returned to the field, he swore that, from here on out, he was going to check the ground very carefully before he sat down on it. For the next few months, before he sat down anywhere, he would smile at us and say, "Getting bit by scorpions is a story for my grandkids someday, but I only want to tell them about it once. Once is enough."

Chapter 19

Wednesday, 8 January 69

I had been one week in the field when Sergeant Lestock told me it was my squad's turn to go on a SRP (short range reconnaissance) mission. He wanted me to lead it. This would be my first mission as a sergeant outside the wire so to speak. I was to take my patrol to a ridge across a valley, about four klicks from our base, stay there on recon for two full days and nights, and return on the third day. I knew a klick was 1,000 meters, or about two-thirds of a mile, so my men and I would hump about five miles for the round trip. The division had reported some infiltration activity along the mountains and Captain Hockett wanted advance warning if any enemy were headed our way.

I was ordered to hump to the location, sit tight, report any movement, and avoid the enemy and not engage in any action unless I had no alternative. Lestock went over the location on the map with me. "Be sure to take Flea with you," he said. "He's been on several SRPs and knows the ropes."

That made sense. I rounded up my squad and told them The Flea was going with me on a SRP and I needed a couple more volunteers. The Flea got a sour look on his face. No one else said a word. Obviously, none of my men wanted to go on a SRP with an FNG sergeant. The silence stretched. I named Spider and Rick Campbell without further ado.

The next morning, at first light, I went over the map coordinates and briefed them on our mission. I knew they already understood the information, but I told them anyway. Spider took the time to help me tighten my ruck so that it would sit quietly in position when I walked and not rub my back. This was critical on an SRP. He told me to bring plenty of writing materials, because we would be sitting for long spells and we had to remain absolutely quiet. He was looking out for me and I really appreciated that.

The Flea volunteered to walk point. Rick brought up the rear. The person in this position is called the drag man and he had to walk backwards part of the time to make sure we weren't attacked from behind. I followed Flea in the slack (second) position, with Spider behind me. We were spread about ten to fifteen meters apart and walked slowly and as quietly as possible, which was hard to do in a dense jungle. I had the compass and the maps, and I frequently checked both.

Walking point is essentially the art of breaking a trail for yourself and for those who followed. Wherever the point man walked, you could safely step. I studied the ground in front of me, wanting to step in The Flea's tracks. It was tricky, trying to watch the ground and also keep a lookout for Charlie and my other men.

After we had walked for five or ten minutes, I began to smell the dampness of the jungle. It was quite a change from the World and firebase, strangely enough I enjoyed it. We were about ninety feet below the treetops, and the sunlight appeared only in patches. Away from the firebase, the jungle was full of natural sounds—rustling leaves, the chirping of birds, and other sounds I didn't recognize.

We had traveled only thirty minutes through the jungle when The Flea dropped to one knee and raised a fist, the signal to stop. I dropped and repeated his signal. The Flea was as motionless as a tree stump; he didn't try to take cover and he didn't look back at me. The patrol halted behind me, waiting patiently for another signal. We were in a slight depression and at the edge of a clearing. Glancing up the hill, to my right, I felt vulnerable. I wondered if The Flea had spotted some NVA and was waiting for them to walk clear of our path.

I thought I heard footsteps. I listened more carefully. Soft footsteps were clearly approaching us. I looked back at Spider, who was partly hidden under some palm fronds. He shrugged his shoulders. I wondered, for just an instant, if they were playing a trick on their FNG sergeant, testing me on my first patrol.

The footsteps were unmistakable now and they grew closer. Suddenly, I saw an old Mama-san step into our clearing. She walked past The Flea as though he weren't there. She headed directly for me. I gripped my weapon tightly, fingering the safety. I frankly didn't know what to expect. How was I supposed to act? What was she doing out in the jungle alone? Without warning, the Mama-san stopped, pulled up her dress and squatted. She never looked at me. When the Mama-san finished, she walked back the way she had come. She never looked back at us. She simply disappeared into the brush.

Now The Flea gave us the signal to proceed.

126

I found that I was quickly adapting to the process. My senses kicked in. There were so many bushes, trees, vines, and hanging jungle debris that the enemy could be anywhere. My eyes and ears became more sensitive. I became more intense. I learned to observe in a new way. I saw the big picture and the details. Any movement, sound, color, tree that appeared unnatural caught my attention. I learned to sense danger as an animal would.

We passed rippling streams, large trees with hanging vines, huge plants with green elephant leaves, and an amazing amount of other beautiful scenery, but every bit of it was fraught with danger. We kept off the trails and humped directly through the bush. It was slow going. We quietly guided each other with hand signals. Every few minutes we stopped and listened, trying to sense anything out of the ordinary. Several times we stopped to check our location on the map. Each time I pointed to our position. I was right on target. Even the Flea and Spider seemed to be impressed with my map reading abilities.

Even as a kid, I had been good with directions, and I had aced the map reading and navigation courses in the NCO academy. I was convinced this talent began in my early days of roaming Charleston, West Virginia by foot.

Finally, The Flea and I saw an area that offered cover and good fields of fire in all directions. In addition to trees and bushes, the area included elephant leaves, which provided excellent shelter. It was a perfect place for two days of concealment. We saw a well-worn path about twenty meters in front of us. It may have been a major enemy infiltration route for the Dak To area. We settled in, spreading out five meters apart, in a perimeter formation.

We removed our rucksacks and immediately set out some claymore mines, connecting them to the detonators and pointing them in a series of directions to catch any enemy who might approach in the darkness of night. I scouted an escape route for any unforeseen emergencies. That done and silently communicated to my team, we settled in. I double-checked to assure myself that everyone had good fields of fire.

The Flea whispered to me, "Sergeant Horton, yer actin' like a little old lady. If yuh don't get killed first, I might like yuh." From The Flea that was the best complement I could ever expect.

I radioed the CP and told them we were set up for the duration.

127

During the daylight hours, SRPs were quite boring. It was essential that we remain absolutely quiet. We could read a book, write home, whisper among ourselves or contemplate nature, but that's about all. We could also sleep. I found myself thinking about home.

Due to the heavy foliage and jungle sounds around us, unusual noises didn't travel far. To hear an enemy approach we had to be alert and quiet. On this patrol, I learned that Lieutenant LePeilbet's RTO, Mike Hughes, would call us on our radio. "94 Sierra, 94 Sierra, sitrep, over."

A sitrep was a situation report. The company radioed each patrol for a sitrep every thirty minutes during the day and every fifteen minutes at night. Our call sign for this patrol was *94 Sierra*. Whenever we heard this signal, our radioman with a handset would key it with two clicks of the mike, which meant *okay*. The signal allowed us to communicate without giving away our position by speaking aloud.

We each stood watch for two hours at a time, both day and night. On the second night, during my watch, I heard the sound of bamboo breaking. The noise seemed to come out of nowhere. It was fairly close by and off to my right. I could hardly breathe. The moment was so filled with tension. After a few seconds, the noise ceased. A dozen explanations raced through my mind and I wondered if I should immediately awaken my patrol team.

The noise returned . . . more bamboo breaking. It seemed to be louder than before. I envisioned an entire platoon of enemy soldiers heading directly toward us. I was just reaching for The Flea's shoulder to alert him when a monkey jumped out of the forest. He ran through our clearing screaming at the top of his lungs, and disappeared into the jungle again. My heart pounded on my chest wall and raced a mile a minute. It took me the rest of the night to calm down.

On the morning of the third day we removed the claymores and saddled up to start our journey back to the CP. Someone suggested that I walk point. Without hesitation, I agreed. Subconsciously, I knew my squad members believed in my ability to get them back to home base safely. I had earned a small measure of their trust.

Just as I was feeling good about my talents as point man, I saw a movement out of the corner of my eye. It was out of place. It happened so fast, I didn't think. My right fist lifted instantly and I dropped to the ground. I could feel the others take my cue. I crawled to the left, taking cover under a bush. I motioned to the others to do the same.

128

There they were, right in front of me. I saw the outline of tan uniforms through the brush. My hearted stopped. I held my breath. I focused on being stone-still, while my ears and eyes were tuned forward. I was an animal on alert. There were at least ten NVA soldiers moving silently, just like we had been only seconds before. Was I just seeing things? *Could this be real?* I wished I could pinch myself to prove I was awake and not dreaming.

I knew enough not to shoot at them. I knew enough to remain calm and quiet or my actions could get us all killed. I waited and waited. I waited at least two minutes after the last NVA had vanished from sight. It seemed like an eon. Finally, I crawled back to The Flea and told him what had happened. The Flea met my gaze and held it. "Thanks for not shootin', Sarge. I don't give a damn if yer a Shake 'n Bake. Yer all right with me!"

When we reached the CP, I reported to LePeilbet and Lestock that all had gone well and that there had been no enemy movement except upon our return route.

Chapter 20

I was hot and sweaty and tired. We had just come in off our SRP and I had reported in to the CP. I was tired and I was a little pissed off. I headed straight to my hooch for a long nap. I did not want to talk to anybody about anything.

But there were Pappy and the Flea, sitting around a hooch, bullshitting with most of the rest of the platoon. Everybody was drinking coffee and hanging out together. I couldn't resist this set-up so I walked over. When I got close, I recognized the familiar smell of candle wax, cigarette smoke and coffee which filled every hooch. The Flea stopped talking, looked at me for a minute and said, "The Sergeant's too happy. He must like this job."

Everybody laughed. I felt embarrassed, but I didn't say anything. I just stood there. Then it occurred to me: if The Flea is right, it means I am in my element, doing the job I was supposed to do.

The guys were telling hillbilly stories. The Flea continued what he had been saying. "Us hillbillies hunt up in the mountains so we are used to mountains. These here in the Nam don't bother us, cause we're hillbillies."

He took a big drag on his cigarette, then removed it from his mouth to watch it burn. He exhaled noisily. He was playing his words for maximum effect.

I was too tired to listen to any of that hillbilly bullshit, but my judgment must have been clouded, because I made the mistake of blurting out, "Shit, Flea, you and Pappy ain't real hillbillies. You don't even have real mountains in Arkansas. The real hillbilly mountains are in West Virginia. You guys over in Arkansas are just in the foothills. Besides, you gotta be poor to be a hillbilly. Hell, I didn't know what socks were till I joined the Army."

I thought this would shut them up and let me get some sleep. But, oh, no.

I had challenged their heritage. Man, you should have seen The Flea and Pappy's faces. The Flea took a big, slow, thoughtful drag then returned with, "Sergeant Horton, glad you could join us. Have a seat."

The Flea pointed a long bony finger at a spot on the dirt. Then he continued, "We were so poor we didn't know what underwear was till the Army gave us some. And Pappy had to have instructions before he knew how to put them on. And these boots they issued to us? These were the first shoes we ever seen."

With that, both Pappy and The Flea lay back against the overhead, smiles of satisfaction on their faces, waiting for my next volley. Pappy took another slug of coffee and belched a good one. Everybody turned in my direction to see what I would say.

I looked straight at Flea and said, "Flea, in West Virginia we were so poor they refused to give us a Sears catalog to use in our shit house. They wanted us to pay for it. So ya know what? A corn cob felt mighty uncomfortable, especially in winter."

Now I had gotten to them. I thought this would end it for sure. Pappy and Flea started to frown. My comeback had drawn appreciative whistles from Ken and Sam and some of the other guys. Flea stubbed out his cigarette. He was getting serious. Then Pappy looked at The Flea and said, "Okay Flea, go ahead and tell them."

Pappy leaned back against some sandbags, just waiting to see what would happen next, a smirk on his face. The Flea's left leg was twitching in anticipation. He leaned forward and looked up at me, "Well, Sergeant," he said, "when I was a kid, we were so poor we only had one meal a day - and that was pretend food."

I was stumped. "Okay, what the fuck is pretend food, Flea?"

This was the response the Flea had been waiting for. "Shit, Sergeant Horton, every good hillbilly knows about pretend food. It's what ya eat when ya're too poor to buy real food."

"For example, my mom would ask me what I wanted to eat for dinner. So I'd tell her that I wanted some of that good pretend steak of hers. Then my little brother would say he wanted some of that pretend spaghetti, the kind with the good pretend red sauce on it. My mom always ate pretend roast beef, herself, but before she took a bite she always served my brother and me first. She was a good mom."

131

The guys started to chuckle at this one. Then, for good measure, the Flea added, "Sergeant Horton, ya know that, after a while, pretend food got too good to eat?"

I said back to him, exasperated, "What the fuck are you talking about, Flea?"

Then he answered, "My little brother, Pee Wee? He gained ten pounds in six weeks off that pretend spaghetti my mom used to fix. Hell, we had to put him on a diet of pretend vegetables after that."

The guys in the crowd groaned audibly.

Tired and sensing defeat, I just looked at both Flea and Pappy and said, "I can't believe you said that, Flea. You can really kick up the bullshit, pal. I guess that proves you guys are real hillbillies after all."

Apparently Pappy couldn't resist, "You ain't just looking up a dead dog's ass on that one, Sarge!"

Hearing that classic hillbilly reply, I chuckled to myself. Then I just shook my head in an admission of defeat, walked over to my hooch, sat down and unlaced by boots. I had to admit that, when it came to hillbilly stories, I wasn't ever gonna out-bullshit those two guys.

Sometimes war had its lighter moments, but most of the time it was just plain hard work. A great deal of my time was spent building firebases, complete with bunkers. A firebase was a perimeter of big holes in the ground where we ducked from incoming rounds and from which we could fight if we were attacked. Sometimes we slept in them. The bunkers were cut into rectangular shapes and faced outward and down the slope of the hill we occupied. Once the rectangles were dug, we cut logs from the surrounding jungle to reinforce the sides and to make a roof, which we called the "overhead." When the overhead was completed, the bunker would have observation slits from which we could shoot our weapons.

A-1-8 Bunkers

The height of a bunker above ground was usually equal to its depth below ground. As we dug, we used the dirt from the hole to fill sandbags, which we stacked above ground. Six soldiers could occupy each bunker. The Flea and several others made beds from wood they scrounged from pallets and ammunition crates. I felt safer sleeping in a bunker than out in the grass on my poncho liner, but I preferred the open air.

My squad members showed me how to drape our ponchos over the bunker's windows and doors at night to cloak the light from our card game, which often continued after dark. Later, when the game was over, each of us would pull guard duty by sitting atop the bunkers for a few hours.

During the long nights, our ten-by-ten bunkers made us feel safer. They were a place of refuge and we didn't dwell on the particulars: mere holes in the ground, with sandbags and green timber for sheetrock and wallpaper. Our bunkers were places where we could laugh, play games, and on rare occasion share a beer. I often lay in my bunker, staring up at the overhead/ceiling and its compacted dirt and dangling weeds, and thought that this must be what it was like to be buried.

The skills needed to build bunkers were handed down from soldier to soldier and war to war. The engineering was conducted by committee, with the strongest personalities having the most input. We learned by doing and by doing what made sense.

At a firebase, standing guard meant sitting on a bunker or standing behind it and visually inspecting a specific portion of our perimeter, sometimes with a starlight scope. When we were on an overnight SRP or an ambush, we would either sit or lie out of sight all night. On any patrol away from the perimeter, we were always hidden.

If we were not on an ambush or on SRP, and we were not humping to another site, we spent our days clearing brush or reinforcing foxholes. Building and repairing foxholes was a never-ending job and always a priority. They were much smaller than a bunker, and used only for fighting purposes. They were usually five to six feet deep and wide enough to accommodate two men in a standup position. We piled sandbags on two sides, and sometimes placed logs across the sandbags to provide overhead protection. If enemy bombardment were likely, more sandbags were placed on the overhead. Usually we could dig a foxhole in an hour, but the time was dictated by the soil condition.

Greg Rollinger by his foxhole in the Plei Trap Valley

Once our bunkers were built, our foxholes dug, and our firebase set up, we began the serious business of looking for the enemy by sending out daily organized patrols and potential ambushes.

When we went out on patrol to set up for an ambush, we could not dig our regular foxholes. At those times we dug shallow foxholes, hoping to finish before nightfall. If an entire platoon were involved, each squad was

134

set up to take advantage of interlocking fire from the other squads. The M-16 riflemen were interlocked with the M-60s. Once these positions had been determined, the digging started. We preferred a tight perimeter. The rule of thumb was boots touching. This made each man on the perimeter feel secure. Each soldier dug a hole deep enough to lie in. Then he filled his sandbags and put them between himself and the outside perimeter, open end facing out. Our sandbags were made of a tough green plastic material. We filled them with the dirt extracted from our foxholes. If we were moving on in the morning, we emptied them and refolded them into our rucks to use on the next foxhole.

As soon as we found a good location for an ambush, we would set up trip flares in a circle. This prevented us from receiving a sudden attack by the NVA from any direction. If the enemy approached, a flare would go off. After the trip flares were in place, the squad leaders would set up two circles of claymore mines, one inside the other, with every claymore backed against a tree, to absorb the back-blast. Claymores were curved objects about the size of a book with short folding legs that held them upright. Every man carried one or more claymores in his ruck. They were detonated by a electro-mechanical trigger we called a clacker that was attached with a long wire. A claymore looked harmless enough, but it fired seven hundred tiny steel balls in a deadly, curving swath . . . like a giant shotgun emits buckshot. The lines extending from the claymores to the clackers ran to the center of our defensive perimeter. In a direct attack, very few NVA would have lived past the first row of claymores.

Once the claymores were in place, we dug our shallow trenches and lay out our grenades beside our sandbags. Grenades were dangerous to handle, but especially so in the woods, where they could bounce off nearby trees and fly back at us. We were instructed to use grenades only on command.

Army life was not without its humorous moments. Ken McCormack, an RTO with 3rd platoon, told us that he had heard that a famous rock and roll band called Martha and the Vandellas would be stopping by our firebase. We were all excited and looking forward to the occasion.

When the USO helicopter arrived late that afternoon, an elderly female wearing Army fatigues deplaned and waved exuberantly at us. Martha was Martha Raye, the famous comedian from Bob Hope's generation not a famous rock band we expected. Instead of a rock band we got a humorous little old lady who walked around shaking hands and giving hugs. She spent considerable time on the firebase. We admired her for coming to the front lines to see us and we told her how much we appreciated her visit. She represented home.

Civilian escort, Sergeant White, Martha Raye, Lieutenant Lepeilbet

When we were not working, or moving from one place to another, or trying to close with the enemy, we spent our time talking to each other about the World and the lives we had left behind. For the most part, we talked about what we were going to do with the rest of our lives. We got to know each other pretty well, whether we wanted to or not. We had no privacy. Only our rucksacks remained sacrosanct.

I was beginning to learn a lot about war. War is hard work, lousy food, no rest, and occasional moments of utter terror.

Chapter 21

I felt pretty secure at our new firebase. Everyone was resting in the sun on the side of the hill. I leaned against a small tree while I wrote home.

"Crack, Crack, Crack." I looked up. It was gunfire. It was enemy gunfire. I dropped my pen and paper and, like everyone else, dove for my foxhole. "Crack, Crack." Again another couple of shots. I couldn't tell where it came from. It seemed to me it was from down the hill over to the right directly in front of third platoon's position. Then it stopped.

It only lasted a few minutes and no one was hurt. I felt a little sheepish as I climbed out of the foxhole. I saw Sergeant White and said, "It's a sunny afternoon, Sergeant White. I thought the NVA only attacked at night." He smiled and replied, "It took me by surprise, too, Sergeant."

It scared everyone. To a man, we had hit the dirt. No one even thought about shooting back at the time.

Later that day, Sam Seldon asked me, "Did you hear about Jerry Loucks (pronounced locks)? I put down my coffee to reply, "no, Sam. Who is he?" Sam said, "He's a Specialist 4th class from 3rd Platoon. He's got a reputation in our company. Jerry cuts notch in his M-16 stock for every enemy soldier he kills. They say he has more than a dozen." Sam went on to say, "Yeah, he's a character. He refuses to wear his Army helmet, even in combat instead, he wears a camouflage-colored, lightweight cloth hat."

"Anyway," Sam went on, "when our position was fired on this morning, Jerry didn't dive for a foxhole like the rest of us. He grabbed his M-16 and left the firebase. He flanked the enemy and after only a few minutes he located the NVA sniper and shot him." Sam said "once Jerry got back he reported that as he approached the dead soldier, he noticed a couple of enemy bunkers. He scouted the area and discovered a huge complex of at least a hundred and fifty bunkers near our perimeter. All of the bunkers had been recently abandoned."

I told Sam, "I guess we built our new firebase right atop a nest of enemy bunkers. I am glad they decided to leave. I guess they left one sniper behind to harass us."

I wanted to meet Jerry so I went looking for his friend Chris to see if he would give me an introduction to the infamous soldier. Before I could locate Chris, Sergeant White ordered our platoon to pack up. We would be flying by chopper to a suspected NVA stronghold. We were ordered to circle overhead while another company launched an attack. If it made contact with the enemy, we would swoop down and join them. No contact was made, so we returned to base later that same night.

I put off meeting Jerry Loucks for another day.

I was beginning to understand what they had been trying to teach me at Camp Enari. They said that the 4th Division's operating strategy in the Central Highlands was called an economy of force mission. We had to do a lot with very little. We were responsible for the largest area of operations of any Army division in the combat zone. Our territory extended from Dak Pek in the northwest corner of the highlands south to Duc Lap, and from the Cambodian border on the west to an area one hundred miles east, Binh Dinh Province. In order to patrol such a huge area, the strategy was to mass our forces in critical areas while practicing a Spartan economy of force elsewhere. Spartan meant what it said. We had to fight with what was available to us and make do.

Little did I realize the impact of this strategy when I had arrived. It meant that my unit would be constantly moving back and forth along the Cambodian border, fighting the enemy on their turf and playing by their rules. The fighting would be jungle fighting in which each individual soldier faced the enemy alone with very little outside support. This was not the type of head-on warfare the Army was accustomed to waging. It was guerrilla warfare, pure and simple, and it tended to nullify our technological advantages.

However, the 4th Division had defeated every enemy threat to any population center in the Central Highlands while providing an outer shell of security ringing the adjacent hamlets, villages, and cities. To accomplish this objective, grunts like us stayed on the move, which required continual personal sacrifices by the men carrying out the operation.

In a conventional war, the objective is to destroy the enemy's force and his ability and will to wage war. In the Vietnam War destroying the enemy's ability to fight was secondary. Our primary mission according to the Brass was to eliminate the social and economic conditions that allowed Charlie to brainwash the South Vietnamese into supporting

Communism. The result was that, in the Central Highlands, we had to fight a war of attrition. We were ordered to protect the population centers and keep the interior roads open.

I often wondered whether our generals and politicians were viewing the war through some sort of magic kaleidoscope which could be twisted until they viewed whatever they wanted to see. Maybe they thought that the Vietnamese social and economic conditions could be molded to match the picture they were viewing. Their kaleidoscope did not show the thousands of hardcore, determined NVA soldiers who were dug in along the Cambodian border. Us grunts did not believe that any amount of social programs, or degree of reprogramming the South Vietnamese people, would help with such a determined enemy encamped at their doorstep. We needed more grunts!

At times we grunts thought our commanders were crazy. We could not understand what we thought were war games and rarely thought that they cared that much for us grunts. As a result, we respected the officers who fought beside us and that was about it. Like a pack of wild wolves, we grunts banded together for our own survival. This is what I came to learn as the real Vietnam, the Vietnam for grunts, and in some weird sense I came to be proud of being one. I often wondered if we were destined to be grunts by some unknown power.

One day when we had set up in the jungle near the Mang Yang Pass, we were informed that some general or brigade commander was going to fly in for an inspection. Our battalion commander arrived first to make sure everything was ready for the visit. When he arrived, he saw that there was paper and other trash littering the area. He tried to get several of the men to pick it up. *Police paper in a war zone? Get real.* No one moved an inch, and besides we were exhausted anyway. The battalion commander wanted our firebase to look pretty for the visiting brass, so he picked up the trash himself! He wanted the foxholes and bunkers to look *pretty!* Never mind breaking his back to see that we got regular supplies of food and water, or clean clothes . . . or socks or mail. We were filthy and exhausted from working around the clock to build the firebase *while patrolling for the enemy.* We watched him collect the trash so he could impress his higher-ups with a neat war zone. I remember looking at some of my men; all they did was shrug their shoulders, no one could comprehend it. This was the first time I saw Colonel Buckner and his boss Colonel Hale Knight.

139

I had been out in the field for two weeks. As had become my custom when I had a break, I sat alone on the hillside, a place I could think. It was late afternoon. Nearby, a couple of my men were working on a bunker. I watched them put the last sandbags in place. They were filthy and wild-looking and looked exhausted. Their appearance reminded me of the soldiers in the trucks that had driven past me the day I was traveling to Enari.

My men had the same wild look, dirty with the thousand yard stare look. As I sat there thinking about it, I realized I was one of them now. I had the same look. It had little to do with lack of soap and water and everyday shaving. It had to do with exhaustion and fear—the nonstop realization that today, any minute, we could be facing the enemy. Kill or be killed. It never left our consciousness. We accepted the bush and everything that went with it. Our numb feelings showed through to a hungry stare that said we were ready for about anything.

I remember my first day in the field. I had just finished digging my first foxhole. I was talking to Joe Shea. He was friendly and helpful and eager to share his belief that there were two Nams. "Listen, Sergeant Horton, there are two Nams." With a sweeping motion of his arm, he indicated both our firebase and the surrounding forest. He smiled warmly, as if he were pleased to be sharing this secret with me.

"There are two Nams? What do you mean, Shea?"

"The Nam that is this hillside in the jungle and probably filled with NVA . . . this is the Nam of the bush. This is the Real Nam. The Nam that is in the base camp at Enari, the Nam that is at Dak To . . . those are part of another, safer Nam. The Real Nam and the Safe Nam are not in the same world. They are totally different from each other. We live in the Real Nam."

At the time, I didn't quite grasp Shea's distinction, but now I did. I saw it in the faces of the men around me. I saw it in the way they talked and how they moved. In the Real Nam—the Nam of the bush—uncertainty was the only constant and death was always present . . . waiting, never far away.

Shea's concept of the two Nams made sense to me now. Coming to Vietnam was like a science fiction movie in which we grunts boarded a shuttle for some distant, untamed planet . . . which turned out to be the

Real Nam. We were sent there to perform war. Some of us would die and some of us would be wounded. All of us would suffer in a myriad of ways. The bases camps—the safest parts of the Nam—were the points of departure and return. The men who traveled to and from the untamed planet were the warriors. No one from the Safe Nam ever visited the untamed planet or cared to learn the truth about it.

Most of the soldiers who were sent to Vietnam lived in the base camps. Base camps had barracks, guards, bunkers, concertina wire, and mines. They had showers, stores, bars and hot food. Base camps were little cities. In the Real Nam we ate cold C-rations, humped hundreds of kilometers through enemy-infested jungles, forded dangerous rivers, dug daily foxholes, and slept in two-hour increments because of continuous guard duty. Our water was usually rationed. We lived in filthy fatigues and often possessed only one pair of socks. Our rucksacks were our homes.

The base camp soldiers lived in and experienced a totally different war. There were far more of them than there were grunts. When they returned to the States, the World learned about *their* war, about *their* Nam, the safe, unreal Nam . . . where everything happened *but* war.

I pulled out my writing materials and finally penned a letter.

We are out in nowhere again, way up in the mountains. I'm glad you can't see how dirty I am now and there is no way to get clean. I do not know how long we will be up here. The Vietnamese Tet Offensive starts soon, so we might be here a long time. If we can keep going till about April, without running into much action, we will be okay. In April, the monsoon rains start.

I added another line to say that as soon as I returned I will earn my engineering degree. My determination for the future gave me the desire and will I needed. The job at hand was the most important I would ever have. I was in charge of a group of soldiers; I had to perform so we all could go back to the World.

Chapter 22

Sunday, 12 January 69

Fourth Platoon humped down a dirt road that ran parallel to Route 14, a road which ran north from Dak To toward Ben Het. It was mid-afternoon. We had spent the morning using tear gas to flush out some old bunkers. We didn't scare up any NVA. Some of the men had become so sweaty in their protective masks that, once the job was finished, they threw them away. Because my mask was soft and I could use it for a pillow, I kept it.

We were on our way to another firebase, with Sergeant White in the lead. We were tired, but nervous. The trail was too quiet, which could mean that NVA were in the vicinity. Our visibility was hampered by shoulder-high buffalo grass which grew on both sides of the road and across the entire valley before us. An entire regiment could hide in that stuff and we'd never know it. Fearing an ambush, everyone was on guard. We were alert for the slightest suspicious movement or sound. We trekked silently. I had point that day, and I was all ears.

Without warning, I heard the steady droning of a plane. It rapidly approached. I stopped to inspect the sky, but due to the towering mountains behind us I couldn't see anything. As I continued to listen, I felt certain the plane was flying toward us and it wasn't a helicopter. Though it was bound to be an American plane and would pose no threat, it could be on a bombing or strafing mission somewhere in the valley, which would bring unwanted attention to our presence.

Suddenly, we felt vulnerable. Taking no chances, Sergeant White ordered the platoon to take cover in the buffalo grass until we could recon the situation. The men immediately spread out on both sides of the road and waded into the grass before flopping down on their bellies in a semi-circle with rifles at the ready.

As the plane appeared over the mountain range behind us it passed directly overhead. I recognized it as a C-123 cargo plane. I was surprised to see how low it was flying— it flew only a few hundred feet above us. What was it doing here? It didn't appear to be on fire or damaged. I followed its progress with my eyes until it disappeared behind the grass.

Suddenly my lower face was covered with a cool but stinky mist. It coated my nose, my cheeks, my mouth—now open wide in surprise—and my forearms and hands. My fatigues were damp. *What was the stuff?* It tasted chemical. I coughed involuntarily because I had breathed in some of the mist and it choked my throat. I heard the other men coughing, too.

After a few minutes, the sound of the plane died away. The valley was quiet again. We reassembled our platoon. No enemy had appeared and everyone felt relieved. Later, when we reached the firebase, we learned that there was nothing to worry about. We had accidentally been sprayed with a defoliant. The Army was using it to cut the triple canopy jungle and make the NVA more visible and accessible to us. Since we could use all the help we could get in finding and destroying Charlie, none of us thought anything further about it. We learned later that the substance was called . . . *Agent Orange.*

Monday, 13 January 69

We were airlifted to Hill 75 near Dak To early in the morning. When the order to move out arrived, we hastily packed our rucksacks, our ammo belts, and whatever food we could carry and hopped on the choppers. Our battalion leaders thought we could anticipate the movement of the NVA and intercept them. When we were chasing enemy like this, we could only bring the essentials, stuff that would fit easily in our rucks.

Now we were in what we called Nowhere Land. There were no roads in or out of this mountain jungle location and the mountain we were located on was so thick we could hardly move. I had never felt so cut off from civilization before. My company was truly on the frontier now.

143

Bill Crockett in Nowhere Land

About seventy-five meters beyond our perimeter was a dense jungle, so dense we could hardly penetrate it with a machete. That's where our job began. We had to clear the top of the hill to make room for the firebase. We called in artillery to blow a clearing for an LZ, then downed the remaining timber with dynamite and chain saws and hacked away the underbrush. Basically we cleared the jungle right off the top of the hill. That left felled trees and broken limbs scattered all over the place.

Next we had to burn the timber. Each tree had to be dragged into position for burning, which often required the entire squad. None of us had bathed or changed clothes in days, and we were a sweaty, stinky bunch.

In the early afternoon, we received a much-needed resupply chopper containing food and water. In addition, the chopper gunners kicked off a couple large bags of clothes which hit the red dirt with a thud and broke open. Everyone in the platoon scrambled to grab and fight each other for a shirt and trousers and shorts that fit. There were no socks, the item we needed the most. For a few minutes it was like sale day at a department store. Crude, but that was the Army way in the bush.

Due to all our hard work we finally completed the firebase. It was dubbed Hill 75 and supported an artillery unit, a reconnaissance unit, and mortar support. The large 105mm artillery weapons had been airlifted during the afternoon using several powerful Chinook helicopters. Chinooks were the very latest helicopter technology, sporting self-sealing

144

fuel tanks, armor plating and the capability to refuel in the air. It was quite a sight to watch them arrive.

Before nightfall, Jerry Loucks arrived at our LZ on a helicopter loaded with a pallet of beer. What a welcome sight! He had been in Enari for medical treatment and, while waiting for his chopper ride back to the company, had spotted the beer, confiscated it, and convinced the chopper pilot that the beer was scheduled to be flown to the field with him. A few days later an officer flew out from Enari to investigate the theft. Nobody in the company knew anything about it. Jerry had taken care to see that every empty can had been properly buried.

Tuesday, 14 January

I was still in Nowhere Land, at a firebase high on Hill 75, with impenetrable jungle surrounding our perimeter. It was five a.m. I had been asleep in my bunker when the sound of a noisy radio blared from outside. I groaned and stretched. The bunker smelled of stale sweat, cigarette smoke, and scented candle wax. I rubbed my face and mumbled irritably to no one in particular, "What the hell is that?"

Spider was already up. He was stretching. "That's Pappy and Flea. They get up every morning to listen to Armed Forces Country and Western Hour. I don't know if they do that to bug us or just to hear the 'Goin' Home Train.'

I couldn't imagine what that was. I groaned. "'The Goin' Home Train?' What's that?"

Spider responded, "yeah, well it's really the 'Orange Blossom Special', but everyone in the Nam calls it the 'Goin' Home Train'. They play it every day."

Then Pappy appeared at the entrance to our bunker. "Hey, Spider, pass me a new claymore."

Pappy and Flea crawled down into our bunker. Flea had a cigarette dangling from the corner of his mouth already. The sweet smell of burning tobacco filled the bunker, covering the stench of old sweat. Flea was yawning and scratching himself, and he started me yawning and scratching too. Everybody moved over to make room for these guys.

Spider reached over into a corner of the bunker and pulled up a claymore. Pappy carefully pried the back off with his knife, and then cut out a small chunk of C-4. Spider looked at me, "Watch and learn, Sarge.

145

Save those heat tabs the Army gives you for emergencies. If you want your coffee fast and hot, there's nothing like C-4."

"Damn, won't it explode when the fire hits it?"

Pappy chuckled, "Watch and learn, Sarge."

I smiled. I had seen this C-4 exhibition at Dak To before I joined the company, but I didn't say anything.

He handed Flea the C-4. The Flea had formed a few rocks into a circle. He quickly lighted the explosive, placed it carefully into the middle of the rocks, and then set a canteen of water on it. Everything the Flea did was real quick. I was always amazed that ten or fifteen seconds later, the water would be boiling. The guys were right. C-4 was fast! They dropped some C-rats coffee into the boiling water and sat back to relax. Soon we all had steaming hot coffee. We drank it gratefully and began to wake up.

C-4 was a U.S. military invention, a plastic explosive that came in two-pound bricks. It was stable to handle and transport, malleable like clay and very powerful. You could hit it with a hammer or shoot it with a bullet and nothing would happen. But with the proper detonator, it would set off claymore mines with a helluva punch.

But when you lit it with a match, C-4 didn't explode. It just burned with a bright, hot flame. A marble chunk of the stuff would heat a canteen full of water to a low boil for coffee or soup in seconds.

A few minutes later, I emerged from the bunker into the early morning light, the coffee in my hand. It already felt like another hot day in the Nam. A four-man patrol was just coming in over the wire. They looked tired. I walked over to the CP to check in with White and LePeilbet. Yep, they confirmed what I was thinking. It was time for four men from our squad to mount up for an overnight. When I returned to the bunker, everyone in the squad was there. "Okay, time to get our patrol saddled up and headed out." Pappy was leaning up against a log near with Churchill and Pinchbug at his side. Churchill had just arrived was a FNG and Pinchbug had been in the rear for treatments of jungle rot and recently returned. Pinchburg was a small guy who kind of looked like a Pinchbug that's why they called him Pinchbug I guess. Both men were part of my squad.

Pappy volunteered, "Me and The Flea are going. Who else, Sarge?"

I was curious. "Why you and Flea, Pappy? You're not the next guys up."

146

Shea said, "Those two hillbillies always volunteer. Patrol for them is like a walk in the Arkansas woods."

He stuck his unlit pipe back in his mouth and chuckled through clenched teeth.

Pappy and The Flea chuckled too.

I asked Pappy, "Are you two guys from the same hometown or something?"

The Flea answered. "Naw, Pappy's from a little town named Kensett - it's hardly a bump in the road - and I'm from St. Louis. But all of my folks are from Arkansas and I've been hunting all my life, so I guess whether it's the jungle or the woods, we're both at home out there."

Then I told them, "Okay. Flea, Pappy, Pinchbug, and Churchill, saddle up."

Pinchbug looked over at Churchill and complained. "You're gonna send this fat FNG out with us? Come on, Sarge!"

Churchill grinned, embarrassed. I told Pinchbug, "He isn't going to learn any other way. You watch his ass for him! I remember when, not so long ago, you were a damn green FNG yourself."

Pinchbug groaned audibly.

As the four of them strapped on their rucks and headed over toward the perimeter wire, I walked along, still explaining the details of their patrol. Then Pinchbug walked over and said to The Flea in a low voice, "No sweat today, Flea, all four patrols are gonna get together at Platoon One's Apple Four and set up a sixteen-man watch. You know where that is?"

"Ya bet I do."

"We'll get plenty of sleep tonight. Only about forty-five minutes of guard duty each."

Flea nodded. He sucked a final drag, tossed his cigarette into the brush, and smashed it with his heel. Cigarettes weren't allowed on patrol. Flea disappeared down the trail in that curious walk of his.

I heard the plan being discussed but I didn't say anything. Patrols were always supposed to go out in different directions, each according to their orders, and set up separately, never together. Later that day, the four patrols met at the prearranged location and set up for the night, together. Everyone sacked out except for the men on watch. In the wee hours, when The Flea's watch was over, he shook FNG Churchill and

147

whispered, "It's time for your watch now, Churchill. Wake Pinchbug in forty-five minutes."

Churchill was half asleep; he mumbled something and rolled over, as if to go back to sleep. But then The Flea ordered him in a stern whisper, "Freeze, Churchill! Don't move!"

Churchill looked over at him in a daze. He thought Flea was teasing him. He whispered back, "Don't do this, Flea. I'm too tired for this shit."

Fleas repeated his order. "Fucking don't move, Churchill!"

Flea slowly slid his hunting knife out of his boot and quickly threw it near Churchill's feet. In the near darkness Churchill could hear the thrashing of the small snake Flea's knife had struck. Suddenly Churchill understood the danger. He had been sleeping with a fucking snake! He jumped to his feet and yelled at full volume, "Holy Shit!"

Now everyone on the patrol was awake. Flea could hear the sounds of a dozen safeties clicking off all at once. Their position had been seriously compromised by Churchill's loud outburst. Churchill asked Flea in a loud voice, "What kind was it?"

Someone in the night whispered, "Shut up and get down, you fucking idiot."

Churchill sat back down and lowered his voice. "What was it, Flea?"

"It's a snake, but he's dead now, Churchill."

Churchill asked in a quavering voice, "What kind of snake?"

Flea whispered back, "Bamboo viper."

Then Churchill exclaimed, "Shit, Flea! What do you do if it bites you?"

"Stick your head between your legs and kiss your ass good-bye." The Flea chuckled to himself.

Pappy whispered over to The Flea, "Hey Flea, was Churchill really sleeping with a bamboo viper?"

The Flea replied, "Damned if I know, Pappy. But Churchill was about to sleep through his watch. A bamboo viper is as good a snake as any to teach that FNG how easy it is to stay awake all night. Now, if anything else happens, anything at all, even if a monkey farts in the jungle, Churchill will wake us up pronto."

Chapter 23

Now here I was in the bush, a Shake 'n Bake Sergeant for real. I was the organizer, director, mother, and leader of our squad. I made sure the men had enough food, ammo and personal supplies, and that they were physically okay. I made sure they were properly trained. When we were scheduled to move out, I had to make sure the men were ready to go.

I was on almost every SRP that my squad conducted. I walked point on most of them. When we moved out, either as a squad, a platoon, or a company, I made sure that everyone kept up, but also that they remained separated from each other by a safe distance. I watched them when we started and when we stopped, and they watched me for instructions.

To navigate on SRPs, I read and interpreted the map and made sure that we were where we were supposed to be. I picked the locations in which we would set up and made sure that everyone was set up properly. I told everyone when to lock and load, and I checked that their safeties were on. I made sure no one did anything stupid.

When we were setting up outside the perimeter for the night, I told everyone where to dig their foxholes and how to do it. Before they went to sleep, I checked to be certain that they had the proper fortifications in place, and that their claymores and trip wires were properly positioned. I double-checked that the men followed the security rules at all times.

I communicated with the chain of command - with Sergeant White and Lieutenant LePeilbet. I communicated to my men the orders they gave me, and made sure they understood them. Within our perimeter, I supervised the construction of the bunkers the men built.

I listened to the men's bitches and when they had legitimate problems, I went to bat for them with White or LePeilbet. I had the balls to deal with White. I was not afraid of him; I think the men sensed that. I also knew that White respected me.

I was responsible for new guys coming to the field; I insured that they kept their weapons clean and in good working order. I helped them with their ruck and watched them learn how to hump. One guy who could not keep up could endanger all of the men. I distributed the M-60 ammo to everyone and made sure our M-60 guy was happy.

I handed out the sequence for standing guard each night and assigned the men going on every SRP. When I accompanied the men on patrol, I communicated by radio to and from the company CP. I supervised some of our search and destroy missions.

On company ambushes, I took orders from the chain of command to set up my men properly and make sure that everyone was in place and remained quiet. I made sure the men had good cover, and were positioned so that they were shooting at the enemy, and not at each other.

If there was a firefight, I would have to supervise the positions and movements of my men. I took orders from the chain of command and, upon engaging the enemy, gave my men fire and movement instructions. As a sergeant except when they were under direct fire, the men could not move without my okay.

In a nutshell, my job was to make sure that every man in my squad would get safely back to the World. I was their leader; I felt responsible for their lives. I took my job seriously. Sometimes that required unusual tactics.

Yesterday we had humped all day and by nightfall everybody was exhausted. It was time to set up for the night, which meant that we had to dig foxholes, fill sandbags with dirt, and put up an overhead, which consisted of cutting logs to place on top of the sandbags. These would create a solid ceiling for extra protection over the foxholes - all before darkness set in. The whole squad was beat, dirty and pissed off. But the men couldn't relax yet. Not until their holes were dug, checked by Sergeant White or myself, and the overheads were in place. It was hell but this was the way to stay alive.

We had positioned ourselves for an ambush near the junction of two trails. Sergeant White had set up an L-shaped ambush plan covering both trails, and he indicated the positions that each of our four squads was to occupy. As usual, he paid special attention to the position and fields of fire that each of our four M-60s would command.

After White moved out of earshot, I could hear The Flea muttering to himself through the cigarette smoke that ringed his head, "The same ol' crap. Dig in, move somewhere else, dig in, move again, dig in - same ol' crap."

I said in a loud voice to no one in particular, "Okay, you heard the sergeant. Start digging in."

150

Everyone had to dig a hole, including me. The foxhole was our only protection against attack. But The Flea wasn't having any. He said, "Fuck ya, Sergeant Horton. I ain't digging no foxhole tonight."

I answered, in a sergeantly manner, "The fuck you're not. Goddammit Flea, we all have to."

After a few more minutes of fuck this and fuck that, and fuck, fuck, fuck, and finally fuck you again, I got really pissed. In fact, I was in a rage. The other guys in my squad were all looking at me, wondering how I was going to handle this situation, in which my authority was being directly challenged by one of my men. This situation would put their new Shake 'n Bake to the test.

I walked straight up to the company commander, Capt. Hockett, to ask him in a loud voice, so that Flea and the other men in my squad could hear, "Permission to kick my man's ass, sir? He won't dig his foxhole."

Captain Hockett looked me straight in the eye and said, "Permission granted, Sergeant Horton."

I turned and walked straight back toward The Flea. I was so mad I couldn't see straight. I was ready to fight. I had every intention of kicking Flea's ass. But The Flea heard me talking to the captain. And he must have seen the determined look on my face, because he started digging as fast as he could.

He must have thought, *there's no reason to kick Sergeant Horton's ass right now. I know I've got to dig a foxhole anyway. Besides, Horton's a hillbilly, just like me.*

The Flea may have thought these things, but when I arrived back at his location all he said was, "Ya gotta do what ya gotta do."

He kept his head down, and went right on digging, quite fast.

The pressure of combat can do strange things to a man. After that incident, The Flea and I began to talk to each other more often. We traded adventures from our hillbilly past. Soon we became the best of friends. Later we laughed about the foxhole incident. I took my job as a squad leader very seriously and now The Flea realized that. As a result, for the first time he took me seriously.

Chapter 24

One of the duties I assumed after arriving in the field was to point. I knew that when I walked point there were no second chances, it was a very serious responsibility.

Sooner or later every man who went on patrol in the Nam was called upon to walk point unless they were a machine gunner, an RTO operator, or just damn lucky. The point man's job was to keep the patrol from being ambushed. He had to spot the enemy before they spotted him. He had to communicate the dangers in front of the patrol in time for it to react. The lives of everyone on the patrol were in the point man's hands.

Walking point was about as dangerous as it gets in the Nam. If a soldier walked point every day, then he was asking to die. At point, a man was ten times as likely to get shot, or to have to shoot someone, as any other soldier on patrol.

Specialist 4 Jerry Loucks was born to be a point man. Jerry volunteered for point every time he got the chance. The very first time I heard his name, he was outside the perimeter killing an enemy sniper. In Vietnam, Jerry was a hunter and a killer. He was a damn good soldier. That's what it took to be a good point man. When it came to walking point, Jerry Loucks was a legend in our Company.

On my first patrol as point man, I remembered some of the rules they taught me in NCO School, and I trusted my instincts. These things got me through. I did okay that day, but I knew, to survive and to keep my patrol alive, I had to do better, maybe much better. So one day I introduced myself to Jerry Loucks and asked him for tips on walking point.

It was about 1600 hours, or about 4:00 in the afternoon. Most of the day's work was done. While the men hung out in their hooches, taking a rest, I walked around the company perimeter to 3rd Platoon. In our Company 3rd Platoon was our sister platoon; they always set up their perimeter next to ours. Naturally many of the guys in 4th Platoon were friends with those in 3rd. When I arrived at 3rd Platoon's perimeter, Jerry Loucks sat in front of his hooch having a cigarette.

I walked up and said, "I'm Sergeant Horton from 4th platoon. I'm from West "By God" Virginia, not far from where you grew up. I heard you were the best point man in the company, maybe the best in the whole division." He looked me in the eye and then said, "Hell, yes, that I am, Sergeant Horton. Have a seat and we'll talk about it."

I made myself comfortable, leaning back against a nearby tree stump and sitting on a soft spot in the ground. Jerry knew I was a FNG, but he never mentioned that fact. Instead, he just started talking about taking the point.

Jerry told me that there were definite rules to be followed when walking point. As we talked, Jerry told me that he had learned a lot about point when he was a young man hunting in the mountains of northern Pennsylvania. He roamed those mountains alone, hunting all types of game. He hunted for survival first, and then to help feed his family. Here in the Nam, it was the same thing. Jerry considered all of us his family and he wanted to take care of us.

Jerry told me, "The first rule I follow is this: I have to see each step I take before I am willing to take it. I look directly at the ground before me to see exactly where I am going to step next. But here's the tricky part. You have to scan the jungle in front of you for anything out of the ordinary at the same time that you examine where to take your next step."

153

Jerry commented that this tactic of double vision, of looking two places at once, was not hard to learn. It was also the only way to keep from stepping on something that would make a noise. Jerry leaned toward me and said, "Sergeant Horton, you can't let the enemy know where you are by making noise when you take a step. If you do, they'll be waiting to ambush you when you least expect it.

"And you can't step on something that will cut you, blow your leg off, or kill you, either. It's against company rules!"

I chuckled at Jerry's joke and thought to myself, *damn, you're right, Jerry. I never thought about this double vision thing before but I guess I did the right thing when I was on point the other day.*

Before he continued, Jerry paused as a way to let me know that this first rule was the most important one. Then he digressed. "I want to tell you a story of what happened to me. Shit, it happened just the other day.

"Do you know anything about the king cobra, Sergeant?"

"You mean the snake?" I asked.

"Yeah, the snake," Jerry replied.

"Not much, Jerry," I admitted.

"Well, it's the world's longest venomous snake, growing sometimes up to fifteen feet long or so. Its head is as big as your fist, and it can rear up and look you in the eye. The fangs are a half-inch long.

"If it bites you, the venom can stop your breathing, and if it spits in your eye, you can go blind. One cobra bite can kill an elephant. Basically, this sucker is nothing to fuck with. Fortunately, it only attacks people when it is cornered or attacked, or to protect its eggs. Cobras lived in the cool undergrowth of rain forests, usually near streams. That means they're all over the Highlands."

Jerry continued, "I was walking point through a shallow riverbed last week. As usual, I was watching where I stepped while scanning across the stream in front of me. But then, just as I was about to step down, a fucking king cobra stuck its body a couple of feet up in the air right in front of me. Hey, I about shit! I froze!

"That cobra started swaying back and forth. I thought the fucking thing was gonna strike me. For the longest time I stood there, frozen, while that snake danced around in front of me. Chris was only a few feet behind me. We were both so still I could hear his breathing."

"By now, the whole goddamned patrol had caught up to us and was watching that snake. After a few of the longest minutes on earth, the cobra went back down again."

Then Jerry said, "I looked back at Chris with a sigh of relief and took a step to move on, but as soon as I moved my leg, that snake rose up in front of me again. I froze again, leg up in the air. Then, finally, after an eternity, the snake disappeared. So very slowly and carefully I lowered my leg down to walk away. But the snake reappeared a third time, swaying and spitting at me."

Jerry commented, "I couldn't shoot the damn thing for fear of giving away our position. And I was afraid to grab it. I was stuck, standing in an awkward position. So I signaled the rest of the patrol to walk around me."

Just then Chris Kruckow walked over and sat down nearby on a tree stump. He sat down with a chuckle and took over Jerry's story. "When I walked up behind Jerry that day," Chris said with a sparkle in his eye, "he and that snake were just standing there, trying to stare each other down. They were locked into a kind of Mexican standoff. I couldn't tell which of them was the toughest."

Chris rubbed his nose, snorted and then continued, "It took a half hour before that snake would let Jerry pass. There was nothing anyone could do about it that didn't make noise."

Jerry added that, after the snake let him pass, the patrol decided to set up for the night. He said, "It was just as well, because I couldn't walk point any more that day."

"I couldn't walk anywhere without staring at the ground the whole time. I was so fucking psyched about stepping on a snake that I couldn't look for signs of the enemy. I mean, I couldn't force myself to raise my eyes off the ground. I couldn't do it! I had to have a rest. I just couldn't walk point. I was no good."

I understood what Jerry was telling me. If you lose your double vision, you can't walk the point. I was all ears. Jerry continued my education. "The next rule is, the point man must hear everything."

He said, "As a point man, Sergeant Horton, you must continually listen for the enemy."

Jerry told me that he always walked about fifty meters ahead of the rest of the patrol so that he wouldn't hear the noises made by his own men. Otherwise he would never hear the fainter sounds of the enemy. Jerry told me, "The point man has to sneak through the jungle alone and evaluate the source of every sound - friend, jungle or foe."

Then he added, "Every now and then the point man must stop, take a soft cap from his ruck, and hold it open behind one of his ears. The rounded inside of the cap creates a listening horn for amplifying sound."

Jerry took off his camouflage-colored cap and demonstrated the technique for me. He added that many times his cap let him hear an enemy who would otherwise go unnoticed. For the first time, I thought I understood why Jerry wore a cloth cap rather than a regulation helmet. The helmet protected his head, but it blocked vital sounds.

Looking me square in the eyes, Jerry Loucks said, "Sergeant Horton, you have to have your eyes, your ears and your nose constantly primed for any new information you can gather. Many times you can't see them or hear them, but you might be able to smell the enemy."

Then Jerry paused and said, "You got that, Sarge?"

I was thankful that Jerry was willing to tell me these things. I guess he figured that, by following his rules, I might save his, mine or someone else's life one day, so it was worth his time to teach me.

Then I asked Jerry a question. "Jerry, is it true what the guys say - that you refuse to wear your helmet on patrol?"

I was pretty sure that, if Jerry did this, he did it for the reason I imagined. But I wanted to hear it from his own lips.

"Sergeant Horton, I don't know about you, but I can't hear with that damn helmet down around my ears. I figure I'll stay alive longer by being able to hear the enemy approach than by trying to protect myself from his bullets after I stumble into an ambush."

That made sense.

Then Jerry told me a hell of thing. Jerry said, "Walking point is like jumping out of an airplane without a parachute. You can never know what lies below you, or what lies waiting around the next bend. The point man is always free falling. Every second you're on point, Sarge, you're up against the complete unknown. To do your job in that situation, you must be willing to die for your men."

I heard Jerry's words, but I was not ready for this. I couldn't take this in. I said nothing.

After a long silence, Jerry told me, "Sarge, this is rule five. You have to believe that, as point man, you are the best man for the job. You must convince yourself that, if you didn't walk point that day, other men would die. You have to feel that your job on point is that important."

Jerry noted that in places the jungle was so impenetrable the point man had to cut his way through it with a machete. This was the worst possible situation. Jerry emphasized, "When this happens, the enemy always knows where you are because of the sound of the machete. The other problem is that, after hacking on the foliage for a while, the point man grows disoriented and no longer knows where he is or where he is going."

His list of rules for walking point was long. He emphasized that the point man had better be in good physical condition. Many times he had walked point when he was absolutely worn out and could hardly raise his arms to use his machete. It was only at those times, when was facing exhaustion, that he would let somebody else walk point for a while to rest.

He hated to relinquish point to any man because it made him feel so vulnerable. Jerry admitted that, when he was not on point, he felt anxious. When I heard this I got a strange feeling. Then I realized that I felt the very same way.

When he walked point through elephant grass, he had to be extra careful. Elephant grass typically grew as tall as a man can stand, and moving through it was a very tricky business. "I can never see more than one or two feet ahead of me. I have to walk very slowly and listen to the grass for any sounds that are out of the ordinary."

One day, while he was walking point through a stand of elephant grass, he stepped right into an open area where a bunch of NVA had camped the night before. The NVA were long gone, but the evidence of their camp was everywhere.

He looked me straight in the eye, "This scared the holy hell out of me, Sergeant Horton."

"I had to keep doing my job, which meant staying on point. With an effort I walked right through that camp and back into the elephant grass again."

"Sarge, it's at those times that you have to focus, maintain control of your body and mind. To survive, you have to learn to deal with it."

"Another important rule for walking point is that your men must trust you. When walking point, trust is everything. If you take your point

157

assignment seriously, you must try to keep your men safe, and the best way to do that is to communicate to them clearly and decisively."

He paused for emphasis, "But trust will not develop overnight. It has to grow. If you are calm and never panic under fire, but work to organize your patrol's response in a firefight, then the men's trust will follow. The men look to their point man as an example they can follow."

"Remember that, Sarge."

Then, after a pause, he said to me, "Sarge, I'll tell you a little story about trust. I have to live with this every day. It troubles me every day and it'll show you what I mean about trust."

He told me that, when he first arrived in the Nam, he would walk point for money. He did this to help the short timers. Short timers were guys who did not have much time left to complete their tour in Vietnam. To minimize their danger during their last few days in the field, short timers would sometimes pay other guys to walk point. "I always took them up on their offer, since I could use the money and I liked walking point anyway."

He went on to tell me about Lou, a particular short timer, a guy who had only two days left in Vietnam. "The guy came up to me one night and told me he had to walk point the next day. He asked me to take the point for him for twenty dollars US. I wanted to, but the problem was that I had already been assigned to another patrol that day. I just couldn't fucking do it."

His voice grew sad. "The kid went out the next morning and within an hour, got blown in half by an enemy ambush. Hell, he only had two days left to go home."

"When I heard that he had been killed, it about killed me. You see, Sergeant Horton, it's all about trust. These guys are my family. I have to take care of them. Sergeant Horton, you have to take care of them, too. It's your job."

I knew he was right.

He confessed that he had to walk point on the very next patrol that day, the patrol that went out and recovered the young soldier's body parts.

Another important rule he told me was that the point man must be able to sneak up on the enemy. He said that this was extremely dangerous, but sometimes it had to be done. He stopped talking for a moment, stood up, motioned for me to follow him, and walked down to the edge of the company perimeter. We stood at the wire, looking out into the jungle. He raised his arm and pointed toward the bush. He paused. Then he said to me, "You must stare through the jungle, that impenetrable jungle, for any movement or any sound. You must see anything out of the ordinary. Your senses must be like that of an animal. Sarge, you must be willing to crawl in absolute silence across unknown terrain, or walk quietly, bent low, in a crouch, for hours, your rifle at the ready."

"Look into that jungle, Sarge. Let the jungle come alive for you. See what I mean? Visualize it, Sergeant Horton. What I am telling you can save your life, as well as the lives of others."

He went on to tell me that sometimes sneaking up on the enemy meant sneaking up on enemy bunkers. "Your only hope is that nobody is in the bunkers. Sometimes they will be, and sometimes not. But just to be sure they are not, always throw a hand grenade into every bunker anyway."

Then he looked at me sternly and said, "Never, Sarge, never turn your back on an ungrenaded bunker."

"There will be times when you will see the enemy. When you do, always engage them immediately and aggressively, because it will no doubt be at close range and there won't be time to take a defensive position. Shoot first and ask questions later. You won't get a second chance."

"But most of the time you will not see the enemy. In fact, you will not see a thing. You might hear them; you might hear their bullets; you might smell them, but you won't see a thing."

When Jerry finished talking, I remembered something Lieutenant LePeilbet told me the day I had first arrived in the field, back on Hill 1049. He said, "Sergeant Horton, there are only two rules from Battalion Headquarters that we disobey out here. "The first rule is never to have a round in the chamber while on patrol. Sergeant, forget that rule. Always keep a round chambered. On patrol, when the shooting starts, you won't have time to chamber a round. Your life will depend on shooting quickly."

Then LePeilbet told me the other rule to ignore. That one was never to shoot until fired upon. The lieutenant said, "Sergeant, that rule is bullshit. Keep one round chambered at all times and shoot anything that moves. There are no friendlies here where we are operating."

Given these comments from both Jerry Loucks and the lieutenant, I thought that now I had enough knowledge to be a good point man. I understood what these men were telling me. It felt right to me. Maybe my NCO training helped, or maybe it was my instincts. I didn't know.

I was grateful to Jerry for his instructions. "Jerry, you're a good teacher and you can bet your ass that I've heard everything you told me. Thanks."

I started to walk away to check on my squad, but Jerry stopped me with a few words. "There is one other thing, Sarge."

I turned back and said, "What's that, Jerry?"

"No matter how busy I am walking point, no matter what unseen dangers are lurking before me, I always have time for a little praying. When I walk point, I always sing a song in the back of my mind."

Then Jerry quietly sang me a couple of verses. They were from the old Baptist song, "Just a Closer Walk with Thee."

As I listened to Jerry Loucks sing, I got cold shivers running up my back. From that moment on we were friends. How would we have ever guessed that our paths would become entangled like this? Or that in the near future, he would play such a large part in my life, as well as in the lives of so many other men. And, yes, we would need God to be hearing our pleas to take "just a closer walk with thee."

I walked back over to my squad thinking about the many things Jerry had told me. Here was the toughest man I had ever known and yet even he needed help, and he wasn't afraid to ask God for it. Maybe I had better try singing that song more often! Hell, I could see that, here in the Nam, I was gonna need all the help I could get.

Chapter 25

We had plenty of leeches in Vietnam. We got them on us anytime we went into the rivers and streams. Once they were attached, the only way you could remove them was by using insect repellent or the burning end of a cigarette. When you sprayed them with that stuff, they disgorged blood and then fell off your skin.

Yesterday, Sergeant White led a five-man patrol down from hill 1049 into the elephant grass. They crossed a river then humped about five kicks, set up for the night, and then returned this morning. They reported in with no contact. When the patrol returned to camp, Sergeant White was carrying a fat FNG by the name of Sump Gut who was very fat. Sump Gut claimed he was too out of shape to make it up the hill with his ruck under his own steam. Some of the guys thought White should have just left him behind.

They guy was called "Sump Gut" because he would, and did, eat anything. Pappy claimed that Sump Gut consumed more than twice the amount of C-rats as any of the other guys.

After a few hours back in camp, Sump Gut found a leech attached to his pecker. He went berserk. He wanted it off but he was afraid to touch it, much less remove it, himself. So in a loud voice he called for a medic. Most of the squad heard the commotion and soon the entire squad was gathered around to witness the unfolding events.

Frenchy was the 3rd platoon medic. He was a skinny guy, full of energy and very spunky. He came walking over to see what the ruckus was about. There were various rumors going around about Frenchy, whose real name was Mike Carlisle. We called him Frenchy simply because he came from France. One rumor held that his father was American and his mother French, and that he enlisted in the Army to escape serving eight years in the French Foreign Legion. Another rumor stated that he was a French citizen all right but after coming to medical school in the U.S and getting his green card, he was drafted. This was a possibility.

Bugs Moran on left and Frenchy on right

The government policy on drafting during the Vietnam War was bizarre, to say the least. Many men found that, far from being impartial, their draft board could be manipulated, could be worked one way or another. And they sometimes learned that, if an official on their draft board got mad at them, they would get drafted.

There were a number of foreign citizens visiting our country who were drafted and sent to the Nam to fight with us. This fact is not commonly known. While we had American citizens fleeing to foreign countries to hide from the draft, foreigners were coming to America to seek a new life but could not escape it. The law said that they had to register with their draft boards, and some of these boards simply gave them a choice, get drafted or go home.

Supposedly, shortly after he arrived in the United States in 1967, Frenchy found himself faced with the prospect that, unless he was willing to fight, he would not be allowed to attend medical school in America. He decided to get drafted and fight with us in order to stay. Hell, one could not help but like a guy for that.

Frenchy had nothing against the Vietnamese, one way or the other. He was not personally committed to the war, so he chose to be a medic rather than a combat soldier. The medical training he would receive at Ft. Sam Houston would help his career. A number of the medics he met at Ft. Sam were conscientious objectors, so during his training Frenchy became a conscientious objector too. Despite this, Frenchy sometimes carried a rifle.

162

After a brief examination down in the bunker, Frenchy announced Sump Gut's problem to the squad and described what he was about to do. He invited us all to watch the leech drop off, if we wanted to. We all began laughing hilariously. It was hard to find good entertainment in Vietnam, so not a one would dare miss an event like this.

Soon the squad was lined up around a bunker and there, down in the bunker, was Sump Gut himself, shaking with fear, with his pants pulled down to his knees. And, sure enough, beneath the rolls of fat, there was a leech on his pecker. What a fucking site - it wasn't pretty.

Frenchy positioned himself down on one knee in front of Sump Gut, holding the bug juice in his hand. He could not convince Sump Gut to perform the little operation for himself. In fact, he registered mild disgust and muttered a few well-chosen French cusswords as he approached the problem. Then he moved into action. He hit Sump Gut on his pecker with the bug spray in one swift squirt! Sump Gut stood with his eyes squeezed shut and the leech fell off. Then Sump Gut looked down to see the blood the leech disgorged flowing down his leg. He let out a moan and fainted. He fell forward, his pants still at half mast, right on top of Frenchy! It was too much for the squad to take. We thought we were going to die laughing, our sides started to hurt.

Here was the passed out Sump Gut overweight, scared-to-death kid, not even infantry-trained, new to the unit, new to the Nam, just in from his first patrol, with a leech on his pecker. It was rumored that he had been sent out to us a few days earlier for failing to salute an officer in Enari.

One minute Sump Gut was standing there with his head down, holding his pecker, watching Frenchy apply the bug juice, and the next minute he was lying flat out on top of him. One minute Frenchy was cool and quiet while Sump Gut was hollering, "Get this thing offa me!"

The next minute Sump Gut was out cold and Frenchy was hollering, "Get this thing offa me!"

Nobody moved to help Frenchy, who was seriously trapped under Sump Gut's weight. Eventually the good doctor worked his way out from under all that fat by himself. Sometime after the Sump Gut incident, Frenchy told us that this was the last time he was gonna help us get rid of our leeches. From now on we were on our own. Frenchy spouted, "fuck it! There oughta be a limit as to what a guy has to do in war."

163

Chapter 26

I had worked for four days straight, cleaning brush, building foxholes, filling sandbags, and cutting overhead to strengthen the foxholes. We shored up our defenses in case of attack. What a job! We worked more than twelve hours each day, with only nights to rest, that were interrupted by the hours we spent on guard duty. This constant activity was exhausting, but we had to do it to be safe.

That morning the first thing I heard was someone yelling, "Sergeant Horton, what the hell is going on?" Someone was yelling at me, "What the hell is going on, Sergeant? Do you think we are running a fucking kindergarten here?"

I was groggy as hell; I was in a deep sleep, no doubt holding someone in my arms, or was it my M16? Sergeant White's words crashed into my ears. He also woke up the entire squad. Once we were awake, he lit into me again, "If I catch any of your men sleeping ever again, Sergeant, I am gonna bust your ass to private." He looked me square in the eyes, not more than six inches from my face. He went on, "If the NVA had been probing our defenses last night, you could have gotten the whole platoon wiped out." I suddenly realized my whole world was watching. Every man in the squad watched. Sergeant White wouldn't quit. "You're responsible, Sarge, you and nobody else. You better have a long talk with your men. The buck stops with you, Sergeant."

It was rare to have Sergeant White chew out any sergeant or any one for that matter in front of the men, but this day he couldn't help it. He was really, really pissed off at me. His face was red as a beet; he simply lost it. My whole squad watched as he reamed my ass out. I stood there and took it. I looked White in the eye the whole time. There wasn't anything I could say. White was right. If the enemy had probed our perimeter, we could have all been killed.

I turned and then looked White directly in the face. I said, "You are right, Sergeant White. It was my fault and it won't happen again."

Then Sergeant White left storming out, cussing and talking to himself all the way.

I turned to the men. They were watching the whole confrontation with great interest and now they all looked like whipped puppies. I could see it their eyes. They gained a new appreciation for their Shake 'n Bake. All of them now knew that I would stand up for them in a crunch and, when necessary, take the heat for them.

Then I asked, "What happened? How did we all go to sleep?"

My men and I tried to recreate the previous night's situation. I had been on watch until midnight then I woke up Rick Campbell. When he started to guard, Campbell had been wide-awake. Once the men began talking things over, we quickly figured out that, even though he didn't volunteer the information, it was "John Wayne" who had fallen asleep. I didn't say anything to him in front of the men, but instead took him aside in private later. I said, "Okay, pal, you fucked up once and that's it. Never again, or I will personally kick the shit out of you and I don't give a damn if they court-martial me. You understand?"

John Wayne, our unenergetic Special Forces guy, looked at me, nodded once and got the message.

I saw Sergeant White a few hours later. He was still pissed. Later I discovered that he never told Lieutenant LePeilbet, and for that I was very thankful. He gave me a second chance. In Vietnam, second chances don't come often. I knew now that I could never let this happen again.

This event made a lasting impression on me. I learned that, as a leader, I was responsible for my men no matter what. As a leader I had to step up and do whatever it took for all of us to survive. My men's lives, and the lives of the company, were at stake. We were just lucky that we did not get attacked while our guard was down. Leadership means just one thing: a leader is responsible for those who follow him.

From that day forward, I never got a full night's sleep in the Nam. From that day forward, I always told several men to wake me during their guard duty. This allowed me to check that everything was okay, but it also meant that, at most, I would get three hours of sleep at a time. That's how I learned to stay alive in the Nam.

Chapter 27

The battalion Brass made a big deal over a program called "Bullets R&R." It was created to give the American soldier an in-country rest and relaxation event. Normal R&R, which every soldier was entitled to for one week a year, involved travel to Japan, Hong Kong, Australia, Hawaii or Singapore. It was expensive because, once there, the soldier had to pay most of his own expenses. But under the new plan, if any man got a confirmed enemy KIA, then he would be rewarded with a three-day Bullets R&R, an in-country vacation which cost him next to nothing.

The battalion Brass wanted their enemy body count higher so that they would look good to their superiors. The Bullets R&R scheme was their incentive program to accomplish that end. It was already in place when I arrived in Vietnam. It seemed a little gung ho to me, but not to Jerry Septino in 3rd Platoon, who earned his Bullets R&R soon after I arrived in the field. This man chose to go to Vung Tau, and basically fucked his brains out for three days. When he returned, he raved about the new program, and told everyone that he had enjoyed himself immensely.

A few days after Jerry returned to 3rd Platoon, he was ordered on patrol, and soon was walking point. After the patrol had gotten off to a good start, and was about five klicks from the firebase, they seemed to be moving real slow; in fact, almost at a snail's pace. Everyone was wondering what was going on, but no one wanted to break silence, which was enforced except for emergencies. Each man thought that the enemy must be nearby, since the point was moving so slowly. Everyone in the column became nervous and jumpy. Then, the entire column halted completely; everyone stood around for a few moments, waiting for orders. When none came down, the men quietly found what cover they could, and finally, the word came down for the column to sit tight. Each man was preparing for the worst. Contact must be imminent.

Then the signal was passed down the line that everything was okay. There were no incidents or hostile actions. It turned out that the column had stopped because, when Jerry the point man came to a cool stream, he walked into that stream and sat down. The cool water felt really soothing to his pecker, so he decided to sit there for a while! Shortly after he had returned from Bullets R&R, Jerry Septino discovered that he had 'the clap.' Within a few days, it was so painful, it damn near destroyed him. That day, when he was walking point, it felt like some SOB was holding a Zippo lighter on his pecker. The only way he could walk at all was to let the pecker hang out of his pants, although that didn't help much.

That night the platoon set up by a creek, and Mr. R&R sat in that creek for a long time. He said to the guys, "You know as I set there, I swear damn near two inches of it just floated away." When he returned to the company at the end of the patrol, he warned everyone, "never, ever get the clap."

Upon his return, he jumped on the first resupply chopper that came in - without getting permission to leave the field. Because of the severity of his clap, he essentially went AWOL, which was a court-martialable offense. Septino located a doctor at Enari and told him to give him the biggest dose of penicillin he had. After the doctor examined his pecker, all he said was, "That's a bad case of clap."

Jerry told the doc that the girls he had sex with all showed him signed cards certifying that the government had checked them for disease.

Of course, when his platoon leader back at the firebase learned why the column had halted on the trail, he blew a gasket. Septino was threatened with an Article 15 for Conduct Unbecoming. Eventually, the Bullets R&R program, while popular for a while, was discontinued.

Chapter 28

We had just moved to a new firebase southeast of Pleiku. When we had our foxholes dug and were settled into our hooches, Lieutenant LePeilbet called a small meeting of the squad leaders. We assembled around the forward bunker, which already smelled of C-4. When we had quieted down, LePeilbet told us that we would be running quite a few SRPs from this firebase. He told us to inform the men that these SRPs would be especially dangerous now because of the tigers. Surprised, I looked at him and asked, "What do you mean, lieutenant?"

LePeilbet told us that a few days ago while on patrol, a soldier was attacked and dragged off into the jungle by a large cat. They thought it had to be a tiger since the animal was able to grab and drag a fully-grown man away. No other type of cat could or would do that.

The lieutenant said that shortly after 0400 hours on 10 January, the other members of the patrol heard the victim yelling briefly. They hurried to his last known location but could find no sign of him or of his weapon. The man had been part of a six-man SRP from A-3-8 (A company, third battalion, eighth infantry). This incident had happened only about eleven kilometers from our present location.

The remaining members of the SRP searched the area, and eventually found his rifle, but could find no trace of the soldier. At daylight, the team made another search of the area. They found the body at 0730 hours. The soldier had been partly eaten.

When I heard this I thought, *Not only do we have to watch out for snakes, scorpions, the water we drink, and the leeches in it, but now we have to contend with tigers.*

I asked Lieutenant LePeilbet, "What would stop a tiger? Would an M-16 do it?"

The lieutenant was not sure, but he didn't think his carbine would. Sergeant Machado of 3rd squad arrived. He was a dark skinned Italian from Massachusetts who looked like he belonged to the mafia and was Lieutenant Lepeilbet's first squad leader. Machado had a sinister look. His input was that it would be damn near impossible to stop a tiger with an M-16, a man would have to be a damn good shot. It was real hard to hit a charging tiger in the heart or between the eyes. You would get off only a few bursts, and then you would be eaten.

Sergeant Lestock said that maybe an M-60 would do the job, but it might take a grenade launcher. Even then, you would have to be deadly accurate. Then Sergeant White said, "Well, if you shoot up the jungle at night, then the NVA will know where you are. Your patrol's position will be compromised, and you'll have to get the hell out of Dodge."

Lieutenant LePeilbet was quiet and persistent. I guess he wanted to bring our discussion back to the point. He repeated that there was a cat out there in the jungle, not too far from us. He emphasized that this cat, this tiger, was a man-eater. The lieutenant held some notes in his hand, which he read to us.

"The male tiger is about nine feet long and weighs nearly 400 pounds. The female is smaller, at about eight feet and 250 pounds. They roam a thirty square mile territory," and he paused and looked at each of us for emphasis.

"So they are right out there where you and your men will be when on your SRPs."

"Here in Vietnam they call them Lord Tigers or sometimes Lord 30 or 'Ong ba mui.' The lieutenant did a fairly decent job of pronouncing the Vietnamese words. The Montagnards believe that they become manhunters on the last night of the last month of the lunar year. They also call them 'chua san lam' which means that they are stronger than any other mountain inhabitant."

The lieutenant had more, "Now hear this. In the dark, tigers see six times better than humans. They have retractable claws two inches long, and thirty teeth each three inches long. They are the baddest motherfuckers in the jungle. You cannot kill them with an M-16 unless it is a very good shot."

I looked at Lestock and said in a loud voice, "Damn, I thought we were the baddest motherfuckers out here in the jungle. Hell, just the other day The Flea told me we were."

This brought a chuckle from the men.

The lieutenant looked at me as if to say, *Get serious Sergeant,* then he added, "That ain't all, men."

"Our Lord Tiger will ambush you. He will stalk you as close as possible and then charge you from behind, silently. He will bite the neck of small prey, but to kill food as large as you guys he goes for the throat, to

169

suffocate you. Then he drags you to a safe location and eats forty pounds of you in one setting. Also, and let's not forget this one, once he has acquired a taste for humans, in all likelihood a tiger will try to kill and eat one again."

The lieutenant also commented that Jerry Loucks had reported seeing what might have been tiger tracks around our perimeter last night. Sergeant White drawled, "Well, boys, that tiger might be stalking 4th Platoon."

That made everyone feel real good.

Then LePeilbet finished up. "Tell your men. Make no bones about it. This is for real. It's a jungle out there, and don't you forget it."

The meeting was over. Just as I was about to leave the bunker, Machado asked, "Lieutenant is there anything good you can tell us?"

As the lieutenant turned back toward us, he said, "Yep. There are reports that they eat a hell of a lot of NVA. We don't necessarily want to kill tigers unless we have to."

I left the meeting and headed back toward my squad's perimeter. The steamy hot jungle sun beat down on me. As I walked, I thought, *I'm not sure what to tell the men. Hell, until the damn thing attacks us we really can't do anything. There's no way we can go looking for it. There's just too many NVA around. We'll just have to be on extra alert, like we were all walking point all the time.*

As I approached my men I said, "Watch out, the NVA has got real help now."

The Flea turned around. He took a drag from his Marlboro and said, "Say what, Sergeant Horton?"

I said, "There are tigers in the jungle near here. Two weeks ago a soldier from A-3-8 got eaten by one. That's no shit."

The Flea looked at me with a doubtful expression and said, "Well, fuck it. What will it be next? Come to think of it, a tiger skin rug would look mighty nice hanging on my wall back in Arkansas!"

I studied The Flea for a moment. I said, "If I were you Flea, I wouldn't shoot unless you can hit a charging cat between the eyes. Otherwise you'll just make the big pussy mad and he'll eat your skinny little ass for supper."

With that, I gathered the men and told them to watch out for tigers. I told them not to shoot unless they had to.

170

The guys didn't say anything, but we all knew that the night jungle noises would tease our senses much more than usual now. The night already played tricks on our eyes and ears. It was always hard to establish what was for real and what was in our imagination. But now, this four-legged enemy brought a new meaning to the old warning, "Watch out, it's a jungle out there."

Chapter 29

The SRP mission was a 4th Division innovation. The theory espoused by the Army's Brass was that continuously-deployed short-range patrols (SRPs) and ambush teams protected the company by detecting enemy movements in advance of attack. Each SRP was composed of three to five men whose primary weapon was reconnaissance and whose primary tool was the radio. Each company in the division manned its own portion of this screen by positioning five to seven SRP teams fifteen hundred to four thousand meters around its location at all times.

In our company, SRPs usually went out only one thousand to two thousand meters, especially when we were high in the mountains under that triple canopy jungle. Our company commander usually designated how many SRP patrols would be mounted each day, and their locations. Most of these were set up on expected avenues of approach to our company's position, or near known enemy pathways.

The SRPs were instructed never to initiate contact, but rather to remain concealed and rely upon indirect fire support from mortars, 105mm artillery or air support to rout or eliminate the enemy. Individual weapons were to be fired only in self-defense, as a last resort.

These SRP teams produced spectacular results for the 4th Division. During the late fall of 1968, in the vicinity of Duc Lap, SRP-directed artillery fire decimated a force of six to seven hundred NVA regulars within hours after the enemy had crossed the border into Vietnam.

By saturating the paths to villages with SRPs, the 4th Division restricted enemy movements and reduced the enemy's ability to acquire food or force the local Vietnamese people to work for them. The theory was that the locals would then be free of the Viet Cong's influence, and would respond positively to the government's pacification programs. Also, by placing these patrols along known or suspected enemy routes, the division could recon an extremely wide front with only a few committed troops. This concept recalls the theory, popular at the time, that one could successfully conduct this war using a Spartan methodology. Commanders even called their operational strategies "Spartan."

This SRP concept might have looked good to the Brass, but it was a scary proposition for the four guys ordered into the jungle looking for the enemy. It was four guys against an enemy of unknown size? No way. Not only were the odds all wrong, but if we made contact, help was thousands of meters away through the dense jungle, which was too thick even for choppers to find us most of the time.

On my first SRP in early January, I adopted the philosophy that the best way not to find the enemy was not to go looking for him in the first place. But we had been ordered to go. So what could we do? Like many SRPs, we traveled only half the distance we were supposed to go, and always set up our patrol in a secure location. Everyone used to say, for a SRP, it was four men, four clicks, for four days.

We thought we had the system all figured out to maximize our chances for survival, but we didn't count on having a visitor. The Flea, Joe Shea, Sam Seldon and I were on a two-day SRP. The first thirty-six hours were uneventful.

But the second night, about two in the morning, while the jungle was pretty quiet, I heard what sounded like a man moving toward our position through the brush. The ground would regularly crackle under foot, and branches would rustle or snap. There was no mistaking it. Something was headed our way. It would move for a while, and then stop. No noise, no motion. Then it would move again.

I gripped my rifle tightly. This was not the time to compromise our position by taking a shot. NVA were probably in the neighborhood, and I would just as soon they remained that way - in the neighborhood, not down our necks.

I was sitting up with Shea. He had the guard duty. We looked at each other, both of us on the alert. Then he and I saw it at the same moment. It was a dark shape, and it was moving. Was it a man? Was it an animal? What? It was moving toward us slowly. Now I could see that it was not tall enough to be a man. Was it a cat? We watched it for a long time. Neither of us were going to go to sleep with a cat prowling around. We might end up as its breakfast.

I kept thinking the animal would get our scent and turn away, but this one just kept coming. Before long, it was nosing around the edges of our cover. Most likely it was hungry. Okay, but I thought they didn't like the taste of humans. If this was a smaller animal - a bobcat or a leopard - I could have easily taken it with my weapon. But if it was a tiger, it would take some straight shooting, even with my M-16 set on full automatic. I was scared stiff, but I was thinking. The cat - whatever it was - was only about twenty meters away now.

A wounded tiger could be extremely dangerous, so if I started shooting, I would have to kill it, and quick. Of course, killing a tiger would also give our position away, and we would have to break location in the dark, which was dangerous too. I decided to lay low, and I tried to signal Shea to do the same. I just hoped the other guys would not wake up and start shooting. I was betting that, given enough time, that animal would leave us alone. I sat there, and I waited.

About this time, the whole darn jungle went crazy around us; it exploded with animal sounds. Every creature seemed to be warning every other creature about the cat's presence; they were all hollering at once. Shea looked at me. I looked at him. Our expressions said, *what the fuck do we do now?*

For the rest of the night, the jungle sounds around us, the yipping and hollering, were so intense; it was impossible for us to hear the enemy. The monkeys, the birds, and God knows what all had a jungle rock concert going on. Our SRP was useless. The enemy could stomp around all night long and we weren't going to hear shit.

Tuesday, 21 January 69

I am out on short range recon mission. There are four of us. We left yesterday and are supposed to be out here for two days and nights. We are careful not to look too hard for Charlie cause then you won't find him and that's the way you stay alive. No one in their right mind would go looking for Charlie with four men.

Last night we had a cat around our position — I do not think it was a tiger — it was a bobcat or leopard probably. We could have taken care of it but a tiger would take some straight shooting even if we used our 16's on automatic. After we heard that cat, this darn jungle got kind of crazy — you'd be surprised how noisy it can be at night. You can hear a long distance too.

Our SRPs had other, more deadly enemies as well.

174

Chapter 30

Frenchy, the medic of 3rd Platoon constantly tried to make the best of a bad situation. He kept inventing schemes to make his life more bearable, sometimes to his embarrassment and often to our utter delight. One day he decided that he had had enough of eating C-rations so he sneaked away from the perimeter and bartered with a local Montagnard villager. In a short time, Frenchy proudly returned to 3rd Platoon's perimeter holding a live, squawking, very plump looking chicken up in the air for all to see. "We'll have a feast!" he exclaimed, beaming from ear to ear.

In order to pay for the chicken he had bought from the Montagnard, Frenchy proceeded to work a business deal. He offered to share his chicken, after it was roasted, with a few of the men - for a fee. Frenchy tried to impress upon the guys that this deal was a real bargain. Immediately, half-dozen guys bought themselves a piece of a chicken dinner. After all, it was a fat chicken; it was obvious there would be plenty to go around. After a successful negotiation which included a small profit for himself, Frenchy proudly took charge of the chicken and brought it to the company's secure area to await its fate. At that time, the secure area was just a bunker with a lot of concertina wire wrapped around it. Frenchy set the chicken down on the bunker holding it firmly by the feet.

Frenchy had never cooked a chicken before. And neither had anyone else, but the first he figured out was that he couldn't cook it until it had been killed. And after that, the feathers had to be plucked.

An amiable conversation as to who should kill the chicken soon degenerated into a debate as to how to do it. Then Ken McCormack - a part owner of the bird - stated that the chicken should only be killed by the guy who knew how to kill it properly, and a fresh debate erupted. Pretty soon, everyone was getting pretty frustrated. The chicken thing just wasn't working out. Someone had to take action, and it was Wild Bill Moran who did.

Frenchy and Ken McCormack

Without warning, Wild Bill grabbed the chicken by the neck and took off running around the perimeter with it. The chicken's wings were flapping, its feathers were flying, and Wild Bill was whooping it up. Unable to resist this foolishness, Chris Kruckow took out running after them both. I just stood there, watching this impromptu circus act unfold.

As he ran, laughing, Wild Bill was trying to wring the chicken's neck. Frenchy was jumping up and down, yelling at Wild Bill excitedly. "Merdre! Sacrebleu! Mon Dieu!" Frenchy was uttering his most powerful cuss words but nobody had any idea what they meant.

I guess he was telling Wild Bill not to damage the bird. "Zut alors, Wild Beel! Don't harm the chicken! Ne fait pas mettre le doight!" he shouted, while holding his head with both hands as though he were watching a disaster unfold.

Bill Moran was a good ole boy from Tennessee who loved to have his fun anytime he could. He was called Wild Bill because he would do anything for a joke. Wild Bill was now running partly because he was frustrated with all the arguing, and partly just to see what Frenchy would do.

Then the bird fought back. It pecked Wild Bill's wrist really hard, and he let go. Now the bird was loose and it started to cluck and flap and run around the perimeter all by itself. At times it seemed to be almost flying. By now, most everybody else in the platoon was running and flapping their arms too. Everyone was chasing that bird back and forth across the firebase. I just stood there, grinning, taking this whole crazy scene in.

Just as someone would almost grab the chicken, it would flap its wings and somehow scoot through the guy's legs. All this time Frenchy was

176

jumping up and down and waving his skinny arms, hollering French cuss words like "Imbeciles!" and "Zut alors!" then mixing them up with "Fuck" and "Shit!" He cussed over and over again, sometimes in French and sometimes in English.

The guys were laughing at Frenchy as much as the stupid chicken. With all his jumping and waving, Frenchy put on quite a show. "Wait! Stop! Wild Beel, Halt! Arrete-vous!"

At the same time, the men were running all over the place, flapping their arms like chickens. Everyone but Frenchy was laughing at this ridiculous scene. For the moment, the cares of the war were forgotten. It was hilarious.

The chicken outran everybody and might have made good its escape into the jungle except that it finally got itself stuck in the concertina wire that surrounded the bunker. It was hiding back in that razor wire where it seemed to know we couldn't reach it. The guys all ran over by the bunker, panting then laughing then panting some more, completely out of breath. They were bushed but so was the chicken. Everybody was resting, trying to figure out how to grab that chicken without getting cut. Concertina wire was nothing to fool around with. Its barbs were sharp; a guy absolutely could not touch it or reach through it without serious injury. But that chicken was too far down in the wire; it was too far away for anyone to reach it with their hands.

Frenchy was about to have a heart attack. He had hollered and yelled until he was red in the face. Now he squeaked at Wild Bill, venom in his high-pitched voice, "Eff that chee-ken gets eway, j'ave vous le nez en marmalade!"

Wild Bill just laughed at him. Of course, skinny little Frenchy wasn't going to kick anyone's ass.

While the chicken flopped around in the wire, another great debate ensued. Everyone was sitting on the bunker now, talking, laughing and bullshitting about how to recapture Frenchy's chicken. Frenchy stood at the edge of the concertina wire, looking down at his chicken with a sullen face. He was just fuming inside. With every passing moment, he was getting more excited and more pissed off. He was pissed at all of us, but he was especially pissed at Wild Bill. "Zut alors! God dammit! Vous etes vraiment le roi des imbeciles! Look at what you've done. You are really, really stupid," he proclaimed in a high-pitched voice.

And of course, whenever he got excited he forgot his English and screeched at us in French. This made everyone laugh all the harder, which made Frenchy all the madder, and even less able to speak good English.

Finally, by throwing rocks at it, the men got the bird out of the wire. To avoid the rocks the chicken just ran out by itself. Once the bird was free, the chase was on again. But this time, Frenchy caught the chicken right away. After that, everybody settled down. Then Frenchy and Wild Bill settled their argument by killing and plucking the bird together.

During the course of plucking the chicken, they realized that it was nearly all feathers; it was the skinniest chicken they ever saw. That chicken was so skinny it was never going to feed all the guys who had paid good money for it.

Rollinger with the Chicken

Of course Frenchy went into a tirade over this too. First he accused Wild Bill of running that chicken until it had lost weight. Then he swore he would get even with the Montagnard who sold him this mirage. When he lapsed into French, he kept repeating the word, "Mirage."

Laughing at Frenchy's distress, Ken McCormack told him, very seriously, "Maybe we can eat the feathers, Frenchy!"

And that was good for another few laughs.

178

Once the chicken had been prepared for cooking, a fire was built and it was roasted on a spit. Then everyone who had paid for part of it got a bite - literally one bite each. Frenchy watched carefully as each soldier took his turn at the chicken, to make sure he did not eat too much.

But before they took their bites, Frenchy calmly and solemnly reminded each guy that he was personally responsible for providing the roasted chicken that day. Then each guy took his bite, smacked his lips, smiled at Frenchy, and dutifully told him just how great that one bite of the World really tasted. Whether the rest of us got a bite of that chicken or not, the hearts of every man in the platoon were lifted by a crazy Frenchman that day. Somehow, through his antics, for a moment we forgot the war, life was fun, and we felt like young innocent men again.

Chapter 31

I had been in the field about one month. My platoon was humping through an area west of Polei Kleng known affectionately as VC Valley, on our way to a place called the Plei Trap Valley. We came to a beautiful, calm, reddish-colored river near Kontum. Everyone was overdue for a bath and Sergeant White agreed we could go for a swim if we were quiet and we hurried. Our three squads flipped a coin. Half the men stood guard, while the other half took off their clothes and slid quietly into the water. The bathers were careful and subdued for fear of alerting any NVA in the area.

In a few minutes Joe Shea waded over to Sergeant White, who was standing on the bank, and quietly told him that he had located a cave in the side of the river bank a little further downstream, and that we should check it out. Sergeant White cautioned the guys to remain on guard and to be absolutely quiet. The men in the water started angling toward the bank where they had stored their weapons. Sergeant White walked along the bank toward the cave, but the bluff was so high above the river at that point that White could not see into the cave, even with Shea pointing it out.

Pappy was standing in the cave's mouth. He had just emerged with a heavy sack of rice in his arms. He looked up at White standing on the bluff and told him quietly that there was a lot more rice inside, as well as a number of tunnels still to be investigated.

Shea, The Flea, and Socks were still in the water, so they entered the cave. In a few minutes they reemerged. The Flea was carrying money—a few coins which turned out to be French—and a black VC pajama-type outfit. He had also found several Chinese-style cigarette lighters. Socks brought out another sack of rice and an NVA flag, and Shea had some NVA grenades and a few knives. He told Sergeant White that Charlie might have been using the place recently, but it was hard to tell. White decided that we should destroy the rice and other goods we had found and set up an ambush.

When they had emptied the cave of all the rice and other items they could find, Socks, The Flea, Shea and Pappy waded ashore. Then Pappy let out a yell, *"Dammit!"*

"What's the matter?" White replied.

Pappy had a disgusted look on his face. "Damn leeches," was all he would say. White and The Flea looked Pappy over. He had nine or ten leeches on his legs and one on his stomach. It took the three of them several minutes to get the leeches off. Remarkably, he was the only one to be attacked. "I'm older, so I'm more desirable," he stated.

My platoon set up ambush positions in the bushes near the cave, but no one saw any enemy activity. The next morning we blew up all the rice with C-4 and humped away from that river. At least a few of my men got a brief bath.

Friday, 31 January

We have been walking from day to night. Right now I am writing by moonlight. The last few days, we have been searching for enemy down by a river. This was my squad's doing, because we found 2000 pounds of rice. I found an NVA bayonet. Every day is like the next.

Chapter 32

Making Soup

It is hard to believe, and most people will think it is a joke, but there was such a thing in Vietnam as shit-burning detail. No matter how hard the grunt's life was, no matter what dangers we had to endure, and no matter what humiliation they subjected us to, there was always something else, something further we had to do that went beyond the believable. The shit-burning detail definitely went beyond. They called it "making soup."

I learned about "making soup" from a grunt in 3rd Platoon. He was unlucky enough to experience soup duty. His name was Christian "Ole" Nelson and he hailed from Effie, Minnesota. I happened to be over near the 3rd platoon positions when Ole was telling his story about "making soup."

Ole, being somewhat of an easy-going north woods country boy, explained that he thought nothing of it when a sergeant stuck his head into A-1-8's temporary quarters back at Enari one morning and said, "Come with me, soldier. I have some work for you to do. You're gonna make soup today."

Ole told us that he had been back in the rear at Enari for two weeks, where he was being treated for a severe case of jungle rot. He was scheduled to return to the field in three days. For the past three weeks, our company had been humping around out in nowhere land and this had given Ole time to recuperate.

Unfortunately, the A-1-8 temporary quarters at Enari was a ready source of slave labor for any work detail a sergeant or officer wanted to dream up. All the dirty work around the base camp was assigned to men who were there for various reasons. A guy might think that, by returning out of the bush back to Enari, he would have a few days off. But then bam! He would find himself stuck on some shitty work detail or guard duty.

Among the many details a guy could get assigned to the shit-burning detail was at the very top - or bottom - of the list, depending upon how you looked at it.

Ole Nelson was quite innocently lying on his bunk when he and two other guys were picked for the lowliest task at Enari – a task the Army had been unable to get even the Vietnamese to do – that of making soup.

The sergeant rousted three men and lined them up outside. He called them to attention and, walking back and forth in traditional military style, explained that he had an important job for them, so they'd better not fuck it up. Then he led the men around to the back of a building next to the A-1-8 temporary barracks and lifted a door in the wall. It was an outhouse. The sergeant told Ole and the men, "Your job is to clean the shit out of this outhouse. You will take these cans out, replace them with empty clean ones and load them onto that trailer over there. Then you are to get in that jeep and pull the trailer over to the edge of the post and burn the contents of all the drums. This will take you all day."

Ole explained, "We all started to piss and moan."

"This is not my job; I'm here on R&R," said one of the soldiers.

"The Army don't pay me enough to haul shit," said another.

The sergeant listened for a minute, then he just crossed his arms as if to say, "You ain't gonna talk your way outta this one, men."

All the men in the third platoon said that there was one thing about Ole Nelson. He was unflappable. He never got shook up over anything. Guys were constantly trying to bullshit him but it would always backfire. When the other soldiers had started to piss and moan, Ole remained silent.

He looked at the sergeant innocently and said, "How are we supposed to get these cans onto that trailer, Sarge?"

The sergeant stared at Ole for a long time, then he said, "I think you're really serious, aren't you, soldier?"

Ole answered with his whimsical Minnesota accent, "Yah, Ya don't expect us to lift those barrels full of shit out of there, do ya, Sarge?"

About that time the sergeant started laughing. He said, "Goddamn, man. You're the guy from Minnesota. I didn't know they had hillbillies in Minnesota! So listen up! First you gotta get your ass down low. Then you scoot the drum out of there. Next, you carefully roll it on its edge over to the trailer. Then you lift it in. You got that?"

When Ole didn't say anything, the sergeant grew frustrated, "You want me to do it for you, or what?"

Ole looked at the sergeant for a while. Then with a straight face he said, "Well, come to think of it, that would be nice of ya, sergeant."

The two soldiers broke out laughing, but the sergeant didn't crack a smile.

Many say that Ole was a rare find. He was a guy who liked everything in its place. He might have been the world's neatest soldier. And he was the kind of guy who looked so innocent that it appeared you could bullshit him. But not Ole, he was born and raised in the Minnesota north woods and was a railroad man, an outdoorsman and an expert fisherman.

In his short twenty-one years of life, he had been on so many hunting and fishing trips that you could say he had seen and done it all. But sergeants loved guys who had an innocent look like Ole, and they constantly picked on them. During Basic Training and AIT, that look had landed Ole on KP detail over and over again. Now here he was in the middle of a war, and that look of his, that innocent, northern, fresh look, had landed him squarely on soup detail.

While the sergeant watched from a safe distance, Ole and the other guys got down on their knees and together rolled that drum out of the latrine. When they got it out, Ole took a good long look at the contents. It was a combination of liquid, paper and brown shit, with about a million maggots crawling around in it.

Ole told the soldier next to him, "Hey man, take a look at this shit."

The guy peeked into the drum and, overcome by the sight and the smell, immediately barfed up his breakfast. The sergeant just chuckled. Ole said, "Now I know where C-rations come from. I had been telling the guys not to eat those meat and potatoes. C-rats meat and potatoes taste like shit. But I didn't realize they mixed maggots in there, too. Damn! Look at those little buggers crawling around."

With that, the other soldier barfed, too.

Ole recounted how the stench from the shit barrel was overpowering, especially after being exposed to the hot Vietnamese sun for a few minutes. It was putrefying. Since the sergeant was fucking with him, Ole told us how he decided to fuck with the sergeant, who was now sitting on his ass, watching the men wrestle with the smelly drum. Ole called over to him, "Hey, Sarge, how many people you reckon took a shit in this one? A thousand? Maybe two thousand? Was this latrine used by both officers and enlisted men? Hell, I bet one officer's shit would be the equivalent to five soldiers'. Wouldn't it, Sarge?"

Then one of the other soldiers wiped his mouth and stood up. He looked a little shaky. But he said, "No, I think it's one sergeant is equivalent to ten soldiers."

The sergeant just looked at them, arms crossed. He said nothing. He didn't have to; he had their asses.

Once they got the drums loaded from the latrine onto the trailer, the sergeant told them to hop into the jeep with him. He said, "I'll drive so I can show you men where we're gonna make soup today."

As they were riding out, the sergeant explained the theory of burning shit to them. "First, you have to realize that shit will burn, but only if you mix it with fuel oil. To get it to burn properly, you have to mix it into a proper soup. Then you light it and, if the soup is right, and if the temperature is perfect, the shit will burn efficiently. Before today is done, I bet you guys will be top-notch shit-burners. What do you think of that?"

Ole turned to the sergeant and said, "Sergeant, I hope ya don't mind if I use your name in my next letter home. I wanna write home and tell them about this. I know they won't believe me, but I will tell them anyway. Maybe I can get a job as a shit-burner when I get back to the World. Can I use ya as a reference, Sarge?"

At this point Ole' humor was wearing the sergeant a little thin. Of course, the other two soldiers were really beginning to like Ole.

But the sergeant continued. "You men will have to mix this fuel oil and shit just right. You use the shit-mixing shovels in the trailer to mix it into a smooth, syrupy substance. Once the mixture is perfect, the shit will burn like nobody's business and you'll be left with a clean drum. If you do not get the mixture right, then after the burn is done, you'll have to scrape the drum out manually and bury the remaining shit by hand. That's a hell of a lot more work. Do you men have any questions?"

Nobody did.

Then the sergeant told the guys, "You see, men, there ain't nothing simple in the Army, especially here in Vietnam. It takes some brains to burn shit. This is an important job which must be done right. You gotta put your hearts into it and do a good job. If you fuck it up, and fuck around, I'll keep you on this detail for a week until you get it right."

Of course at that threat Ole could not restrain himself. He looked at the sergeant and said, "I can't speak for the other guys, Sarge, but I know this will be an experience I will never forget. The Army has given me so

185

many memories. I hardly know what to say. There are almost no words to describe how I feel. I'll tell my grandchildren about this one day."

After this comment, the sergeant decided he didn't like Ole. His Minnesota humor was irritating.

Now they were approaching the shit-burning location. For the obvious reasons, this was at the very edge of Camp Enari. The jeep pulled up and the soldiers were instructed to get the drums off the trailer. When they were all set, the sergeant showed them how to mix their first can of soup. When the mixture was right, he lit the drum and, sure enough, all the shit quickly went up in flames.

While the men watched the shit burn, Ole said, "Now I know why Vietnam smells like shit."

The sergeant then ordered the men to mix the rest of the drums.

Ole took up the shit-burning shovel while another guy added the fuel oil. As Ole stirred the soup, he said to him, " I can't believe I'm doing this. If I 'm not humping in the jungle getting shot at, or growing jungle rot, I'm burning shit. I thought this kind of thing was reserved for someone who went to Hell."

After a few hours Ole and the other men got used to the smell and the mixing process. Their concoctions actually started to look like soup. They felt some weird sense of accomplishment. After they had mixed about five drums, the moment of truth was at hand. It was time to find out whether their mixtures would burn properly. Ole rolled up a newspaper, pulled out his Bic lighter and lit his paper torch. Then he tossed it into one of the drums. The mixture slowly went up in flames. A black cloud of stench boiled out of the can and filled the air. All three of the men cheered as though they had just scored a touchdown.

The sergeant smiled at them and said, "You men are gonna make first class shit-burners. From here on out, you're on your own. I want you to empty and burn every latrine in the battalion area."

Then he told them, "The bad news is, this will take you three days; the good news is - well, I guess there is no good news."

So Ole and the other two soldiers spent the next three days making and burning soup. Since they had to hang around and do nothing while the shit was burning, it was boring work. To pass the time they laid in the sun to get a tan. On the third morning Ole was so sunburned he could not get out of his bunk.

That morning, when the sergeant came to get him, Ole told the sergeant, "I got to go to the infirmary today, sergeant, because I can't move. I am seriously sunburned."

Then Ole added, " I can't go back to the field today either because I can't put a rucksack on."

"Soldier," the Sergeant said, "don't you know that you are Army property and, as such, you cannot purposely destroy, harm or otherwise make yourself unusable as a piece of Army equipment? I'm gonna see to it that you get an Article 15 for this. You men should have kept your shirts on. That is why, soldier, the Army issued you a shirt in the first place."

The sergeant marched off, threatening to court-martial Ole. But Ole and the other two guys just spent the next two days fucking off around the base until their sunburns peeled. Soon after that, Ole returned by chopper to A-1-8 in the field.

He arrived in the early evening to find Jerry Loucks and Greg Rollinger just hanging around with some of the other guys at 3rd Platoon, taking it easy. They had strung several poncho liners together between the trees and were sitting in the shade, bullshitting and having a smoke after dinner. As Ole approached his friends, Chris Kruckow looked up from a conversation he was having with Jerry Loucks and said, "How's it going, Ole?"

To which Ken McCormack added with a chuckle, "Get your rot healed yet?"

"Yeah, man." Ole replied. "Enari was great! They healed me right up."

"Hey, Ole!" Jerry Loucks acknowledged him with a nod. He was sharpening his big knife.

"But ya know," Ole continued, sitting down on a stump, "Army life is wonderful, isn't it? I mean, I go back there to get my rot doctored and the Army voluntarily teaches me some new skills that might lead me into a career path someday. It's damned exciting!"

"I mean, most of the time when ya get to Enari, ya just lay around on ya'r ass, right? Just wasting time. It's boring. But I got a chance to do something important that also taught me some new skills."

"Yeah, like what, Ole?"

"I learned how to make soup."

"Shit, they put your ass on K fucking P man," Rollie exclaimed through his cigarette. He exhaled loudly.

"You mean you ate real food instead of C-rats?" Ken wondered. This might be news.

As usual, Jerry Loucks didn't say anything; he just kept sharpening his knife. But Ole could tell he was interested to hear more, as were the other guys. Chris teased, "Gonna open you a restaurant back in the World, Ole?"

"Actually it's something like that. But ya know the Army; I had to mix the soup in big vats. It was a bit difficult to season at first, but then I met this sergeant who helped me get it just right."

"A fucking sergeant helped you? No way!"

Ken was sure Ole was bullshitting them now.

"Yeah, Ken, I know what ya mean. But this guy was different. I'm telling ya, the guy was really helpful. And he even told me I could use his name for a reference for a job when I get back in the World."

"No fucking way!" Chris exclaimed.

"Shit, Oley, I can see you now, opening the biggest restaurant in Duluth next year," Ken said with a grin. He scratched at something on his leg.

"Well, I might not be ready for the big time yet, but I definitely have a new skill. Making soup is not for everybody."

"What kind of soup was it?"

"I think they called it outhouse soup."

"After spending a week on this, I think it was one of the most important jobs I've had since being in the Nam. I'm planning to write my mother about this tonight. I know she will be pleased."

"Then, if I get back to the World and need a job, this might just be the kind of career start I would need. The beauty is, not everyone can do it. I mean, the two guys on detail with me dropped out. They just didn't have the stomach for such an important job."

The guys looked at each other and started to dust themselves off. Ken raised his eyebrows in disbelief. Rollie frowned at Ken and said, "He finally went over the top. I never heard anybody bullshit like that." Then to a man they had fallen silent and never took their eyes off of Ole.

"I urge each and every one of you men to find a way to get back to Enari sometime during your tour so that you can volunteer for the soup-making detail. I mean, this is definitely something to remember something to tell your grandkids.

188

"Heck, on my way over here, I met up with Sergeant White and I told him about my soup-making experiences. He promised to try to get it on my service record."

Ole looked at the faces seated around him. Ken McCormack, Chris Kruckow, Greg Rollinger and Jerry Loucks, four tough soldiers, all were looking at him with expressions of utter disbelief. But he had them. He had told them an outlandish story, and they didn't know whether to believe it or not.

A long line of Nelsons had spent countless hours telling stories in bars and fishing holes all over Minnesota, and now Ole was living up to the Nelson family legend. Here he was in the Nam, holding his own with the rest of the world. Those many hours spent fishing and hunting with his dad and his uncles had paid off. Ole was a survivor. No one could touch him, no one could bullshit him.

"You know, when I get back to the World, as time passes, I may not remember the countless hours and days I spent humping all over this godforsaken nowhere land. And I may not remember the terror of walking point, or of the ambushes we have staged. Or the deprivation I experienced so many times going for days without food or water.

But I will always remember doing something so valuable for the Army that I received the complete co-operation and admiration of a sergeant. And guys, I will always remember you all, my buddies. But most of all, I will remember the days I spent making soup, and what making soup taught me about life."

Chapter 33

Saturday, 1 February

The last time I wrote I was at kind of a secure place and was getting ready to go on a 24 hour recon mission and would be able to write some letters. Well, they changed that because we volunteered for a mission. So now we are almost at the Cambodian border after walking about 15 miles in two days. I have been through hell these last two days. This is the worst yet. We walked over the roughest place you can possibly imagine. Had to go across rivers by rope and we had to go up one mountain that was so steep that we had to use a rope to get up it. It took 3 ½ hours to climb up - it was straight up! When we set up for the night, I was so tired I sat down and almost could not get up.

They won't give as a break. They walk us into the ground every day. Plus, after we got to where I am now, the stupid colonel stopped the helicopters from flying and now we don't have any food and little water unless we get a bird in today. I'm going to teach my kids to hate the army and hate war. It is the most disgusting thing a person can go though and none of my kids are ever going to experience it. We get volunteered for all the missions. Well I shouldn't talk about it too much but I want people to know how the infantry gets messed over like a bunch of animals.

When we arrived at our nighttime location, we found a level, protected area with a natural LZ nearby. Thankfully we didn't have to chop and clear trees in our exhausted condition. We could barely muster up enough energy to dig foxholes.

Just before dark, a Slick arrived with the mail. Unfortunately I got no letters from home. Joe Shea received three packages though, including a large box of cookies. There was enough to pass around. Sergeant White sampled one and declared, "The wives and mothers of America must send more cookies, the infantry is powered by cookies from home!"

. The pilots on the Slick had assured us that a second chopper would be flying in with food and water later that evening, but the battalion Brass stopped all helicopters from flying that night. Except for Joe Shea's cookies, we had no food or water for almost twenty-four hours.

Sergeant White commented that if it hadn't been for wives and mothers sending food and cookies the Army could not operate at all.

Chapter 34

Massing Forces

Because of this huge area of responsibility and the limited helicopters available, the 4th Division established a policy of massing forces in critical areas while practicing Spartan economy of force, which in laymen's terms meant they tried to stick "five pounds of shit in a one pound bag."

In conventional war, the Army tries to find and destroy the enemy and their will and ability to wage war. In the Central Highlands we operated differently. We operated in a counterinsurgency environment. The destruction of the enemy's will and ability to fight was secondary. Our mission was to eliminate the conditions- socioeconomic as well as military- which gives rise to insurgency and to motivate the South Vietnamese people to rout the enemy and therefore prevent the enemy from succeeding.

To accomplish this goal the 4th Division was to provide an impenetrable protective screen which would allow the Republic of Vietnam to control population centers. The idea was to instill and bolster a sense of security among the South Vietnamese people. If we could contain the external threat from the North Vietnamese Army (NVA) regulars, the South Vietnamese government could systematically eliminate the conditions which allow the Viet Cong to exist. It was complicated to say the least.

To put it simply, our mission was to intercept the NVA and force them to fight in remote areas away from the population centers. We were to provide a protective screen to permit government and commerce to continue un-abated in the Central Highlands.

This is where we came into the picture. We were the screen. Our Commanders maneuvered us along key terrain areas that block the enemy's routes to the major population centers. We were the pawns in a giant chess game to be moved to protect the Central Highlands. It was a life and death game.

We would do this by what the Army call "reconnaissance in force" operations. We would find and destroy enemy base camps and eliminate enemy caches. We moved companies and battalions throughout various

Areas of Operations (AO's) in these operations. Thus, we inhibited movement of large NVA units and reduced the enemy's influence upon the civilian population.

For me, my part of this plan began in Plieku.

Chapter 35

Monday, 3 February

I was in Pleiku, and I was very drunk. Bullets, Lieutenant Colonel Buckner our battalion commander, had ordered our company to hump over the hill to rendezvous with some deuce and halfs. We then convoyed into Pleiku. After we left that last firebase, north of Dak To, the NVA infiltrated the area in force. With all the trouble brewing in the Central Highlands, the Brass knew that sooner or later we would have to take care of it, so Bullets, our Battalion commander, brought us down to Pleiku to get re-provisioned first.

We were scheduled to return up north right away, so the company quickly re-provisioned with food, ammo and some supplies for headquarters, and stood ready to move out at any moment. But then there were reassignments, transfers, and other paperwork to be done, and meetings were held to determine how our company could best co-ordinate its efforts with the other companies in the brigade, especially C Company, who we would be joining up with in March for some combined operations in the Plei Trap Valley. As time passed it became apparent that this re-provisioning would take days, a thought we very much welcomed. It would give us a break before we started a new, more aggressive phase of our campaign against the NVA. During this time there was more Brass around us than I had seen in one place so far in the war.

Two days later, on 5 February, though the rest of the company was gone, our platoon was still in Pleiku. Now we were really beginning to enjoy ourselves. Two companies of South Vietnamese soldiers were posted to the site next to us, and the earthy scent of their food, sort of a combination of ginger and rotting compost was difficult to miss. The 4th Platoon was the only platoon in our company securing tactical operations command. We had to stay within the perimeter at Pleiku, close to battalion headquarters while the rest of the company humped back out into the bush looking for the enemy. This light duty was a pleasant change, in comparison to so many days spent humping all-day and on guard all night, surrounded by NVA. For the moment life was pretty easy.

I made a nice tent from my poncho, and slept on ground that was very soft. After so many weeks spent humping in the bush, this place was great. The company's re-supply work was completed so we were just hanging out. Don White, our platoon sergeant, told us that we might be here for one to three more weeks. This was very good news, since we knew we were relatively safe at this location.

Our rest did not last that long. On February 6 we were ordered to join the rest of the company to conduct Search and Clean operations. We moved to Polei Kleng to the vicinity of LZ Mile High and then we were to walk the road where we meet five slicks. We were transported to an area west of Kontum near Soui Doi for a stand down on 9 February. From there we were to reorganize for assault missions into newly assigned Area of Operation. The objective will be to conduct reconnaissance in force and ambushes to stop enemy infiltration.

Chapter 36

Like Ole and his friends, Spider was once drafted into the soup-making detail. But in true pirate fashion, Spider found a way to make soup while executing the well-known maneuver called "getting over" at the same time. When one "gets over," one takes a situation in which one is being "fucked over" by someone else and turns it to his own advantage. Hence the term "I am getting over" means "I am getting away with something, something I'm not supposed to be doing."

Typically the other guy would be a sergeant, an officer or just anyone who wanted to fuck with you in some way.

Not long after he had transferred out of the field to the rear at Enari mid-January, The Spider found himself in a situation in which he needed to "get over." At the time, Spider was in a transition period. He was still getting the lay of the land - learning how things worked in the rear - and that made him vulnerable. He had tried guard duty for a while, but that sucked. And he had not yet developed his carpentry schemes which eventually lead to the creation of his successful private venture, which was a bar for warriors called Your Father's Mustache

Spider at Your Father's Moustache

During this transition period, Spider stayed alert for some permanent job that would be fun and still keep him out of the front lines. Very adept at "getting over", Spider was continually inventing plans for getting off the base so that he could go "downtown" to Pleiku City where the girls were.

At the time, Spider was working KP in the mess hall. He knew a guy there who had access to the battalion mess truck. His name was Hubert Smith III. Soon Hubert and The Spider would go downtown anytime there was a reason to take the truck off the base, whether it was to go to the dump or even to make a quick run over to the air force base. Hubert and Spider would always take the truck together. And they would always make a detour downtown to pay a visit to the girls - for their personal development, of course.

One day they were set for a run downtown when Company A sergeant walked by and spotted Spider sitting in the mess truck. The sergeant smiled, crossed his arms, and walked over to the truck. He said, "Meli, it's Company A's turn to burn the battalion's shit. You have the honor of the day, soldier!"

Of course Spider had broken one of the golden rules learned by every grunt early in basic training. This rule was so important that it was actually rule number one – become invisible, and remain invisible. It was Spider's fault for letting the sergeant see him. So now he was stuck with the shit-burning detail and he had to forfeit his ride downtown.

But in a moment of inspiration, Spider remembered that there was a guy in the battalion who was actually the regular shit-burner. His name was Dwayne something or other. Shit-burning was always assigned to Dwayne when the available workforce of transient GI's were too busy with other things, such as guard duty or KP. And Dwayne always had Montagnards assigned to him. In fact, Dwayne worked with his "yards" on a daily basis, and he had them doing the lowest jobs around the base. Burning shit would certainly come under the category of a lowly work assignment.

Now the thing about Dwayne that stuck in Spider's mind was that while the shit was burning, Dwayne would disappear. Actually no one knew where he went. While the shit was burning, there was no one around. So Spider decided that he had to contact Dwayne, but quick! He thought, *In this situation, there's got to be way" to get over." Dwayne will know how to do it.*

196

Most of the guys around the battalion didn't think much of Dwayne, probably because he was a permanent shit-burner so they never took him seriously. But The Spider knew that Dwayne was crafty enough to finish out his tour, avoiding combat by doing the dirty jobs no one else wanted. Besides, Dwayne was good working with the Montagnards and he was good to them, they liked him. They worked hard for him. In Spider's book, Dwayne was one smart dude and because of that Spider always made it a point to get along with Dwayne. After all, you either have friends in low places or you don't. Of course, Spider always did.

After telling Hubert to wait in the truck for a minute, Spider walks over to the barracks and found Dwayne. He said, "You gotta help me, Dwayne. They got me burning shit! You're the expert on the subject. What's the secret?"

Dwayne gave Spider a big grin and a pirate's wink. Spider thought, *That look, that grin. Yes! Santa Claus really has come early this year!*

Then Dwayne answered, his expression turning into a leer, and his eyes narrowing, "The secret is plenty of diesel, that's the secret all right. Give it enough diesel and it will burn all day. Ya ha ha!"

Dwayne loved to mock Spider's imitation of Long John Silver. When he did, the two of them would break out laughing. After they had a good laugh, Dwayne gave Spider more detailed instructions.

Now as he left the barracks, Spider's step was a little lighter. He was about to get over on the sergeant who was harassing him. This made him happy and he halfway double-timed into a slow jog down to the end of the dirt street. There, just as Dwayne said, stood a granddaddy of an outhouse. It was a grand six seater, and it was built away from the other buildings, with its own shit-burning area. Without stopping, Spider immediately went around behind the thing to the, let's say, the business end.

About fifty feet away, Spider saw six burned-out "honey pots." These were fifty-five gallon drums cut down to approximately one-third their full size. They had two holes cut opposite each other just under the top edge so that they could be hooked and dragged from the latrine. Their contents had been burned down to ash. Two long metal hooks lay nearby. Spider grabbed the longest one and dragged the empty honey pots into position behind the shithouse. There were three trap doors in the shithouse, each with two pots in it.

Spider stayed carefully up wind of the situation while he hooked the doors up and dragged the first two full drums out.

Then he heard a voice from above say, "Hey! I'm up here trying to shit!"

Humm, thought Spider, *A voice seems to be yelling out of this ass hole covering one of the shit holes.*

So Spider yelled back up at the ass hole. "You better fuckin well shit then, cause I ain't down here posing for animal crackers."

Then he dragged the first two cans over to the burning area. By the time Spider had hooked the fourth can, the ass hole had disappeared. When Spider saw this he thought, *Well, I'll be damned! It's a funny thing about the Army. There have been plenty of times when I thought I was talking to an asshole, but today is the first time I ever knew it for sure.*

As he was hooking the last two drums, Spider was trying to decide whether he should begin by burning two at a time. Then he decided, "No, it's better not to get too 'cocky.'"

In less than ten minutes, the new cans were in place, the doors were down, and Spider was pouring on the diesel. As Dwayne had suggested, he was really, really pouring it on.

Dwayne's words were now teasing Spider's brain. They told him, "Spider, get lazy now. The shit will have to burn all day so keep pouring it on."

Spider followed Dwayne's instructions carefully. When one is about to get over, one has to follow instructions to the tee.

When the cans were filled with what Spider thought was enough diesel, he added more, and still more. Finally he backed upwind, lit some paper and fired 'em up. A huge black cloud of burning shit poured forth from the honey pots. It was like Pearl Harbor in the middle of the base. In fact, the cloud was bigger than even The Spider had expected. That cloud was so thick; nobody would be able to tell that he wasn't there. This was just as his buddy Dwayne had predicted. Now it was time to move onward, to bigger and better things!

Spider went back to the barracks, grabbed some clean clothes and headed for the showers. He was careful to stay invisible this time. The Spider was going downtown!

After he had reconnected with Hubert and the mess truck, and they had driven a few klicks beyond Camp Enari, Spider leaned out of the truck window and looked behind them. The smoke was so thick, pouring right from the middle of the camp that it looked like there had been an air strike! Spider yelled out, "It's gonna burn like that all day, Spider, so you can party in Pleiku all day. Fuck 'em if they can't take a joke!"

Spider had a great time downtown. When he returned to Enari, the cans were still smoldering. And he never heard a word of complaint about the shit he had burned. Spider realized then that there was this funny thing about shit. While it was burning, nobody would come anywhere near it. Therefore, nobody would know that Spider hadn't been there the whole time.

A few weeks later, Spider became a carpenter. Now he was on his way to developing his warrior's bar, and his troubles for the remainder of his tour were over. Guys like Spider were truly gifted. They had the will to get over even if they had to burn shit all day.

But it turned out that Spider's antics were just the opening act in the Enari soup wars. A few weeks later, the most memorable event associated with making soup in the history of the 4th Division occurred.

This event was not reported in any newspaper, Army log, or official government document and yet it actually came to pass. It was an event beyond comprehension, and as such, it was swept under the officers' rug.

At Camp Enari, believe it or not, the officers had their own swimming pool. It was a really large, Olympic-sized pool, and it was built and being operated right in the middle of the war. It had been built with the labor of grunts that were on temporary assignment at Enari, supposedly getting a much-needed rest. Of course, a few combat engineers planned the thing during their off hours. As far as the official records went, this pool did not exist. But there it was. It was an affront to every grunt in the Nam. Such extravagance was just another slap in our faces.

Well, one day this extravagance ended. One day shit fell from the sky. Drums of shit fell out of the sky and landed directly into the officers' swimming pool. An entire palette of honey pots dropped directly into the pool. The shit, the maggots, the paper and the liquids all mixed together in the beautiful, green Olympic pool to form a thick brown soup that was immediately sucked into the pool's expensive water filtration system. They said one could smell the stench 100 meters away.

Witnesses say they saw a helicopter, maybe it was a Dustoff, in the vicinity of the pool one minute and the next thing they knew, barrels of shit were falling at high speed (32 feet per second). Those barrels exploded on impact with the water's surface into a spectacular brown mess. They were like large brown bombs going off, turning that beautiful Olympic-sized pool into a giant, Olympic-sized cesspool.

When The Spider heard this news, he couldn't believe his ears. He immediately walked over to the officers' compound to take a look for himself. Yep, there it was all right, a shit-filled swimming pool. The Spider had to work hard to keep himself from laughing. But as the days passed and the stench spread, various engineers were consulted. The conclusion was unanimous - all that could be done was to plow the pool under. It was a total loss. Spider set up a grapevine to help spread the news about this incident back out into the field. The universal response from the grunts was a smile and the simple statement, "We got over."

Years later, it was alleged that a Dustoff pilot might have dropped that palette of shit in retaliation against one of the officers at Enari. It seemed that there had been a fight at the officers' club the night before, and the pilot had come out second best. Of course, it just goes to show you, one shouldn't fuck with the warriors in the Nam, especially with the Dustoff pilots, who lay their ass on the line every mission. They don't give a shit. If you do fuck with them, you're liable to end up with shit all over your face, and in your swimming pool too.

Chapter 37

Early Saturday morning Lieutenant Lepeilbet called me to his foxhole for a briefing. Steve Benyshek was there, stretched out on his rucksack. Steve was about six foot four, blonde, and looked like a California surfer. I had seen him brought in on as helicopter sling a few days before. "Okay, guys, I want you to hear this," the Lieutenant said. "Maybe we can all learn something that may save our lives. Beneyshek is going to brief us on the contact his SRP made on Thursday."

I sat down and leaned on a pack to the left of Sergeant White as Beneyshek told his story.

The SRP had started February 16 when Bill Crockett, the RTO: Charley Storm, the squad leader and Beneyshek set out on a two-day SRP to recon the enemy. All three were from 3rd squad of our platoon.

Steve Beneyshek   Bill Crockett

After lunch, Crockett set up the radio to report their position to the company. But the battery was dead. Bill had failed to check it before they left camp.

"We better be damn careful now," Storm said. "We ain't gonna get any help out here by ourselves."

They continued on the two-day SRP without incident and then left the night location to come back to the company. On the morning of 18 February they headed back to the firebase.

They worked their way through the dense bushes and grass down one long ridgeline. Bill said to Steve, "We're on the wrong side of the ridge, Sergeant Storm."

They stopped and looked at their map. All the ridges looked the same from their location. They realized that they were in deep shit. After much discussion, they decided to move down that ridge they were on but they were not sure that this was the right thing to do. They were lost and they knew it. Worse, they had no radio, they couldn't call for help.

As the patrol moved down the ridge, Beneshek walked point with Bill following and Charley on drag. They humped in the same direction for about four hours on a clearly marked trail. The only problem was that they walked deeper into the mountains.

About noon, Sergeant Storm pulled up. "Okay, time for a break. Let's have some lunch and think about this." Beneyshek stood guard while Bill and Charley ate just off the trail. The enemy was in the area so they wanted a position that allowed a hasty retreat, or an ambush, if needed.

Suddenly there was movement. They saw two NVA headed down the trail. Beneshek whispered to Bill. "Look, shall I shoot?"

Bill whispered, "Hell, yes, they are the enemy, aren't they?"

Beneshek opened up and dropped both NVA. He recalled that he was so nervous that he was lucky to hit anything.

Storm said, "Okay, let's move back in the trees in case there's more of them. Let's go."

They moved quietly. They went fifty meters further back from the trail and set up a defensive perimeter in case they were counter-attacked, a loose circle pointing their rifles outward. They were ready.

Sergeant Storm

After an hour and no sign of the enemy, they moved back toward the site of initial contact. When they got close, Bill threw a grenade to clear the area and they set up another defensive perimeter.

Nothing happened, so they searched for the two NVA and found them dead near the trail. There was nothing of any military significance on the bodies, but they discovered a blood trail left by another NVA who must have been wounded by their ambush or hit by the grenade explosion.

They followed the blood trail slowly but they found nothing.

They decided to continue their journey back to the company, keeping off the trail in six foot tall brush to avoid the enemy. That didn't work; it was almost impossible to move through the bush so they followed another trail.

After they humped about two hundred fifty meters from the initial ambush site, they saw signs of the enemy's presence again. Beneshek stopped. He picked up something white. "It's a cigarette butt and it's still wet."

Then all hell broke loose.

Bill saw a flash out of the corner of his eye. He jumped out of the way but was too slow. The first bullet ripped into his hip. AK47's firing from all directions.

The men did what they were taught. They moved then assaulted the enemy returning fire immediately. Their fire was intense as they had their

M16's on full automatic firing. After several minutes, they managed to quiet the enemy.

Beneshek had killed one of the NVA. Then they decided to break contact with the enemy since they did not know how many NVA were really there.

But as the shooting stopped, Bill lay wounded. During the firefight Bill had managed to take his ruck off and crawl off the trail. He had moved over the side of the hill and down into the brush to hide. Beneshek followed Bill down into the brush and attended to his wounds as best he could. Bill was wounded in the hip so he could not travel. They had a wounded man, they were lost, and had no radio. And there were plenty of NVA in the area. So Sergeant Storm and Beneshek decided to split up and search for help. They knew the firebase was not too far away; they just had to locate it.

As sergeant Storm headed over the hill, unbeknownst to him two NVA followed him.

Beneshek humped back down the trail the same way they had just come and soon got stuck out on a ledge that was also surrounded by NVA.

All three of them were now split up and NVA crawled all over the place.

At the time of the ambush our company sat on a high ridge overlooking the valley where the patrol had been ambushed. I remember the sounds of the shooting. We knew the patrol was in trouble but couldn't raise them on the radio. And our lookouts couldn't see them. We studied our maps to determine the route they should have traveled. Once we determined approximately where they should be, Sergeant White called in a rescue helicopter. I saw the helicopter flying into the valley along the ridge. The helicopter had loudspeakers they used to try to make contact with the SRP. We saw the helicopter, heard the speakers and the shots. The drama unfolded before our eyes.

Even though their suspected location was in site, it would have taken a full day to hump the rugged mountains to them. Every man in the company sat on the hill watching the rescue helicopter search down the hill into the valley. Many said silent prayers for the lost men. It was a serious situation to be lost in the middle of enemy action without support. SRP patrols were never supposed to make contact with the enemy. This was an infantryman's worst nightmare.

Benshek eventually found his way down off the ridge without alerting the enemy. He kept walking, trying to find his way back to the firebase. Then he started climbing again and got lost on another high ledge.

All the while this was happening, Bill still lay in the brush, wounded in the hip, hiding from the enemy. He didn't move for fear of being discovered.

Sergeant Storm discovered NVA were following him and played hide and seek with them all day. He couldn't shake them.

The drama extended into the night. Bill lay in the brush without his rucksack - no food, no water. Beneshek spent the night on a ledge, while Sergeant Storm hid from the enemy.

The next day Bill heard loudspeakers: "Shoot twice if the chopper is near you. Shoot once otherwise, at short intervals, so the pilot can spot you."

Bill crawled painfully out of the bush to retrieve his ruck, but it was gone. But he still had his weapon. Lying on the trail with his shirt off, he rolled over and fired twice in the air.

The pilot heard the shots and flew the chopper overhead. The pilot spotted Bill lying on the trail. The chopper crewman lowered a hoist with a sling and hoisted Bill safely out of the jungle.

From our location, all of us saw the chopper carrying Bill in the sling flying toward us and we started to cheer.

Bill Crocket on a sling rescued

Once Bill was safely back at the firebase, the helicopter lifted off to find the other two men.

About noon Beneshek saw the helicopter heading toward his position. He stood high on a ridge and waved at the pilot, but the pilot didn't see him. As the chopper passed over, Beneshek set off a CS grenade. The gas drifted up into the chopper and caused the pilot to look down. Soon Beneshek too was hoisted up into the air and flown back to our location on the ridge. Now only Storm remained.

The chopper searched for the rest of the day, but couldn't locate Storm. At nightfall, the chopper returned to its base.

The next day, Beneshek climbed aboard the chopper to direct it to the last location he had seen Storm. They spotted Storm humping through the jungle at a fast pace, as though someone chased him. The chopper signaled him to an open area and hoisted him aboard.

Storm was exhausted. He had played hide and seek with the NVA for two days and nights. He had tried to find help for Bill while the NVA hunted him. On the second day he had turned on the NVA and set up an ambush and killed one. The other NVA disappeared.

As Storm was lifted out, many NVA were spotted running toward him from the surrounding jungle.

It had been a narrow escape. The men had gone without food or water for two days. All three of them were airlifted to a hospital in the rear. Bill's hip wounds were bad enough to send him back to the World for treatment. Beneshek rejoined us and Sergeant Storm was so short they let him rotate back to the World right away.

Chapter 38

Our Enemy, the 66ᵗʰ NVA Regiment

In early December, the number of intelligence reports of enemy activity near the Chu Pa Mountain area of Pleiku Province had been increasing. Intelligence reports of enemy activity were also surfacing along known or suspected trail systems to the west and southwest of the Chu Pa. The information from these reports was plotted on maps but gave inconclusive evidence, so attempts were made at visual and photographic reconnaissance of the infamous Plei Trap Road. The trails branching from this road led directly to the Chu Pa area, and the Chu Pa Mountain itself.

Reconnaissance showed movement along the Plei Trap Valley. Recent improvement along the network of trails in the Plei Trap had been easily spotted, and almost daily Snoopy flights confirmed its increasing use. Fourth Division engineers tried to close the high speed infiltration route by attempting to blow up trails, but their success in stopping movement to the Chu Pa remained inconclusive. This area was too vast for adequate visual observation, and the surrounding jungle, with its triple canopy, was too thick to allow trail observation by aerial photography.

Concurrent with the Chu Pa operation was the threat posed by the 66ᵗʰ NVA Regiment, which consisted of about 1,500 men. This unit with supporting engineers and artillery, targeted Polei Kleng, Plei Mrong, and Kontum City.

The 66ᵗʰ NVA was a favorite fighting unit of both NVA commanding general Vo Nguyen Giap and North Vietnam's President Ho Chi Minh. It was better known as the *Tiger Regiment*. Among its warriors were an ethnic group called Nungs, which had its roots in China and had settled in Vietnam hundreds of years earlier. It was not known if Ho Chi Minh was descended from the Nungs, but he considered this regiment his "honor" unit. The Nungs were bigger and stronger than their counterparts and took pride in their reputation as fighters. Also, it was the death of some Nungs in the Battle for Hill 947 that led to the belief among some that the Chinese had entered the war on behalf of North Vietnam, though such was not the case. At any rate, the 66ᵗʰ was a tough outfit and was the unit that we faced. The presence of this crack enemy unit triggered immediate response by battalion commanders of the 1st Brigade and our company, the A-1-8, part of the 1st Brigade. It is for this reason they moved us from Dak To in January after our company completed 15 months of continuous operations in the vicinity in that area.

We redeployed to a new base at Soui Doi near the Mang Yang Pass and in early January then we operated south of Soui Doi near the Dak Payou Valley commonly referred to as VC Valley. Then in anticipation of a renewed enemy offensive which was expected in the Lunar (Tet) new year, our brigade was alerted to deploy anywhere within the 2d Corps Tactical Zone on short order. On the night of 24 January the order came, and we conducted a tactical road march from Soui Doi to Kontum and participated in a combat assault the following morning to secure the high ground southeast of Polei Kleng.

In late January and February the 66th NVA Regiment immediately probed our positions. Sightings and minor contacts were made with the battalion's SRP recons indicating that the enemy was trying to skirt north-westward around our blocking force.

Another battalion was moved by truck to Polei Kleng and combat assaulted into blocking positions while an additional battalion from the division's 2nd Brigade was airlifted to an area north of Polei Kleng to protect the northern flank from infiltration.

The 4th division was now aligned with the 2nd Brigade controlling three battalions west of the Ya Krong Bolah River to block the enemy's advance, and with elements of the 1st Brigade protecting the approaches to Kontum City and readying themselves for a combat assault either to smash the enemy or to cut him off from their sanctuaries.

This was our plan of attack in late January and February.

Enemy Offensive

Once the blocking forces were in place, the enemy initiated extensive reconnaissance efforts against our positions and became more aggressive in their movements. On 23 February, the NVA launched a new phase of their offensive in the Central Highlands, beginning with attacks by rocket

208

fire against the population centers of Pleiku and Kontum and against US fire support bases.

Meanwhile, having received supplies and replacements following their retreat from the Chu Pa, the 24th NVA Regiment had now infiltrated back across northern Pleiku Province into positions east and west of Highway 14. On 24 February, elements of this regiment sprang two abortive ambushes along the highway. The 3rd ARVN Cavalry dispersed the attackers, killing 63. Farther north between Kontum and Dak To, Viet Cong local force battalions emerged from the mountains and forests to attack lightly defended villages along the eastern side of Highway 19.

In the tri-border area of Vietnam, Cambodia and Laos west of Dak To, enemy artillery began heavy bombardment of the Ben Het Special Forces Camp. To counter these threats, the division immediately deployed elements of an armored battalion to Ben Het and Dak To, and simultaneously sent an infantry battalion into the Chu Prong Mountain complex east of Highway 14. At Ben Het, US tanks throttled an NVA infantry-tank assault, killing 42 enemy and destroying two of eight Soviet PT76 vehicles and turning back a battalion of ground troops. At Chu Prong, our infantry battalion rooted the enemy from caves and captured large supplies of munitions.

The 66th NVA Regiment still was the principal threat to Kontum Province and continued to probe Polei Kleng in an attempt to penetrate the blocking force. At that time, the average infantryman knew nothing of the nature of these events other than the day to day existence and struggle for survival. In retrospect it was a good thing that we didn't; fighting the toughest unit in the North Vietnamese Army would have been a very disquieting fact to know indeed.

Chapter 39

Tuesday, 23 February 69

Because the company had been on the move constantly, I had not written home for several days. Many NVA were coming down the Ho Chi Minh trail now; we were making contact daily. Charlie had been hitting the big base camps and the major cities all over South Vietnam. In the Central Highlands we kept busy trying to kill the enemy before they could reach their targets. Third platoon had lost Sergeant Grinstad to a logging accident and had no lieutenant so Sergeant White was made 3rd Platoon Leader and Lestock was our Platoon Sergeant in 4th. Lestock was a good leader; he was experienced and by now we were well-trained, and operated smoothly as a unit.

A week ago we pulled out of our firebase on foot. Then we humped across some of the most difficult terrain we had yet encountered. The jungle was very thick and the ground constantly changed; we humped up, then down, then up, then down, high in the mountains. First we humped ten or twenty klicks away from the scene of an air strike only to be told that we had to return the next day to assess the damage. To return we had to hump back through the mountains again and then we found ourselves at the scene of an arc light air strike, surrounded by huge bomb craters and hundreds of blasted trees, fallen and stacked like the kid's game, pickup sticks.

That last hump almost killed us. Our company didn't make it to our destination; we just dug in on some unknown hill and rested. This didn't happen very often, but we had reached our limits and could go no further.

The next day we moved off the hill and down through a valley, then up over to Hill 1044, and from there we humped over to Hill 1018. By this time we had gone a number of days without hot chow of any kind. While on 1018, we discovered a high-speed trail used by the enemy. Captain Hockett's RTO, Charles Webb, known to us as "Slim" or sometimes "Tex," radioed this discovery in to headquarters. Bullet, the battalion commander, radioed us back to set up on 1018 for the night, to search for any enemy that might be passing through.

To dig our foxholes, we had to shovel hard soil so it took a long time to dig in. Before we were done the Brass flew us in some water and C-rations. It was a damn good thing, because we were almost out of both.

On Friday we settled further into Hill 1018. We began to clear fields of fire and dig deeper foxholes. After that, we had to expand the LZ for the choppers to land. Our field position was starting to look like a firebase. The Brass apparently wanted us to stay put for a while, to block the NVA returning from Pleiku after their recent attacks. They had been trying to rocket Camp Enari.

We also got mail and some clean clothes. But even with all this attention, we got no socks again. I began to wonder if the clerks in the base camps were selling our socks on the black market. Most of the men had not changed socks for months. Also, since water was so scarce, and had to be flown in, no one had shaved in a week, despite Sergeant White's admonition that, "Shaving was good for your face." We had begun to look like the wild men we really were.

Three days later our company was still dug in high up on Hill 1018 west of Pleiku. From this position we could overlook Highway 14. We were supposed to support the second brigade, who was in contact with the NVA. Our mission was to be the blocking force for any NVA attempting to return to Cambodia. Because Charlie had blown some big holes in our supply road, no supplies or mail had been able to get through since Friday. I didn't know which was worse - to lose my food or my connection to home.

Then, unexpectedly, we received food, water and mail delivery by chopper. I got a nice package containing several cans of fruit and a new Bowie knife, which was just what I wanted, and which I immediately strapped to my right leg. The knife was perfect. The blade was eighteen inches long, so it was more like a sword. And it had a beautiful ivory handle with brown imprints in it. When the guys saw this they about shit. I now had a man's knife. Hell, I could almost use this as a machete. I let a couple of the guys hold it for a few minutes, but only for a few minutes.

I did not have time to write home, we were to move out of the firebase with my patrol, and I had to eat something first. We were going on a three-day recon looking for those NVA who had been firing mortars on Pleiku.

We carried out the SRP recon, but we didn't find a thing. It was quiet and peaceful, and there were no signs of enemy activity. It was the kind

211

of patrol we always hoped for. We were by ourselves, there were no signs of enemy activity, and there was nobody to mess with us for three whole days.

When we returned, I wandered over to 3rd Platoon's area. Third Platoon always set up next to our location; they were our sister platoon in the company. Not much was going on so I watched Chris Kruckow and Sergeant Woodall throwing a knife at each other's feet. It was a simple game that was popular among the men. The game of Knife worked this way: the players took turns throwing the knife. The object of the game was to see how close the thrower could come to his opponent's feet without actually hitting them. It took guts to stand there and let someone else throw his knife as hard as he could, right at your feet. Only the tough guys played this game.

Chris was pretty good at it, and he used to terrorize the FNGs by challenging them to a game of Knife. Most of them were afraid to say yes, but also afraid to say no. Chris had nerves of steel, and he always let the FNGs have the first throw. He never flinched, no matter what. When it was his turn with the knife, he would throw it real close to the FNG's feet. The pussies would always lose their nerve and jump away, losing the game and revealing their true natures.

But today, Chris had been playing with another tough guy, Sergeant Woodall of 3rd Platoon. Chris threw first. His knife landed several inches from Sergeant Woodall's boot. Woodall, being a good ole boy from Georgia, was not to be outdone. For his turn, he carefully planted his knife an inch from Kruckow's boot.

I stood there, watching this game in awe. I saw Jerry Loucks standing on the other side of the players. With each throw, the knife kept getting closer to someone's foot. I thought, *I've seen this game back home but never played this seriously — these are some crazy fuckers.*

Now Chris, being a country boy from Minnesota, retaliated by throwing his knife so that it stuck in the dirt touching Woodall's jungle boot. Chris looked at Woodall with a grin and said , "I guess I won, Sergeant. Ya can't get any closer than that."

But Sergeant Woodall was not through. He scratched his head, "Hell no, Chris! It's my turn and I may be able to tie you. Us Georgia boys can't let ourselves get beat by a northerner. I don't care if you are a damn country boy."

212

Woodall had to try to tie his opponent. He could do nothing else. But his next throw missed. It sliced squarely through Chris' boot and down through his foot to the board he was standing on. In fact, the knife nailed Chris' foot firmly to the ground.

Chris was caught by surprise. He hollered at Sergeant Woodall, "Ya fucker! Ya ain't supposed to stick it in my boot. I won, ya fucker."

Then he grimaced in pain and stood there, looking at his foot with the knife sticking out of it.

I saw it happen but I couldn't believe it. I'd seen people do dumb things before but this game took the cake. I figured that both these guys would be in deep shit now.

Sergeant Woodall didn't say anything. I looked over at Jerry Loucks; he just shook his head and walked away. But since it was the least he could do, Sergeant Woodall walked over to Chris and pulled his knife out of his foot. Blood squirted out the top of the boot where the knife had gone through. Seeing this, Sergeant Woodall calmly wiped his knife clean and re-sheathed it. Then he suggested to Chris, "Let's go find Frenchy, Chris. Tell him you dropped your knife on your boot; otherwise Hockett will bust us both back to private. We ain't supposed to play games up here."

Both of these good ole boys had stepped over the line and now they had to work their way back.

Chris said, "Well, okay Sergeant. But first - ya gotta admit that I won."

And he just stood there, with his foot bleeding all over his shoe, waiting for Woodall's response.

Woodall thought about it. He was not one to concede easily. But in this instance he was caught in a jam. With a sigh, he relented, "Okay, Chris, dammit. You won, man."

With that both men set out to find Frenchy; Chris was hobbling along and Sergeant Woodall was helping him walk. I didn't follow them over to the medic's hooch, but I heard what happened from Chris later.

When they approached Frenchy's location, they saw him lying back in a very relaxed state, catching a few Z's. Chris hollered, "Wake up, Frenchy. Ya gotta customer."

Frenchy slowly opened his eyes. He took one look at Kruckow and Woodall standing there and started cussing. "Zut! Mon Dieu! Sacrebleu! You fuckers, eh! I was dreaming of a girl now, and she had such big tits."

213

Frenchy used to lecture the men that it was not healthy for a man to be without sex for any length of time. He was always talking and dreaming about getting some.

Chris looks straight at him, saying, "We don't care about your sex problem, Frenchy. I need your help."

"It is terrible. It is not natural. I should not have to suffer like this, eh?

"Frenchy, goddammit! Listen to me!", Chris interrupted.

Frenchy replied, "Okay! What do you want? The doctor, he is in. What is the matter?" and he sat down on a nearby log.

Chris lifted his bloody boot and said to Frenchy, "I got my knife stuck in my boot, accidentally."

Frenchy glanced down at the top of Chris' boot, which was now completely covered in blood, and said. "How in the Hell did you do that?"

Chris responded, "My knife stuck me."

At this point he put a kind of dumb look on his face, trying to appear innocent.

At first, Frenchy didn't say anything. He just watched the blood gushing out of Chris' foot. Then he began to mumble in English, "Fucking hillbillies, fucking country boys, and fucking southerners too, eh? How in the Hell did I get stuck with all three of them? You never even got shot but you were wounded playing a fucking country boy game. Mon Dieu! Zut alors! She had such big tits too."

Then Frenchy pulled himself together and looked at Chris. "Okay, take the boot off, Kruckow."

Chris untied his boot, pulled it off and stuck his foot up in the air for Frenchy to see. Frenchy leaned forward to begin his examination, but as soon as he got a whiff of Chris' foot, which smelled strongly of blood, sweat, dirt and decay, he almost fell backwards from the stench. "Whew-e-u-u!" he exclaimed.

"Mere de Dieu et sacre nom de nom, eh? That stench could kill a horse. Don't you guys ever change socks and wash your feet?" mixing his French and English phrases.

Chris looked at him and said, "Hell no, Frenchy. None of us do. We haven't had any clean socks in the company for months. You ought to know that."

Frenchy scratched his head. "Damn!"

Then Chris leaned over close to Frenchy's face and stared him right in the eye. "Hell, Frenchy, I just got used to the smell."

Chris grinned threateningly, showing his teeth. "You can too."

Frenchy jerked his head back, seriously offended, and said with contempt in his voice, "I don't mind being the medic, Kruckow, that's bad enough, eh? But why do I have to put up with this stench?"

Chris just shrugged, started laughing, and stuck his smelly, bloody foot up into Frenchy's face again.

He replied, "Well, Frenchy, you're the medic. But I ain't hardly had any water to drink for the past two days, let alone enough to wash my feet and socks in."

With a sour grunt, but without another word, Frenchy pulled Chris' sock off. It disintegrated into filthy rags in his hands. He threw the bloody mess away, brought out some alcohol and poured it directly over the knife wound. Chris jumped a little but he didn't say anything. Then Frenchy got some bandages and wrapped Chris's foot carefully.

He looked up at Chris. "You guys were playing that country boy knife-throwing shit again. The next time I catch you at it, I tell Captain Hockett. But this time, this time I let it slide. But I'm not gonna put up with this stench just because you guys want to stick knives in your feet. Next time you doctor yourself; don't bother me. Doctor your own wounds, or I go to Hockett."

Kruckow and Woodall didn't say a word. They just walked off in silence. Neither of them mentioned their knife-throwing contest again except that every now and then, Chris would subtly remind Woodall what a lousy knife-thrower he was. Chris would say, "Woodall, you're just a city boy, not a country boy like me. What can you expect?"

Woodall would be just trying to forget about the whole thing.

On Thursday, right after our patrol returned the company left Hill 1018 and humped into the valley below where we were loaded into Armored Personnel Carriers (APCs) that drove us through the jungle to Firebase Marylou. Mary Lou was a permanent firebase, complete with 105mm howitzers and a mortar company. In fact, as we approached the firebase we could hear the artillery booming away.

APCs were a kind of combination tank and truck. The guys who drove them called them "fighting foxholes." They were made of aluminum lightly armored against attack but were specially designed to haul squads of soldiers around. Once on board, it was like riding in a large metal coffin. We couldn't see where we were going or what was happening outside.

When we reached Firebase Marylou we were able to buy cold Coke and beer. That sure hit the spot. We spent the night at Mary Lou, where we got showers and then, the next day, were loaded onto trucks that were to take us to the Polei Kleng Special Forces Camp.

We had been told that the 1969 Tet Offensive was now in full swing. The NVA were coming! And, to top that, we were going to go looking for them! Sooner or later, the shit would hit the fan.

Chapter 40

Sunday, 24 February 69

Once loaded on the trucks, we were convoyed through Pleiku, where the convoy stopped to pick up a couple of soldiers from C Company. The soldiers climbed into the truck transporting the guys from 3rd Platoon and a few of us from 4th platoon.

I asked, "Where you guys from?" One of them responded, "Hey, man, we jumped off of the C Company convoy an hour earlier to buy some dope and beer and got stuck." There were peddlers alongside the road. Someone said, "So you guys are AWOL." Ken McCormack looked at one of them and asked, "Where have you been? Boonies?" The other one who was a large black guy responded, "Bridge guards, man. What's it to you?"

We soon realized that both of these guys were high, and that they had been drinking, too. They started mouthing off to everyone in the truck. The first one looked up and said, "We're some bad motherfuckers, so don't fuck with us." The other one said, "Hey man, what the fuck are you staring at? We're gonna kick Charlie's ass and yours, too, motherfucker, if you don't stop staring." He looked straight at me when he said that.

Nobody said anything. I looked at Ken McCormack and shook my head. I whispered, "We gotta fight Charlie and put up with this kind of shit at the same time?"

Every guy on the truck tried to ignore them. The last thing anyone wanted was to spend time and energy kicking these guys asses. Of course, we could get a court martial for shooting them.

Both of these guys were fucked up, looking for trouble, and that was all there was to it. The other thing about them was that they were really dumb. I thought, "Since these fuckers are so dumb, how can we reason with them?" Then McCormack looked over at me and stated, "I guess we can overlook that some people are just born ignorant. Sometimes you have to cut them some slack now and again. These guys are asking for too much slack."

One guy stared at Ken McCormack, who had 3rd squad's radio, and yelled, "Where in the fuck we going, Man?"

Ken responded. "Polei Kleng."

Then the other one asked me, "Man, have you done any real fighting?"

I just stared at them and said nothing, and thought, *Wonder why they think they are so bad? I never thought that bridge guarding was all that tough.*

We ignored these assholes, and after a while they shut up again and things quieted down. For the next few miles Jerry Loucks and one of the bridge guards had a silent staring contest. The pot had started to boil - - a silent boil.

About five miles from Polei Kleng the two bridge guards started whispering. Then they loaded their weapons. As we drove past some civilians on the road, one announced, "We're gonna shoot some gooks."

Jerry Loucks put his hand in front of their weapons. "These people ain't the enemy. They're civilians."

It took a while, but Jerry finally convinced them not to shoot anyone. Then things settled down again. Jerry then asked, "I want you guys to remove the rounds from the chambers of your rifles, please." He was polite, but direct.

"You want my weapon unloaded, you'll have to take it from me, motherfucker," One of the guards responded.

"Hey, these guys are looking for a fight," I said to Ken "They don't give a damn who with, either. They want to be tough, but now they are fucking with the wrong guy."

"Unload the fucking rifles," Jerry said.

"Fuck you, motherfucker," the biggest one growled.

As the truck bounced down a dusty road, the other guard swung his weapon. The sight end struck Jerry's face. Blood poured from Jerry's nose. He jumped to his feet, his eyes narrow with rage. I had never seen it before, but Jerry flew into a rage. He went berserk. He was going to kill the both of them. In an instant someone was going to get killed.

Chris Kruckow was sitting beside Jerry. He was a tall, lanky guy and was one of the machine gunners for 3rd platoon. Chris had been listening to these insults without saying a word.

As soon as Jerry jumped them, Chris grabbed one of the guards, jerking him away from Jerry and knocking the rifle from his hands. He lifted the guy off the bed of the truck.

Since Chris had spent his life in the World as a logger in the Minnesota north woods, he was as strong as an ox. And hiding behind his boyish face was a killer instinct.

218

While the convoy bounced down the road, I saw Chris carry the bridge guard the length of the truck. He slammed the guard onto the truck cab, bent him back over the top of the cab, ripping open his shirt.

The soldier was powerless to move. "Get this crazy motherfucker off of me!" he screamed.

While he held the guard down with one arm, with his other hand Chris drew the large hunting knife he kept strapped to his leg. He raised the knife above his head. "I'll teach you to fuck with Jerry," He yelled.

I saw Chris's arm and hand start to move in a downward stoke toward the guy's chest.

"Don't kill him! Don't kill him!" someone yelled.

Sergeant Dave Muck, who had been quietly watching the whole thing from a back corner of the truck, jumped up. He lunged toward Chris. Everyone was yelling and screaming. Just as the knife was about to make its mark, Muck deflected the blade.

Chris and Sergeant Muck locked into a tense arm wrestle, the knife poised in the air menacingly, hovering over the guard's chest. "You're crazy!" Muck hollered. "Stop, Chris, they'll send your ass to jail."

This was one of the few times that Sergeant Muck took the liberty to use cuss words. As they struggled over the knife, the two men stared hard at each other.

Finally, Chris got Muck's message and calmed down. He put his knife away and Sergeant Muck backed off. But then Chris pulled the guard down from the truck cab and beat him to a pulp.

I noticed that Muck had no problem with this. It was the proper punishment for messing with any of the guys in the platoon. Only after Chris had completed his lesson did Muck and Ken McCormack pull Chris away. I guess they figured the guard had had enough.

While this was going on in the front of the truck, Jerry Loucks had disarmed the other guard and had him down on the truck bed, knife at the man's throat. He cut him enough to draw blood. The guard's eyes were wide with terror. His hands were shaking and sweat was rolling off his forehead. Someone yelled, "don't do it, don't do it." Jerry was about to take his head off, but at the last moment he stopped. Jerry then came to his senses and realized that things had gone far enough.

When the truck reached Polei Kleng, Sergeant Muck spoke to Sergeant White, who had been riding in the cab. White looked at everyone's faces, listened to the men's story, and then took the guards off the truck. He led

219

them across the landing strip to their company commander, cursing them all the way.

At first the Company Commander did not want to do anything, but Sergeant White insisted. So he brought Jerry and Chris into his office and chewed their asses out. Then he asked for their side of the story. He had Jerry Loucks fill out an accusation report. The Company Commander filed charges against the guards for inciting a riot and striking a member of the armed forces. Both men were busted; justice had prevailed. We heard the guy that hit Jerry Loucks got thirty days in the Long Binh jail. I thought, "Those guys got off easy." If the other men hadn't been there to control Jerry and Chris, they would have killed them both. Those bridge guards had tangled with the wrong warriors, and they were lucky to have lived through it. They picked the wrong truck to ride in that day.

Chapter 41

We were on constant patrol hunting for the enemy. It was a deadly cat and mouse game. Sometimes they were the mice and sometimes we were. We both understood the game. *Be quick. Don't hesitate, or today may be your last.*

We were involved in another game, too. Chess. We were the pawns of the Brass: the generals, the colonels, and the majors. When they said, "Move my pawn over there," it meant an all-day ass-kicking hump for us grunts. Our lives were at risk, not theirs. Our endurance was being tested, not theirs. Our successes would earn us another day to live. Another day to dig another foxhole.

Wednesday, 26 February

I am out on a 3-day recon mission, looking for the NVA who have been firing mortars on Pleiku. There are five of us and, so far, we have not seen anything.

Thursday, 27 February

The 1st Brigade's overall operating plan for the month of March was code-named *Operation Wayne Grey*. It was developed from intelligence that indicated the enemy, during the winter of 1969, was preparing to carry out a mini-Tet offensive against the major cities of the Central Highlands.

Intelligence indicated that the 66th NVA Regiment and the 24th NVA Regiment, with supporting artillery elements from the 40th NVA Artillery Regiment, and sapper units (which were elite enemy infiltration units) were preparing for attacks against Kontum City, the Polei Kleng Special Forces Camp, and our fire support bases west of Polei Kleng. They also planned to attack civilian locations from Pleiku north to Kontum and Dak To and west from Kontum to Polei Kleng.

In late February captured documents, POW interrogation reports, and aerial reconnaissance of the Polei Kleng area and the firebases lying west of Polei Kleng all pointed to an enemy buildup for offensive operations. The K25 NVA Engineering Battalion was directing the construction of new roads that branched off from the Ho Chi Minh trail and also deep into the mountain range east of the Plei Trap Valley. They had improved many trails and roads from the Cambodian Border. There were signs of vehicular traffic in the northern Plei Trap Valley, as well as east of there, indicating heavy supply activity and the probable use of artillery and tanks in their operations.

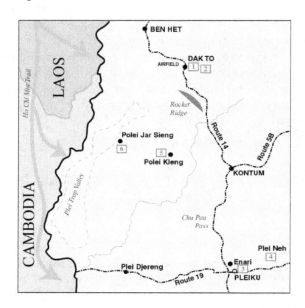

Suspected enemy strengths in our area were estimated to be:

Unit	Strengh
The 66th NVA Regiment	1275
Headquarters & Support Units	550
The 7th Battalion	240
The 8th Battalion	250
The 9th Battalion	235
The 40th NVA Regiment	unknown
The K25 Engineering Battalion	250
The H67 Dispensary (NVA hospital)	unknown

For us in the A-1-8, this news meant that we would have to move to the Polei Kleng Special Forces camp. We would have to assault the Plei Trap Valley.

The mission of the 1st Brigade was to conduct offensive operations in the Plei Trap Valley area in order to destroy enemy forces, prevent their reinforcement and re-supply, and also prevent their withdrawal into Cambodia.

The concept of this operation was organized into two phases.

In Phase I, the 1st Brigade, numbering about thirty-five hundred men, was to conduct offensive operations with its four associated battalions: 1-8th Infantry (which included my company), 3-8th Infantry, 3-12th Infantry, and its direct support artillery battalion (called the 6-29th Artillery). Initially, these battalions were to conduct air combat assaults into previously-held firebases on the eastern Plei Trap to establish adequate artillery fire support positions. With artillery support established, rifle companies were to assault the western Plei Trap area by air behind main enemy forces and along the enemy infiltration routes. Upon landing, the companies were to move eastward into the base areas and disrupt known enemy lines of communication. Maximum use of artillery and air strikes, to interdict enemy movement, was to be used. Once our patrols located any enemy force, all available firepower was to be brought to bear upon them.

In Phase II of the operation, the 1st Brigade, to prevent enemy withdrawal, was to continue its offensive action by establishing company-sized blocking positions astride known access routes. Ambushes and short-range patrols would be placed along enemy routes of withdrawal. Artillery fire programs and chemical drops would be used to cover routes of egress not under direct observation by our ground troops.

Enemy troop concentrations would be struck from the air by B-52 bombers. Air cavalry would be available to screen the western operation area and to detect and interdict enemy movement into or out of the area. Artillery would be used, with a maximum force on all suspected and confirmed enemy locations. Air strikes would be employed to destroy all enemy bunker complexes; saturation bombing was to be used on any concentration of enemy troops. Once resistance was broken, U.S. infantry would sweep through the area in a clean-up operation.

The 1st Brigade received orders to deploy to Polei Kleng, where we would stage an assault into the northern Plei Trap area. Reliable

223

intelligence indicated that two regiments—the 24th NVA and the 66th NVA—were preparing for an attack on Polei Kleng and Kontum. The Brigade mission was to prevent the withdrawal of these regiments back into Cambodia and to cut their lines of communication with the Ho Chi Minh Trail.

All battalions were to be marshaled for deployment to the Plei Trap. The 1-8th Infantry and 3-8th Infantry were convoyed to Polei Kleng. We were trying to trap the enemy before they could return to Cambodia. The operating assumption was that if we caught them on the move or in temporary locations after they attempted a mini-Tet offensive against the major cities of the Central Highlands, we could wipe them out.

This was the essence of Operation Wayne Grey, the brigade operation that put us in the Plei Trap Valley. We were told the reason we were going into the Plei Trap was to catch the tired and beat-up NVA leaving the area after staging their Tet offensive. We were also assigned to hit their replacements as they arrived from Cambodia before they had a chance to join their units.

This was a good strategy in theory. The facts were that, when we count the number of grunts who were fighting on both sides, the NVA grunts outnumbered the American grunts by between seven and ten to one. We had air power and artillery on our side, which was powerful when we could use it, but when we were out in the bush, thrashing around in that triple canopy jungle, engaged in one-on-one firefights with the enemy, air power was useless. In the bush operating on the ground as a separate company unit, alone against the NVA, we were vastly outnumbered.

Friday, 28 February
Operating in the Plei Trap Valley was tough going. We had to penetrate deep into enemy territory and operate in an area in which it was very difficult to maneuver. Throughout the Plei Trap Valley the terrain consisted of steep slopes, deep valleys, and triple-layered jungle canopy, with trees growing one hundred fifty feet high in many areas. This dense jungle greatly reduced observation from either the air or the ground, which almost completely prevented our customary surveillance of the enemy's movements. The local jungle density restricted the effective use of rifles and machine guns in the type of defensive perimeters we usually set up, except at very close range, requiring extensive clearing of the brush to create firing lanes.

224

On the other hand, the steep hills, deep ravines, and dense vegetation provided us with good protective cover throughout the area, except along the Plei Trap Valley floor, which had relatively flat terrain. In these areas, the cover was only fair.

Throughout the Plei Trap Valley the jungle and the broken terrain provided excellent concealment for the enemy. Enemy bunkers and trails were completely hidden from us until we stepped on them. Sometimes these bunkers and trails would be found later, after artillery, air strikes, or chemical defoliation had destroyed the jungle canopy.

Charlie Company C-1-8 captured a Russian-made truck filled with 105mm howitzer rounds on the Ho Chi Minh Trail. The NVA truck crew had stopped for lunch only a few yards from where a Charlie Company platoon had set up. A short ambush dispatched the NVA and a "Flying Crane" was called in to lift the truck and its load out of the jungle.

The jungle and the steep slopes were severe obstacles to our vehicular traffic. In the steepest areas, even movement by foot was tough. And their steep banks made most streams difficult to cross unless extensive preparatory work was done to build a fording site.

The enemy traveled by foot through the valley areas and crossed the mountains through any saddles or passes they found. In other words, they stayed in the lowlands. Enemy trails extended from the Cambodian border at the northern end of the Plei Trap Valley out along the valley floor and then south to Firebase 20. In the Plei Trap Valley, the Ho Chi Minh Trail was never more than fifty or one hundred kilometers from our company.

During the month of March 1969 we expected the weather to be clear, which would permit the use of helicopters and jets, except where the terrain was covered by ground haze. The question on everyone's mind was how effective we could possibly be on an enemy hidden under dense foliage. The answer: probably not very effective.

The bottom line for my platoon and my squad, was that we would be humping in this rugged terrain without our customary air support. We would face a well-equipped enemy in their own backyard. At the time, I sensed that events were escalating and leading us into vastly increased danger but, of course, I couldn't forecast just how difficult or treacherous our mission would really be. Only the Brass knew the big picture.

On 1 March, elements of the 1ˢᵗ Brigade combat assaulted to the west of the 66th Regiment to effect a vertical envelopment and cut the enemy's lines of communication. Heavy fighting erupted. One of our battalions drove an NVA engineer unit off its primary landing zone, killing 30 while losing only one man.

Unable to attack Polei Kleng because of the division's blocking forces to its front and discovering that US forces had been airlifted behind it, the 66th Regiment shifted southward to attack Plei Mrong, only to find the 1ˢᵗ Battalion, 35th Infantry, poised to its front along the avenues of approach. To escape envelopment and cover withdrawal, the regiment turned to a series of harassing attacks. What was left of the 40th Artillery shelled US bases from Ben Het to Polei Kleng.

Chapter 42

Saturday, 1 March

Our entire company was now located at Polei Kleng, a Special Forces camp about fifty miles west of Kontum. At Polei Kleng we dug our foxholes beside the airfield into hard, clay-like soil. Without any overheads for protection, we waited for our turn to be flown into the Plei Trap Valley.

Greg Rollinger digging in hard ground

The air was filled with the smell of fuel and the sounds of planes and choppers steadily coming and going. A dry, choking dust fell on everything and everybody. When I closed my mouth, I bit down on grit.

The camp had a good landing strip with a PSP runway. PSP was pierced steel planking which, when interlocked and laid over the dirt, would support heavy cargo planes . . . an instant runway.

From my foxhole I had a good view of the field's activity. I watched helicopters line up on the far side of the metal grid. They stretched as far as I could see. Many of them were powerful Cobra gunships, sleek, three-foot wide airships with mini-guns in the nose and rocket launchers down each side.

S

Greg Rollinger with Cobra

A Cobra could hit two hundred miles an hour in a dive and lay down a blistering fire over an entire football field-sized area in seconds. Only the best flight officers got to fly the Cobras; among chopper pilots, flying them was an honor.

Huey helicopters lined up behind the Cobras. The so-called Slicks were mainly used as troop transports, but many of those were armed with mini-guns and most also had M60 machine guns mounted on each side manned by gunners from inside the cargo holds. The Hueys were used to ferry troops into and out of an LZ quickly, and to provide fire support for deplaning troops when necessary. If we were taken into LZs that were under fire, we couldn't hear if the enemy was shooting at us or not because of the helicopter's noise.

Some Hueys were used as Medevacs (medical evacuation helicopters) or Dustoffs, and had a large Red Cross symbol. They were used to fly wounded men from areas of fighting to intermediate aid stations. They were, essentially, flying ambulances.

Except for the infantryman's job, the Medevac pilot's job was the most dangerous in Vietnam. Many times Medevacs landed in the middle of firefights to extract the wounded. The NVA soldiers had no respect for the Red Cross symbol painted on a Medevac and would try to shoot these choppers down whenever they had the chance.

The Chinook CH-47 was a large, twin-rotor workhorse helicopter that could lift almost anything into or out of the forest, including troops, artillery and APC's. From my foxhole, I could see a couple of them at the far end of the landing field. The Giant was also used to extract damaged helicopters out of the jungle after a firefight and take them in for repair. When a Jolly Green Giant went down, a special Sky Crane chopper could lift the Giant and ferry it back to base for repairs. The Army tried to cover every possibility.

The Plei Trap Valley was located at the end of the Plei Trap Road. The road went to and ran through the entire length of the valley so it was one of the main arteries for NVA infiltrators coming down the Ho Chi Minh Trail through Laos and Cambodia. The NVA used this road to deploy troops for attacks against such population centers as Kontum, Pleiku, and Dak To. They also used the mountainous terrain and jungle canopy cover to move troops and supplies east or south undetected toward the low-lying coastal areas.

The Plei Trap Road varied from three to five meters wide, and every low spot and stream crossing had a bridge or culvert built over it. Side-hill cuts were recessed to keep them from crumbling, and steep shoulders were marked with sturdy wooden stakes. About every fifty-five meters along the road protected bunkers sheltered three or four men each. This sophisticated road had taken untold man-hours by the NVA to construct and even more to maintain. Almost all of the work was done during the night.

This remote area, the Plei Trap Valley, in the Central Highlands, where we would soon be headed, had a long wartime history. In both 1967 and 1968 major battles had taken place in the area. It was well-known that the enemy moved a large amount of war material down this road on foot and by truck.

Now my company was waiting to fly deep into this NVA territory.

In addition to all the enemy activity in the Plei Trap Valley, we were informed that the NVA had recently captured Dak To, which was supposed to be defended by the South Vietnamese army. Word came down that we might have to straighten out what the South Vietnamese had messed up. It was obvious to us that the ARVNs would never be able to defend their country by themselves.

Once we were airborne out of Polei Kleng, the 3rd Platoon was the first to touch down in the combat area. The landing zone, called LZ Turkey, had been blasted out of the top of a hill by artillery and the surrounding brush had caught fire. Since it was 2nd Squad of the 3rd Platoon's turn to take point, they went in on the first bird. Greg Rollinger, Harold Proctor, and Sergeant White were part of that squad. They had been warned that the LZ was *hot*, meaning that the enemy might be waiting for them.

Greg Rollinger and Harold Proctor

Flying into a hot landing zone was exceedingly dangerous. Even if you arrived on a chopper after the LZ had been secured you were not safe. Charlie would often allow the first few choppers to arrive unmolested, then unleash furious fire on the next ones. If this happened, only part of the unit would be on the ground and it would be difficult or impossible for additional troops to land due to the heavy small arms and rocket fire.

No one knew what to expect at LZ Turkey so we expected the worst. When the first chopper arrived, the pilot had to hover over a small opening in the jungle and slowly lower the helicopter between the trees. He couldn't maneuver due to the intensity of the brush fire burning at the perimeter of the clearing and, while trying to avoid that, he took a

232

blade strike on a tree. The pilot immediately lifted the bird back up to treetop level and announced that, due to the damaged blade, he might have to return to Polei Kleng.

Sergeant White shouted at the pilot. "Can we make it back to Polei Kleng?"

"There's a fifty-fifty chance. What do you want to do?" the pilot shouted back over the whump-whump of the blades.

"What's the turn-around time, if we get another bird?"

"About forty minutes."

Sergeant White thought for a minute. "Let's go ahead and jump," he shouted, and he gave the jump signal to the others in his squad. The pilot dropped back down into the clearing, until they were about ten or fifteen feet off the ground.

Loaded Chopper into LZ

Greg Rollinger sat on the edge of the chopper door with his feet hanging over the side, the big M-60 cradled in his arms and a full rucksack on his back. The door gunner tapped him on the shoulder and gave him the jump sign. Greg looked down at the ground, then back to the door gunner, and shook his head firmly. He couldn't possibly jump such a distance with his equipment. The door gunner spoke into his mike to the pilot and then ordered Greg to jump again. Greg jumped without tossing his rucksack first. He hit the ground hard and rolled. With all the weight he carried, he could have easily broken his legs. It's a good thing that the LZ wasn't hot, Greg would not have had time to recover. Despite its damaged blade, the chopper was able to hover until everyone had safely jumped off.

The men on the ground had been told to put out the brush fire and enlarge the LZ so that the rest of the platoon and the company could land. Rollinger and Proctor's mission was to secure the LZ and give cover to the firefighters.

The hilltop was thick with smoke from the burning wood. Sergeant White positioned Rollinger and Proctor on one side of the hill and showed them their field of fire— it happened to be the entire side of the hill! Since Rollinger and Proctor had only one M-60 for the squad's

234

protection they were the only ones on guard, the rest were fighting the brush fire. To have more protection, they had to put out the fire so more men could land. Even if we had arrived, we could not land because the LZ was too small and on fire.

Meanwhile, in an air assault mission north of our location in the A Shau Valley, the 1st Air Cavalry had lost a number of helicopters. The 4th Division commanders loaned the Air Cav most of the 4th Division's choppers. Our battalion had very little in reserve to carry out our air assault, and there were no gunships available to support us.

White's radio operator for this mission was new to Vietnam that very day. After they had jumped from the chopper and run for cover on the LZ, he started to cry like a baby. White stared at him in disbelief. "Dry up!" He yelled. "In war, when you cry, you cry alone." While White was not two inches from the soldiers face staring him in the eye, the soldier calmed down. That's all it took, after that the soldier was ok.

While Rollinger and Proctor kept everyone covered, the other men cut trees frantically. A few hours later, the landing zone had been cleared; the other birds were radioed to come in. With that, we were introduced to the Plei Trap Valley.

Sunday, 2 March 69

It was late in the afternoon, just after six o'clock. During the afternoon there had been a light drizzle, there was dampness all around us. My platoon packed up slowly getting ready to move out on patrol. Our mission was to patrol for about six miles along a river close to where our company set up. It was getting dark with a chill in the air. We moved out as quietly as we could, but since there were about twenty of us, it was damned near impossible to do. I heard someone complain, "fuck, it's gonna be dark I won't see a goddamned thing."

I could barely read my compass, if I held it right up to my face. I had to rely on my internal sense of direction as we moved through the underbrush. All we could see was each other's silhouette as we moved slowly beside the river.

After we had been walking for a half-hour, the soldier beside me disappeared. I think he strayed to the right a little maybe to take a leak. I finally saw him moving to my right, his body made a silhouette against the jungle mist. All of a sudden three shots rang out, a deafening crack,

crack, crack of an M16. I heard the guy to my right cry out, "It's me, stop shooting!" I yelled "cease fire, cease fire!" Instantly, I knew what had happened. One of our men thought he was NVA and shot him. We scrambled to the soldier as fast as we could and found out it was Sergeant Machado, he was ok but was shaking all over. With luck the three bullets hit his canteen with a repeated WHANG! Shrapnel wounded him in the ass. I heard some commotion toward my rear and saw three members of my squad holding another soldier down on the wet ground. It was the soldier who shot Machado, he had gone into a fit once he learned what he did. Several men had to control him to keep him quiet since we were in the middle of NVA territory. It took 15 minutes to calm him down.

With the dense jungle and the darkness, the entire platoon had to return to our company's location and wait until daylight before we could call in a Dustoff to airlift Machado to the rear. Sergeant Machado remained cool. He knew that he had bought a ticket back to the World. When the Dustoff arrived, Machado held up his riddled canteen for all of us to see. "My lucky canteen!" he said, grinning. When his chopper finally pulled away, he popped a smoke grenade and it left the traditional trail of smoke. He would not be back. The soldier that shot his canteen took a great sigh of relief. Most of us were envious, Machado had his ticket home.

My platoon was ordered to conduct a sweep of the area directly across the Dak Hondrai River from our base camp again. Since NVA had opened up on the company the day before with machine guns, Captain Hockett wanted our platoon, twenty of us, all three squads, to conduct a sweep. We were ordered to leave before we had finished digging our foxholes.

It was a hot day. We were exhausted from yesterday's sweep and the Machado incident. Ronald Westbrook and Rick Campbell were walking point. My squad was leading the platoon, and Rick was leading my squad. For some reason Rick was carrying an M-16 that day, instead of his M-60, which he had left back in the perimeter. Within a few minutes of starting to sweep, we discovered a wide path which had been recently graded and used by the NVA to move supplies during the night. Then, as we walked over the crest of a small rise we came under fire.

I don't remember who fired first; it seemed as though Ron, Rick, and the NVA saw each other at the same moment and opened up simultaneously. I heard the shots and immediately joined in the battle. The NVA were so well hidden I couldn't tell how many of them were firing. We were receiving intense automatic weapons and grenade fire on our position. I hit the ground seeking cover but there was none, just grass and weeds.

Rick Campbell worked his way over to the right of the enemy position and laid down heavy fire with his M-16. In his initial bursts he killed one NVA. This gave us a chance to seek better cover. Since we were caught between the enemy location and the river, we could not maneuver.

My squad was pinned down in crossfire between two enemy positions. We were receiving intense fire from our right flank and from our left front. The enemy was really close—maybe only thirty meters.

Crouching, I moved closer to Don Cheek, who was shooting his M-79. As I moved closer I got a better picture of the enemy's location where I was in position to direct my squad and provide needed flank security. Bullets were zinging past my head as I came closer. I started to return fire on the enemy directly to our front. All of a sudden, Don yelled, "I'm hit!" He was lying in the path, right beside me. I could see he was hit in the arm. I scanned his wound and unbelievably saw that bullets had gone through both of his forearms. I yelled for a medic. The enemy machine

237

gun fire continued while I was trying the best I could to help Cheek. Don remained relatively calm.

Sam Selden was lying in the weeds beside us at the time, and he and I used our bodies to shield Don from the enemy's fire while the medic worked his way forward. Sam hastily wrapped Don's arms with his torn shirt to stop the bleeding. I noticed that the same bullet that penetrated his arms had ripped his shirt, but it had not hit his torso. I kept firing at the enemy while Sam worked on Don's arms. Once these makeshift bandages were in place, we turned our attention back toward the enemy. No one of us said anything even though the bullets were landing just a few feet ahead of us. We just focused on the battle.

Once I knew that Cheek was ok, I grabbed his M-79 grenade launcher, rose up and fired it at the enemy. *Poom!* I had never used a bloop gun in combat before and was surprised when the shell hit a tree branch high overhead and burst with a loud noise. Shrapnel rained all over us and the enemy. Harmlessly, thank God. For a moment, the burst scared everyone. I decided not to try the launcher a second time!

I grabbed back my M-16 and joined Sam and the other men in laying down heavy fire on the enemy. Socks, Roman Rostinoff, ran up the road in an erratic, dodging motion, while under fire, to reach Don Cheek and carried him back out of harm's way. Sam and I kept focused to the front while Socks was able to evacuate Cheek to the safety of a fallen tree to our rear. The enemy maintained crossfire on us. Socks, a FNG had become the gutsy soldier in just a few short weeks. Without hesitation, and while under fire, he had helped to rescue Cheek.

Then Ed Weaver, the 4th Platoon medic, treated him. Weaver gave him morphine which sent Cheek to La La land until he could be evacuated to a field hospital. All Cheek wanted to do was eat a can of fruit cocktail he was carrying in his ruck and so he did, right there in the middle of a firefight. Ed who was there beside him was a conscientious objector and never carried a weapon in the Nam. He was the replacement for Doc Driver, who had finished his tour and rotated back to the World.

Weaver and Socks carried Cheek to where John Gray and Lieutenant LePeilbet were located. John was the first to tell him the good news that came after the bad news. "This wound is your ticket home, Cheek."

While Cheek's medical evacuation was taking place, I kept firing at the enemy. Gradually I worked my way closer to their location to allow my squad members to improve their positions. Flea and Pappy had worked their way forward by this time, and had joined Rick, Ron, Sam and me in the fight. Pappy yelled, "Damn, Flea, looks like we finally found 'em! Let's kick some ass!"

"Yuh gotta do!" the Flea hollered back as he blazed away at the enemy.

A few minutes later, in the middle of the firefight, with everyone shooting as fast as they could, Pappy's M-16 had jammed! The Flea gave Pappy hell for not cleaning his gun!

"Dammit, Pappy, I told yuh to clean that rifle yesterday! These things jam up fast. Have I gotta watch yuh every minute?"

Within seconds, Flea's rifle had jammed, too.

To get us out of this predicament, Lieutenant LePeilbet worked his way up to our position. After surveying the scene, he crawled toward the enemy and silenced the machine gun with a grenade. This allowed our platoon to organize a flanking movement that resulted in breaking the crossfire and routing the enemy.

About this same time, a Light Observation Helicopter ("Loach") chopper came to our rescue. The pilot buzzed in close and hovered over the trees right in front of the enemy. A machine-gunner, hanging out the door, fired his M60 machine gun on the NVA. He was so close to us I could have thrown a rock and hit him. While that gunner was firing at the enemy, the impact of the bullets sprayed the ground close to us.

Once the Loach had made a few passes the enemy positions were silenced. The chopper flew toward our perimeter, but stopped and hovered over the middle of the river, spewing water everywhere. Don Cheek ran splashing out to meet it. Since he couldn't use his arms, he found he couldn't climb aboard. After a few minutes of frustration, he was pulled into the chopper by the gunner. He was flown to the hospital at Camp Enari and never returned to the field. He had his ticket back to the World.

The 3rd Platoon heard all the commotion while my platoon had been conducting its sweep across the river. They had been taking a bath in the river. As usual, they had split their platoon and were bathing in two shifts so that each group had a heavy guard on the bank. When they heard all the shooting, the soldiers in the river moved quickly. They scrambled up onto the bank and into their clothes in record time.

Finally, as my platoon withdrew from the battle scene and returned across the river to its perimeter, we called in air strikes on the NVA. Soon, Air Force jets laid napalm along the path, where the enemy had

239

ambushed us. Napalm was a form of thickened gasoline like jelly; it stuck to everything it touched and caused an intense fire.

Greg Rollinger sat atop a bunker dug into a riverbank and watched the napalm canisters tumble as they fell. They seemed to move through the air in slow motion. For one panicky moment he thought they were going to land on the wrong side of the river. But when the canisters finally hit, they were right on target. Rollie saw a huge explosion and fireball. Then he felt the terrific heat and smelled the strong odor of burning gasoline.

A few hours later, after the fire had died out, Sergeant White led 3rd Platoon back across the river to make an assessment of the bombing and to take a body count. Frank Novotny, squad leader in the 3rd Platoon, walked on line by the creek, with Jerry Loucks in front of him. Sergeant Muck covered the right flank with Henry Scarver, rifleman, on the left. The rest of the platoon followed behind. When they reached the graded path, the platoon moved cautiously. The dirt was still warm from the napalming. When they came to the crest in the hill, they spotted two dead NVA. Each NVA carried a brand new AK-47 rifle, identifiable from its telltale collapsible metal stock. The NVA were still smoking from the blast of the napalm.

The platoon searched the area and found more dead NVA in bunkers. They had been burned to a crisp from the heat of the napalm. Their dark brown skin looked thick, like leather. Some of them were lying naked next to their weapons; their clothes and body hair had been entirely burned off. One soldier was lying on his back with an AK-47 in his right hand. The skin on his face looked drawn up, like beef jerky. His teeth peeked out through his lips, which were frozen into an evil grimace. For some reason these men hadn't been totally cremated. Maybe others had been and nothing remained but ashes. The platoon dubbed these NVA the "crispy critters." For the first time the men saw firsthand the impact of Napalm bombs on the enemy.

The next day, 3rd Platoon swept through the same area without resistance.

Chapter 43

Wednesday, 4 March 69

We had been in the Plei Trap Valley for four days and had made contact with the enemy every day. My company left its location by the Dak Hondrai River and humped up a hill for the night. The 2nd Squad from 3rd Platoon stayed below, on ambush, to cover our move. They set up out of sight, back in the brush. As a safeguard, they had placed claymore mines in front of them. From their concealed position, they could scan a clearing which was backed by a hedgerow.

Snook (George Sams) was on watch at dawn when an NVA came walking through the hedgerow toward him. As soon as Snook saw him, he automatically lowered his head. He waited, alert, silent, and scared, to see what the NVA would do. The enemy was very cautious and moved slowly. Snook was patient; he just waited and watched. The first NVA was soon followed by a second and then a third. Each of them stepped slowly through the hedge. Snook had the clacker for a claymore in his hand. He waited for the right moment. Suddenly the first NVA stopped and peered directly at Snook. At that moment, The Flea's favorite phrase popped into his mind, *Yuh gotta do what yuh gotta do.*

Snook squeezed the clacker and blew the claymore.

Sergeant White heard the explosion up on the hill and came running from his hooch. He awakened the rest of the guys in 3rd Platoon and told them to saddle up, they were going up the hill to help 3rd squad.

Meanwhile, Snook laid there in anticipation not knowing how many NVA were on the trail. He knew he had killed the first two and, in the pre-dawn light, he thought the third had gone through the hedgerow. The third soldier must have been wounded.

Finally, Sergeant White and the rest of the 3rd Platoon arrived at Snook's position. White and Snook examined the two dead NVA. White reconned the area and decided to lead the men through the hedgerow. The field before them was empty. Using a quiet voice and hand gestures, Sergeant White ordered the men into a formation to make a frontal assault. In this formation, each man in a parallel line started across the next clearing. They moved slowly towards the next hedgerow, their rifles ready to fire. Without warning, the wounded NVA rose out of the bushes with his hands in the air. The instant he appeared, every man fired. White yelled, "Dammit! Cease fire! Dammit! Cease fire!"

Miraculously, the NVA soldier was still alive. Several men made a quick litter out of a couple of sticks and a poncho. Almost as soon as it was called in, a Huey landed in the clearing and the men loaded the wounded NVA into its cargo hold. One of the men hopped on the chopper and flew back to Polei Kleng as the wounded NVA's guard.

Later in the day, Sergeant White informed the men that the captured NVA had died.

It was common, in a war to take souvenirs from the enemy dead. Snook, by tradition, had his pick from the two dead NVA soldiers. He saw a canned ham that one of the NVA had been carrying. He grabbed it thinking that he scored a big prize. He stuffed the ham into his rucksack so that the other men wouldn't see it.

For a couple of days afterward Snook humped the jungle with that ham in his rucksack. He dreamed about it constantly. He treated it as though it was his greatest treasure. Eventually he told every guy in the platoon about it—how much he loved to eat ham, how he had once considered being a hog farmer, how easy it was to raise hogs, and on and on.

After a while, Snook had every guy in his squad salivating over that ham, even though he had made it clear that he was going to eat all of it himself. He was saving it for a special place and time. He wanted to sit down and enjoy the ham on his own quietly, without being rushed by the unpredictable pressures of war in the bush.

Finally Snook decided conditions were right. His squad was between missions. For the moment, there was no pressure. He found a nice spot under a tree and laid out his poncho in preparation for a feast. He took out the canned ham and, using his knife, started to pry the container open, but no matter how hard he tried, he could not get it to open.

Pretty soon, Snook was cursing in frustration. For several days he had been dreaming of this feast, and now that the moment had arrived he couldn't get the damn package open. He was fit to be tied.

He turned the ham container over to study it closer and, to his amazement, noticed a red dot on the back of it. Snook was stunned. He couldn't speak. For the past forty-eight hours he realized that he had been humping around with a two-pound NVA land mine in his rucksack!

242

A mine that was large enough to blow him all the way to hell . . . and 3rd Platoon with him.

While our company was set up in the Plei Trap Valley, several changes in command were announced. Sergeant Grinstead returned to the World and Sergeant White took his place as 3rd Platoon Leader and Sergeant, reporting directly to Captain Hockett. Sergeant Lestock was to returned to the World in a few days, and I was to replace him as Platoon Sergeant of the 4th Platoon, reporting directly to Lieutenant LePeilbet. I had been in country just 75 days and now I was Platoon Sergeant.

Sergeant Lestock's had done a good job. I was glad for what I had learned from him. I would have responsibility for three squads and three of the men I had led were now the squad leaders of my platoon - Pappy, Sam Sheldon, and Ron Stone. It gave me confidence knowing how capable they were.

Since we had arrived in the Plei Trap we had received very little re-supply. There were times we had to patrol all day with little food. Captain Hockett had just explained to us that all of the battalion's resupply helicopters had been shut down.

Wednesday, 5 March 69

Ken McCormack was not on the ambush with 3rd Squad when Snook blew the claymore on the NVA. Instead, he was with the rest of 3rd Platoon, led by Sergeant White, who charged down the hill to reinforce 3rd Squad after the ambush occurred.

After the smoke cleared, he saw two dead NVA lying there that were killed in the ambush. The men were edgy; they all were pumped up with adrenaline. More NVA could show at any time and every man knew it. No one wanted to stay at this location and the sun was coming up. They felt vulnerable to attack.

Sergeant White ordered the platoon to form a defensive perimeter - all except for Ken McCormack and Chris Kruckow. He gave these guys different orders.

White knew it had to be done. He knew it when he first saw the dead NVA lying there; he knew something had to be done. It was not right to leave dead men like this. Sergeant White thought, *After all, we are*

243

Christians and every man deserves a burial. So he decided then and there, *I'm gonna have them buried; they're warriors just like my men. It's the right thing to do.*

Unfortunately, when he looked up, Ken and Chris were the first two guys he saw. Chris and Ken violated one of the rules learned from Basic Training – stay invisible. White looked directly at them, "Okay, Chris, and you too Ken. You guys are elected. Bury these men after you strip and search them."

The standing orders from 4th Division were to follow the four 'S's (Secure- Seize- Search- Strip). It had to be done but this was the first time that either Ken or Chris had carried out that fourth 'S' - to strip and bury someone.

When Sergeant White first ordered them to burial detail, the gravity of the task had not sunk in. Yeah, someone had to do it and yeah, it happened to be them, but they were numb at that point, feeling no emotion, not knowing what this was, and on an adrenaline high besides. They did not comprehend the job that they had been ordered to carry out.

So Chris and Ken ran back up the hill grabbed some shovels and returned to Sergeant White's location. They started to dig the holes. The first part of the job was not too bad. They had been digging holes since they had arrived in Vietnam. By now it was automatic. At first they were just scooping the rich, hard, red dirt up into a pile, but the more they dug, the more they thought about what they were doing.

Ken was thinking, *Hell, I'm digging a grave. Damn, I'm digging a grave for someone who tried to kill me. Why? I'm supposed to shoot them, not bury them.* He started bitching about it to Chris "This is not my job."

He kept on shoveling. But then in a minute he added, "Why do I have to do this? I didn't kill these guys."

Chris was disgusted with this assignment too, but for a different reason. He told Ken, "Damn. I don't like to be around dead bodies of any kind. Now I have to bury one. It ain't right. I did not come to the Nam for this."

"Shit, they don't pay me enough to be on a fuckin' burial detail," Ken complained as he shoveled.

Sergeant White was standing close by. He walked over. "You guys keep quiet or you'll bring the NVA down on your necks. Then I'll have to dig a hole for you."

He made his point.

For some reason, Army style I guess, the burials had to be completed in a hurry. This made both Ken and Chris grumpier still. Ken suddenly whispered, "The fucking army didn't train us to do this."

And Chris added in a low voice, "I'm a machine gunner. They pay me to kill 'em, not bury 'em."

With Sergeant White watching them out of the corner of his eye in the background, they dug as fast as they could, but they continued quietly bitching all the way. The ground was hard and soon, even though the air was chilly, both guys were sweating.

"Enemy or no enemy, we shouldn't have to sweat this much so early in the morning," Ken argued.

Sweat drops were rolling off his forehead. The more they dug, the more pissed off both men got.

Finally they had a dirt pile and a hole, and were ready to bury the first guy. The next step was to strip the two dead NVA. They had to take all their clothes off down to the underwear and send the clothes and possessions to the rear for examination by Army Intelligence. This was standard operating procedure but both Ken and Chris thought the clothes would be of little value. Nevertheless, they went along with the program. Ken looked at Chris and said, "You take this one and I'll take the other."

At that point both Ken and Chris got down on their knees next to the two dead NVA and proceeded to undress them and throw the bloody clothes in a pile next to the graves.

As Ken undressed one of them, he noticed that the NVA had a picture of his family in the pocket of his khakis. Ken spent a moment looking at the picture, and as he did, he wondered what that family would feel when their husband or father did not come home from the war. It was a disturbing thought. But Ken soon snapped out of it; he realized where he was — in the middle of an NVA-infested jungle. In this war, life and death were so closely connected that there was no time to consider the consequences; one's survival was always at stake. Ken threw the picture in the pile of clothes and proceeded to undress the NVA.

In the final step, Ken had to unbutton the NVA's pants and pull them off, leaving the NVA completely naked except for his underwear. By that time both Ken and Chris were sweating profusely. Pulling a dead man's pants off was no easy matter. They both finished this task about the same time, and then they stopped and stared at what they had done. Chris

245

muttered a few words like, "I can't fucking believe we are doing this" as he shook his head in disgust.

Next they had to lift the body into the hole. First of all, the guy was dead; therefore lifting him by his arms and legs was extremely difficult. As he started to lift, Chris wondered, *why is it that dead people are so heavy?*

As Ken grabbed the arms, he said, "I guess this is what they mean by dead weight."

Chris was holding the legs. They lifted up but the dead NVA kind of slumped in the middle, so they half dragged and half carried him into the hole. Once he was in, Chris looked at Ken, and both of them said it at the very same instant: "Fuck!"

The hole was too shallow. Of course, while all this was going on, both men were expecting to be hit by the NVA at any minute. It was nerve-wracking to say the least. By now, both of them had had about all they could take of this burial thing. They didn't want to screw around with this detail very much longer. So they both stood there, staring at the NVA lying in the hole. Chris poked the guy with his boot and whispered, "Let's force him in. Hell, I ain't digging it any bigger."

They got down on their hands and knees and started pushing and tugging to get the guy to fit into the hole. They pushed and shoved and bent and squished the body with their hands to make the body fit.

Finally they stood back to admire their work. Chris was ready to be done. "Okay. That's that."

Ken looked around. Sergeant White was nowhere in sight. "Good enough," he agreed.

The guy was in the hole. Now they hurriedly covered him with dirt.

Once he was covered, they stopped to rest. Ken said, "Wish I could have a smoke."

And that's when Chris said, "What the fuck!" and pointed at the grave.

Now Ken saw it too. He saw it but he couldn't believe it. The NVA's toes were sticking out of the ground! Ken closed his eyes for a moment, hoping that this was just one bad dream. He wondered what kind of madness had brought him to this point in his life. He felt angry, and felt sick inside. But, hey, orders were orders. Ken said, "Fucking army, fucking war, why me? God, how will I ever tell anybody about this? I can't believe I'm doing this! We are fucking animals."

Chris looked at Ken with his innocent Minnesota face and mumbled, "Well, I guess we should have dug it deeper, huh, Ken? We gotta fix it."

While they were debating what to do to get the toes covered, Chris rummaged around in the brush and found a couple of big rocks, which he placed on top of the guy's toes. He and Ken looked at each other, smiled, considered the job done, and moved on to the next NVA.

Afterward, as Ken walked up the trail to join the rest of the platoon, the impressions he had of these dead men would forever be burnt into his memory. Except for the crispy critters this was the first time he had ever seen a dead guy up close and personal. He thought about those coal black eyes that did not look away nor blink. He thought about the straight, black, coarse hair on those dead NVA's heads.

This was very sobering. Ken realized that, although he had bitched about having to dig those holes, in the back of his mind was the realization that this war was becoming all too real. People were really dying. And with a little less luck on his side, he could have been the dead guy that morning.

Thursday, 6 March

In my last letter I said I was going into the Plei Trap Valley, which is turning out to be a very bad place. Well, while I am here you won't get many letters from me because I will not have the time. I have been in about 10 firefights since I got here and our company has killed about 15 NVA. Only two guys have gotten wounded out of our platoon and only four in the whole company. One of the guys that got wounded by an enemy machine gun was beside me and we had to shield him from the fire. I had to bandage one of his arms while the enemy was still firing at us. We had machine guns open up on us two straight days. We are better soldiers than the NVA so we always come out on top in firefights. It is a very weird feeling to have bullets flying over you. The worst thing I guess is that you don't know exactly where the enemy is. The only way to think about it is that you are better than Charlie and then keep your eyes peeled. You have got to want to kill him. You must always get the jump on him. Right now I know my squad has killed two.

I can't write you lies that there is no fighting. I want everyone to realize the only people doing hard and dangerous work over here is the infantry. We work harder, we get the worst on supplies, but we fight more than anyone else. It makes me mad the way the guys back in the rear have it so nice, including the air force and the navy. They can't even or don't even know what war is like.

Maybe all this contact has affected my mind a little but I think I have become oriented to jungle warfare. I can't even daydream anymore. All I do is think about if

247

the squad or the platoon is set up right or moving right or trying to out-guess the enemy. I will definitely need help to get oriented back to society when I come home. I feel so hard now, just like an animal.

I can't wait till the monsoons start; maybe I can snap out of the way I am. I had better sign off now cause I might not be able to finish.

Friday, 7 March

Sergeant Lestock had made it. It was time for him to return to the World. He had his early out and was leaving on the first bird. He and Lieutenant LePeilbet had been training me to take over as Platoon Sergeant of 4th Platoon.

Since the company had arrived in the Plei Trap Valley, Sergeant Lestock had mostly hung around the company perimeter, not doing much and certainly not going out on patrols. He was protected. We wanted it that way. Whenever a soldier was *short* (with little time left on active duty), we treated him with special respect. He must not be killed. He was one of the chosen ones. He would return to the World and tell the truth about an infantryman's life in the Nam.

As Lestock packed up and said his last good-byes, there were tears in his eyes. His heart was heavy for us. As he walked toward the chopper, he carried the weight of our dreams on his shoulders. How many of us would die or be wounded after he left? What would happen to the platoon? It was hard leaving his family . . . his men. In combat, he would have died for us. I knew that. We all knew that. Now he was on the chopper sending us his farewell smoke signal. *I won't be back.*

As the chopper lifted off, we waved and cheered. Lestock waved back at us. He was crying. Sam, Shea, Pappy, The Flea . . . all of us stood and watched until the chopper climbed out of sight. We felt hopeful. Another one of us had made it out.

Reality returned. There was no time for dreaming in the Plei Trap. We had orders to find the enemy. The NVA owned the Plei Trap, and they weren't going to give it up easily. I reminded myself that if I wanted to survive, if I wanted to keep my men safe, I had to step up and take charge. I was the platoon sergeant now. A lot more was expected of me.

My platoon now contained twenty-two men. Specialist 4 Ron Stone reported to me from 1st Squad, Specialist 4 Sam Seldon from 2nd, and Specialist 4 Pappy Rawls from 3rd. I had been in the Nam almost eighty

248

days. Twenty-two men depended on me—a twenty-one year old buck sergeant.

I didn't feel twenty-one. My sense of humor had been blunted. It was hard for me to imagine being young. My innocence was to be lost forever. My mind drifted into deeper places. War does that. It was hard to imagine being anyone other than a sergeant who thought about nothing but war . . . and about living, one more day. How could I feel this way in just a short period of time?

I met with my squad leaders. I told them I took my new job seriously. Since Lestock had trained me, they could expect the same type of platoon operation from me as they had received from him. My number one priority was for everyone to get home in one piece. I also reminded them that this was the Plei Trap. We were expecting heavy contact with the enemy and we could not be lax in our duties. Everyone had better be ready. When it was time for action, there must be no hesitation.

I had just finished the meeting when I heard shots. Everyone hit the dirt. We saw The Flea flying toward us in his unique hopping motion, hollering. White sprinted over to him and caught him by the arm, swinging him around to slow his pace. "What the hell's going on, Flea?"

The Flea was so excited he could hardly talk. The cigarette fell out of his mouth. Then he managed to gasp, "Brown Mexicans."

"What? Brown *what?*"

The Flea gulped another swallow of air. He was excited and his skinny chest was heaving, but he couldn't stop jumping around as he tried to talk. "Either they were the brownest damn Mexicans I ever saw, Sergeant White, or they were NVA. I fired at them, but they got away."

White looked at us and said, "Get your weapons, men! Let's go."

Flea had been on guard at an observation post about seventy meters in front of our position. Captain Hockett had established the post to give us an early warning of any NVA headed our way. If the forward observers were to see the enemy coming, they must pull back to give us warning. Flea was on guard in the post when three NVA came walking into view. When he got over his surprise, he shot at them but missed. The NVA took off running . . . and so did he. Sergeant White, Jerry Loucks, Chris Kruckow and a couple of others quickly crossed the perimeter to track the intruders, but they soon lost the trail.

In the Plei Trap, NVA walked the trails openly, without fear. They were, no doubt, more surprised to see The Flea than he had been to see them.

Saturday, 8 March

Even though our commanders knew where we were, most of us were becoming disoriented, our surroundings all looked the same, our days were running together. What was the same was the humping, the moving, the digging in, the setting up for guard duty and SRPs, then moving again—day after day, day after day. This had us so tired that, if we came close to encountering the enemy, we wouldn't have even realized it.

On this day, Captain Hockett was ordered by radio to send 3rd and 4th Platoons on an overnight mission to check out an abandoned French plantation house near the Cambodian border. To get there we humped down a long ridge, then across a saddle, and up another long ridge, before stopping for the night. Our destination was to move to the top overlooking a valley where the old plantation was supposed to be located.

Lieutenant John Andrews, with 1st Platoon, and Lieutenant Tom Porter, with 2nd Platoon, remained at the company base in the Plei Trap Valley. If the 3rd and 4th platoons ran into trouble Andrew's and Porter's platoons would be airlifted to our rescue. My platoon had been on point all day. Then toward evening, Hockett called a halt. Sergeant White passed with the 3rd Platoon on the forward side of the trail. The 3rd platoon would take the lead position when we entered the valley the next day.

Lieutenant Tom Porter *Lieutenant John Andrews*

When night fell, our platoons were put on fifty percent alert. Half of each squad was on guard duty around the perimeter while the other half slept. The men would change guard halfway through the night. We never got much sleep since we knew NVA were all around us. No one wanted to be surprised.

During the night, I heard the damnedest noises in the valley below. They were low, extended moaning sounds. I listened carefully, sitting stone-still, trying to interpret them. Animals, I guessed. Then I remembered a conversation with Sergeant White a few days earlier. A military intelligence report had stated that large NVA forces transported their mortars and mountain artillery by elephant.

About this time, an FNG in White's platoon whispered to him, in a shaky voice. "What's that sound, Sarge?"

"They're just mating peacocks, Private. Relax."

White knew they were elephants. So did I. Others knew better, as well, but no one said a word in contradiction. No one wanted an FNG freaking out in the middle of the night. Hour after hour, we listened to the elephants make a tremendous racket down in the valley. The FNG kept quiet. I can only imagine what his imagination conjured up.

The next morning we moved out. We scanned the jungle from side to side, our eyes tried to interpret every blade of grass moving in the breeze.

251

We had only thirty-two men, rather than the forty-four that made up a fully manned platoon. We were short of manpower and we all knew it.

When we reached the valley floor we found no NVA, but plenty of elephant dung. The elephants had made a clear path through the thick bamboo forest. They had flattened three and four-inch thick bamboo trees with as much ease as a tank. The path was so slippery with downed bamboo we couldn't walk on it.

We all stood at the edge of the bamboo forest and stared in awe at the power of these massive animals. Greg Rollinger remarked that he felt more secure carrying his M-60 instead of an M-16. He figured it could stop an elephant, whereas the M-16 couldn't.

As Jerry Loucks was making his way through the beaten down path White's RTO handed him the radio. We were given a recall order to return to the company base and rejoin 1st and 2nd Platoons.

But before we could hump back up the hill, we needed a re-supply since we were out of water and C-rats. Battalion Brass agreed to fly in some water, but that was all. It arrived just in time in cans improvised from 105mm shells. Since there was no landing zone close to us, the helicopter gunners kicked the shell cans out of the chopper cargo hold. Most either tumbled into unreachable crevices or broke apart on impact. There was no time to bitch about it. We rounded up as much as we could and moved on. Finally, after we had humped back up the saddle between the two hills, we reached an open area and the chopper returned for another try. It hovered closer to the ground and we were able to salvage more of the 105mm containers. We got our drink of water, enough to keep moving.

Sunday, 9 March

As I sat on the side of the hill, reflecting on the events of the day, I was so tired that I was unable to move. Splintered trees lay all around me and far down the hill. Where the company had gouged a hole in the jungle I could see the sky. For a while I simply stared across the valley floor. It was nice to focus on something distant. In the jungle I could only see a few feet in any direction. The sky was clear. It looked great. Soon, stars would pop out. I looked forward to seeing them. They were the same stars that shown in the West Virginia sky. Like the others in my platoon, I was tired and sore. Sitting there, I was covered in dried sweat, and red

252

dirt caked my face and arms like a powdery mask. I had no energy and no will to clean up. My men were sprawled, singly and in small groups, down the hillside in front of me. It had been a long day.

While we were on patrol, the NVA were moving through the jungle all around us. No one could sleep. The enemy knew we were there and we could hear them moving through the brush. They knew our company had moved into the area, and of course this was their territory.

When the sun finally came up, our situation was the same. We expected to run into the enemy so we were hyper-vigilant that day. By the time we reached camp, I was so tense I would have shot anything that moved.

Monday, 10 March 69

Today, we received food, water, ammo . . . and mail. If it were possible to be content in the jungle, then we were content that night. There were no hot showers and pillows, but, hell, we couldn't have everything.

Ken McCormack's foxhole was next to mine, where the perimeters of the 3rd and 4th platoons met. We had just finished digging in and filling sandbags and started to talk. Ken had raced stock cars for one season in the World, and he hoped to return to racing when he left the Nam. Although he was a skinny kid, he was tough. Ken mentioned that he was grateful to be in Jerry Loucks' squad. Jerry had taught him things the Army hadn't . . . things he needed to know in order to survive in the Nam.

Ken was married and he called his bride Sunshine, in honor of the sunlight he experienced in San Diego, where he was born and raised. Thirty five years later while researching this book, Ken let me read a letter he had written to Sunshine that day.

> *Hi Sunshine!*
> *Here is your official dirt-covered grunt letter of the tenth of March. Just five months and eleven days to go. My Darling, this will be fast, as we're just stopping for an hour or so to drop some food and repack our rucksacks. We're getting ammo, too, and we need it. I just got mail for the first time in five days. I got five from you but haven't time to read them. Will find time tonight, or tomorrow. Things are hectic. We are really moving around, kind of a game of chess with the NVA. It's rumored that somebody*

253

captured three Russian trucks and also an NVA Major with attack plans for Firebase 20. Sergeant Muck, Kit Carson, Chuck and one other guy were wounded, but only slightly. Don't worry, it's about over.

Of course, you've probably heard about the NVA tanks at Ben Het, Kontum and here in the Ia Drang. Now we are carrying LAW rockets, too, to stop the tanks. By the time you get this it will be all over and I'll be somewhere else, so don't worry. I love you. Ken.

The Ia Drang Valley, which Ken mentioned in this letter, lay east of Route 14 and southeast of Pleiku in the Central Highlands. It was hallowed ground. Here, from November 14th to 16th, 1965, the 1st Air Cavalry had met the 33rd and 66th NVA regiments head-to-head in a conventional battle. The Air Cav killed two thousand NVA regulars.

The night was cool, it was now going on three in the morning, and it was my turn to stand watch. I could see clearly across the front of the perimeter for maybe fifty to seventy meters. I could see all the way to the beginning of the scrub brush, which was thick enough to hide the enemy.

I thought about Sergeant White and Jerry Loucks being so close to enemy artillery on their most recent patrol, that they could hear the NVA's 105mm breeches close before they fired the weapons. They were pissed because the Army Brass would not allow them to go after that artillery. We all wondered why. Those 105s could be killing our men.

My watch was almost over. It was close to dawn. As I turned to get a cigarette, BOOM! I was rocked back on my feet. The ground shook. Dirt and rocks exploded in front of me. In a split second the entire company came alive. Someone called out, *"Incoming! Get your head down!"*

This was the first time I had been shelled. I hugged the ground, waiting. Then I spotted my foxhole and scrambled into it. Oops! When I jumped in, I found it was already occupied. There were *three* of us in it. The Flea was one of the occupants. "Remind me to kick your ass the next time you argue about digging a foxhole, Flea," I groused at him.

We were both learning exactly how important foxholes were. BOOM! The ground shook again. Our worst fears had been realized. Those 105s had us pinpointed. We were sitting ducks. The enemy was lobbing rounds at us every four to five minutes. Somebody had to do something.

The incoming subsided for a minute. When I raised my head above ground I saw Lieutenant LePeilbet running toward me. "Saddle up! We're moving out! Quick, before we get shelled again!"

I dashed around to every man in my platoon. "Get your asses moving!" I never saw them pack up so fast. The whole company was in motion. We were all asses and elbows, staying low, scrambling away from LZ Turkey. It took only fifteen minutes for the entire company to vacate the premises. The enemy had been watching us, waiting for the best moment to strike. The entire company moved along at a trot. Our eighty-pound rucksacks, completely filled with re-supplies, weighed nothing. We moved more quietly than ever before. Charlie had put the fear of God in us!

When we reached the top of that mountain, we felt safe. With a little scouting of this new location we discovered we had natural protection from attack on all sides, a good place to dig in, and nice soft dirt to sleep on. As we secured this new perimeter, we heard more shelling below us. We had gotten away just in time.

Once we had settled in, Sergeant White came to Lieutenant LePeilbet and me with a request. He wanted two men to go with him on a patrol back to LZ Turkey. In his hasty retreat Lieutenant Smith, our company's pay officer, had left the mailbag behind. All of our money orders were in that pouch, ready to be mailed home. Normally Lieutenant Smith would not be in the field with us, but he had missed the supply chopper back to Enari. He was stuck with us for the night.

Jerry Loucks and Ken McCormack volunteered for the patrol; Ken had over two hundred and fifty dollars in the lost mailbag. As they started down the trail, Jerry and Ken picked up Chris Kruckow and Rollie. Jerry walked on point. It was about five-thirty in the morning, and the fog had not lifted. They moved at a fast clip and the mist helped to hide them from Charlie. It also made the trail seem eerie. The mission was a dangerous one. To recover the mailbag without incident, they would need lady luck on their side.

LZ Turkey looked like an infantry ghost town. The four men spread out and searched the perimeter for the mailbag. The men moved as quickly as they could. Visibility was nil. They knew they needed to leave before the mist lifted and Charlie's opportunity to find them improved. Out in the open, they were easy pickings.

255

Ken found the mailbag. Everyone took off as fast as they could run. They made it back up the hill in record time. As they dashed through our perimeter, holding the mailbag aloft for all to see, the troops let out a cheer.

Later that night, Jerry Loucks shared *his* prize with the rest of his squad. Jerry had stumbled on a whole case of beer at LZ Turkey. He had stashed as many cans in his rucksack as he could. As evening approached, he lifted his beer in salute. "Here's to Lieutenant Smith and his lost mailbag."

Chapter 44

Monday, 10 March 69 Letter Home

Well, I have only 164 more days left in Vietnam, at the most. We are still in the Plei Trap Valley, and there are still NVA all around us. We have not had any big firefights since I last wrote on 6 March.

At our last location, we spent several days next to the Dak Hondrai River. There were NVA bunkers right across the river, but we swam, bathed and cooled off in the water anyway. Of course, we always posted a heavy guard. Then yesterday we humped up a hill and dug in at this location. We have good cover here, because it is another triple canopy jungle situation. You can't see farther than a few meters in any direction. We are safe for the moment.

The Brass is still talking about moving us up north again, near Dak To. The only good thing I can say about my situation is that the monsoons will start in two months' time, and things will settle down then.

I have a ten-day growth of beard. Since we have been humping through the jungle and living on rationed water, I have not had a chance to shave.

All I can do is dream, and sometimes I can't even do that, because I'm too tired. Lately, when I go to sleep at night, I am out like a rock.

With all the NVA around us and the daily firefights we have had, there is a great mental strain on me now. We have to be constantly on guard against attack. Plus, I have been promoted to Platoon Sergeant. This means that I have twenty-two men to take care of instead of seven. Many of my friends, Pappy, The Flea, Rick, Shea, and Sam Seldon are still with me, but Ron Lestock left. Sergeant White was made Platoon Leader as well as 3rd Platoon Sergeant, because they lost their Platoon Sergeant, and I was made Platoon Sergeant of the 4th Platoon. I have to step up to the next level now and do my best with this new job.

Infantry is the hardest job there is. I do not care what anyone says, it takes brains to chase Charlie around the jungle, and meet him on his own terms. An infantryman is the only soldier who faces the enemy where he lives, on the trails and in the bunkers. We don't sit in a secure area behind wire fences, big guns and land mines. We don't sit in an airplane, a tank or a helicopter. Our only protection is our M-16s. We rely on nothing but our jungle skills to keep us alive. I wish to God that everyone who complained about our boys in Vietnam could know what it is really like to fight over here.

I am not trying to feel sorry for myself, being in the Infantry. I just want to point out that out of 524,000 soldiers in Vietnam, only about 75,000 are ground pounders.. That's us, and we are the grunts. We get no breaks. Still, Americans should wake up to the facts. Maybe if we had less bullshit and more infantrymen, this war would be over by now.

Our platoon is down to twenty-two men, when we are supposed to have forty. We get no hot food, no clean clothes, or any "non-essential" re-supply at all. We only get mail every two to three days, but at times, I have gone ten days without mail. That's hard on our morale.

I would write my congressman, but I know it wouldn't do any good. I could write about the fact that I have not had any clean socks for a month and a half, or that there are two men in our platoon who can barely walk. We cannot send them to the rear, because we are so short of men already. We hardly have enough equipment to fight with. Why can't we get more grunts to help us?

Chapter 45

Monday, 10 March 69

A Tracer reconnaissance platoon had been assigned to our company at the beginning of March. It had been acting as forward point while we were moving and as a reconnaissance element.

The Tracers were elite soldiers who were specially trained for Long Range Reconnaissance Patrols (LRRPs). They saw a lot of action since they operate totally within enemy territory. Their mission was to protect our company by providing early warning of enemy activity. They were trained to operate in small teams and to recon the enemy deep in their own territory.

John "Pee Wee" Pizarski was one of the Tracers. He arrived in Vietnam almost thirty days before I arrived. He had married exactly thirty days before he arrived in the Nam. As luck would have it, both of us were assigned to the same company. Our destinies would cross in a most unusual manner in the next few days, a manner that neither of us will ever forget.

As we moved from firebase to firebase and mission to mission, I saw Pee Wee many times around the company perimeter. Initially he had been assigned as a rifleman in 1st or 2nd Platoon, but he hated being a grunt. The constant digging and other manual work in the hot sun bothered him. By the time I arrived in the Nam, he had volunteered for the LRRPs, where he would not have to dig foxholes. Rather he had to reconnoiter the enemy, as dangerous a job as one could find in the Army at that time.

Sergeant Randy Chrietzburg (LRP)

One day he was conversing with Jerry Loucks. As I was walked past Pee Wee's hooch Jerry introduced me to "LRP" (pronounced Lurp), as Chrietzburg was called, and to Pee Wee. In the course of the ensuing conversation, I asked them what it was like being a LRRP.

LRRPs traveled through the jungle, deep into enemy territory. They reconned locations where we would not normally go without a platoon for backup. They silently watched the enemy's daily activities. Sometimes four to five would undertake a mission together, but most of the time only two or three men patrolled as a team.

"Don't you ever worry about getting captured?" I asked Pee Wee.

"The thought is there, but we have to forget about it and stay focused on the job at hand," he responded.

Jerry Loucks stepped up to say," I was on a mission to Dak To in May. There were six of us. We were trying to rescue a captured rifleman from 2nd Platoon. It was an ugly situation. Second Platoon was on an ambush that had gone bad. During the firefight and the resulting withdrawal, one of our men turned up missing. We went looking for him the next morning. I was walking point. We had been out all morning, combing the area. I was walking parallel to and about ten yards away from a major trail. When I reached a clearing, I saw him. He was blindfolded and tied to a post. I did not move forward, there was something not right, something held me back. He was still alive and I saw him move. But, my instincts, told me to back off."

260

"I backtracked about twenty or thirty yards to where the rest of the squad was waiting, and got on the horn to the company. The Company Commander agreed that the setup was a trap. He had seen this kind of thing before. Normally the NVA would kill the men they captured and move on. The Company Commander told me, 'I hate to say this Jerry, but that kid is dead already. The minute you try to rescue him, he's going to be killed. If you go into the open area after him, you will be killed, too.'"

After thinking about it a few minutes longer, Jerry realized the only possibility for a rescue lay in their ability to sweep in from every direction around the open area, and find and kill the enemy before they killed the captured man. He split the squad. Three men circled to the left and Jerry and two others swept to the right. Halfway around the clearing, firing erupted.

The NVA shot the kid, who was now lying grotesquely on his side, arms still tied to the post. Jerry and his men retaliated, but no firing was returned. The NVA simply vanished. Apparently they were hoping to set up a successful ambush. When that didn't happen, they shot their captive and left the scene.

"I'd rather die fighting than get captured," Jerry added quietly. "It would be hard to take, knowing I was being used for bait."

As I returned to my foxhole, Jerry's words echoed in my mind. "I'd rather die than be captured."

I had just finished writing my longest letter home. I was tired of the Army and tired of war. The way they kept us searching for the enemy for a fight, I knew we were going to get it - probably a big one. The men didn't want to fight any more, they wanted to survive and go home. But there was nothing we could do about it. It was going to happen; I could feel it. Maybe this time the bullets wouldn't just whiz by me, like they did when Cheek got shot. If that was what it would come to, then I was ready no matter what.

The Army was treating us like a pack of wild dogs, sniffing out the enemy, and chasing the NVA all over the Plei Trap. We humped all day on C-rats and rationed water, dug in after dark, then had to mount constant patrols or watches through the night. I was tired of it. I wanted to find the enemy, have a shoot out and get it over with. I was tired of worrying about it. My mind, my body and my spirit were exhausted. How could I be expected to fight for my life in this condition?

261

We were truly, truly animals now. That's all we were worth to the Army. At least, if I died, I would be treated like a person. Maybe my funeral would be as good as his, that soldier's from Texas, the guy whose funeral haunted my memory but whose name I could no longer remember.

We did a good job of burying him that day - when I was on funeral detail from flight school. I was proud of that. That little one-room church was so beautiful. I could see it in my mind, and feel all our spirits soaring. I remembered the sweet sounds of the choir and how much his family loved the guy. It was an honor to be there to represent the best in him and to be a part of that moment.

As I sat there on the hillside mulling things over, feeling so pissed off, I got to thinking about life and death. I began to think about being buried. What if my time was about up? I ought to think about that.

Then I did a very strange thing. I pulled out some paper, the kind I used to write home on, and I started to write. I started to write my last wish. If anything happened to me, I would have it there in my pocket, next to my other letters. When somebody read it, they would know that I was not an animal, that I was human, and that I had felt strongly about my life. Then I proceeded to write down my last wish, and I hoped that, whatever world I would go to in my death, I could see the smiles on my friends' faces when they carried out this wish.

My Last Wish

Make my funeral just like the old-time ones. I want black preachers; men who preach with their hearts. I want a black choir too; they will sing with their hearts. I want laughter and I want tears. I want people to feel, sing and pray to whatever God they may worship. I want to be remembered with a smile and a tear and I want people to walk away celebrating how wonderful life is.

My funeral can't be formal - the ministers can't read from the Bible - I don't want Bible lessons, and there should be no reason for anyone to repent anything. Save it and turn it into good deeds for the living.

I want my funeral to be held in an old church. I want old church music, the music that is sung by the poor people of the mountains and, once heard, remembered by everyone. It's got to be the kind of music that makes you cry anytime you hear it. The Old Rugged Cross, Amazing Grace and the like are starters. But at the end I want the choir to sing an old one that lifts the spirits, causes the toe to tap and the soul to reach out and say "I am glad I'm alive, and I thank Jerry one last time for making me feel good."

I want some of my friends to speak at my funeral. I don't care if they're nervous - that won't matter. I want my friends to tell the audience how happy I was to know them and that they made my life full and wonderful. I got so much from being their friend. And if I could do it over again, I would pick each and every one of them to be my friends again.

And lastly, I want it known that I felt like I had even chances with God. I have sinned a lot, started out tough in life and on the backside of things. But I treated everyone with a lot of respect and kindness, and tried to make the world a better place. On the one hand I got my sins and on the other I got my deeds - hopefully the sins weren't bad enough to outweigh the deeds. At this point, it's too late to worry about it anyway.

And in the last farewell, announce that I have allocated $200 of my estate for a happy hour at the local bar, until the money is all used up - so here's to you.

Your Friend,
Jerry

I carefully folded my Last Wish and tucked it into my pocket.

Chapter 46

Mission: The 3rd Battalion 8th Infantry had the mission of conducting a combat assault into the southern portion of the 1st Brigade's area of operations and to conduct reconnaissance in force and ambush operations along enemy infiltration routes in known or suspected base camp areas.

Execution: Company A-3-8 was commanded by Captain Isom who was new and inexperienced. He assumed command on 12 Feb 69. The company performed a combat assault from Polei Kleng into the Plei Trap at location YA784979 on March 2.

They moved to location YA804878 on March 3 and set up a SRP from 3rd platoon. Shortly after 1600 hours the SRP encountered an NVA and the platoon leader in charge of the patrol informed Captain Isom.

The forward observer assigned to the company recommended to the Captain that artillery be called in on the enemy positions. Instead of taking the advice, Captain Isom decided to investigate without artillery support and directed the third platoon to move forward to follow the NVA.

The enemy did not fire upon the platoon until they were in a killing zone of an ambush that covered three sides of the trail the platoon walked. The NVA let the platoon move into an area where they were waiting and prepared. Once they were in the killing zone snipers opened fire from the trees, then booby traps were encountered and the platoon was mortared. The enemy closed quickly on third platoon. As a result, the enemy had the third platoon surrounded, cutting them off from rest of the company.

The rest of the company then moved up to help the platoon and began to receive heavy enemy fire. Soon most of the third platoon, the company commander and the second platoon leader were killed. What was left of the company withdrew down the hill and to establish a makeshift perimeter as best they could. They were still under fire and greatly outnumbered.

The soldiers of the A-3-8 endured two nights of terror. They started out March 2 in the Plei Trap with 123 men and lost 35 killed, 48 wounded and four missing. Half the company was wiped out.

The location of this battle was less than 10 kilometers or six miles from where our company was headed. No one told us about the A-3-8's tragedy, we could have learned from their mistakes.

Chapter 47

Tuesday, 11 March 69

Ben Het was under attack. The enemy had brought tanks down the Ho Chi Minh Trail for the first time, and they were attacking our forces throughout the Central Highlands. Our division was on the defensive and spread thin all over our operating area. Our battalion was being used as a blocking force to bottle up the NVA before they could move back to Cambodia.

My company was operating in Kontum Province, about ten miles southwest of the city of Dak To, near the Cambodian border. We were advancing on an area that contained a suspected enemy hospital complex. We had been assigned ten Tracers who were organized into two teams of five men.

Team One, led by Randy "LRP" Chrietzburg, was ordered to travel directly ahead of us. LRP was an expert at Long Range Patrols, and James "Frank" Franklin, John "Pee Wee" Pizarski, Floyd Robinson, and Wayne "Jocko" Joslin were glad to be under LRP's command. All of these men were to write themselves into the company history books in the next few days. Their mission was to move to Hill 783 and make bomb assessments of the B-52 strikes that were planned for later that night. LRP was ordered to follow a strict 150-degree azimuth and to avoid trails.

Team Two was ordered to protect our left flank. Sergeant Bahr led this team, which included James Fullerton, Joe Thomas, Dan Potterfield, Kemer Runckle, and Steve Windham.

As we moved toward our destination, Captain Hockett became increasingly convinced that the enemy was watching us and that we could be attacked at any time. There were signs of NVA everywhere. Except for 3rd Platoon, the company moved together, spread out in single file. Third Platoon had been on a five-day ambush. They were scheduled to link up with us later at an abandoned firebase.

My men looked and moved as though they were weary. There were no smiles and no joking. Not now. This was serious business. We all sensed the danger. We were beat from the long humping, but there was no time to relax. Something was going to happen. We just didn't know when.

Once we arrived at the firebase, we had to set up. We dug our foxholes and formed a perimeter, as usual. In the early afternoon we got an unexpected resupply from a helicopter drop. In addition to ammo, water, food, and mail, we received our first change of socks since early January. Many men had worn their jungle boots without socks and dealt with the pain of continual blisters; others had worn socks that were completely rotted. Some of the men had wrapped their feet in rags.

Third Platoon showed up late in the afternoon with nothing unusual to report. Captain Hockett (our CO) ordered Sergeant White to keep 3rd Platoon moving and to set up on a high hill overlooking the firebase. White gazed at Hockett with tired eyes. "My men are beat. They can't move out again without a rest."

Hockett's eyes narrowed. "I don't care how tired they are. Move them out anyway."

Third Platoon moved to the higher ground. At dusk, Hockett suddenly called the other platoon leaders together and announced, "Saddle up and move out as quickly and quietly as you can! We're moving in the dark to 3rd Platoon's location!" There were no questions. The platoon officers got the message, loud and clear.

Lieutenant LePeilbet showed up at my position—the one I had just settled into. "We're moving out, Sergeant Horton! Saddle up your men. Make it quick and make it quiet. We've got fifteen minutes. I'll explain later."

Instantly I switched gears from being Jerry to Sergeant Horton. I had my orders. I dashed to each squad's position and made the announcement. One would have thought the world was coming to an end. There was a renewed level of moaning, but my men got the message. We quietly moved out of the abandoned firebase.

It was eerie—surreal—moving up the hill in the dark. I could barely see the outlines of a few men in front and back of me. I had the impression we weren't real . . . that I was dreaming.

When we reached the top of the hill, there was confusion. It was dark and hard to figure out where to set up. The men were tired and stressed out. They would have flopped on the trail if granted permission. Like a broken record, and for the umpteenth time, I issued my instructions. "Okay, men, set up and dig in. This time, shallow foxholes are—"

267

Kaboom. Kaboom. Kaboom. The sounds of a bombardment swallowed my words. I ran with many others, to stare down the hill at our former location. I saw explosions of dirt and trees. The whole area was under heavy mortar attack! *Kaboom! Kaboom! Kaboom!* Muffled explosions reverberated through the night air. I was awed and muttered aloud. "I'll be damned, Shea. We moved up here just in time." Without another word from me, my men started to dig their foxholes.

Sergeant White moved past me, wearing a sheepish expression. "The CO moved us out just in time. He saved our asses, didn't he?" He kept on walking until he reached Captain Hockett. He thanked the CO, for making his tired platoon move out of the firebase. Hockett's maneuver had worked. It was a brilliant move . . . one the enemy hadn't counted on.

The evening wasn't over yet. Our B-52s bombed the area of our next mission. In the crisp night air we sat atop the hill and watched the bombing. The whole sky was a giant light show. The B-52s flew at a high altitude, we could not see them. All we could hear was the rumbling of the bombs dropping and exploding. Each bomb caused a brilliant flash, one after another, in staggered patterns that marched across the jungle canopy. In the white and red light of the blasts, I thought I saw shock waves moving through the air. It was awesome. Then more B-52s came and the cycle repeated. The ground rumbled continuously all night long, like an unceasing earthquake.

Someone mentioned that this type bombing was known as an Arc Light. The bombing always followed a specific pattern. It destroyed the jungle and left craters the size of small ponds. I spent the night lying under my makeshift tent with open eyes. I felt the ground shake with each explosion, watched the night flash continually, a man-made storm.

Nobody slept much that night. Everyone knew that, with the morning light, we would travel to a dangerous place of the Plei Trap Valley. Pappy called it "The Valley of Tears." Someone else said, "It's the place the NVA call home!" We were about to find out what that name meant, one way or another.

My company was ordered to hump into the heart of The Valley of Tears, to assess the bomb damage and mop up the enemy troops left behind.

Wednesday Morning, 12 March 69

This morning started like every other morning for the past months. We had a stand-to thirty minutes prior to sunrise, then a quick breakfast, before everyone geared up for the day's hump. After a sleepless and worrisome night, our company was packed up to move out early in the morning.

For this mission, Captain Hockett had ordered Tracer Team One to travel six clicks in front of the company—much further than usual. He wanted them to follow a specific compass heading and to avoid trails, hoping to prevent an ambush. "We shouldn't be that far ahead of the company, sir," LRP had argued with Hockett the day before after hearing his orders. "If we are cut off by the enemy that distance, we will be sitting ducks."

Hockett was firm about his plan. "I want your team out there and that's that. The company must have early detection of the enemy in order to successfully complete our mission. If your Tracer team makes contact, the rest of the company will rescue you."

The two Tracer units conferred. They had recently moved through the area without detecting the enemy. They felt fairly confident that they would be safe. LRP had to follow Hockett's orders and Team One moved out, well ahead of A Company, which included my platoon.

It was a clear day, sunny and bright, with a few scattered high clouds in the deep blue sky. A gentle breeze blew intermittently and the warmth of the sun indicated it would be another hot day. We were in the middle of the dry season. The company broke camp and moved off the hill approximately fifteen minutes after LRP's team. The Tracers moved quickly and soon they were about fifty minutes in front of us.

We traveled across a field covered in medium high grass and reached a wide trail which headed into the jungle. As we walked, the sky slowly disappeared and the forest closed in around us. One of the company RTOs, Charles Webb, walked beside Captain Hockett and maintained frequent contact with Tracer Team One, which had now reached the first bomb crater. It took guts to be an RTO, because the radio was cumbersome and heavy and made its carrier an easy target. Webb's job was to follow Captain Hockett so that he could remain in contact with battalion headquarters and the two Tracer units operating forward and left of our position.

Webb was a close friend of Joe Shea, they went to basic and AIT together and were in the same squad and platoon and came in country in August 68 with Shea. Webb was called Slim and was in my squad when I first arrived, he was then reassigned as Hockett's RTO. He was from Texas and had that Texas drawl, tall with sandy brown hair that was curly and he told me that he was called Spiderman also but mostly Slim. That day I had Webb's camera in my ruck, I had taken many pictures and was waiting to send the film home before returning his camera.

In the first two hours of our humping, Webb made and received four or five routine radio calls from the Tracers informing us of their locations. They had not detected any enemy.

My platoon (4th, Lieutenant Lepeilbet's) was walking point. We were followed by 3rd Platoon (Sergeant White's), then the company HQ group (Capt. Hockett and RTO Webb), then 1st Platoon (Lieutenant Andrew's), and then 2nd Platoon (Lieutenant Porter's) bringing up the rear. As our company moved toward the bombed area, we were stretched into one long column about 100 meters long. As we moved to our Bomb Assessment destination the column stretched and contracted as a large accordion, stopping, starting, moving quickly in dry areas and slower in other terrain. It was the way we had to move to prevent us from being surprised and surrounded by the enemy. At about 0930 we came down the side of a hill through a small creek and marshy area that started climbing to a small rise. There was low ground with standing water that was angle deep and high buffalo grass on either side of our trail. Our company took a break at 1000 hours at the lower reaches of the hill.

Sitting there, I remember gazing into this shallow valley, the small creek flowing through it. *So peaceful*, I thought.

Sergeant Horton and John Gray taking a break

Soon we were moving again. As we walked, I spoke to Domingo Correa. "This place is too beautiful," he said. "It's too quiet, too. It's like walking point down a trail where no birds are singing. When nature is too quiet, trouble is on the way. I don't feel right about this, Sergeant Horton."

RTO Webb received another report from LRP, who reported that the first bomb crater was about twenty-four feet wide and twelve feet deep. They had been walking through heavy vegetation blown down by the bombing. The terrain was mostly small hills that were created by the bombing and triple-canopy jungle. The only time they saw the sky was when they were walking near the bomb craters.

About 1045, as we started up the rise Airborne thought he saw something. Then he pointed to two enemy soldiers about one hundred meters ahead of our platoon. He took a shot at them, but missed. They took off in the direction of Tracer Team Two's location. LePeilbet guessed that they were either trail watchers or scouts. He was concerned

271

they would lead us into a trap. Either way, part of the company's mission was to destroy any enemy troops it located.

Shortly after we crossed a hill top and started down a southeasterly finger. Our surroundings changed, from bright sunlight to the filtered light that streams through bamboo and brush. We were in the twilight of a thick triple-canopy jungle. At the same time, the trail turned into a path. The terrain and the trail turned the company to the right off the crest of the higher ground. The vegetation was fairly thick with trees that thinned out as we climbed the hill. At the top the trees were father apart and taller and over the hill and down the trail of the saddle or finger area were large thickets of bamboo interspersed among the trees.

This saddle area was about 250 meters in length; the valley was about 100 meters long. There was high ground to our left and behind us. In front of us, a flat open area sloped gently upward. We walked on into a lower area that was covered with a thick layer of dead leaves due to Agent Orange defoliant that stripped the leaves from the trees. It was impossible to walk quietly since they were at least a foot thick in places.

We sensed the enemy was all around us. It was now almost noon. Every man was silent, eyes and ears straining . . . on maximum alert. We continued on. After another few minutes, we saw what we thought was an NVA cemetery with little markers for each grave. Someone said it could be enemy signs marking an NVA encampment. Nobody said anything. As we entered the valley, we smelled an odor, like something dead. Maybe dead bodies . . . from the bombing.

The Tracers proceeded in a zigzag reconnaissance for about thirty minutes, observing no signs of the enemy. The team took a 15 minute break, during which Hockett told the Tracers that a bunker complex with enemy soldiers had been spotted from the air. The Tracers noted the coordinates and computed that the complex was about 600 meters along the direction of our travel. They started out with caution, proceeding another 200 meters through thick vegetation. At the same time we entered the saddle-shaped area in the center of the depression. It had been well bombed. Huge craters, maybe thirty to fifty feet in diameter, were everywhere. The ground consisted of dry, hardened clay with light brown dirt thrown over it from the bombing. Piles of leaves covered the ground so completely that we couldn't see anything beneath them. It would be next to impossible to spot a machine gun nest, or a bunker, or any ground fortifications. Despite this devastation from the bombing, the jungle was still so thick. The trees were still not bare.

Once we walked into this saddle-shaped depression, we couldn't see very far in any direction. As we walked across the saddle, we came upon a large bomb crater to our left.

Airborne was leading on point, followed by Ron Stone. Domingo Correa was about fourth or fifth in this line of men leading the company. The platoon stopped. As Correa looked around behind to the rear, he saw some of our platoon lying and sitting on what he thought was the top of a bunker. Correa, a machine gunner, was searching the area for signs of the enemy. Suddenly, he saw an NVA soldier come out of the back of the bunker. The NVA looked straight at Correa and Correa saw what he could not believe. The NVA's dark black hair stood straight up, two inches off his head. The NVA was as scared as Correa. Correa points to the soldier and hollers at our men, "watch out, there's a fuckin' NVA." The NVA was not six feet away from the men on the bunker. Quickly, Ted Kaiser raised his M16 and started shooting at the NVA but missed. Unbelievably, the NVA recovered enough to crawl back down into the bunker.

Correa shouted to Shea, "did you see the guy's hair, he was scared shitless."

Domingo Correa

For a second, all we could hear was the sound of Ted's rifle fire. Then all hell broke loose!

Bullets came at us from every direction. Everyone hit the dirt. Tense and automatically assuming a firing position, I scanned the forest to see where the shots were coming from and, at the same time, to see whether any of my men had been hit. Everyone I saw was hugging the ground.

Airborne was standing on an enemy bunker. Then he noticed that there were some cut logs, but the camouflage made it impossible to distinguish that it was a bunker . . . even standing on it. The enemy shot at him through the top of the bunker. Fortunately they missed. He backed off in a hurry as the firefight began.

Ron Stone—Tennessee—was squad leader of the point squad in my platoon. He had taken over after Sergeant Machado was wounded. Walking slack behind Airborne he, too, had decided to take a break. When the shooting started, he discovered he was sitting right on top of an NVA bunker too! In a wink he dove for cover. Just then, an NVA popped his head through the bunker and Ted Kaiser started shooting at

274

him. Airborne threw a grenade, but it bounced off the bamboo overhead with no effect.

The Flea had been walking flank. He heard shots and peered around his surrounds. We had been getting so much enemy contact in the previous week he was used to it. At first he did not think much of it. Since no one was shooting at him, he waited to see what was going to happen. Within seconds his ruck received three hits. Flea tightened with fear, almost swallowed his cigarette, and jumped off the rucksack. "This is the real thing!" he yelled. "This is *war!*" He took off on a run toward the action.

Ted Kaiser laid down a steady base of fire with his M-16, which permitted my platoon to take cover. He remained standing and continued to fire after reloading until he had killed several NVA. Immediately thereafter, my platoon was under intense enemy small arms, automatic weapons, grenade, and rocket fire. Ted tried to fire an M-72 LAW rocket at the bunker, but just before he pulled the trigger he saw Airborne and Lieutenant LePeilbet charging it and held his fire.

Off to my left were deep woods and off to my right the terrain dropped off into thick bush. The whole platoon was hugging the ground on the trail. Bullets hit the ground not five inches from me and little puffs of dirt were flying up. I could not see where the firing was coming from. I knew we were in real trouble lying there like sitting ducks.

Each time a bullet hit, the ground beside me exploded. I lay there for what seemed like an eternity, unable to move. I couldn't see the enemy. I didn't know where to shoot. I didn't know where to move. At first I thought the enemy were all in the trees, but later I realized they were everywhere—under the ground, above the ground, *and* in the trees.

The sound of the shooting barrage was deafening. I couldn't hear myself think. One thing I was finally able to ascertain . . . 4th Platoon was not doing the shooting. It was the enemy. We were caught in a storm of lead.

Chapter 48

When the firing began, 3rd and 4th Platoons were stretched into a column heading toward the bomb crater, 4th Platoon was on point, with most of 3rd Platoon walking the down-slope of the hill, heading toward the saddle. The company commander and 2nd Platoon were located behind 3rd Platoon, and 1st Platoon was defending the rear.

My platoon made the first contact, but soon 3rd Platoon was sucked into the fight. When they first started to take fire, they didn't realize how serious the battle was. They quickly positioned themselves near the front of the bomb crater and to the left of my platoon while returning fire. As soon as they could, both 3rd and 4th Platoons pulled back and formed an irregular U-shaped perimeter to the side of the bomb crater at the bottom of the saddle.

First Platoon was still climbing the hill when initial contact was made. As the fire intensified, Captain Hockett called Lieutenant Porter and told him to move up and secure the 9:00am -3:00pm positions with 12:00 being toward the top of the hill. The 3:00pm position corresponded to the trail disappearing down the finger through the bamboo. The small arms fire accompanied by B40 fire was intense as Porter's platoon scrambled to their positions. At that time there was heavy fire coming from further up the hill, both from bunkers and spider holes as well as from snipers up in the trees. There was very little cover or concealment on the 1st Platoon side as the shrubbery was thin and the trees much further apart. NVA were observed moving from right to left across their front (from the 3:00 toward the 9:00 position). The enemy intended to flank them and establish a line that anchored on the stream/marsh we had crossed earlier.

Lieutenant Andrews's 2nd platoon was in the 3:00pm to 9:00pm position, lower down the hill and in a more shrubby area, although there was almost no cover or concealment there either. He was facing more toward the stream/marsh and his 3:00 position also faced toward the bamboo "wall" at the beginning of the saddle. Hockett and the CP were in the center, closer to Lieutenant Andrews than to Lieutenant Porter's position.

During the initial attack, the NVA had managed to cut our company in half—2nd Platoon, Headquarters, and 1st Platoon were cut off from 3rd and 4th Platoons. The enemy let the first two platoons walk deep into their area, before starting the fight. The enemy's plan to defend their base camp had worked. It was the same strategy the enemy used on the A-3-8 that wiped out half the company March 3.

Gerry Richardson of 2nd Platoon had begun the day's hump early. He and the men in his squad were bone tired. His squad was traveling in the mid part of the company's column, and once again they seemed to be stalled. Gerry was standing in the middle of a small stream on the way up a low knoll. His squad members had closed ranks as they always did, when fatigue set in. The day was exceptionally clear. Suddenly they heard a barrage of gunshots. The men reacted as one body. Their first instinct was to get low, but as they crouched in the water, word was passed back to them that 4th Platoon had run into the enemy positions. Second Platoon immediately took cover, alternately facing outward. It was not unusual for the point men to see and engage a small group of NVA. Gerry and his platoon waited for the "all clear" signal to be passed back to them.

The intensity of the firing increased, and it was punctuated by the sound of rockets and grenades. Clearly it was more than a short skirmish. Lieutenant Porter surmised that 3rd and 4th Platoons were heavily engaged and that his platoon would soon be in the fight. He had his men form a defensive perimeter as best they could.

The enemy was all around and on top of us. Both the 1st and 2nd platoon positions and the 3rd and 4th platoon's positions were completely surrounded. This was our worst nightmare. We could be totally wiped out.

Second Platoon tried to improve its position, but the enemy fire was too intense. The knoll in front of them was small and its sides steep. Headquarters was already set up on the crest of the knoll, which was elevated several feet above their position and to the left. There was a narrow, unoccupied point on the front of the knoll that was not protected by the makeshift perimeter, but they were pinned down. They took heavy fire from the hill and from the trees above them so they could not move.

In basic training we had been taught to judge the distance to the enemy by listening for the snap-crack of incoming fire. The snap was the sound

277

of the bullet breaking the sound barrier overhead and the crack was the sound of the weapon being fired. The enemy was so close, the snap and the crack were virtually indistinguishable! Lieutenant Porter and his men realized they were trapped. The easiest way to describe it is a sick feeling in your stomach filled with tremendous anticipation mixed up with terror.

Sergeants George Adornetto, David Heyward, and Robert Moen took instant charge of their squads, organizing their men and their fields of fire. Adornetto and Heyward were Shake 'n Bake sergeants, like me. Moen, originally the platoon's machine gunner, had been promoted to E-5 and a squad leader position.

Caught in the open, there was not much cover to be had. Gerry Richardson wished he could crawl inside his steel helmet. He found a rock no more than six inches high and tried to duck behind it. Turning his head in any direction, he could see puffs of jumping dust. He heard the unmistakable pops of multiple rounds firing directly over his head. He lifted his head and searched his surroundings. The snipers had buried themselves in the thickest vegetation. He saw several in his platoon pointing at the trees overhead. Together, the men rose from their positions and moved swiftly toward the trees, taking random blind shots, hoping to flush the snipers.

Through the vegetation, Lt. Porter saw NVA troops attempting to move behind 2nd Platoon and seal the path out of the valley. If they succeeded, the company would be totally trapped. Lieutenant Porter ordered his two machine gun teams to positions that covered the path and this prevented the NVA from accomplishing a potential fatal maneuver.

Meanwhile, Lieutenant LePeilbet received fire from the bunker directly in front of him. He and a few others immediately returned fire. The lieutenant ordered Pappy to put a few grenades into the bunker. Ted fired repeatedly, but the grenades missed the narrow bunker slits. They bounced off and exploded . . . harmlessly.

LePeilbet grabbed several grenades from the men nearest to him. He and Airborne started to charge the bunker. Then an NVA soldier tossed a Chicom grenade at them and it landed a few feet from LePeilbet. The lieutenant jumped away instinctively shielding Shea, his radio operator. Once the grenade exploded, LePeilbet looked at Shea and asked. "You okay?"

278

Shea nodded and pointed at the lieutenant. "But you're not!" He reached behind the lieutenant and touched the blood coming from a shrapnel wound in the lieutenant's back. He showed LePeilbet his own blood. The lieutenant was shocked. He felt no pain. He didn't know he had even been hit. He kept repeating, "I'm not hit. I'm not hit." Then he discovered his legs were numb and he couldn't walk.

LePeilbet realized he needed help so he radioed for Sergeant White and 3rd platoon to come forward. When White got LePeilbet's message, he ordered my platoon to sit tight and to keep firing. He thought the worst was over. He was going forward to help the lieutenant. When he approached LePeilbet 's location, he found him flat on his stomach, bleeding from his back. He gently rolled Lieutenant LePeilbet over. LePeilbet acted as though he had not been wounded.

John Campbell was lying in a firing position beyond but near LePeilbet. The rest of the men in the 3rd and 4th platoons were stretched out in a single file back down the trail. In front of White were the bunkers and a large bomb crater to the left facing down the trail.

All the time the rest of my platoon was taking heavy fire from the enemy bunker complex in front and to the left of us. I was toward the rear of the platoon and was firing at the enemy and watching for muzzle flashes, and trying to figure out where the enemy was located. The area we were forced to fight in had been cleared of underbrush. The enemy's field of fire was clear. They were shooting at us from the safety of their bunker complexes and trees and they had surrounded us. They had orchestrated a deadly attack on our entire company, a plan they had in place if their enemies were to enter their base camp areas and of course, we were their enemy.

The bunker complex in front of my platoon was extensive, well-planned, and well-constructed. Partly because of the thick layer of leaves, visual surveillance to locate entrances proved fruitless. Our lead element had tried to maneuver toward the first bunker, but was now pinned down. We had already been under continuous fire for what seemed like an hour but was only minutes.

After Lieutenant LePeilbet was wounded, Pappy ordered Domingo Correa to take his M-60 and find a place to shoot up the forward bunker. Domingo reloaded his weapon with a full belt and ran forward. He spotted a little hillock to his right where he could set up, but got himself entangled in wait-a-minute vines. His momentum carried him forward

279

and for a brief moment he was dangling in the air, an easy target for the NVA. He struggled to free himself and promptly took up a position on the hillock and laid down heavy fire. It was to no avail.

Sergeant White appeared beside me. "Sergeant Horton, we're going to take out those bunkers. Get some men and follow me." I knew we had to do something; we couldn't just lay there and get killed. I moved up the line of men to the front leaving my rucksack behind.

I wanted to see what we were up against first. I moved to the front with White, near Lieutenant LePeilbet. He lay helpless on the ground and Joe Shea was still beside him to provide radio communication. The enemy was firing from a bunker directly in front of us and from another to our left. At that time no one knew that the bunker in front of us was part of a large complex housing a battalion size NVA force, we could only clearly see the one bunker.

Lieutenant Lepeilbet and White devised a plan of attack. Campbell, my platoon's machine gunner would lay down suppressing fire from a position to the right of the bunkers, while Sergeant White, Flea, Airborne and I would charge the bunker straight up the middle and wipe it out. The bunker was 50 to 60 meters in front of us at 11:00 from our position. When Rick Campbell came forward, the lieutenant issued his instructions.

Rick maneuvered about 20 meters in front at the 1:00 position. Lieutenant Lepeilbet yelled at him to aim directly into the bunker's opening. At first Rick couldn't see it, but the lieutenant spotted it for him. He started laying down a heavy fire that forced the NVA inside to back off.

When he first moved into his position, Rick didn't have enough ammo. After he started his barrage, others from my platoon threw him the belts of machine gun ammo they were carrying. At last, all the extra weight they had carried through the mountains was paying off! Rick laid down a devastating fire on that bunker.

The other men in the 4th platoon were preoccupied with defending their positions. With Rick Campbell in action with his M-60, the four of us moved, with The Flea and me taking point.

Once Campbell moved up and started doing his thing, we started out. We could see Campbell laying down heavy fire as we moved. The thought crossed my mind that he could shoot us by accident.

My adrenaline was in full effect. I never moved so quickly in my life, not even while playing basketball as a kid against the big guys at the playground. This time, the ballgame was for keeps and the enemy was ahead on points. We had to stop them. We were playing a deadly game, where the points were for life or death.

We could hear bullets coming at us from every direction. Leaves, dirt, rocks and tree limbs were flying, falling, and exploding all around us. The noise was continuous and deafening.

An NVA soldier appeared at the rear of the forward bunker. He fired at us with his AK-47. We killed him. The Flea and I laid down fire, while Airborne and Sergeant White rushed ahead. They took cover and laid down fire, while we dashed ahead of them. We played leap-frog all the way to the bunker, alternately firing and running. Sergeant White moved with us, directing us as we advanced.

When we reached the bunker, we came on-line for a frontal assault. On White's command, we slowly walked forward, firing all the way. We made it to within five meters of the bunker complex and had positioned ourselves between the enemy and our perimeter. Rick Campbell and Domingo Correa were still laying heavy fire on the bunker with their M-60s. They did a good job of keeping the enemy's heads down while we assaulted the bunker.

I was on automatic. My instincts were in full rage. I was so scared and so excited that I instinctively performed as I had been trained to do. I was running the fast break in basketball, everything was automatic but at the same time I felt a rage that I had never before experienced. I wanted to kill the enemy, and get it done as quickly as possible. I thought about death . . . the enemy's. I wanted them to die, all of them.

At this moment, I noticed the bunker had a gun slit that was low to the ground. I was almost standing on it. I backed up and took a position with my left side against a tree. The Flea was just to the left of me. I yelled at him, in a fighting rage, "Shoot, dammit, *shoot!*"

Flea and I were standing straight up not five meters from the bunker firing directly in it while White and Airborne were to my right, seeking cover behind a couple of small trees, as they fired. "We're too close!" I hollered at White. In our charge, we had almost overrun it.

We didn't know it at the time, but the enemy bunkers were interconnected by tunnels. When we killed the enemy in one bunker, more NVA would move up, to take their place. They kept appearing and

281

we kept shooting them, as though we were in a shooting gallery, playing the game for life or death. It happened so fast, we didn't have time to aim. We pointed and shot and hoped we wouldn't mess up. One mistake could be our last.

While we were charging the bunkers the rest of the platoon was busy defending their positions. Before we left Sergeant White had organized them into an oblong perimeter behind their rucksacks. At that time Tracer Team two was positioned off to our left, their job was to provide security to our left flank. Once the firing started Joe Thomas of Tracer team two had a clear view of the bunker complex from his vantage point. He pointed at us as we assaulted the bunker and said to another Tracer, "The enemy must think we are crazy, look at those guys – they are crazy. They will think twice about trying to overrun us."

While Flea and I laid down heavy fire from the left side of the bunker complex, White and Airborne assaulted it from the right. White rolled in behind the bunker, and I yelled and fired on full automatic. He attempted to storm the bunker, but an enemy soldier appeared at the side of the bunker. He shot at White. White pushed his rifle barrel aside with his left arm, moved to the side and shot him. He continued to shoot into the bunker through a matted bamboo door. He maneuvered himself directly on to the bunker and knelt to pull the pin from a grenade.

The Flea had engaged an NVA in a deadly duel. The two of them were shooting at each other, at close range. The Flea was so excited that it was hard for him to shoot straight. Both he and the enemy were in constant motion. Finally, the enemy made a mistake, and popped his head up one too many times. The Flea blew his head off.

While The Flea was having his duel, I had continued laying down heavy fire directly through the front of the bunker complex. I knew I was hitting my targets. I was shooting on full automatic bursts. My weapon and I were in sync. I had gone through several magazines when my M-16 jammed. I looked up and saw The Flea. He was just in time.

As I got my weapon re-engaged and started firing, I saw a flash off to my left about 40 meters from a ridge. Then an explosion went off to my right and almost at my feet. The shell landed between Sergeant White and me. I was thrown into a complete somersault which seemed to occur in slow motion. Time stood still. It was as though I had entered another world. Everything was totally quiet. I felt no anxiety or pain. My

282

somersault could have lasted an hour or only a second. Then I struck the ground.

A Ricky rifle (recoilless rifle) shell had exploded at our feet. The enemy had fired it in a desperate attempt to stop us, even though it was atop their bunker. Their ploy worked. The four of us lay on the ground in front of the enemy bunkers, wounded . . . but still fighting.

Sergeant White took the brunt of the explosion. He was severely wounded in the right leg. From his knee down, his leg was shredded and hanging by a mere thread of bone. Although he was in severe pain, White kept his presence of mind. He called to the rest of our platoon to come get us and to The Flea and me to crawl back toward our perimeter.

His muffled voice and message reached my brain but I was still in a fog and wasn't sure who he was. As sound returned, I heard the continual bombardment of weapons.

We were in bad shape. White had a crippling leg injury and was unable to return even small arms fire. Airborne had suffered a sucking chest wound; he was totally quiet and in life-threatening danger. The Flea had been blown quite a distance away from me. He was in a daze and bleeding from a wound in his side. As soon as the shell exploded at our feet, the NVA started their assault. They were pouring up the hill in waves toward 3rd and 4th Platoons.

I pushed myself to my feet and tried to continue to assault the bunker complex. My head, right hand, shoulder, thigh and leg had been blasted with shrapnel from the explosion. Blood poured in my eyes from my head wound. Death was all around us. Our lives were on the line. There was no time to think about anything, just time to react.

The Flea had recovered from the shock of the explosion and staggered over to me. Amazingly, his rifle was still firmly grasped in his hand. The blast had knocked his belt, canteen, and all of his equipment right off his body! White hollered at us for the second time. "Get out of here. Get back to the perimeter!"

Because of the adrenaline flowing through my veins, I was able to keep walking and fighting. I felt no pain from the many pieces of shrapnel lodged in my body. Adrenaline was at work, doing the good. Then I fell and could not get back onto my feet. The Flea's adrenaline took over. He grabbed both Airborne and me by our belts and dragged us away from the bunker. *"Medic!"* he yelled, at the top of his voice. As he was dragging me, I tried to fire at the enemy positions. Airborne was unconscious.

Correa remembered our frontal assault on the bunker. He saw us move right up on it. Years later, he remembered mumbling, "What the fuck did they do that for?" And when he saw us get blown up, he remembering muttering, "It is truly unfucking believable, if they live through that shit." He saw us help each other back from the bunker, hobbling back. NVA were all over the place.

When he reached the perimeter, The Flea let go of Airborne and me and fell to the ground. For the first time, he could feel the pain in his body. Shrapnel had pierced both of his knees, both thighs, and his right side. He looked down at himself, then over at me. It finally dawned on him, he was seeing his own blood.

Rick Campbell had seen the explosion that hit the four of us. About the same time, another explosion had occurred near my platoon's perimeter, peppering three soldiers near Rick with shrapnel. He saw three or four explosions, one after the other. Rick remained in position, laying down covering fire allowing The Flea to drag Airborne and me away from the bunkers. At the same time, he spotted two NVA in front of the bunker complex. Rick cut them down with his M-60.

Sergeant White could not move. Pappy crouched near the rear of the platoon. He heard the explosions and then our calls for help. He moved forward, saw that White was down and, without hesitation, left the safety of his covered position to rescue him. He stuck a magazine in his belt, loaded a magazine into his rifle, and took off running. He sprinted approximately forty meters across our perimeter. He was exposed to small arms, automatic weapons, and grenade fire. He reached Sergeant White unharmed, slung him over his shoulder in a fireman's carry, and ran back to the platoon, stumbling and falling a couple times. The enemy was shooting at them as Pappy was carrying Sergeant White back; one round ripped through Pappy's fatigues without wounding him.

Ken McCormick of 3rd platoon recalls how the third platoon was in single file and recalled all hell breaking loose ahead of them. They stopped for a few minutes, in place, but did not form a perimeter. And then Jerry Loucks gave the word to drop their rucks and that White had been wounded. They had to help out 4th platoon. Ken moaned, "Oh, shit, if that tough old bastard could get hit, and then anyone could. This is gonna be bad." Sergeant White was 34 years old at the time.

284

They started down what they thought was a road but could have been a well-worn path or trail, at a fast pace, an area without a lot of cover. Ken remembered this because he had not been in a serious fire fight at this point and protocol to this point had been to _back away_ and call in air or artillery. But this time they were moving, deliberately, and fast, _toward_ the shooting. Ken said to himself, "this is very - very bad, we are going to get hurt." As they moved down the saddle they found some trees for cover and formed a perimeter with the 4th quickly. There was not a lot of resistance from the enemy, the enemy stopped shooting and let them in. But then all hell broke loose again.

Greg Rollinger, 3rd platoon machine gunner, yanked his ruck release and hit the ground when the shooting started. In a matter of minutes he was up again running to reinforce the 4th platoon. He grabbed the rest of the M60 ammo and left his rucksack where he dropped it.

Jerry Jensen, assistant machine gunner for Harry James in the 3rd platoon remembers moving forward and hitting the ground on a small hill. Soon after Jensen spotted some NVA in the trees and began firing at them. They were in the trees tied up in the tops. He remembered that the men in the perimeter shot a countless number of them but never did quiet them all. Jensen saw one NVA throwing several hand grenades in the middle of the perimeter. The NVA was in a spider hole, he kept popping out of and tossing out a new grenade. After a while that stopped, someone in the perimeter must have gotten him because it did not last very long.

In the middle of the confusion one frightened soldier in the 4th platoon yelled, "We're all going to die!"

Courageously, White lifted his head to yell at him. "No, _we're not!_ The men in the bunkers . . . the ones in the brown uniforms . . . are going to die today. _We'll_ die in the cardiac ward as old men! We are _not_ going to die today! _Get out there and kill the enemy!_" Even though he was seriously wounded, Sergeant White hollered to everyone in the platoon, exhorting them to kill the enemy. He was determined to rally the men and trying to save lives. I will never forget his words that day.

While The Flea and I lay in the dirt, wounded, we had continued to fire at the enemy. But I was growing weaker with each passing minute; my wounds and the continual loss of blood were overcoming my adrenaline. I could no longer stand up. But as long as I had the strength to shoot I

285

kept firing into the bunkers. Flea yelled for a medic again, but no one came forward.

Flea was beside me. I saw him move to a crouching position, to better spot some of the snipers. All of a sudden, I heard a crack. Flea was knocked off his feet. Stunned, he pointed to his leg. "I've been shot *again*! " I just gazed back at him, maybe I couldn't grasp it, and I had nothing to say.

Before the bullet hit The Flea, it snapped a branch on a bush beside him. Flea had the presence of mind to notice the branch and to trace the path of the bullet from it. He drew a straight line from his leg to the broken branch, in his mind, and spotted a sniper in a tree. He hollered at Lieutenant LePeilbet, who was propped against a tree about ten meters away. "NVA . . . in that tree. Shoot him!" Seriously wounded in the back and unable to walk, LePeilbet still had his carbine in his lap. Following The Flea's instructions, he raised it up and shot the enemy soldier, the AK-47 fell out of the tree bouncing harmlessly across the dirt. The dead man hung in mid-air, swinging from a rope. He had been tied to the tree directly above Lepeilbet.

While this was going on, Jerry Loucks was positioned at the rear of 3rd Platoon. As he came forward, he tried to assess the situation and to figure out what to do next. He did not have too much time to think, heavy enemy fire was coming from every direction. Jerry met with Sergeant White. Even though White was badly hit and in immense pain, he kept his wits about him and told Jerry Loucks to assume command. As he laid there wounded, Sergeant White said," Several of our men are on the verge of panic, Loucks. Our company has lost three leaders in the span of thirty minutes. We need leadership immediately, or we'll have widespread panic. Everyone will die if that happens."

Jerry Loucks moved up near us to assess the situation; he saw that all of us were seriously wounded, with the enemy still laying down intense fire on our perimeter. He spotted me, lying near the front of the large bomb crater. My hands and face and clothes were soaked in blood. He knelt beside me and asked for a situation report. I rolled over and I told him about the bunkers and other locations of the enemy. "Sergeant White and Lieutenant LePeilbet need a medic, Loucks. I'm not hurt badly. What do you want me to do?" At the time, I was bleeding profusely from the head and, with all the blood pouring into my eyes; it was getting hard for me to see. I calmly told Jerry, "the only reason why the shrapnel in my head did not kill me is that I am so damned hard headed." He laughed but then I saw Jerry's eyes move toward my hand and he quickly looked away. I felt fear for the first time when I saw fear in his eyes. The look on his face told me he thought I might die. I knew he couldn't stand to look at my wounds. For some reason it did not freak me out, I just kept going.

I was lying about thirty meters to the left of Sergeant White. Lieutenant LePeilbet was against a tree to my left near the enemy bunkers. The Flea was lying beside me. He was bleeding from his right side. Airborne had a sucking chest wound and was lying quietly beside Sergeant White, who was now in so much pain he could barely speak. He summoned all his energy and yelled one more time, "Loucks, get us out of here!"

The firefight had its own personality – an organized panic with flashes of terror and urgency where we had to focus just to maintain our sanity. Our situation was desperate.

Regardless of our condition, we continued to hold our portion of the perimeter. Each of us was looking out for the others. We would not give up until it was all over. Jerry Loucks shouted back at Sergeant White. "We have to take out these bunkers first, Sarge, or we will all be killed!"

White just nodded his okay.

Jerry Loucks took over. First he ordered Chris Kruckow to get a medic to attend to our wounds. Then he organized a fire team and began to assault the bunker complex. There were three enemy bunkers to our immediate front, and more set in the hill behind.

Kruckow turned to Frenchy, who was hugging the dirt a few feet from him. "Hey Frenchy! Get your ass forward on the double. They need you!" Then he jumped up and scrambled spider-like along the ground to our position.

Frenchy treated White and Airborne and then came over to see me. He was calm even in the middle of the chaos. We were both in the prone position since the sniper fire continued. I sat up as Frenchy approached. He wiped the blood from my head and tied a rag around it. He asked me if I were in pain and I said I was okay. "Where are you hit?" he asked.

"I'm not sure. I think in the leg and the shoulder."

Frenchy took the right side of my shirt off to check out the damage to my shoulder. I tried to look, but really couldn't see. My shoulder was peppered with small holes as well as my thigh, I noticed my Bowie knife had large chunks of shrapnel in the handle.

Frenchy asked, "How is it? Is it OK?" I mumbled.

He didn't answer me. I decided not to ask anything more. I didn't want to know.

As time went by, things became distant and surreal. I heard Frenchy tell someone, "No, he can't have morphine. It's too dangerous. He has to get out on the first Dustoff."

In the next few minutes Sergeant Woodall had moved forward from 3rd Platoon to join Jerry Loucks. Jerry yelled at him over the deafening rifle fire, "we've got to take out the bunkers so we can get the wounded safely back to the platoon." They had to do it. There was no other way out of the situation.

Loucks and Woodall assaulted the left bunker. Woodall charged up one side while Loucks charged right up the middle. They were both in a killing rage. As they charged, there was a loud explosion between the first and second bunkers. A recoilless rifle round had hit a nearby tree. The impact threw Jerry Loucks backwards, wounding him in the face. He recovered, got up, and recharged the bunker again, shooting all the way in.

The NVA laid down automatic fire at Loucks, their rounds missing him by mere inches. He scrambled straight up the middle, through a hail of bullets. Somehow—by some miracle—the enemy never hit him. Jerry got on top of the bunker and threw a grenade into it. He finished the first bunker. The enemy was still coming up the hill. The NVA in the second bunker were still firing at them.

Sergeant Woodall moved up from the left and reached the first bunker. Both he and Jerry stood on the now silenced bunker, firing at the NVA, who were advancing up the hill. They were like ants pouring out of a disturbed anthill. The minute they fell to their deaths, others kept coming behind them. Jerry Loucks' weapon was firing at them continuously. As soon as this NVA ground assault slacked off, both Loucks and Woodall jumped over to the second bunker and fired their rifles into it, killing the NVA who were inside. Then they checked out the third bunker. The enemy soldiers in it were already dead. Sergeant White, Flea, Airborne, and I had knocked that bunker out.

All the bunkers had been quieted, but the enemy was still firing at us from the hillside and from the trees. Loucks and Woodall moved back to the perimeter. Then Loucks decided that it was time to move the wounded back to the cover provided by the rest of the platoon. Loucks, Raul Baeza, Frenchy, and several others carried Lieutenant LePeilbet, Airborne, and Sergeant White on stretchers improvised from our ponchos. While they were being moved, none of them uttered a sound. The Flea roused himself and helped me to my feet. Then he helped me back to the others.

Once we were in a safer position, Jerry Loucks worked his way back to tell Rick Campbell, our machine gunner, to leave his position and pull back. I saw Rick running towards us with his own M-60 and five or six rifles in his arms and quite a few bandoleers of ammo draped over his shoulders. He was carrying the entire squad's supply of munitions.

Too much was happening too fast for me to keep track of it. I knew that what happened in the next few minutes would determine whether we all lived or died. The enemy kept coming and our men were tiring and running out of ammo.

We had walked into something important and the NVA didn't want us there. Their huge enemy force was prepared to destroy us . . . or die trying. Later we learned that they had neatly placed their personal items—wallets, pictures, shoes, and letters from home—beside their fighting positions. They intended to hold their positions until they died.

Chapter 49

Noon Wednesday, 12 March 69 Organizing the Wounded

Once the enemy bunkers in front of our position had been neutralized and the wounded carried back to the relative safety of the combined platoons, Jerry Loucks drew the rest of the men in 3rd and 4th Platoons into a tight perimeter. I and the rest of the wounded were surrounded by them. We were at the bottom of the small ridge we had descended before the enemy contact, and our rucksacks were stacked around us for protection. Jerry left us with our M-16s and used every able-bodied man for the continuing fight. Bullets were still flying back and forth from both sides. Some of us were still shooting at the NVA.

Captain Hockett and the 1st and 2nd platoons were positioned near the top of the hill. The enemy had moved between the two halves of the company and to the top of the hill. Both elements of the A-1-8 were completely surrounded.

Hockett understanding the gravity of the situation ordered 3rd and 4th to join back with the company. Jerry Loucks radioed for help in moving back up the saddle but Hockett wouldn't allow either the 1st or 2nd to do that. The 3rd and 4th were going to have to walk back right down the middle of the finger to rejoin company.

While the 3rd and 4th platoons were fighting the enemy near the bunkers, 1st and 2nd platoons were fighting a pitched battle with NVA moving in on them from three sides. There was fighting on the top of the hill, and just off the left side of the finger as the NVA were moving up a little draw. Enemy machine gun and rifle fire was coming from the left, right and rear of the platoons. The NVA had a blocking force with the bunkers at the end of the finger and were moving in on the Company Command Post (CP) from three different sides. The entire company was really in a bad situation.

We were lucky that the NVA did not mount an all-out attack to overrun our positions. No doubt the reason they didn't was the fierce fire we directed at them and because of poor terrain.....steep, woody slope on the right side and a pretty large clear (bomb blast area) area on the left. After we had charged the bunkers, the NVA knew we would fight to the death.

Even though we were wounded we had our weapons. We were ready if the enemy were to overrun the perimeter. Everyone was relatively calm. Lieutenant Lepeilbet was lying there smoking a big cigar perfectly calm saying that he was going to get to go home. He appeared to be in a good mood which instilled confidence in all the men. Someone tore the Lieutenant's pants open and his ass was hanging out the whole time.

I was lying there stunned, I had lost a lot of blood with head wounds, shoulder wounds, leg wounds and hand wounds. I, no doubt, was the closest to the blast and had the most shrapnel in me, whereas Airborne had a sucking chest wound, was the worst one wounded and in the most danger of survival. They would not give morphine to me or Airborne because of the nature of our wounds. White was in the most pain but he was his regular self. We laid there within the rucksacks.

I had stopped firing my weapon. I was too weak to use it. From time to time the battle seemed to grow more distant. I struggled to keep from passing out. I wondered if I would I ever see home again.

The strategy was to keep the two platoons moving back up the hill, meter by meter, while protecting the wounded men in the middle. Loucks acted as Lieutenant Lepeilbet's arms and legs. The company moved very slowly. It took hours to reach the high ground, and we were under constant heavy enemy fire all the way. We had to reach higher ground . . . or die.

Because of the enemy fire the 3rd and 4th were pinned down and could not move at all. Then slowly, men of the 3rd and 4th platoons gathered us wounded and moved back to the CP a few steps at a time. We would start to move and the shooting would start, we would stop and take care of business for a while, start to move and stop, and do it again. The wounded were dragged by ponchos and carried. It was painful for the wounded but that didn't matter – it was life or death. We got shot at each time we moved. Jerry Loucks would go nuts each time the enemy fired and start yelling, and then we would turn our attention back to the fight for a while, but carefully because by then we were running low on ammunition. Loucks demanded that the men aim at the enemy not just spray fire at them. He yelled, "Look for the muzzle flashes. Shoot the motherfuckers!" Jerry's fighting rage was contagious. What was first fear now turned to being pissed off as our men were inspired by Jerry's words.

291

Loucks led the way, many times he would run toward the enemy standing straight up while firing at them, while the men on the perimeter covered him. He would stand straight up, fire a few shots, run a few steps toward where he thought the shooting was coming from, stopping, shooting a few rounds, running forward, stopping, shooting a few rounds, and so on until he decided they'd had enough. And then when they would start shooting again, he would get pissed, almost like "haven't you learned your lesson yet?"

The fighting continued to be intense and everyone focused on the job at hand. At that moment, Domingo Correa realized he was exceedingly thirsty. He stopped shooting to holler at Stone and Kaiser, "Hey, you guys thirsty?"

The men closest to him realized that they were also thirsty. Soon everybody began to shake their canteen to see if they had any water left. Somebody yelled at Domingo. "I'm dry. Throw me some water!" Domingo had plenty. In a momentary lull in the battle, he pitched his canteen to his thirsty comrade. Pretty soon, canteens were flying back and forth among the men. Even though they were in a life and death fight, the men found brief light-hearted relief from this simple act, performed in the middle of the battle.

By now, Sergeant White was in unbearable pain. The blood had dried on my wounds and I felt no pain. I kept telling myself that my wounds were not all that bad, even though I had caught a glimpse of many little holes in my flesh. I was lucky, if I hadn't had my Bowie knife, I might have lost my leg.

My platoon—including Pappy, Shea, and Sam—were now taking directions from Jerry Loucks. They were laying down fire outward from our perimeter, protecting us by keeping the NVA's heads down. I wished I were with them, fighting. I was their sergeant. I was their leader, their brother. I saw desperate faces. My men were intensely focused on killing the enemy and on surviving at all costs. Minutes seemed like an eternity. Every man in my platoon was seeking a way out of our disastrous predicament. The only problem . . . we would soon be out of ammo.

We definitely needed help. Thank God, we got it in the form of Specialist 4 Jerry Loucks. He directed the men's fire while shooting up the jungle like he was in the old Wild West. He was a pure fighting machine. He must have thought he was wearing body armor, because he seemed unmindful of the bullets flying all around him. Without his helmet, he wore only a red bandana tied around his head, using it as a bandage for his head wound.

Under Jerry's direction, the men in my platoon and 3rd Platoon rallied. They fought bravely and with determination against an overwhelming enemy force. They made the move to higher ground by integrating the two platoons into one unit. He had supervised the construction of litters for the wounded. Yard by yard we maneuvered our way up the slope. He raced from man to man, directing their fire toward NVA positions in specific parts of the jungle.

While placing rucksacks around the wounded for protective cover, Jerry was wounded a second time. In pain and exhausted, he refused to stop and continued to carry out his mission. By carefully directing the platoon's fire, he was able to help the men succeed in temporarily silencing the enemy. For a moment, the jungle was almost quiet.

Too soon, the enemy force regrouped and again launched an all-out assault on our position. A long, vicious fight ensued. Unperturbed, Jerry Loucks repeatedly checked every man on our makeshift perimeter, helped to evacuate the wounded, and kept the perimeter tight by physically repositioning the remaining platoon members.

Jerry Loucks saved our company on March 12th. For his heroism, he should have received the Medal of Honor. Without this brave man, our company would have been overrun. It's as simple and as horrifying as that.

Chapter 50

The NVA had us pinned down but the men of the A-1-8 fought like heroes.

Greg Rollinger, a machine gunner from 3rd platoon, spotted three NVA approaching their position from the right front. Rollinger knew he had to move fast. Rollinger and his assistant machine gunner, Harold Proctor, who fed Greg's ammo belts, were located behind a big hardwood tree. Rollinger swung his M-60 around the tree and started to fire at the enemy. He shot the first NVA. The NVA was dressed in a brown uniform and had a 9mm bolt action rifle with a grenade launcher attached to the front. It was an easy kill. Then Rollinger's machine gun jammed.

By now the other NVA soldiers turned and opened fire on Rollinger and Proctor. They were firing their AK47's on full automatic. Rollinger worked frantically to get the M-60 going again, but to no avail. The enemy's bullets hit closer and closer. He was cursing that big gun. "You big dumb son-of-a-bitch; this is no time to jam up! Get it together or we are gonna buy it!" At that time Rollinger was cussing his machine gun, Proctor returned fire at the enemy with his M16 and killed the second NVA.

Then finally Rollinger got the belt set and raised the weapon to a firing position and opened up with all it had. As the third NVA continued to shoot at them, Rollinger saw the muzzle flash from the AK and shot him with a burst from the machine gun on full automatic of at least 40 rounds nailing the NVA to a tree. Rollinger ran out of ammo and started yelling at Proctor again without knowing Proctor had dispatched the other NVA. Proctor yelled back," I got him God Dammit!" For good measure, Rollinger lobbed a grenade on top of the dead soldier's body. Wham! Even though Rollinger had been trying to quit smoking, he turned to Proctor and said, "It's time for a cigarette."

In the heat of the battle, Rollinger and Proctor sat there, relaxing with their smokes. They noticed that the now-dead enemy had shot the bark off of one side of their tree, and that his bullets had dug a big hole in the dirt right in front of their cover. *Close call*, Rollinger thought. He shrugged it off and took another drag.

While Rollinger and Proctor were busy with their own battle, Sergeant Novotny was in another life and death struggle. Frank Novotny was a squad leader in 3rd Platoon, was married, lived in Austin, Minnesota, and he and his wife were expecting their first baby sometime in March. Just as the 3rd and 4th Platoons were forming up their U-shaped perimeter, an NVA threw a grenade at Frank. In an act of spontaneous bravery, Frank's assistant, Richard Mathews, a religious guy from North Carolina, jumped on top of Frank to shield him from the brunt of the explosion. When the grenade went off, Mathews was hit in both legs. At that Frank got pissed off, sighted his M-16 on the enemy's head and blew it apart. The NVA's head literally exploded.

In the 4th platoon Pappy entered into a one on one firefight with the biggest NVA he had ever seen. Pappy thought the NVA was Chinese. The dueling firefight started when Pappy got shot at from about forty meters up the saddle. Pappy spotted the huge NVA firing from behind a large anthill. Pappy fired back at him. The NVA responded by bobbing to one side of the hill and shot back at Pappy. So Pappy as the Arkansas hillbilly he was, took a long breath to relax and counted 1001, 1002 ... On 1004, the enemy popped up and Pappy shot him square in the forehead. Pappy no doubt killed a Nung, one of the NVA 66th regiment's elite soldiers.

Our M60 machine gunners were distributed around the perimeter, their ammo was running low. Chris Krukow, 3rd platoon machine gunner, was on the left side of the saddle looking down it toward a small ridgeline. He used his ammo wisely and watched for the muzzle flashes of the enemy weapons just as Jerry Louck's ordered. From his position he saw a number of NVA firing at some of the 4th platoon soldiers and with several quick bursts dispatched them. Krukow with his boyish face, his country boy patience and tenacity operated his M60 calmly and accurately to save many of our men's lives.

There was nothing us wounded could do. We were trying our best to stay alert. We knew our lives were on the line. Because of the wounded, Loucks realized the urgency of moving to Hockett and high ground. Our only choice was to do it the hard way ... an inch at a time. We left our rucksacks, fought, moved a little, stopped to fight some more, and moved again. We slowly moved up the hill.

Rollinger and Proctor moved their M60 back up the hill and maintained the perimeter only five to ten feet at a time. They had to step over dead NVA as they went. The dead enemy were huge in size compared to normal Vietnamese, dressed in full web gear and uniform each with three banana clip magazine ammo pouches for their AK-47s around their chests.

Jerry Loucks skillfully kept those of us who were wounded in the middle of our defensive perimeter. Each time the perimeter moved, we were carried or helped to a new position. While we were moving the enemy were still in the trees firing at us, while others threw grenades.

Due to the heavy machine gun fire we then halted. The machine gun fire came hurtling down at us from a thick bamboo thicket. We were now pinned down. The NVA really had us. We had come too far to return to the valley below, and there was little cover on the hillside. Each shot we fired went into the direction of 1st platoon located straight up the hill, but there was nothing else that could be done.

With the battle raging, our dilemma had been broadcast throughout the brigade operating area. The battalion commander, in the rear, was monitoring updates from our location and figuring out what to do. The brigade commander was circling our area in a command helicopter, reviewing the situation. The word was out that the A-1-8 was in danger of being wiped out and somebody, somehow, had to do something . . . quick.

Since the division had troops thinly spread along the entire Cambodian and Laotian borders, no other unit could come to our rescue. We were trying to contain and destroy a fierce enemy with only limited resources, and there wasn't enough manpower to go around.

Afternoon Wednesday, 12 March 69   Cobras – the Tide Turns

While we were stuck on the side of the hill, it seemed that no one would be coming to our aid. Just then, Joe Shea—LePeilbet's RTO—tapped Jerry Loucks on the shoulder and handed his radio handset over to him. Shea yelled over the heavy sound of fire, "A helicopter gunship pilot is on the horn. He heard about our desperate situation from battalion headquarters. His gunship is a Cobra. He's in the air and he wants to bring a rain of fire down on the enemy!"

I heard Jerry radio back to the pilot. "Can you help us? We're up to our asses in NVA!" A smile spread over his face and he hollered over to us, "He's on his way!"

Cobras are specially-designed ground attack helicopters capable of diving at almost 200 miles per hour. Sometimes called "Snakes," Cobras are armed with 2.75-inch rockets, rapid fire mini-machine guns, and 40mm grenade launchers. They are formidable flying weapons.

Once the Cobra reached us, the pilot radioed Loucks. "Throw some smoke to mark your position. I can't tell you from the enemy!" The Cobra pilot had only two rockets, but he had his mini-guns, which were powerful weapons by themselves. He had, however, brought a friend with him. *Another Cobra.*

Loucks threw his smoke a few meters ahead of us and the other men around the perimeter threw smoke in front of their positions. The smoke was very thick and most of the smoke grenades only went 15 to 20 feet in front of the perimeter. Almost immediately, two Cobra gunships came roaring in, one after the other, laying down fire at our smoke line and all around our perimeter. They pounded the enemy with their 20mm rockets and mini-guns in a storm of lead. The sounds of destruction were so loud we were deafened. The sights and sounds were petrifying, but our hearts leapt with joy. The cavalry had arrived, and these horrific sounds were their trumpets' battle charge. Their bullets were right on top of us, literally no more than five or ten meters away, but none of our men got hit. It rained lead. It rained fire, smoke and hell. The NVA were showered with rockets and bullets.

It was as though a black, fiery, death machine had appeared out of nowhere to fight on our side - a big bad flying dragon raining death and destruction on the enemy. Even though I was weak and dazed, I could hear myself hollering uncontrollably, "Kill the motherfuckers. Kill 'em and win!"

It was strange lying there, watching these pilots do their jobs, cheering them in my heart, wanting to live so bad but knowing that with just a little bad luck I could be killed in seconds. The rain of bullets was intense. It was like hell, but I must have been close to God. My life was fragile now; at the wink of an eye it could all be over. I knew deep within me that I had to fight to the very end. I knew I would never let go of my weapon. Life and death and whatever comes next were all mixed together now, in a unreal surreal drama, where an instant lasted for hours. I was ready to travel to the next world but yet, I was willing myself to live with all my might. I was ready for whatever came next, life or death. I guess, if that was my fate, I was ready to die.

While I was hollering, "Kill the motherfuckers," everyone else on that hill seemed to be hollering too. Guys were yelling just like this was a basketball game, except in this game we all wanted the opponent dead.

Those two Cobras executed a perfect slam dunk in the enemy's face, and, in this ultimate game of life and death, we were now in the lead. I was sure glad that those big, black, mean, flying machines were on our side.

The Cobras wreaked holy hell on that jungle. It was truly awesome. To this day I don't know how they could lay that much fire down that close to us without hitting us. In the middle of the battle, even though I was scared, I cheered the Cobras out loud. We all did!

About this time, Rick Campbell spotted a Loach helicopter off to our front. It had been fitted with an M60 machine gun and a door gunner. The Loach fired its M60 at treetop level, just in front of the bunker complex that we had charged. The door gunner hung out the door and threw grenades at the enemy bunker. The chopper hovered so close to the action the NVA could have thrown rocks and hit it! That door gunner had balls of steel.

Near Dusk Wednesday, 12 March 69   Making it to the Company CP

The Cobra attacks had pretty much cleaned the snipers out of the trees, as well as the machine gunners out of the bamboo thickets. The Loach had cleared the last of the forward bunkers. And sure enough, once the chopper attacks were over, the battle quieted down. This gave us a much-needed break, allowing us to move up the hill.

What was left of 3rd and 4th Platoons now moved quickly to higher ground, stepping over NVA bodies strewn everywhere, most of them lying there with their full equipment on. The enemy wore pith helmets, which offered no protection against our bullets, and web gear holding banana clip magazines to re-load the AK-47s strung across their chests. Each man only carried about fifty rounds which was not much for an extended firefight. Perhaps their leaders expected they would not need more, since they wouldn't live long enough to use them? It seemed that the NVA put less value on the individual soldier's life than us. That day we found out they were ready to die.

We worked our way back up the hill trying to rejoin the rest of our company. Lieutenant LePeilbet, Sergeant White, Airborne, The Flea and I were carried, helped or dragged on our ponchos. In addition to his machine gun, Rick was carrying five or six rifles which belonged to the men who were assisting the wounded. It was late afternoon.

During this small lull in the fight, we moved as quickly as we could. Every man's face looked desperate and each one's soul beckoned to ask, *Is this it? Is this my last day on earth? I must fight on.. I must not fail.*

As we approached our headquarters' position, someone radioed Captain Hockett that we were coming up to him from the south, and to suppress fire on that side. Don't mistake us for the enemy. Hockett replied "Okay, come on in." Finally we rejoined with the 1st and 2nd platoons.

In the melee our rucksacks had been left at the bottom of the hill. I thought about all the stuff in my rucksack, including letters from home, but I decided it didn't matter. I wanted out of that place as fast as I could go. When we finally rejoined the company, I felt a small glimmer of hope. We just might make it now.

Someone was dragging my poncho, pulling me along, I was not sure who. I was very weak. My face was covered with dried blood from the wounds on my head. While we were being moved into position near Captain Hockett, Sergeant White looked up from the poncho on which he was being dragged, and saw dozens of NVA bodies strewn all down the ridge where we had been. Captain Hockett had taken cover behind a big tree, and directed the company's efforts from there. Even under such intense fire, he was cool enough to formulate a good strategy. Captain Hockett co-ordinated this exchange, then he organized a counterattack to clear the LZ so the Dustoff air ambulance could land.

Third and 4th platoons now shared a perimeter with the 1st and 2nd, many of the men were set up in the right side of the hill where the ground was hard and rocky. No one could dig in so they had to hug the ground as best they could.

Our men tried to enlarge our perimeter, to provide more room for the Dustoff, which was trying to descend into a very small area. The M-60s laid down heavy fire and several of the men tried to move forward. Then, for a few minutes everything was quiet. But once we let up on our firing, the enemy started to fire at us again. They just would not give us a break. There were too many of them. Our plan to silence them had succeeded briefly, but then the NVA counterattacked. Their rifle and sniper fire grew intense for a while, but our men beat them back again.

It had taken us more than six hours to cover the two hundred meters separating the two elements of our company. There were a lot of NVA we had to eliminate to do it. Even though the enemy had us dead to rights, we fought as fiercely as humanly possible. The enemy found out that day what the men of the A-1-8 were all about.

We got word that the Tracers, being on point, had been trapped between the enemy and us about one hundred meters to our front. They had spent the day attempting to fight their way back to us, and still had not succeeded. Although the rest of the company was now re-united, the Tracers were still trapped in the middle of 'NVA city.'

We also learned of casualties. One was James Fullerton from the second Tracer team lead by Sergeant Bahr. After the company's initial contact with the enemy, Sergeant Bahr ordered his team to pull back from their flanking position onto high ground in order to join up with 1st and 2nd Platoons. Joe Thomas remembers that when the 1st and 2nd Platoons joined together, they began taking intense sniper fire. Joe reacted instantly and jumped one way while his buddy James Fullerton jumped the other. Fullerton got hit by a sniper's bullet and he died shortly thereafter. Steve Windham of the Tracers was fighting nearby, and he helped carry Fullerton's body back into the makeshift perimeter.

Randy Chrietzburg was listening over the radio when he heard the battalion commander, "Bullets", ordered Captain Hockett to have the company line up and execute a frontal assault on the enemy. The two men argued about the situation for a while, then Randy heard Hockett tell the colonel "Get fucked!"

Randy Chrietzburg of the Tracers had advised Captain Hockett that a frontal assault was not a good idea. When the battle began, his team had been trapped about one hundred meters in front of our position. They were cut off from our company and hiding in a bamboo forest, literally in the middle of the enemy forces. Randy told Hockett that if he performed a frontal assault, the entire company would be killed. The Tracers estimated that there were hundreds of NVA waiting in bunkers and trees just beyond the saddle where we made contact.

Captain Hockett's decision to disobey the colonel's order may have saved the entire company that day. Although a normal company would field one hundred-twenty men, before the attack began we numbered only about seventy-five. Counting our killed and wounded after the attack, we would have been able to field only about sixty fighting men against all those entrenched NVA. They would have had us at least ten to one.

After our artillery shelled the NVA's positions, Captain Hockett kept calling in the Dustoff, but the chopper could not descend. It had circled our position for more than an hour. Each time the pilot tried to land, his chopper started taking intense NVA fire, and he had to lift back up again.

Chapter 51

The 1st and 2nd platoons had their hands full in a separate life and death battle with the enemy.

After 4th Platoon was first attacked, 1st Platoon, led by Lieutenant Andrews, began drawing fire from the NVA. The enemy fire was coming from a flat valley area to the right of the saddle as 1st platoon looked down the trail. 1st Platoon knew they had a big problem when they heard over the radio that 4th Platoon had run into bunkers and several were down and wounded. They could hear a hell of a lot of shooting going on down the saddle.

Lieutenant Porter of 2nd Platoon was in the last platoon in the column. When the firing began, his platoon moved up and secured the eight o'clock to twelve o'clock position of a hastily-formed perimeter on the side of the hill leading up to the saddle. This perimeter was set up near a bamboo forest. There was lots of bamboo around, and also heavy brush. The men took positions behind their rucksacks and Lieutenant Porter organized them into a perimeter capable of supporting interlocking fire. He saw many NVA moving up from bunkers and his men immediately engaged them.

After Lieutenant LePeilbet was wounded he called Lieutenant Andrews and told him that he was wounded and asked for help. Andrews radioed back LePeilbet that he would sweep down the hill toward him. At that time 1st Platoon was then positioned in the elephant grass a few meters from a set of thick trees at the edge of the jungle. There was not much underbrush there, so Andrews got everyone in a line for the sweep. They began sweeping down the hillside, firing down towards a flat area at the bottom of the hill. Lieutenant Andrews planned to sweep all the way down, then move left on the saddle and perform a flanking maneuver on the enemy bunkers located in front of the 4th platoon.

First Platoon had swept about fifty meters — and they were about halfway down the hill on the saddle - when the guys in the 3rd and 4th Platoons started calling over the radio, telling them to stop, that they were firing too close to their own positions. Then Captain Hockett ordered Lieutenant Andrews to stop his sweep and move back up the hill. Once back on the trail, 1st platoon took positions nearby the CO to protect the headquarters unit. Captain Hockett was yelling for help. He was caught between 3rd Platoon and 1st Platoon, about thirty meters down the saddle, and he had been isolated from each of them as 1st Platoon moved away from him for the sweep.

As 1st Platoon moved back up the trail they started to take fire from the enemy, to their front and to their right. The fire coming at them from the right was intense. Some of the men were hit. Sergeant James Olson and Infantryman Charles Revis of 1st Platoon got hit when the NVA came up that side of the finger. Sergeant Olson was shot in the hand. He was one of the walking wounded. He could not fire his weapon, his wound was minor. Charles Revis was hit in the forearm and he was told he would be evacuated on the first Dustoff.

A 1st Platoon's soldier spotted a sniper in a tree and shot him with a round from his M79 grenade launcher. The enemy's entire body virtually exploded.

As they moved to protect headquarters, Lieutenant Andrews told Frank Runge to take his M-60 and his squad and secure the high ground, in effect to secure the top of the hill. At that time, 1st Platoon had to regroup to protect their wounded. Frank was reluctant to take his squad to the top of the hill, but orders were orders. Someone had to secure the high ground, to protect the rear, or 1st Platoon would soon be in big trouble.

Frank Runge and Herbert Pulk of 1ˢᵗ Platoon

Second Platoon was located in a bamboo forest and 1ˢᵗ Platoon was on a part of the trail where there was not much cover; there were only a few trees nearby, and they had an open bomb blast area with several craters to their left. That was about it. The enemy was firing at them from the other side of these blast craters.

The firefight now reached a crescendo and Lieutenant Andrews remembered lying flat on his stomach with his face in the dirt, waiting for a chance to act and wondering why he had not been shot yet. His radio operator, Herbert Pulk, yelled at him that they had to move out, and they did so, quickly. Lieutenant Andrews remembered that they had to move more than once away from the heavy enemy fire. Pulk kept yelling "we have to move when the bullets hit too close." This no doubt saved the lieutenant's life each time Pulk yelled. As they changed positions, the lieutenant heard shooting from the top of the hill from Frank Runge's location.

When Runge approached the top of the ridge, he interrupted an enemy platoon just as they were maneuvering into an ambush position. The enemy opened fire on Frank and the men behind him. As a result the

304

men behind Runge were alerted to where the enemy was located. The rest of his squad was able to take cover and return fire. Runge's maneuver kept the enemy from concentrating their fire on the company headquarters group and the rest of his platoon.

Gerry Richardson saw Frank move forward toward the NVA position. As usual Frank was leading his squad, his M-60 braced on his hip, advancing while shooting randomly into the trees. A moment later Frank suddenly turned, ran back, pointing to a sniper tied to the top of a tree. One of the men fired and killed the sniper. The sniper just hung there by a rope up in the tree.

But as Frank was moving back, Gerry realized that there was something wrong with him. But then he thought it was okay, since Runge was carrying his M-60 as he was running. Gerry noticed a blood stain on Frank's right side, slightly above the waist. The wound didn't seem to be serious because of the location. Gerry heard someone yell that Frank was shot.

Lieutenant Andrews looked up the hill, he saw Frank walking down toward him, holding his side, his M60 lying on the ground. Because he was walking, the lieutenant thought that Frank was okay too. But Frank didn't make it down the hill. He collapsed before the Lieutenant.

Andrews and Pulk ran up to Frank to see where he had been hit. There was not much blood on his uniform but Frank told them that he was in pain. The bullet hole was small but when they rolled Frank over, they saw that a lump the size of a grapefruit had formed just above his right kidney. The lieutenant immediately called for a Dustoff. The RTO Pulk reported that, because of the intense enemy fire, Frank could not be evacuated right away.

Ralph Zerr, the platoon medic, had been in the field for only two weeks. He was at Frank's side; Frank was the first patient he had treated in combat. He tried to help Frank but, without sophisticated medical equipment, there was not a lot that he could do.

As Frank was in constant pain, Zerr and Lieutenant Andrews held him and tried to comfort him as best they could, even though they were crouched in an open area, at the edge of a bomb blast crater, without any cover.

The enemy was positioned just on the other side of the crater. Shots were whizzing all around the place, so they were vulnerable in the open area. Lieutenant Andrews stayed with Frank as long as he could, but finally left him to set up the platoon's defensive positions. Ralph Zerr was still holding Frank when he uttered his last words: "You guys take care of yourselves."

For Gerry Richardson, the hours seemed like minutes; everything was happening real fast. When Gerry returned to his perimeter position, he asked someone if Frank Runge had made it out on a Dustoff. The man just looked at Gerry and pointed to a body lying on the ground nearby, covered by a poncho liner. Gerry walked over, pulled back the poncho and recognized Frank. He was devastated. Gerry's world instantaneously went silent. There was a sudden hole in reality, and an intense grief overcame him. Even though the firefight was in progress, he could not hear a sound. All motion ceased as well. Even the smoke on the battlefield froze. Frank was more than a squad leader, he was older, over thirty years of age and he had been the go-to guy for the guys in our company. Unassuming and a good listener, he was like a father figure to the men. The guys regularly went to him for advice in personal matters. Here was a man everyone in the company would sorely miss.

Before Frank joined the Army and was shipped to Vietnam, he had been an electrical engineering student, like me. He had volunteered for the Army and wanted to do his part to help the boys in Vietnam. That day he paid the ultimate price for helping his men and his country. His actions in noticing, then cutting off the flanking NVA saved many American lives that day. Frank Runge died a hero.

Gerry's biggest single regret was that, during Frank's final few moments, he didn't go to him and try to comfort him, as Frank had comforted and counseled Gerry for his fear of being killed, so many times in Vietnam. Now Gerry sat there in the middle of the battle stunned. He knew Frank had single-handedly charged an unknown enemy position and saved 1st Platoon's flank. This courageous act had cost him his life. Gerry Richardson just sat for a long time and looked at Frank's body. He totally forgot about the firefight, and he totally forgot his fear of dying.

Lieutenant Andrews moved near the perimeter and was firing at the enemy. He looked for the NVA, but he never really saw them. They were too well concealed. He fired in their direction, but never really knew whether he was hitting them or not. It seemed like eternity – hours passed.

After the Cobras had bombed and strafed the NVA positions, Captain Hockett ordered Lieutenant Andrews to form a tight perimeter around the Company HQ. Both 1st and 2nd platoons moved in, forming a tight perimeter. The enemy's fire had died down. No one had any concept of time.

The firefight had been so sudden and so intense, they had no idea how long they had been in contact with the enemy. Time stood still for everyone in both platoons.

Second Platoon was taking fire from the tree line at the top of the hill. Third and 4th platoons were still pinned down on the finger, still in contact with the NVA, but a lot of their firing had died down.

After Frank Runge died, Lieutenant Andrews checked on who else might have been hit. He was working to get the men to move into better covering positions. Third and 4th Platoons were working their way back up the finger, along with their wounded, to join the rest of the company.

As the men were trying to get organized, there was a lot of confusion. Sergeant Adornetto and some of the men were busy clearing a landing zone so the Dustoffs could retrieve the wounded. Everyone was low on ammunition and water and were praying for a re-supply, probably from the same Dustoff they expected to land.

First Platoon took up a new defensive position across from the landing zone. Lieutenant Andrews told Charles Revis who was hit in the right arm him that he should leave on the first Dustoff because they might not get any other evacuations that day. Revis was feeling okay, but he agreed to go.

Charles Revis and Carey Pearce ("The Flea")

When our platoon reached the company headquarters position, I saw Frank Runge. He was just lying on the ground covered with a poncho. I asked who it was, and learned that it was Frank Runge. It did not seem real, seeing him lying there, covered with his own poncho. My mind would not let me think about the implications of his death. I was dazed and almost completely numb to my emotions.

Chapter 52

Near Dusk, 12 March 69 Dustoff Three Seven as recounted by Mike Rinehart and Others

Captain Hockett kept calling in the Dustoff, but the chopper could not descend. It had circled our position for more than an hour. Each time the pilot tried to land, his chopper started taking intense NVA fire, and he had to lift back up again.

The battle had been raging for six hours now, and it was beginning to get dark. All the men were very tired, and the seriously wounded men were really suffering. After the Dustoff's third attempt to land despite our low ammo situation, Captain Hockett decided to have the entire company fire out of the perimeter all at once for a Mad Minute, to see if they could quiet the enemy long enough for the chopper to land.

The Mad Minute idea came from Ft. Benning, Georgia, where the Brass used to impress visiting dignitaries by having an entire company on the firing range fire their weapons as fast as possible for a "mad minute." The terrific noise, the smell of the powder, the huge volume of fire and the destruction of the targets was very impressive. Even though they were facing the night without resupply they fired straight out of the makeshift perimeter. Rollinger aimed his M60 straight at the bamboo thicket near the CP and began firing blindly into it. Their fire was devastating. A few minutes later, when the firing stopped, the surrounding forest was completely quiet. It looked as though the Mad Minute idea had worked.

While the NVA were keeping their heads down, the Dustoff was able to descend and load the wounded men on board. As the chopper lifted us out of the jungle, even in my weak and dazed state I was swept away in the emotion of the moment. The sounds of the battle were still ringing in my ears. During this time, my wounds didn't hurt. In fact, I couldn't feel a damn thing.

I had done my job as a soldier; I was part of the team, the brotherhood. Our lives had depended on teamwork and we had come through for each other. Teamwork saved my life.

The men had fought like heroes. Even though we were outnumbered at least six or seven to one all day, we held the enemy off. The company was still surrounded, but at least the platoons were re-united. At this point everyone was nearing exhaustion, but a glimmer of hope kept us going. The A-1-8 was united. We could stand together and fight as a unit. The NVA had a formidable task trying to wipe us out now. This day was full of heroes.

Lieutenant Porter moved up to the CP area and then walked up to Lieutenant Lepeilbet and asked, "How's it going Andy? Are you alright?" Lepeilbet with some pain said," I can't move or feel my legs." As Porter walked away he saw Pappy and said," here is a real man, a former rodeo bull rider in great shape and he's gonna be in a wheel chair the rest of his life." As Porter returned to the perimeter he saw Frenchy starting an IV giving human serum albumin to one of the wounded. It must have been Airborne. Porter remembered the sight and smell of the bloody bandages on the wounded and this remained with him for years to come.

Sergeant George Adornetto

Sergeant George Adornetto, a squad leader in 2nd Platoon, was a cocky Italian guy from New Jersey. He was short and dark. He always had a "five o'clock shadow," even right after shaving. He was also an effective squad leader and, following Tom Porter's orders, he and Sergeant Moen had quickly organized their men to clear the bamboo and brush with machetes so that the Dustoff could land. I will never know how he and his men did this, as they were under almost constant sniper fire while they chopped and broke down the heavy limbs and thick bamboo stalks, working completely out in the open, heedless of the NVA shooting at them. While this was going on, the rest of 2nd Platoon was returning fire toward the enemy.

It was a miracle that no one was hit during this maneuver. Their bravery allowed the company to evacuate the wounded. With the clear spot on our perimeter, the Dustoff was able to hover, very close to the jungle, and on the slope of the hill. When asked later why he had exposed himself to such intense enemy fire, Adornetto stated, "It seemed like the right thing to do at the time."

Mike Rinehart was the Dustoff AC (Aircraft Commander) that day. He and his team were attached to the 283rd Dustoff (Air Ambulance) group, a part of the 498th Air Ambulance Company stationed in Qui Nhon. Mike and his group flew all over the Central Highlands for II Corps. His call sign was Dustoff 37 (pronounced "three seven").

Medevac was performed by practically all re-supply, or "ash and trash"helicopters in Vietnam at one time or another. In fact if it weren't for all the slicks taking care of the light-weight sick calls, Mike and the other Dustoff teams would never have been able to handle the more serious cases. The difference between a Medevac mission and a Dustoff's mission was that the Dustoff was used solely for evacuating combat wounded, usually during, or immediately after, intense firefights. Also, the Dustoffs were the only ones who would fly at night. They flew under great risk of taking fire and they always carried trained medics on board. The Dustoff pilots themselves had gone through medical training at Fort Sam Houston, had become certified medics, and had received extensive instrument training before being sent to Vietnam. This wasn't true for most other helicopter units.

The Dustoff call sign had been adopted by all Helicopter Air Ambulance companies in Vietnam that were a part of the 44th Medical Brigade, except the Air Cav and the 101st Airborne, who had their own medical evacuation helicopters, which were known as Medevacs.

The Dustoff crews were completely volunteer, a distinction these men were proud of. A typical Dustoff team consisted of four men: the Aircraft Commander, a pilot, a medic/gunner and the door gunner. The

311

pilot that day was Lieutenant John O'Connell who was a brand new squeaky clean Lieutenant just out of flight school.

At the time that Captain Hockett's RTO called for medical help, Mike and his crew were temporarily based at Kontum on a three-day stand-down at the 44th Medical Corps base camp, having just flown there from Dak To.

The information that was initially called in, ordering Mike's team to our location in the Plei Trap Valley, was sketchy at best. All Mike heard was "6 US… 2 critical… unit in light contact… gunships on call… red leg off."

From this communication he knew that he would be flying into a hot zone to rescue six wounded men. This transmission invoked his most common dilemma - either take the mission without waiting for air cover or let the wounded men die while they waited for support. Mike rarely, if ever, waited.

Even though Mike's information on our situation was sketchy, but he preferred it that way. He had learned early in his tour that having too much information could be dangerous. Knowing the details about enemy strength, weapons and locations just made him anxious. He thought, *Hell, I know we are in a damn dangerous country. Why make it worse by thinking about it?*

When a mission was called in, his crew hauled ass and got airborne immediately, heading in the general direction of the mission. As they flew, they received additional information from Dustoff control, including:

- The exact location co-ordinates for their target.
- The number of wounded to be evacuated and the types of their wounds.
- The type of soldier being evacuated: US/ARVN/Green Beret or who?
- The ground unit radio frequency and call sign.
- Is the unit still in enemy contact? If so, is there any air support on location?

(If there is no enemy contact, then why is the RTO whispering?)

312

- The location of the artillery to target line (so Mike could keep from flying across it, and maybe catch an incoming round.)

Once all of this information was collected, Mike would either call for artillery to be lifted just before he arrived, or call for aerial support over the LZ in the form of gunships,

Initially, when Dustoff 37 approached our area, the battalion or brigade commander in the command and control ship circling overhead wanted to tell Mike what to do and how to do it. But Mike told them to fuck off. He needed direct contact with the men on the ground. He then contacted Captain Hockett's RTO and determined that we were in more than just light contact with the enemy, and had six seriously wounded men. Mike asked whether we needed a Dustoff while still in contact, or if we could wait until it broke off. The RTO said right away. By that exchange, Mike saw how desperate we were.

But, this was serious business. Mike had to make the right judgment call because, if he took the mission, and his aircraft came in under really heavy fire and got shot down, then instead of six wounded we would have ten, as well as a crashed and burning aircraft blocking the LZ. Then no one would get out. Upon determining that our situation was critical, Mike wanted to talk directly to our CO, Captain Hockett. He didn't want to have to relay through the RTO. Hockett got on the radio immediately.

When Mike and his team arrived at our location, the jungle canopy was so thick that all he could see was several gunships circling about, the command and control ship diddling around, and intense smoke pouring from a forest fire nearby started by our firefight.

Mike and his team circled the area, trying to figure out exactly where our LZ was. Captain Hockett kept asking Mike if he saw us. Mike could hear us, but all he could see was smoke, ash, and jungle. Finally after fifteen or twenty minutes, he realized that they had been circling the outside of a donut, directly over the NVA who were firing up at them, and that we were in the middle of it, shooting out. About this time a gunship helped to point out our location by firing several rounds in the right direction.

To be sure of our location prior to making his approach, Mike asked Hockett to pop some smoke. When we did, Mike identified it and promptly reported the color to Hockett, who responded "Nope. Wrong color, try again."

313

When Dustoff Three Seven approached the LZ, two gunships cleared a path on either side of them, and kept the NVAs' heads down so that Mike could make a landing.

It turned out the NVA had popped their own smoke! They were obviously listening to Captain Hockett's transmission, and were trying to get Mike's chopper to hover over their position so they could shoot it down. Anyway, once Mike got the colors straight he started circling, looking for the LZ. What at ground level looked like a field that could be spotted from ten miles away, wasn't even visible to him when he was only 150 feet above it. That's how dense the gray smoke was. But after he had started his landing approach and got within about seventy-five feet of the company, he saw our unit scattered out more or less in a circle.

Mike's evacuation mission was originally designated as a "hoist mission" because there was so little room to land in the valley where the NVA had us trapped. This meant that, to get us wounded men out, the chopper team would have to hover, and carefully lower a sling into the jungle. This was a time-consuming and dangerous procedure, usually reserved as a last resort, because both the chopper and the men in the sling would make easy targets for the NVA. But when Mike's team arrived over our location, he saw that a hoist mission wasn't feasible; the firefight was too intense.

Approaching a hot LZ was usually done in "combat assault" style, which meant staying above small arms range until the last possible second, then chopping power and falling into a screaming, spiraling dive right to the touchdown. However, the opening above the LZ in our case was so small that Mike couldn't use the combat assault type of landing. Instead, he had to gently settle down through the jungle, a risky landing any time, even without hostile activity all around him.

As Mike flew in, the shooting which had slowed, started up again. Our company was still surrounded. After clearing the LZ, Sergeant Adornetto's squad and the rest of the company were busy shooting at the NVA moving up the hill toward them. Even though the whole company was laying down heavy fire on the enemy, in a fanatical combat assault the enemy kept coming. Finally, the shooting momentarily died down.

At that point Lieutenant Porter, checked with his squad leader who was on the LZ and blurted out, "Are there any more? How many were there? Did you get them all? Why did they stop?" Adornetto shouted back, "All

I can say is that we kept shooting 'em until they stopped. Maybe we got 'em all."

Mike made repeated attempts to land but each time he drew too much fire from the enemy. After this routine had continued for more than an hour, he was starting to get low on fuel.

During this period, Mike Rinehart and Captain Hockett were in constant communication. They both knew that it was imperative to get the wounded men out, some could die. In an act of great personal bravery, and using a coordinated effort, Mike brought his chopper down just as our company, in their "mad minute" and aided by fire from a nearby Cobra gunship, poured intense covering fire on the enemy. To lower the chopper into the clearing, he had to hover under the jungle canopy and slide over close to the hillside. In the process, he mowed some jungle brush down with the chopper's rotor. Luckily, it didn't break anything. But Mike did manage to hover a few feet above the hillside, in a hole in the jungle just large enough to fit his machine into.

Mike saw that the LZ was on a pretty steep slope, and, from the rotor wash, smoke, ash, limbs, leaves and jungle debris were flying everywhere. He tried to land right away, but the slope was just steep enough that hovering eight feet above the ground, the main rotor would have only cleared the men's heads on the high side of the hill by about six inches. Mike couldn't move forward because the bamboo and the trees were too thick. So he backed his machine up until they reached a place where the slope wasn't so steep, but even there he had to hold a five or six foot hover.

Mike always worried that, under those conditions, someone in the heat of the firefight would panic, stand up and run up the hill right into the rotor blades. The resulting crash would be more destructive than if the chopper had taken a direct hit from a B-40 rocket - not to mention the loss of the man.

Once he was hovering, and his crew had started loading the wounded men, time stood still. For Mike Rinehart, what must have been five minutes or less felt like fifteen, or thirty, or more. The risks of being shot down while hovering were just that great.

A small forest fire was burning nearby. The intensity of our shooting had caught the underbrush on fire, and it was pouring out dense black smoke. So as the wounded men approached the Dustoff, the helicopter's blades were blowing leaves and soot and dust and smoke and loose dirt everywhere.

While the Dustoff was hovering, the ship's intercom was switched to "HOT" so that the whole crew could talk to each other without having to press the intercom buttons. It was important that the crew could talk to the AC because the AC didn't know, generally, what was going on behind them, or whether they were drifting around into the trees or, even worse, if they were about to stick their tail rotor into a bamboo stand or something.

Since the bird could not land, our buddies lifted each of us wounded up after they carried us to the Dustoff. This was at some personal risk; in fact, it was strictly a volunteer mission. A number of men, including Gary Feldman, RTO Joe Shea, Gerry Richardson, Jerry Loucks, and several others volunteered to load us onto the chopper.

Standing with the wounded men was Charles Revis. He had been wounded, but not severely. While he would eventually need to leave the field, he would not have been a priority for evacuation. But Lieutenant Porter, thinking that the "hellhole" seat might be empty, encouraged Revis to go down and get aboard the Dustoff if there was any room at all.

While they were loading the wounded men, there was a continual conversation between the Dustoff's crew, their medic and the AC. "Hold what you got..."

"Okay..."

"You're drifting left; come back to the right..."

"You're too high. Come down..."

"Okay hold what you got..."

"We're taking on wounded..."

"Hold your hover..."

"Okay, we got three more to load..."

"Steady..."

"Okay, they're bringing up three more to load..."

"You're drifting back, move forward... steady ... hold what you got."

During the loading procedure, the AC, Mike Rinehart, and his pilot were both at the controls. That way, if either of them got hit, the other could take over and immediately fly the ship out of there.

The Dustoff is an amazing machine. The aircraft commander and the pilot sit in a small cabin forward, then a huge rectangle is cut out of the

316

side of the aircraft. This is the cargo hold. It often has no doors and is so large that enemy shells can whiz right through without touching a thing. It makes the Dustoff look like a flying square donut. Normally the cargo hold houses two M-60 gunners and their weapons, or, in this chopper, one gunner and a medic. The hold is also where we wounded were destined to end up, hastily piled on top of one another by the men loading us aboard. Then behind the cargo hold was the engine, the transmission and the fuel tanks.

Everything happened in a mad rush. The enemy was still shooting at us, of course. The volunteers were loading the wounded guys on the pilot's (right) side of the ship. They were standing on the skids, pulling the men up into the cargo hold. As soon as someone would get aboard, they'd push them to the left, or yell for them to move to the other side, then load another man.

Gerry Richardson was carrying one end of Sergeant White's litter. He saw that White had an ugly compound fracture of the right leg. All he could see was bones and blood. Gerry had bent over to dodge bullets and he was trying to run fast while also carrying the litter. Sergeant White was heavy. As they carried him past the company commander, Sergeant White yelled "You're a great group of soldiers. I am really proud of you guys! Give 'em hell!"

Gerry thought, *"What a time for accolades. White is seriously wounded, we're getting our ass kicked, and still he praises us"*

Revis was loaded just after Sergeant White and, since he was ambulatory, they told him to get in the hellhole, which was the gunner's seat. On a gunship helicopter configured as a Dustoff the gunner's seat became the medic's seat, except when the chopper was loaded with wounded men. At those times, the medic rode in the hold, caring for the more seriously wounded soldiers, and the hellhole rode empty. But today they put Revis in it, since his wounds were so minor that he could sit there without any problems.

As he was being loaded aboard the Dustoff, Lieutenant LePeilbet told Country that he was in charge of 4th Platoon now. He offered him his carbine rifle. Country replied, "No thanks, Lieutenant. I don't want it because it would make me look like a lieutenant, and I'd be NVA bait."

With that comment, Lieutenant LePeilbet realized how anxious his men felt, and he decided that, in this situation, he could not leave them. He had Country and Joe Shea carry him back off the chopper into the field

317

where, despite his paralyzed legs, he volunteered to remain on the perimeter with his platoon all night. At his urging the men used their helmets to scrape out trenches deep enough to cover their bodies, and held their positions. Lieutenant LePeilbet was finally evacuated on a Dustoff the next morning.

They loaded Richard Mathews last. He had been wounded in both legs by an NVA grenade when he shielded his friend Frank Novotny from the blast with his own body. Frank was holding Richard's hand as they loaded him. Then Frank returned to the firefight.

The Dustoff crew had loaded our wounded in less than three minutes. When everyone was on board, the crew yelled to the AC, "Okay!"

Mike Rinehart simply replied "Coming up."

The crew continued talking to Mike, guiding him backwards out of the LZ. It wasn't until we were clear of the slope that he could turn the aircraft around. We were staggering under max power, trying to hold a hover. Once Mike pulled pitch and started to nose down to gain speed and lift, the Dustoff began taking fire from the left side of the aircraft. Now zings from hits but the supersonic popping sound of rounds breaking the sound barrier as they passed clean through the hold without hitting anything. At that point, there was lots of yelling. Mike thought, *Damn, those guys are in the trees.*

The Dustoff had successfully backed carefully out of its hole in the vegetation, and turned to fly away. But a Loach helicopter gunship was hovering directly overhead blocking our flight path. At first Mike Rinehart said "What the hell, great! He's providing cover for us."

But as he ascended, he realized that the Loach was in the way. Our chopper slowed down to a crawl, waiting for the Loach to move. But apparently that pilot did not see the Dustoff underneath him. By the time Mike yelled at the Loach pilot over the emergency frequency, telling him to get the hell out of our way, we had rounds incoming from the left again. The Dustoff was a tempting target for the NVA, who opened fire on us as we hovered there just above the trees.

Suddenly Mike's armored seat took two hits that felt to him like blows from a sledgehammer. Under the impact, the ceramic coating popped off the inside of his seat, and he later discovered that he had a purple ass. In fact, for this action Mike subsequently received a Purple Heart.

318

The pilot thought that Mike had been hit, and tried to take the controls away from him. For a second, the two men had a misunderstanding. Mike said: "I got it."

The pilot misunderstood him: "You got hit?"

Mike replied: "No, I got the controls. Loosen up."

Pilot: "Right, you got it."

Mike asked the pilot to concentrate on the instruments, and issue a May Day call over the air. The gunner in the cargo hold screamed as he was firing his M-16 on full automatic, "Let's go! Let's go! Up! Up! Up!"

Now there were rounds hitting in the hold all around the wounded men, but fortunately most of them just went zinging through the open cargo bay. We could tell by watching the green tracers flying around us. Everyone except the seriously wounded men were yelling at the pilot to get us out of there. I was scared shitless, as were the other men, but at least I was quiet about it.

I was in a cold sweat. But my body was telling my mind to relax, to float, to let things go. My mind was telling my body, *"Don't go into shock, Jerry. You can handle this. Hang on until you reach the doctors."*

We roared out of there with the skids whapping the trees. I thought we were going to crash, but, to everyone's surprise, the damn thing kept flying, despite the best efforts of the NVA to shoot us down and the Loach above to block our escape.

While our Dustoff was making its getaway, I rolled slowly over to look out the cargo hold door back down at the ground. Although my vision was blurry, I saw the company perimeter. Then I spotted Raul Baeza standing up, out in the open. With his shirt off and a bandoleer across his chest, he was busy focusing his camera on our chopper. Right in the middle of the firefight, this crazy guy was filming our escape. I thought to myself, *Damn, this really is just like in the movies!*

Once the chopper cleared the top of the trees, the enemy really let us have it. We were now being hit with intense sniper fire from trees higher on the hill. So many bullets were flying our way, it seemed like the entire eight hundred NVA on the ground were shooting at us. I heard bullets just raining on the Dustoff in a continual patter and saw green tracers flying everywhere. The Flea was lying beside and on top of me. Everything was happening so fast. I could hear the bullets; I thought I could see them. .... then I saw it, a bullet went right through the Flea's arm in slow motion. It must have been an optical illusion. He got hit in

319

the arm by a shot that pierced the cargo hold floor – not two inches from my head.

While this rain of bullets was falling on us, Charles Revis, sitting in the hellhole in front of us, was laughing "I'm going home! I'm out of here! Goodbye Nam!"

He was holding up his wounded arm for all of us to see. He was very relieved that he had escaped the Nam with such a superficial wound.

Short-timer Revis was twenty-years-old who hailed from Old Fort, North Carolina. He was very short time. During February he had been sent to Cam Ranh Bay preparatory to heading home, but at the last minute he decided to come back into the field for an extra sixty days. If he agreed to do this, he would not have to spend five and a half more months in the Army once he returned to the World. By extending his tour in the Nam a month or two now, the Army would give him an early out.

Revis had gone to Japan on R&R and bought a nice ring for his sweetheart back in North Carolina, whom he planned to marry on his return. Now he sat in the hellhole and waved down to his buddies. He flashed his "million-dollar wound" for all to see. "This is my big ticket home!" he yelled.

But, a few moments later, just as we were about to break away, Revis was shot twice in the chest, and fell out of the hellhole, and right across our wounded bodies. The Flea, with wounds himself, climbed over everyone to reach Revis, to see if he could help him. Guys were piled so thick in the cargo hold that, on his way to Revis, Flea hurt somebody everywhere he stepped.

Looking forward beyond The Flea, I could see the AC, Mike Rinehart, and thought that he had been wounded in the shoulder. The helicopter was rocking and rolling all over the place and everybody was yelling, but despite this terror the rest of us felt lucky. We had made it out alive.

Chapter 53

Wednesday, 12 March 69 the Drama in the Air

The battle had the full attention of Brigade Headquarters. Even though they couldn't reinforce or extract us from the battle, they were able to provide us with various types of air support and, throughout the day, many helicopter pilots performed heroic acts on our behalf. These pilots commanded the Cobra gunships that silenced the snipers pinning us down, the Dustoff helicopter that pulled the wounded men out, the Command and Control helicopter monitoring the battle while circling overhead, and a lone supply helicopter that brought the company much needed ammo at the last minute. In every instance, heroic actions by these pilots resulted in many lives saved.

The Cobra gunships arrived about an hour or two after the battle began, and they turned the tide in our favor by breaking the attack of the NVA, and giving us a chance to regroup. These powerful choppers were very precise fighters; they wreaked havoc on the enemy just a few meters from our own position. They also helped the Tracer recon team break contact after they were pinned down, and they killed many NVA snipers. They shot them right out of the trees before our eyes.

A Command and Control (CC) helicopter had been closely monitoring the situation from the air all day. The passengers in that CC were the Brigade Commander, Colonel Hale Knight, Major Albert Sheehan, Brigade S-3, and the Command Sergeant Major , James Gilbert. Sergeant Major Gilbert had heard about the battle when they left Camp Enari that morning. Gilbert volunteered to go on the mission. Gilbert knew some of the men in our company, including The Flea, and he felt invested in our well-being. For one thing, he had helped The Flea get out of trouble by overriding an Article Fifteen disciplinary action earlier in the year.

The pilot of the Command and Control helicopter, Clifton L. Chambley, was a 1st lieutenant who had been in-country for less than a month. His chopper circled the battle zone for many hours. Colonel Knight and Sergeant Major Gilbert were in constant communication with the company RTO on the ground. They could not get a good status report from the ground, since the RTO they were in communication with was overly-excited. Each time Gilbert radioed, the RTO kept telling them that NVA were trying to shoot his head off and told them he would not stick his head up above cover. The RTO sounded scared to death, and was probably in shock.

Realizing that the Dustoffs would not be able to return to the LZ, and that our company was pinned down securing it's wounded, Sergeant Major Gilbert urged the Brigade Commander to use their helicopter to complete the Dustoff mission. Only when the company was freed of its casualties could it maneuver against the well-entrenched enemy positions.

So they tried. The first time that the ship went into the landing zone (LZ), enemy fire had the company pinned down and it was impossible to get the wounded to the craft. Sergeant Major Gilbert ordered the craft out. As they were ascending in the air using his M-16 Gilbert fired at the enemy who were at tree top level. He also directed the door gunner to fire his M-60 at the enemy located in the trees.

Then they made another attempt to get into the LZ. Once again heavy enemy fire kept the company down, unable to move the wounded. On the second try, the enemy now focused all of the attention on the C&C ship. The pilot was forced to take evasive maneuvers. Sergeant Major Gilbert and the door gunner again laid down heavy fire toward the enemy. They were unsuccessful and so they had to order the ship to lift off again.

Then after this second attempt, in spite of a number of bullet holes in the fuselage, Sergeant Major Gilbert directed the craft to over-fly the enemy positions nearest the LZ in an attempt to silence them. During this time Sergeant Major Gilbert exposed himself to the return fire of the enemy by leaning out of the doorway and firing directly down into the enemy positions.

The ship was hit by heavy fire. When it was 50 feet from the ground, automatic weapons fire smashed into the pilot's plexi-glass, slashing him severely in the face. Other automatic weapons raked the side of the ship, wounding the door gunner and putting his M-60 out of action. The C&C ship was effectively blind and defenseless on its right side, and while the co-pilot wrenched the ship into a series of violent evasive actions Sergeant Major Gilbert detached his harness and blocked the doorway, placing himself between the enemy rounds and his Commander. Enemy fire continued to damage the ship, and several rounds impacted in the radio console within the ship's cabin. Command Sergeant Major Gilbert moved into the doorway, bracing himself as best he could, in an effort to shield his Commander from the enemy's automatic weapons fire.

From Gilbert's position he could see that the aircraft was directly over the casualties on the ground and that it was impossible to land. He ordered the helicopter out of the LZ, guiding it through the dense jungle and rough terrain surrounding the LZ. On the way out, the craft continued to take direct hits on its right side as Sergeant Major Gilbert fired into the enemy positions, succeeding in silencing one of them in spite of the unstable and precarious position he occupied.

As he was firing into another position, he was hit by enemy fire and killed instantly. His cover fire had allowed the aircraft to safely gain enough altitude to clear the LZ and move to a secure position.

Sergeant Major Gilbert had only thirty days left until his retirement. This was his fourth tour in the Nam. After retirement, he had been planning to live in Australia.

Once Sergeant Major Gilbert was hit, the chopper took off in a hurry, and Chambley told Colonel Knight that he might have to land early because the instruments were showing zero oil pressure. Knight told him to keep flying anyway. So Chambley headed for the nearest medical facility, and hoped for the best. After they landed safely and Sergeant Major Gilbert was offloaded, Chambley discovered that the ship had a circle of thirty-caliber bullet holes torn through the fuselage around his seat.

At dusk the company was extremely low on ammunition again. They called for re-supply. It was critical for them to get re-supplied before dark, in case the enemy decided to attack during the night.

Another helicopter piloted by Lieutenant Michael Ward responded to this dire situation. About dusk, he flew his Loach helicopter into the LZ and brought the much-needed ammo. He tried to land several times but, because of the intense fire, could not make it. In his last attempt, in the falling darkness, he succeeded in unloading his chopper by kicking water and ammo out the door. While hovering at the LZ, his machine was pulverized by enemy gun fire. Miraculously, Ward was not wounded and the chopper was able to fly away. At least the company had enough water and ammunition to make it through the night.

Chapter 54

Midday Wednesday, 12 March 69 as Recounted by Randy Chrietzberg and Pee Wee Pizarski

At the same time our company was in our battle, the LRRP teams own dramatic struggle ensued. For hours Randy Chrietzburg (LRP) and his Tracers team - James Franklin (Frank), Pee Wee Pizarski, Floyd Robinson (Rocky) and Wayne Joslin - zigzagged silently back and forth over treacherous terrain, assessing the damage to various enemy locations which had been pounded by B52 strikes the day before, and reporting their findings by radio to Captain Hockett.

During this time they were repeatedly notified of possible enemy bunkers by the Forward Air Observer, and were ordered to check them out. Apparently, from their well-camouflaged bunkers, the NVA allowed the Tracer team to move about at will for several hours so as to catch the company, advancing behind them, by surprise. And since the Tracers had been positioned by Captain Hockett so far in advance of the company, when fighting broke out, they found themselves separated from our company's location by at least 200 yards, trapped on the far side of the enemy's position.

Rocky (Floyd Robinson) was walking point. The team had been taking turns on point all morning, and it was Rocky's turn. Frank (James Franklin) usually walked point since he was the most experienced at it. Floyd Robinson had just been assigned to a Tracer unit, a fact of which he was terribly proud. He had begun his tour in Alpha Company, 3rd Platoon in February and reported to Frank Novotny. Floyd's nickname was Rocky; he was a big guy from Burlington, Kansas, and he looked like a boxer. He also had a brother stationed in Vietnam. When his brother volunteered for reconnaissance, Floyd volunteered too. At the time he was just twenty years old.

Even though he was less experienced than any other member of the team, Rocky kept bugging Sergeant Chrietzburg to let him walk point and finally Chrietzburg gave in so Rocky was serving as point man for one of the two five-man Tracer teams protecting the company.

When the team advanced up a ridge, Rocky had silently signaled the men that he had spotted some NVA nearby.

Sergeant Chrietzburg signaled, "How many and where?"

To which Rocky pointed repeatedly to his right and held up enough fingers to signal, "Twelve, I think."

When they received this message, one by one the guys moved to take up a firing position in the direction Rocky indicated. Just then, klackity klack, klackity klack, all hell broke loose. Bullets were flying all around them. The Tracers returned fire as best they could but as usual it was hard to see where the fire was coming from. Then Pee Wee looked up. He caught something out of the corner of his eye, and he started shooting straight up into the trees. Jocko, who was closest to him, hollered, "What the hell you shooting at over there, Pee Wee?"

Pee Wee yelled back, "Its hard to see 'em but they're in the trees too."

The team had caught seven enemy out in the open. Four of them were huge, giants over six feet tall, and they wore olive-drab uniforms. They towered over the other three men, who were dressed in the traditional NVA drab-tan attire. Pee Wee thought, *Damn, look at the size of those guys. Those are Chinese. Hell, we're fighting the damn Chinese here!*

The team directed fire at these enemy and dispatched them all. When the shooting stopped, the team could hear sounds as though other soldiers were being dragged away, so perhaps they had killed or wounded more than seven. There was no way to ever know.

For a moment things grew quiet. The team held their positions, waiting. From his location, Frank was able to observe several of the NVA they had killed. These soldiers were wearing green uniforms, web gear and entrenching tools. Frank noticed that several were armed with AK-47's while others had Chinese SKS rifles which had bayonets that folded up under their barrels. Frank also spotted one rifle grenade. All of these dead soldiers looked well-fed, clean shaven, and had recent haircuts. They appeared to be in good physical condition. He concluded that these were NVA regulars, well-trained and recently arrived from the North.

LRP radioed the company. He and Frank were trying to figure out what to do next. While they were on the radio to Captain Hockett's RTO Charles Webb, Pee Wee whispered to Jocko, "Ya know, we're in a world of shit out here." They were completely surrounded by the enemy. The thought that they might not make it back to the company had now crossed everyone's mind.

Then firing broke out again, but not against the Tracer team. This time snipers positioned in the trees about one hundred fifty meters away were firing on the rest of the company. Randy Chrietzburg could see them clearly, so he called RTO Webb and requested permission from Captain Hockett to direct gunship fire down on the enemy positions. When he received it, Chrietzburg called the Forward Air Observer and, by throwing smoke, accurately directed a Cobra gunship on four passes over the snipers.

When LRP got off the radio and whispered to the team. "Okay, men. You can hear the firing. That's Alpha Company. They are under heavy fire and we have to make it back to them. This place is crawling with the enemy. And it ain't your normal troops here; it's an elite unit complete with Chinese advisors and everything. We'll never make it if we stay here through the night. We gotta go back. Are there any questions?"

The gunships temporarily quieted most of the snipers who had the company pinned down. There was still sporadic gunfire they could hear in the distance. Only problem was, by directing this attack, the team's position had been compromised even more than it had been. Nevertheless, they remained in place for another hour, during which time they observed little enemy fire.

The Tracer team planned to link up with the company at an agreed-upon location later that night. The men moved carefully toward the company's position by moving generally toward the firing. They were in single file, separated by about ten to fifteen yards. This was standard operating procedure to prevent the whole team from getting wiped out in an ambush.

But on the way there, they happened upon a camouflaged NVA bunker complex.

Frank spotted it first. He whispered, "Bunkers."

While the other team members flanked them to provide cover, Chrietzburg and Franklin moved in quietly to check the bunkers out. They discovered a half dozen well-camouflaged, entrenched bunkers which had been partly blown away by the recent heavy gunship fire. They did not appear to be occupied. These bunkers were constructed of six-inch round logs and had a foot of dirt packed on top of them. They appeared to be built for protection against bombs, and were not used for fighting. While the rest of the team stood guard, Chrietzburg and Franklin searched all the bunkers in their immediate area. They found some mortar rounds, some AK-47 rounds, and two or three coconut-shaped canteens. Some of them were connected together by small tunnels.

Unexpectedly an NVA pooped out of a bunker in front of Sergeant Chrietzburg. LRP reacted quickly, fired a six-round burst and killed him instantly. About that same time, LRP heard a shot from down inside the bunker. He prepared to shoot only to find Frank emerging. Frank reported he had killed another NVA. Both of these soldiers were dressed in black pajamas, neither appeared to be armed, and neither wore a helmet.

The team continued to search bunkers for a distance of forty meters, and they could see that the bunkers continued into the distance much further than that. Then they found a spider hole at the base of a clump of bamboo trees. A spider hole was a hidden passageway leading away from a bunker. It was an escape hatch, and probably meant that there were NVA nearby. Chrietzburg had barely uttered a warning about this to the team when heavy automatic weapons fire opened up, klackity klack, klackity klack, firing erupted. For the next fifteen minutes, the jungle erupted with the deafening sound of M-16s, AK-47s and grenades all exploding at once. It was an intense firefight. Then, abruptly, all was quiet again.

Chrietzburg turned to give a vocal command to his team, but they were nowhere to be seen. In the dense vegetation, he had lost visual contact with them.

Pee Wee who had been walking drag bringing up the rear looked up and around carefully. He was alone too! When the firefight began everyone scattered. Pee Wee could not hear or see any sign of them. Now he was caught in the middle of the enemy, alone, with the smell of spent ammo hanging in the air. A haze of smoke was slowly flowing up from the ground, right through the thick brown and green foliage. Otherwise, there was only an eerie silence just for a moment.

Suddenly there was an explosion, Chrietzburg saw Frank double up and fall into an enemy foxhole. Then Chrietzburg jumped for the hole just as two B-40 rocket rounds exploded with a characteristic thud, one after the other, about fifteen meters behind him. The force of these explosions blew Chrietzburg's helmet right off his head, and the radio, which he had in his hand, took a couple of shrapnel hits but he was okay.

He turned Frank over to examine him and render first aid. Frank said he was okay. Intense enemy fire was still coming in on them, they were caught in a cross-fire. Frank radioed the company for help. But at this point, the company was pinned down by their own battle, and it was impossible for them to give the Tracers any assistance. Captain Hockett ordered the Tracers to return to the company perimeter on their own.

The two men carefully raised their heads up out of the foxhole and spotted a machine gun nest about fifty meters to their front. They ducked down, looked at each other for a moment, and then simultaneously lobbed grenades at the enemy. The machine gun fell silent. Within seconds Frank killed two more NVA soldiers who charged straight at them through a nearby heavy bamboo thicket. After that, the firing ceased.

Chrietzburg and Franklin waited for about ten minutes, but there was no further fire on their position. Together they crawled out of the foxhole toward the machine gun nest they had silenced. There were three dead NVA in khaki uniforms in the nest, each armed with Chicom grenades stuck into their pistol belts.

The other members of their team were nowhere in sight, and since the others didn't have a radio, there was no way to tell if they were dead or alive. While they were discussing what to do, Frank spotted an NVA dressed in black pajamas with a bandaged forehead walking toward them, and he killed him with a single shot. The men laid low in the machine gun nest for a while, fully aware that they were in a precarious position.

Then Sergeant Chrietzburg rose up to look around. He spotted another enemy in a dark brown uniform walking across their flank. He also had bandages on his head. Chrietzburg killed him with a five-round burst. Another radio check with RTO Webb revealed that the company was still pinned down under heavy fire.

From their position in the enemy machine gun nest, Chrietzburg and Franklin were vulnerable. They decided to move into the jungle. But when they stood up and started running for the cover of the forest, they found themselves being fired at by both machine gun and small arms fire again.

Fortunately, the vegetation was so thick that, once they dove for cover, they were invisible to the NVA. They managed to silence the machine gun with grenades, but then Frank found himself exchanging rounds with another NVA shooting an AK-47. Frank expended two magazines and three hand grenades, but he failed to silence the enemy. Then, a few minutes later, he was seriously wounded in the right leg. Chrietzburg looked at the wound and saw that Franklin had lost a four-inch chunk of his leg above the kneecap. The wound was bleeding profusely.

Chrietzburg grabbed the radio and called in a Cobra gunship, and after three passes, it finally silenced the enemy's fire. Because the enemy was so close, the gunship's rounds struck the ground and sprayed volumes of grass and dirt all over both men. But the two Tracers had to lay there and take it. To jump up and run would have put them in another NVA's sights.

Once the gunship flew away, Chrietzburg called the company for a medic. He quietly reported their position, and whispered that he and Franklin could not move. The NVA were all around them. He whispered into the radio that he and Franklin were hiding in a bomb crater and, since it was growing dark, had so far remained undetected.

Chrietzburg reported to RTO Webb that Franklin had been hit and was losing blood. Captain Hockett's reply was that the company was taking many casualties and he could not send a medic at that time. Unfortunately he told Chrietzburg and Frank would have to work their way out of enemy territory alone, wounded or not.

Afternoon 12 March 69 Pee Wee as Recounted by Pee Wee Pizarski

Pee Wee snapped out of it. His animal instincts subsided and his brain started working again. Now he had to decide what to do. It was simple, *Continue working my way back to where the firing is, but move quietly without being seen. When I get close, I will have to crawl.*

Pee Wee moved as quickly and silently as he could. Pretty soon he had come to within 100 yards of A company. Sergeant White, Airborne, The Flea and I had already charged the bunker and had already been hit by a rocket. We were lying there wounded while the enemy's fire was raining down on the company from all sides. Jerry Loucks and Sergeant Woodall had already cleaned out the bunker complex but the enemy was still coming up the hill at us. In short, our company was experiencing hell on earth.

As Pee Wee approached our position, he saw the NVA at work. They were firing from bunkers about thirty yards from his position, off to the right. Other NVA were located about forty yards from the company, off

329

to Pee Wee's left. Pee Wee was facing us about 80 to 100 yards away. Suddenly he observed the whole side of the hill behind him erupting with fire. Ka-boom! *Damn,* he thought. *What was that?*

The NVA up there were raining rockets down on the company! Pee Wee crawled closer to get a better look. Soon he spotted a Ricky rifle team firing on the company from the top of a small ridge.

The Ricky rifle was actually a Soviet-made B-10 Recoilless Rifle. It was not a rifle at all but a portable cannon, capable of firing 57mm, 75mm and 105mm shells. It was usually mounted on a tripod like a mortar. In other words, it was heavy artillery in a portable form. It had the same effect as an RPG (Rocket Propelled Grenade) , which means that it was deadly as hell. An RPG was basically a shoulder-fired anti-tank rocket launcher. If this weapon could take out a tank, imagine what it could do to a group of guys.

This was the same Ricky rifle that had hit me, and had also injured Sergeant White, Airborne, The Flea, and a number of other guys in our company. Later, it wounded Jerry Loucks in the jaw. From his cover in the foliage, Pee Wee witnessed a number of rockets being fired down on the company. Something told Pee Wee to go after that Ricky rifle. *Fuck it, they're killing my buddies.*

Although he was exhausted, Pee Wee started crawling toward the ridge. As he crawled, he thought, *I'm gonna blow those fuckers to hell.*

He got within twenty or thirty yards of the ridge undetected. At that point, the sound of rockets firing over the top of him was deafening, and the smoke was thick. He calmly and carefully removed two grenades that were clipped to his pack and laid them in front of him on the ground. The foliage was so thick around him that he had to be careful not to lose the grenades. Judging the distance between his position and the Ricky rifle on the ridge, Pee Wee realized that his toss had to be just right. And he had only two chances, because these were the only grenades that he had.

Pee Wee grabbed the first grenade, pulled the pin and carefully counted, "1001, 1002, 1003" and then let the grenade fly toward that Ricky rifle. He heard an explosion and he waited. But hell, there went another rocket. The enemy was still firing! He had missed. So he thought, *This next one is my last chance. It has to hit the mark.*

Pee Wee pulled the pin and started counting again, "1001, 1002, 1003."

This time he stood up out of the foliage, then heaved his grenade. When it exploded, he knew it was right on. With his mind and body on automatic Pee Wee scrambled up the ridge M-16 in hand. When he looked into the Ricky rifle bunker, he saw four NVA. Two of them were dead and two were just dazed. So he fired two bursts from his M-16 to kill the dazed ones and then, for insurance, he fired a burst into each of the dead ones as well. He later said he wanted to make sure all of them made it safely into the next world.

Once this mission was completed, Pee Wee scrambled back down the ridge. He lay down in some dense cover and turned over on his back just to rest for a moment. The adrenaline that had been pumping, the stress on his body and mind, were catching up with him. Pee Wee was tired. He felt a deep satisfaction. He thought to himself *job well done*. While he lay there, Pee Wee dug into his rucksack, pulled out some rations and ate them.

After a few of those kinds of minutes that seem like hours passed, Pee Wee's mind started to work again. *Survival! That's my new mission,* he thought.

I have to make it back to the company.

Pee Wee started crawling again.

He was damn near totally exhausted from the fighting, and he was thirsty as hell. Pumping adrenaline will do that to you. He felt dehydrated; he needed water badly but his canteen was empty. He continued crawling slowly through the brush with all his might.

The enemy was still close by. In fact, they were all around him, even right above him. As he was crawling along, he heard such a racket of firing erupt that he could not any longer tell the enemy's location. They must be everywhere. But he didn't care about the NVA; he didn't want any more encounters. He just wanted to make it back to the company in one piece. Pee Wee figured, *enough is enough*.

His job was done.

But suddenly, as he was crawling through all the noise, Pee Wee felt a burning sensation on his back, as though he was on fire. The burning sensation was so hot, he couldn't stand it. Ejected shell casings from an AK-47 were falling directly onto Pee Wee's Pizarski's back! An enemy soldier was firing at our company right over the top of him! The spent shells hurt like hell. Pee Wee moaned involuntarily.

Then it was too late. Before he knew it, an enemy emerged from a camouflaged tunnel and grabbed his rifle while two others grabbed Pee Wee from behind. He struggled but he was tired. He couldn't evade them, and he was too tired to subdue them. He was captured. The three NVA proceeded to drag him off into the jungle.

Pee Wee was physically beat, and his mental state was not much better. In fact, his mind was almost totally blank. He gave up struggling and just let the NVA drag him away. His survival instinct told him to conserve his energy. He wasn't dead yet, so there was still a chance. They carried Pee Wee about 100 yards into the jungle, into a small clearing. He was now about 200 yards from the company's position. As they were dragging him along, Pee Wee looked up. He could see helicopter gunships overhead working the area with rockets and mini-guns, blowing off the tops of trees, wreaking hell on the enemy. But there was no way he could signal them. He watched them disappear over the treetops.

The three NVA soldiers who had captured Pee Wee were NVA regulars. They wore the standard NVA attire, off-color tan, and they were fully outfitted. They were North Vietnamese soldiers this time, not Chinese. Once they had dragged Pee Wee to a clearing, they forced him to sit down. They beat him about the head and face a few times. Then they tried to interrogate him. They wanted to know who he was, what his unit was, their strength, and where they were located.

Pee Wee could not understand them very well. He spoke only a few Vietnamese words and the NVA spoke only a few English words. Besides, Pee Wee's mind was lethargic; he was trying to recover, to regain his strength. At this point, anything he could do to buy time would keep him alive. Instinctively, he knew if he could get through the next few minutes then he would have a chance.

Somehow, during the interrogation he mentioned the word "Tracer" and the three NVA soldiers immediately became interested. It was as though they knew all about the Tracers. Pee Wee thought they might have been monitoring our radio transmissions and heard the word used there. Without knowing it, by uttering the word "Tracer," Pee Wee had saved his life. The enemy now thought they had a valuable catch. They thought Pee Wee was in intelligence and that he was worth something.

With that knowledge gained, the three NVA seemed satisfied not to kill Pee Wee right away. One of them pulled some rope out of his belt pack. This was a blue and white nylon rope just like the ones we used in the company. It looked suspiciously like it came from U.S. Army supplies. The NVA used it to tie Pee Wee.

First, they tied his ankles together and then they tied his wrists behind him. He struggled, but he was tied too tightly. The NVA had done a good job on him. Then the three NVA dragged him over by a big tree laid him down with his back against it. And lying there, Pee Wee was in an extremely painful position but he was still alive. Now he watched the three NVA dig into his pack. They were pulling everything out on the ground to see what they could find. Soon they found his LRRP rations and started eating them. As they ate, they were laughing and joking. It was almost as if they were celebrating. Their battle with our company was still going on not 200 yards away, but these guys were laughing and eating as though they had found a great prize, and their day's work was done.

Pee Wee was now starting to recover. His mind was coming into focus. As he lay there in pain, he remembered what Jerry Loucks had said. "I'd rather die than get captured by the NVA, cause then I'm gonna die anyway."

So far Pee Wee was alive because he was a Tracer. When they found out that he didn't know any secrets, he would be killed. He remembered Jerry's story of the kid who was used as bait. *There is no way I'll let that happen to me,* he told himself. *I gotta do something.*

Pee Wee noticed that the NVA were so busy with the items in his pack, they were not paying much attention to him. He also remembered the knife he had hidden in his boot. When they had searched him earlier, the NVA had missed it. Because of the way he was tied, his hands, which were bound to his feet, were near his boot. And because he was left propped up to that tree on his back, the NVA would not be able to see him reaching for the knife. As he lay there watching the NVA go through his pack, he thought that maybe he could reach it.

Without moving, Pee Wee quickly scanned the clearing he was in. He spotted his M-16. It was ten to fifteen feet to his left, just leaning casually up against a tree. Pee Wee had reloaded it just before being captured. His rifle was ready to fire. All he had to do was to reach it and flick the safety off. Now Pee Wee had a plan.

Despite being tightly tied, Pee Wee slowly wiggled his hands down to his boot. The pain in his wrists was almost unbearable, but that was all right. It meant that he was still alive. In his tied position it was difficult for him to move anything, but he could barely touch the knife now. Pain didn't matter. It meant nothing to him; he was entirely focused on reaching that knife. Then he got a hand on it. This was a small hunting knife his wife had sent him for Christmas last December. The thought occurred to him that this might have been the best Christmas gift he had ever received!

Most of the LRRPs carried small knives hidden in their boots just for this type of situation. Now Pee Wee was in that situation. The knife was halfway down in his boot with the other half hidden up under his trouser leg. When he finally got his hands on it and pulled it out, he felt very relieved. He cut his ankles free first. Now Pee Wee was no longer tied but still he didn't move. Now he flipped the knife around in his hands and worked on the ropes tying his wrists. This was the hardest job of all and he had to exercise great patience. A couple of times one of the NVA glanced over Pee Wee's way so he paused, holding his breath, making sure he displayed no movement. When it was safe, he resumed cutting. Finally, the knife cut through the ropes around his wrists.

He was free. Now Pee Wee thought, *No, don't act yet. Let me rehearse this plan once through in my mind first.*

Pee Wee watched the NVA for a moment. They were still enjoying themselves, eating his rations. They looked as though they didn't have a care in the world. Pee Wee glanced quickly over at his rifle. He knew he had to be real quick to jump up and reach that weapon in time. And once he had it in his hands, he had to be deadly accurate with his shots. He would have to dive ten feet, grab the M-16, take the safety off and then kill three men. This was no small undertaking. But he had no alternatives now, so each move had to be perfect.

As he contemplated his plan, Pee Wee's adrenaline was starting to build. His survival instinct, his animal instinct to fight to the death, was surfacing. Adrenaline is a wonderful body chemical. It works on the heart, blood vessels, lungs and muscles to get us ready to fight.

But the body contains more than one kind of adrenaline. Noradrenalin (known in the medical world as NA) is a form of adrenaline found in the brain. This chemical messenger clicks on the fight or flight response switch. It enables a quick and fearful retreat or, if necessary, the aggression to prevail in combat. It worked for Pee wee.

As Pee Wee jumped up and dove for his rifle, the word "bastards" boiled up into his throat like a scream. At that moment his NA must have been pumping full bore.

In one lunge, Pee Wee reached his weapon. As soon as he touched it, his hand automatically flicked the safety off. In one motion he raised the rifle and fired a perfect burst into the chest of each of his three captors. It happened that fast. Pee Wee was quick, his aim was perfect and the action was violent. As he fired, he couldn't hear the shots go off. All he could hear was his own voice yelling, "You dirty bastards! Go to hell!"

It was over. Pee Wee was standing there in the clearing, shaking like a leaf. All he could see was blood erupting from each of the three enemies chests. He walked over to each one and, to make sure they were dead, shot them carefully in the head one more time. He stood over them a moment, watching. No, they really were dead and now it was over. Pee Wee waited for his heart to stop pounding. He felt real satisfaction.

Once he calmed down a little, Pee Wee gathered up the items in his pack, dropping the uneaten rations back into it. Reconning his own position, he estimated that he was about 200 yards from the company and in no immediate danger. As he was about to leave the clearing, he noticed some communication wire strung through the trees down into the area. He thought, *While I am here, I might as well fuck up their communications too.*

So he took his knife and cut the two wires, then carefully spliced them back together the wrong way. He crisscrossed the wires and hid them so the enemy would never discover just where the problem was.

With that done, Pee Wee headed down a trail, moving in the general direction of the company position. His objective was to make it back to the company before dark, but he wasn't sure how to accomplish that with so many NVA around. He moved in the general direction of the firing.

Afternoon, 12 March 69 Pee Wee joins Jocko and Rocky as Recounted by Pee Wee Pizarski

As Pee Wee worked his way cautiously down the trail, he ran into Jocko, who had been hiding nearby the whole time, waiting for the right opportunity to return to the company's position. After a whispered conference, the two Tracers decided it would not be feasible to head

335

directly back to the company. To avoid the enemy, they would have to work their way around the enemy's flanks. They did not know the company was surrounded.

As they moved out together, they discovered Rocky hiding in the brush, also near the trail. None of the three men knew what had happened to LRP, or to Franklin. They decided that the best thing to do was to travel together and began to move out. But before they had gone more than fifty yards, Rocky signaled to stop. He pulled out his map and compass and suggested that they circle to the north and then west and come into the company from that direction. But Pee Wee and Jocko both preferred to head south first, and then circle west to the company's perimeter. Pee Wee and Rocky could not agree so they split up again. Rocky headed north and Jocko and Pee Wee worked their way south. This was the last time Pee Wee or Jocko ever saw Rocky Robinson.

Now it was just the two of them, they moved south in their roundabout way, using the traditional escape and evade techniques they had been taught in their LRRP training. They traveled as quietly and cautiously as possible.

At one point in their journey, both of them stopped. They heard a strange sound coming from the top of a nearby hill. They listened closely. They could clearly hear it over all the shooting. It was a whistling sound. Someone was whistling at them. "No, it isn't an animal," Jocko whispered to Pee Wee, "It is definitely human."

Pee Wee whispered to Jocko, "Jocko, I have heard that sound before. I swear it's my dad. Listen, it will be two longs then a short and then two longs. It's our call, the one we always used with each other."

They both listened. The whistling continued, just as Pee Wee had described.

Cold shivers ran down both the men's spines. "How can this be? Your dad's not in-country!"

Pee Wee said. "My dad died eight years ago."

Then he thought to himself, *Is he calling me from the other side? Is this his way of telling me that I will be all right, that he is here looking out for me?*

Both men stood still, puzzled, listening. Then the whistling stopped. Both Jocko and Pee Wee would keep this mysterious event a secret. There was no way to explain it, and who would believe them anyway? They moved on.

336

After getting off the radio with Chrietzberg, Captain Hockett told Lieutenant Andrews to take some of the men from 1st Platoon and some from 4th Platoon, since 4th knew the area better, and work their way down that saddle again to rescue the Tracer team.

The rescue party consisted of three guys from 1st Platoon, plus Lieutenant Andrews, and four guys from 4th Platoon - eight men in all. After they had spent the whole day fighting their way up that finger to safety, going down it again in their exhausted condition was the last thing these men wanted to do. Lieutenant Andrews told every man that they would have to cover each other's moves. They would advance down the saddle by leap-frogging, running from tree to tree for cover.

As the rescue team moved out through the darkening sky, they constantly watched the sides of the saddle off to the right and the brushy area on their left, to make sure that the enemy wasn't sneaking up on them. The lieutenant was worried that the enemy had moved out of the bunkers, and that, at this very minute, might be heading directly toward them.

Andrews and his men were advancing from tree to tree. Every time he moved, he thought he was going to get shot. He tried not to show it, but he was more scared on this mission than he had been in his entire life. But the team made it down the saddle without contact, and soon reached the first bomb craters at the end of the saddle.

Ronald Enser was the patrol's point man. Before starting across the open area in front of him, he stood behind his tree a long time, watching the jungle for movement or any other unusual activity. To advance further, he would have to sprint thirty meters in the open without cover.

Ron Enser was a tough guy, and he wasn't stupid. After reviewing all the options carefully in his mind, he left the safety of the trees. Enser glided as silently as possible along the right side of the saddle, hugging what little cover there was, making his way toward the tree line on the other side of the bomb blast area. He figured this to be the quickest and the safest route he could take. When he was about halfway across the clearing, a Cobra gunship suddenly appeared over the treetops, made a pass at the clearing and laid down a burst of fire from its miniguns. The bullets exploded in the dirt just in front of Enser. He cursed under his breath, dove to the ground, and rolled and crawled for cover.

Seeing this near mishap, the rest of the patrol ran back to the safety of the trees behind them and radioed the Cobra to stop firing into their clearing. Then Lieutenant Andrews looked for Enser and spotted him lying in a pile of leaves, trying to camouflage himself as best he could. Andrews moved forward, edging quietly into position to talk Enser back to the tree line, but before he could make contact, the enemy opened up on Enser. The Cobra's strafing run had called the NVA's attention to that clearing, and now Enser was caught in the open.

Unwilling to lay in the leaves and risk getting shot, Enser jumped up and ran back up the saddle toward the patrol, all of whom were watching his progress. The NVA started shooting the second Enser showed himself, but the patrol could not return fire or make any noise that might reveal their position. Enser was on his own.

When he was about halfway back to the tree line, Enser took a hit in the legs from machine gun fire spurting from the brushy area to the patrol's left, and went down. Lieutenant Andrews was also caught out in the open now, so, when the enemy started firing, he hit the ground and crawled quickly behind a big anthill.

With the patrol back in the trees and Andrews behind the anthill, there was no one to help Enser. But after Enser went down, the NVA ceased firing. Since they did not finish Enser off, it was obvious that they wanted the men in the patrol to try to rescue him so they could shoot them too. But the men would not take the bait; Enser was left to lay there. Enser had to crawl, pulling himself along with his hands, most of the way back to the patrol before anyone could reach him.

Pete Gedvilas from 1st Platoon had been walking slack behind Enser when the trouble began. He and Enser had been leap-frogging each other, trading point. And he and the rest of the patrol had been waiting in the tree line when Enser had tried to cross the open ground. After Enser got shot in the legs, and Lieutenant Andrews' rescue attempt failed, Pete started to crawl out into the clearing to get him. He had advanced no more than five meters into the clearing when an NVA pineapple grenade hit him in the arm and bounced a few feet away. Pete froze, just staring at that grenade, absolutely the worst thing to do in a situation like that. But the grenade didn't explode!

After saying a silent prayer, Pete continued crawling toward Enser, reached him, and pulled him back to the tree line. About that time, Lieutenant Andrews crawled away from his anthill and rejoined everyone in the safety of the trees. The patrol regrouped. The NVA had momentarily stopped shooting at them and the jungle was relatively quiet.

Then the patrol spent the next few hours attempting to cross that open ground again to rescue the Tracers. But each time one of the men showed himself, he received immediate and heavy enemy rifle and machine gun fire. The patrol called in a number of Cobra gunship runs trying to clear the NVA out of the area between the patrol and the Tracers. Each time the Cobra ceased fire the men tried to move forward, they drew intense enemy fire again.

After a few hours spent pinned down by the NVA, Anderson decided that the patrol had to return to the company empty-handed. They radioed the situation to Captain Hockett, and then moved in the dark back up the saddle to the company position. About halfway back they came to the area in which 3rd and 4th Platoons had abandoned their rucksacks. They searched through most of them for ammunition and water, taking what they could carry, before returning to the relative safety of the company position.

At dusk and into the night, 12 March 69 Chrietzburg and Franklin as Recounted by Randy Chrietzbergi

Randy Chrietzburg and James Franklin were still trying to work their way back to the company's position and they were short on ammunition. With only a little effort, the enemy could have easily surrounded and killed the two men, but for some reason they did not do so. Since it was growing dark, the Tracers rolled down their sleeves to cover their light skin and darkened their faces with charred leaves. They realized that they might have to fight their way out by hand. Even though he was wounded in the leg, Frank decided to continue carrying his rucksack so that the enemy would not get his food or claymore mines.

Both men were in excellent physical condition but as darkness approached they were becoming exhausted from this continued ordeal. With the NVA all around them, they had to move slowly through the jungle toward their rendezvous point, and Frank needed a rest break

339

every fifty meters or so. Finally, during one rest stop, Chrietzburg convinced Franklin to give up his rucksack. Sergeant Chrietzburg then carried both men's rucksacks, their two rifles, the radio, and Frank too.

The men stumbled together through the darkness. Frank was lying partially against Chrietzburg's back and shoulder and he shifted his weight every few minutes by hobbling along. The men traveled about seventy-five meters like this, and then they stopped. They could not continue because, as they approached the enemy positions surrounding the company, they were making too much noise in the heavy underbrush, and would be discovered. Also, Frank was now getting noticeably weaker.

They took a break. Frank whispered to Chrietzberg, "I can't walk, I gotta crawl. It's the only way back. You walk." Frank had to go first crawling so that Chrietzburg would not lose him in the darkness. They moved for fifty or seventy-five meters like this and then stopped for a fifteen minute rest.

When they set out again, an NVA soldier spotted Chrietzburg's silhouette in the dark. The NVA mistook him for another NVA because he did not shoot. Instead, he whispered the Vietnamese words "Lai Day" ("Come here").

Without a word Chrietzburg leveled his weapon and fired at the NVA, killing him instantly. The NVA was thrown back about five feet by the bullet's impact, and then crumpled. Although Chriestberg had fired on semi-automatic, only one round had discharged; his rifle was now empty. A quick check revealed that Frank's weapon was out of ammo too. During this time, Frank just lay on the ground, resting, and in a daze.

After killing the enemy soldier, Chrietzburg fell to his hands and knees and scooted over toward Frank. Due to the loss of blood, Frank's eyesight was failing and he had to be told things several times. Nevertheless, he and Chrietzburg managed to crawl away from the scene together. As they maneuvered through the forest undergrowth, suddenly four grenades exploded in front of them. Two were nearby. The flash from one of these temporarily blinded Chrietzburg.

After a few minutes, when he regained his vision, Sergeant Chrietzburg spotted Frank dragging himself up to the bunker from which the grenades had been thrown. He had a grenade in his hand. Suddenly there was a bang and a flash, and then silence. No sounds issued from the bunker. Franklin was also lying very still and when Chrietzburg reached him, he knew that Frank had been wounded again, perhaps this time by fragments from his own grenade.

Chrietzburg tended Franklin's wounds as best he could and the two friends lay there together beside the bunker for a few minutes, resting. Franklin whispered to Chrietzburg, "LRP, I think my arm is gone."

In the distance, they could hear the occasional small arms exchange between our company and the NVA. They figured they were only about seventy meters from the company position. Chrietzberg grabbed the radio and called Captain Hockett again. He whispered their position and their situation, detailing the extent of Frank's wounds. He asked Hockett to send a couple of men but the captain refused, saying that the company was still under attack. Once again, even with Frank in serious condition, the Tracers would have to rescue themselves.

Chrietzburg knew that if he and Franklin stayed in their present location until daylight, the NVA would certainly discover them. But at this point, Frank could not continue to move on his own. So Chrietzburg made a difficult decision. He told Frank that he would make his way back to the company alone and return with help, in a few hours at the most, but certainly before daybreak. Franklin liked this plan, and he nodded his approval.

Chrietzburg gently moved Franklin into some brush for better cover and carefully noted his location. Then to comfort him he lay down beside him and held his hand for about fifteen minutes. He left Frank their empty rifles, both canteens and the radio. Frank also had his big knife. Then the two men said goodbye. Randy repeated to Frank that he would return. James Franklin slowly whispered, "I trust you, LRP."

Then he smiled and closed his eyes. Randy Chrietzburg turned and carefully crawled toward the company's position. At this point, Franklin was trusting Chrietzburg with his life.

When Chrietzburg reached the company's perimeter, the Tracer immediately asked Captain Hockett to be allowed to gather volunteers to rescue Franklin. But Hockett said no, insisting that the men wait until daylight. He would not give a reason for this decision.

This made no sense to Chrietzburg, since Franklin's location was crawling with NVA, and he had been seriously wounded. He needed medical attention soon, and he was not that far away. Chrietzburg only needed a couple of men to help carry the Tracer about thirty meters back

341

to the company medics. He and Hockett had harsh words, but Hockett would do nothing to help Frank.

Charles Webb, the company RTO, was in whispered communication with Franklin all night. The Tracer was in great pain. The men in the company had to listen to his voice all night knowing that that he could be dying. They tried to offer Franklin what encouragement they could. And despite his precarious situation, James Franklin never complained.

Chapter 55

Dusk Wednesday, 12 March 69 from the Plei Trap 44th Medical Aid Station, Polei Kleng

Once we were safely away from the battle, the medic yelled at Rinehart that Revis had been hit bad. Mike decided he had to make it to the nearest air strip at Polei Kleng, where a company of the 44th Medical Battalion had recently moved. Mike flew flat out, but the chopper was loaded down. The chopper had red-lined at about 140 knots and held maximum power all the way to Polei Kleng. Mike expected an engine failure, and he wanted the engine rpm and airspeed as high as possible in case we lost power and had to autorotate to the ground.

Coming into the airfield, Mike dropped the collective and we glided toward the ground. He made a running landing, sliding in on the skids, right onto the PSP (perforated steel plates). This was the fastest type of landing, but it was dangerous. The skid boots were known to snag on the PSP and either flip helicopters or rip off their undercarriages. However, Mike took the chance. He'd already radioed the 44th Med that we were coming in. The Polei Kleng air strip had just taken a mortar attack. Despite the attack, the medics and doctors were on the flight line with stretchers.

As soon as we landed, Mike and his pilot jumped out to help unload the wounded men. After the medics had pulled two or three of us from the chopper, they reached an unconscious man and gently placed him on a stretcher. That was Charles Revis. While the medics examined Revis's wounds to assess the damage and stop the bleeding, Mike kept trying to get the sand out of Revis's eyes. Suddenly the medics stopped their attempt to revive Revis. He was dead. Mike absolutely could not accept the medics' pronouncement. He continued to remove sand from the soldier's eyes. Revis had survived the battlefield and been killed while being evacuated from the landing zone. A bullet had found him through the cargo hold of the helicopter. It wasn't fair. It wasn't right. The boy deserved to go home. He had served his time. Mike was devastated.

On the tarmac, where I had been placed after being pulled from the Dustoff, I watched several paramedics working on Revis. The air was thick with the smell of mortar smoke. I was weak and fighting shock. I knew that the 44th Medical Aid Station was a temporary stop. They performed hamburger surgery, temporary first aid, and bandaging and evacuation preparation for the more seriously wounded. Once they had a full load at the aid station, they would either transfer us wounded back to Pleiku or, if there were more than fifteen or twenty of us, the triage sergeant would call in an Air Force C-130 to take us to Qui Nhon.

Two men carried me to the aid station on a stretcher. I joined about twenty other wounded men, including Sergeant White, The Flea, and the other wounded. I remember the tent being olive drab, dark and damp; it didn't seem like a hospital, it was more like a morgue. A doctor walked up and down the aisles between the cots, looking at the various wounds. At times, he shook his head, clearly affected by the sight. While we were waiting to receive medical attention, several men died. I could hear the frustration of the doctors and medics in the background.

Lying in that musty hospital tent, my mind tried to wander, I tried to think about something besides the war. I tried to do my out-of-mind-and-body thing, but vivid, intense images of the firefight kept flashing through my mind. It seemed that I relived that firefight a dozen times lying there in that cot. I tried to sleep. But each time I closed my eyes, they would fly open and I'd be right back in the thick of things. My heart pounded, and I worried about the other wounded men and about my men still in the Plei Trap.

Finally, a doctor gave me some morphine and I was able to float away. I was away from the battle to a peaceful place . . . to thoughts of home. I was seriously wounded. I was also in battle shock. I needed someone to tell me it was all right. I needed someone to tell me that it was okay to leave, that someone else would step up and finish my job.

Dusk Wednesday, 12 March 69 71ᵗʰ Evacuation Hospital Plieku

The medics at Polei Kleng did not operate on me. They cleaned my wounds and made sure that I was stable enough to transfer to the next hospital. The next morning I was shipped out on a Dustoff to the 71st Evacuation Hospital at Pleiku.

Once I reached Pleiku, the nurses removed my clothes and wheeled me into the operating room to prep me for surgery. They opened all my wounds, removed the shrapnel, and left the flesh exposed. Where I had been peppered with dozens of small holes in my shoulder, I ended up with most of the shoulder sliced open, like a side of beef. Then they gave my arm and my leg the same treatment. When I awakened and saw all this exposed flesh, I was afraid to move.

After a few days I was flown to Cam Ranh Bay. I had come full circle now and was back at the spot where I had first entered Vietnam less than four months ago. I lay there in my gurney with my Bowie knife at my side, it being my only possession. The doctors and nurses had placed it there for me to have just before the flight to Cam Ranh. Just then a clerk showed up at my side and began to ask questions as part of the out of country clerical processing. Then he saw my knife and told me that he would court-martial me if I took it, he said it was impossible to travel with a weapon. At the time I went along with him without argument, my mind was thousands of miles away.

Looking back on it now, I know he was bluffing. How could they court-martial a seriously wounded soldier for keeping the knife that had saved his leg? That knife was the only reason my leg was not entirely gone. Since I had been standing closer to the explosion than Sergeant White had been, without the protection of my Bowie knife I would have been wounded as badly as he was . . . or worse.

Thirty years later, I will never forget the sight of the large pieces of shrapnel that were embedded in its handle. It was by sheer luck and the knife, that I did not lose my leg.

Evening Wednesday and night, 12 March 69 Aftermath in the Plei Trap

While I was being airlifted on Mike Rinehart's Dustoff out to a field hospital, the men that remained on the ground were still under attack and they were facing a desperate situation. They were low on ammunition, food, and water, and were surrounded by a large enemy force. They had to do something or they would all likely be killed. But what?

Evening approached, the firing slowed to a halt, but still the situation remained unchanged. They waited for the NVA to make their attack. To try to forestall this inevitability, they called artillery in on the enemy positions all night long. The shells sometimes exploded very near the company's perimeter, and the noise and shock waves were deafening.

While they waited, the men tried to figure out how to defend themselves. Nobody slept. Even with the two recent helicopter re-supplies, everyone's ammunition was low. The men were very thirsty; many were dehydrated from the day's long battle. But they were very tense and ready to fight. However, getting anyone to conduct a recon, to move more than ten feet beyond the company perimeter, was impossible. The men all wanted to stick together.

The company conducted no probes, but strangely, they received no probes from the enemy either. The NVA may not have known it but, if they had wanted to, they could have overrun the company in short order. The men could not dig in because there were only two shovels in the whole company and the ground was too hard to dig using anything else. So the men lay there, on the surface, without much of anything for cover, waiting for the enemy to strike. Waiting, in fact, all night.

As night fell, Gerry Richardson noticed that the jungle had become very quiet. He hoped maybe the enemy was tired too. Quickly twilight turned to standard jungle black, and darkness consumed the company. Gerry felt numb from the day's battle. He was so tired that he couldn't stay awake. He realized that, at that moment, he didn't give a fuck what happened. He was just too tired.

Lieutenant LePeilbet, who had refused to be evacuated that day, scraped out a position for himself in the dirt with his helmet, pulled his helmet down tight around his ears, and settled into a prone fighting position. He still could not feel or use his legs, but he was able to issue commands and he continued to fire his carbine when necessary.

As nightfall approached, Domingo Correa was busy praying. He prayed to the Lord every day that he would not get hurt. Now he thought that that was why he had survived this firefight. He had not even been wounded.

But his prayers were disturbed when he heard something unusual. He raised his head to look around. He thought it might be someone in the platoon who had been lost and was now trying to find his way back to base. As he listened, he realized that he was hearing a musical sound. He listened more carefully and thought it was whistling, so he whistled back to them. He whistled one note, like "Whe-e-et!"

Some moments passed and then whoever it was whistled "Whe-e-et!" back at him.

So Domingo was sure someone was lost and signaling to him. He unhesitatingly replied by whistling the way a man would whistle at a girl "Whe-e-et Whew!"

346

Silence. No answer. Suddenly Domingo realized that he had been whistling to an NVA soldier.

Ronald Enser had been lying on the ground, bleeding. He was badly wounded in the leg. Nevertheless he couldn't wait any longer. He had to get up and take a piss. He struggled to stand up, and he held onto a tree for support. His leg hurt like hell. He started to piss but then he passed out from the pain while he was pissing, and fell down. Somehow he made it through the night.

Chapter 56

The next morning, right after sun up, Jerry Loucks, Ken McCormack and Sergeant Muck organized and led a patrol to rescue James Franklin. Even though he was totally exhausted, Randy Chrietzburg came along too. He was the only man who knew Frank's location. Randy had given James Franklin his word that he would return to rescue him. The last time he saw Franklin he was seriously wounded, Frank had looked his friend Randy in the eye and slowly whispered, "I trust you, Sergeant Chrietzburg." This bond between the two men sealed Chrietzburg's determination to bring Frank back.

The patrol started out making its way quietly through the jungle that morning, but as they approached Frank's position, the men ran into intense sniper fire. They took cover, at least until they could locate the source of the hostile fire.

After a few minutes spent returning fire, then waiting and watching, they were able to determine that the enemy fire was coming from a number of spider holes in the ground. A spider hole was a small, well-hidden tunnel entrance Charlie used as a doorway into and out of a bunker, but in this case, the spider holes were manned by NVA gunners. The rescue patrol had to silence the spider holes or they would be cut to pieces. They could not move forward.

After studying the situation, Jerry Loucks came up with a plan. He had noticed that the spider holes were positioned in such a way that each one provided covering fire for the next. Their fields of fire were all interlocked, which made them very difficult to attack. Jerry's plan was to move very quietly up to each spider hole from behind. Then lob a grenade down into it. To insure that it did not get thrown back he would have to hold his grenade until the last few seconds before lobbing it down the hole.

The patrol talked it over in whispers and agreed that this was the only way to beat the spider holes that had them pinned down. And time was of the essence in this rescue. James Franklin needed to get medical attention soon.

Sergeant Muck volunteered to help carry out the plan. After gathering everyone's grenades, they ran from tree to tree until they were positioned behind the closest spider hole. Then Jerry Loucks tiptoed up to it and pulled the pin on his grenade. After long anxious seconds while Jerry just stood there, Ken and Randy were relieved to see Jerry drop the grenade down the hole at the last second and fall to the ground for cover. BAM! The grenade went off in the hole. While Jerry checked the spider hole carefully for survivors, Sergeant Muck moved up behind the next spider hole, which was no longer protected by the one Jerry took out.

The two men leapfrogged each other down through the web of spider holes, dancing on their toes while the fire team watched their backs ready to shoot anyone that might pop up. One man would locate a hole, pull his grenade's pin, wait out the count, drop the grenade down the hole at the last possible second, and then step back. After the grenade exploded, the other man would run ahead of the now dead hole and prepare to blast the next one. Meanwhile the first guy would get another grenade ready. He would move behind his partner over to the third hole and, when the second one was blown, blast that one too. The rescue team watched holding their breaths as Loucks and Muck performed this spider-hole ballet down the line of holes.

When they got a fix on a new hole, Ken or Randy would yell the location to Loucks and Muck. But when they saw how long that Loucks and Muck held their grenades before dropping them down those holes, the men grew worried. Sometimes they would spontaneously holler, "Drop it! Drop it, Jerry! Drop it, Dave!"

A grenade could have easily gone off at any time in their hands. It all came down to timing. The patrol watched in awe as these brave men did their stuff.

At one point in the process, an NVA suddenly appeared out of a spider hole and took a shot at Jerry Loucks. This got Jerry pissed off. He dove headfirst down into the spider hole, knife in hand. He went right down into that hole after the NVA. The rescue team could see Jerry's feet sticking up in the air, wiggling, as he struggled to kill the enemy.

When Jerry emerged again, his face and chest were entirely covered in blood. But fortunately, it was the enemy's blood! Jerry was only wounded in his ear lobe.

When this awesome grenade ballet was over, and the spider holes had all been silenced, the patrol left that area in a hurry. They knew the noise of their grenades would bring the NVA down on their necks. After advancing silently through the brush for about thirty more meters, communicating only with hand signals, Randy Chrietzburg called a halt with his upright fist.

He needed a few minutes to orient himself. Somehow the forest looked different in the daylight than it had the night before. The four men quietly crouched down on their haunches, listening to the jungle sounds for any sign of the NVA, and waiting patiently for Chrietzburg to reveal which direction they should follow. After a few minutes, Chrietzburg spotted the bunker Franklin had silenced the night before, and he knew they were close to him.

Randy Chrietzburg walked over to the bunker, looked to his left and slightly behind himself, and pointed to some bushes nearby. Jerry Loucks knelt down and lifted the bushes aside. James Franklin was lying there, hiding from the NVA, still alive. Jerry gently rolled him over. Frank stared up at Jerry for a moment, seemed to recognize him, and then he closed his eyes and died. James Franklin had lain in the dirt all night, with his leg torn up and one hand blown off and the flesh gone between the elbow where the hand used to be.

Mid-morning Thursday, 13 March 69 Dustoff for the Other Wounded

Another Dustoff roared in and hovered while the wounded men were loaded. Several volunteers hurriedly carried the wounded men onto the Dustoff. To give protection to the helicopter, everyone was firing into the jungle in another Mad Minute, but no NVA fired back this time.

Now Lieutenant LePeilbet, twenty-two hours after he had been seriously wounded, agreed to leave the company. But first he distributed his useful stuff to other guys. By his order, he was the last of the wounded men to be loaded onto the chopper. The Dustoff cleared the area about ten in the morning, without incident.

The day had started out quietly enough. But after the Dustoff left, there were a few incoming grenades, and then the NVA mortared the company. The men tried to dig in on the hard surface, but all they had to dig with was their helmets. It was difficult to know which would be more dangerous - to dig with your helmet and expose your head or keep your helmet on and be subject to a mortar hit.

350

Despite the mortar activity, there was no ground assault from the NVA. By late morning, the company finally got re-supplied by chopper with ammunition and water. Most of the men who were still on the ground were scared. Very scared but resolved. They expected a major attack at any moment. What was the enemy doing? That was the great unknown. The company badly needed information.

Afternoon Thursday, 13 March 69 Attempted Recovery of Rucksacks

In the early afternoon Lieutenant Porter of 2nd Platoon led a squad on a short recon. As soon as they left the company's location, they walked into the enemy complex. They found bunkers and tunnels everywhere. The enemy had even run field telephone wire between the bunkers, and constructed mortar pits. This preparation was proof of what the company had already discovered; that the enemy was well entrenched.

When Lieutenant Porter's recon turned up only empty bunkers, Capt. Hockett ordered 2nd Platoon to advance back down the saddle, recon the area, and recover the men's rucksacks which had been abandoned the previous day. Before he left, Lieutenant Porter spoke with Lieutenant Andrews, who told him where the rucksacks were located.

The entire company watched silently as 2nd Platoon moved cautiously down the saddle, hoping that nothing would happen to them. The platoon reached the rucksacks without incident. But when they tried to get stuff out of them, they found the rucksacks had been badly shot up. Many had caught on fire from the heat of the bullets, and had burned up. The company had lost their extra radio batteries. But the rucksacks had been shot up and burned for a good reason; the men had used them for cover. Those rucksacks were all that had stood between them and certain death. Soon after examining all the rucksacks, the NVA began firing on the platoon. Second platoon ran back up the saddle as fast as they could, bringing only a few rucksacks, those which could be easily salvaged.

Then 2nd Platoon performed another reconnaissance. This time they penetrated about three hundred meters into the jungle before the enemy started hammering them with intense fire again. They could advance no further. During this recon, Lieutenant Porter shot a sniper close by, and the man fell to the ground, so the lieutenant walked over to him. The dead NVA was dressed in a new uniform, his web gear appeared new and unscratched. Lieutenant Porter rolled him over and discovered a new

351

Chinese SKS rifle lying under him. It was the type with a silver bayonet that folded up underneath the barrel. The guy appeared to be asleep. Dead asleep.

Lieutenant Porter grabbed the rifle and started trotting back toward the perimeter. As he approached close enough to see the faces of his men, he tripped over a root and fell headlong. To the men in his platoon, it appeared as though the sniper had nailed him. They looked very relieved when he got up, dusted himself off and, with embarrassment mixed with relief, entered the perimeter. He carried the Chinese rifle around for several days before sending it back to his locker at Enari for safekeeping. But later he discovered that it had been stolen by someone working at the camp.

After the information gathered from these various recons was reported to the Brass, the commanders at Enari decided that our firefight was not an incidental ambush. Instead, we had marched right into a regimental NVA command post, and that the enemy had no choice but to fight us. So the Brass concluded that it would be best if two companies, Company A and Company C, attacked this NVA strongpoint at the same time.

Late Afternoon Thursday, 13 March 69 Withdrawal under Fire

Our Company had been decimated; the men were exhausted. They did not have any energy left with which to conduct any kind of effective operation against the enemy, not without plenty of reinforcements and substantial additional firepower. So our company was ordered to move out of its location, in marching order - 4th Platoon on point, then 3rd Platoon, then Headquarters, then 2nd Platoon, and finally, 1st Platoon.

Capt. Hockett told Lieutenant Andrews that 1st Platoon had rear guard, and that they had to stay on the battlefield until the entire company had vacated their positions. First Platoon set up a small defensive position shaped like a "J," with the bottom of the "J" pointing down the saddle. Each man in the platoon sought whatever meager cover he could find. The company left the area by humping back down the trail from which they had arrived the day before. The men left behind in 1st Platoon to guard the rear were scared as hell.

While 1st Platoon was waiting to pull out, Mike Moran, who was in position facing down the finger, turned to Lieutenant Andrews and reported that he saw NVA coming up the saddle. A few seconds later,

Paul Beck, a machine gunner, turned to Lieutenant Andrews and said that the NVA were coming up the left side of the finger too. All hell broke loose. The enemy was all over the place again. Every man was firing everywhere as fast as they could.

Lieutenant Andrews ordered the platoon to move out immediately. They ran so fast that Andrews left his rucksack, with eight hundred dollars of his R&R cash money in it, as well as his undeveloped rolls of film. His rucksack was too heavy because it also contained extra ammunition. He simply had no time to grab it.

When Gerry Richardson of 1st platoon awoke that morning, it was just before dawn. The company was already making preparations for a withdrawal. Gerry was in 1st Platoon, and his squad would be the last in the platoon to leave. He was stationed near the point where the saddle connected to the knoll. In the final minutes of the withdrawal, Lieutenant Andrews passed by, leaving only he and Paul Beck left to protect the rear. At this time, Gerry had an M-79 grenade launcher while Paul was firing his M-60 machine gun. The company was moving out slowly, and they periodically stopped to check their progress.

Then the enemy appeared to the front of Gerry and Paul. At first they were just so many shadows in the trees. But as they moved closer, these shadows had faces, then uniforms, then helmets - just like real soldiers. Gerry wondered why he was sitting there, holding a breech-loading single action weapon, facing such a large number of the enemy. Then he calmed himself down, extracted a spent shell, inserted the new round, closed the breech and aimed carefully, then squeezed the trigger. All he could remember was a center of mass in his sights and an explosion of red. With his M-79 grenade launcher, he had killed an enemy who had advanced to within several meters of his position,. The enemy just exploded before his eyes.

Gerry didn't remember whether it was his suggestion to run or Paul Beck's, but they both knew it was time to get the hell out of there. They ran toward the end of our company's column. The company was moving as fast as they could since they now had a large number of enemy chasing them.

To reach the rest of the company, the men had to run up the saddle and across the landing zone. Paul Beck tripped over some cut brush in the LZ as he was running from the enemy, and fell down. Lieutenant Andrews turned back to cover Paul, and he could see the NVA firing

353

directly at both of them. It was surreal. Everything moved slow motion. Andrews thought he could even see the bullets coming at him. He stood his ground and emptied two or three magazines at the NVA on full automatic, giving Paul time to get back on his feet. Full automatic allows you to fire an M-16 at 750 rounds per minute, or twelve and a half rounds every second until your weapon jams. That was the only time in his life that Lieutenant Andrews had ever fired his weapon on full automatic. But it didn't jam, and it saved Paul's life.

As he ran up the trail to catch up with the company, Lieutenant Andrews was calling Fire Support to drop artillery on their night position, and do it RIGHT NOW. He figured that, by the time the rounds landed, everyone would be out of the area.

The platoon soon halted along the trail to see if they were being followed. Mike Moran was explaining to Lieutenant Andrews that, in addition to his rucksack, which had burned up on the finger, he had also lost his bush hat. About that time a Chicom grenade exploded. Mike got hit in the upper arm with a piece of shrapnel and the force of the impact threw his arm back which automatically hit Lieutenant Andrews right in the family jewels. For several minutes the lieutenant was incapacitated. Mike didn't know who was hurt worst - himself or the lieutenant.

The NVA were in hot pursuit of Alpha Company. Second Platoon began yelling to the headquarters guys ahead of them to get moving faster, the NVA were breathing down their necks and 1st Platoon was taking fire. This was not an orderly withdrawal. It was a retreat!

Chris Kruckow, the M-60 gunner in the 3rd Squad, was one of the last men to leave the saddle that day. As the other guys, whom he had been covering, pulled back, he was left unprotected. The enemy opened up on him in a hail of fire. The ground around him was boiling with hits from NVA bullets. Just about the time Chris was about to leave a bullet penetrated his gas mask, which was tucked under his belt, and bore into his leg. Luckily he was not bleeding that much, but Chris couldn't walk. He tried to move on his own but couldn't.

Word got back to Jerry Loucks that his friend Chris had been wounded. Jerry and Ken McCormack immediately ran back down the trail to rescue Chris. When they found him, he was still being fired upon from the trail behind them. Ken McCormack quickly fired a burst toward the muzzle flashes and shot the NVA who had been firing at Chris. With that Jerry told Chris leave his rucksack and other gear behind, and the three of

354

them got the hell out of there as fast as they could. Ken gave Chris his D-handle shovel as a crutch and between them they carried the M-60 with Chris hobbling and leaning on Jerry's shoulder. For cover, McCormack fired a few bursts down the trail as they were retreating.

Once out of harm's way, Chris found that he could hobble around slowly on his own using Ken's shovel as a crutch. He was still not bleeding very much. A few hours later, a Loach helicopter with one pilot and a gunner flew in and picked Chris up. When the Loach lifted off, the enemy really opened up on it. Watching all that fire the chopper was attracting, Jerry Loucks was in agony. He worried that Chris must have been killed. The enemy just peppered that chopper. As the bullets struck home, Jerry could see bits of the chopper's metal body flying off. Fortunately the chopper stayed in the air until it was out of sight.

While the NVA was chasing our Company down the trail, Captain Hockett was being instructed to leave the area entirely and rendezvous with Charlie Company (C-1-8). The two companies were to join up and regroup on top of a wide, flat hill a few klicks from their current location.

Charlie Company had recently been in a big fight too. Between them, the two companies could only field enough men to form one full-strength unit. Our Company had entered the Plei Trap Valley with seventy-five guys, but came out with only thirty-six. Three of those were KIA; all the rest of the men had been wounded, many of those seriously. Fourth platoon started out in December with thirty-two guys but by the end of March had only twelve men left.

Our Company had attacked, been surrounded by and then fought off the NVA's crack unit, the Tiger Battalion of the 66th Regiment. We had gone up against the elite of the NVA. These were well-outfitted, well-trained NVA regulars. They were among the best fighting men the North Vietnamese had, and they were waiting for us. For most of the fight, they had us trapped. We were lucky to be alive.

Friday, 14 March 69 I am still a Virgin

Company A and Charlie Company rendezvoused together and formed a combined perimeter once our company moved several kilometers from the battle area. Both companies dug in anticipating attack from the NVA. It was here that several of the men from our company volunteered to make a water run down the hill to a stream they had crossed the

355

previous day. Someone had to go; the work was hard and hot and the men were all running out of water again. Stream water in Vietnam was polluted with some very unfriendly bacteria, so the men would have to use their Army purification tablets, but that was better than having nothing to drink.

Several men from each platoon collected canteens; then, for protection, they made the run together. While this group was down at the stream, the NVA began firing on the company perimeter.

Sergeant Dave Muck was a Mormon. It was well-known in the company that he didn't drink either Coke or coffee. He kept reassuring the men in his platoon that they were safer to stay near him because he was a virgin, and God would not let a Mormon die a virgin. After all, he pointed out, he had survived the 12 March firefight without a scratch.

When the shooting began, Sergeant Muck spotted an NVA machine gun position and began firing repeatedly at it with his M-16. Then the NVA gunner apparently spotted Sergeant Muck shooting at him and pretty soon, the two men were firing back and forth at each other, Muck from his foxhole and the enemy from his bunker. The machine gunner would rake the front of Muck's foxhole, each round as it hit spewing sand from the bags, then, when the firing had passed, Muck would leap up and get off a few rounds before the next rake came in. Soon these two men were engaged in a personal, fierce firefight, each focused entirely on eliminating the other.

Then Sergeant Muck was hit; as he jumped up to fire he took an NVA round through the flesh of his upper arm. This made him furious. Ignoring his wound, he leapt up on top of the sandbags surrounding his foxhole, in plain view of the enemy, and started cursing that NVA machine gunner, giving him the finger and then shooting at him again with his rifle, while screaming, "I am a virgin! You cannot kill me! God will not let me die a virgin!"

The other men in his platoon were astonished. Domingo Correa blurted out, "Look at that crazy Muck!"

They all expected him to get killed any minute. But Muck just stood there, cursing and firing, firing and cursing.

When Sergeant Muck jumped back down into his foxhole a few minutes later, the enemy machine gun position had been silenced. And Muck had suffered only that flesh wound in his arm. The men in his platoon were really inspired. Not to be outdone, they began to shoot at

356

the enemy furiously. Pretty soon, the entire platoon was having a personal Mad Minute. When it was over, the NVA attack around their perimeter had been silenced. A bunch of the guys in 3rd Platoon were wounded in that firefight, but no one badly enough to need a Dustoff. And once the coast was clear, the guys on the water run made it safely back inside the perimeter.

The new combined company remained at this location until March 15. They began to take incoming 60mm rounds and that night, the NVA probed their positions. By now all the men were mentally as well as physically exhausted.

Shaky, the Battalion surgeon had been flown in to help treat some of the walking wounded. After talking to some of the officers about the men's condition, he called Battalion HQ to report that neither company was fit for combat. Unfortunately, what a surgeon said didn't make any difference to the Brass. The day after Shaky's call, both companies were ordered to move out toward Battalion HQ, to take out some big NVA mortars.

Colonel Buckner, Bullets, told the two company commanders that first they should form up and assault the area where we fought the NVA on the 12th. Captain Hockett told Bullets that he refused to go! Everyone in the two companies knew that the NVA would be waiting for them, well dug in and ready to fight. Both of the company commanders were relieved of duty, and Bullets sent out a major to replace these men. The combined company, under the major's command, was then renamed Task Force Alpha moving over to Hill 467, another very dangerous area. In time Task Force Alpha was moved to An Khe for duty guarding a bridge because the Major recognized the condition of the men, and finally convinced Bullets to accept Shaky's recommendation.

In two days, 12 March and 13 March, the two companies, A-1-8 and C-1-8, had each lost half their men, either killed or wounded. Both companies had been surrounded. Such was the success of Operation Wayne Grey.

Chapter 57

It was another hot day in Vietnam, I lay on a stretcher in Cam Ranh Bay. My body was cut open and I felt weak and vulnerable. But there was not a moment's peace. Powerful jet engines roared overhead, one after the other. Trucks and jeeps whizzed back and forth. Men walked or ran in all directions, shouting to be heard over the noise. Helicopters took off or landed in a non-stop pattern of activity. It was a busy day at the base. In the midst of this organized bedlam known as war, I waited with my wounded comrades to be flown to a hospital in Japan.

The 249th Army Hospital had been operating at Osaka, since the beginning of the Korean War. To get there, we would have a two-hour plane ride from Vietnam.

I struggled to lift my head from the cot. I could see a cargo plane nearby; one with a ramp that opened downward from the tail. Normally, it would be loaded with jeeps or trucks, but, today, it would take on human cargo. Eventually, my stretcher was wheeled toward the plane. Once inside, it was dark and cool. It was a welcome relief. When my eyes adjusted to the gloom, I saw that the plane looked like a huge tunnel filled with straps hanging from the ceiling.

The medics rolled me deep inside the plane. There were stretchers all around me, and slots on both sides for stacking the stretchers, one on top of the other. Each slot contained a wounded man. The medics lifted me up, and then I was one of them . . . just another guy on a shelf. From my stretcher, I could see a few of the wounded with IV bottles hanging above their arms. Each man had a different set of wounds to cope with and a different story to tell. It was noisy and smelly in the plane with nauseating odors of fuel oil and medications. While the plane was being loaded, all I could do was lay there and bear it.

Finally, the ramp closed, the air conditioning came on in the darkness, and we took off. Our flight seemed like a very long two hours. The soldier in the bunk above me kept yelling to the medic that he was getting wet. From what I could gather, condensation from the plane was dripping onto his face. The medic gave him a towel and told him that it wouldn't be long until we landed.

A soldier in a nearby stretcher said the plane was loaded entirely with broken soldiers. Hundreds. The thought was too powerful to contemplate. Some of the time, I drifted into a dazed half-sleep. Some of the time, I thought I was floating instead of flying. I tried to figure out whether or not I was happy. I was glad I wasn't dead yet. I knew that some of my comrades in A-1-8 hadn't made it, but I tried not to dwell on it. This wasn't the time.

Eventually, we arrived at the hospital. It was small, but very clean. Everything was white. There were about twenty men in my ward. Our beds were arranged in two rows with heads against the wall and feet toward the middle of the room, just like in the movies. Across the aisle from me, a soldier had a stump for a leg. The medics helped him into bed. I couldn't stand to look at it. Raw meat. Why didn't it bleed? *I hated the war.*

I had been trying to sleep all afternoon, but was disturbed by the commotion accompanying a new arrival. He was given the bed to my right. He had giant blisters all over his face, hands, and arms. Someone told me, later, that he had operated a flame thrower and, when he was using it, something had gone wrong.

Frank occupied the bed to my left. He was from Kentucky. Since I was facing him, we struck up a conversation. Frank had lost the use of his right arm. He said he was shot a total of seven times in a recent battle, and each time he had been wounded, it had felt different. Finally, the enemy had overrun his company's position. They blew his arm away and left him for dead. He had four other bullet wounds in his body.

The next day they brought in a guy who looked like he had been burned all over his body. He was also missing a leg. Why wasn't he in a burn ward? His limbs and stump looked completely charred. I couldn't believe he was still alive.

This ward was hell. I wanted to go home. I had had enough. I asked the nurse for some sleeping pills. She obliged me and for the next couple days, I drifted in and out of a drugged sleep. It was better than facing the reality of the ward and the war.

A few days later, the doctor told me that I would be going home right after they sewed me up, which would be the next day. I asked him why my hand was numb. He said I had median nerve damage. The nerve was almost severed. He said he didn't know whether it would ever get better, but maybe the doctors could do something when I got back to the States.

359

Upon learning the true condition of my hand, I felt surprisingly resigned. I was surrounded by men with severe injuries of all types—amputees, terrible stomach wounds requiring colostomy bags, the list went on and on and got worse. I could look forward to a better life in the future and whatever happened, things would never be as bad for me as the agonies experienced by my wounded comrades. I felt lucky and I was thankful.

Written between the lines of my doctor's words was the clear message that the Nam was over for me. At last, I could turn my thoughts towards home and towards building a new future. A thousand questions flooded my mind. *Will I be accepted? Am I damaged goods? How can I explain what has happened to me?* These thoughts must have run through the mind of every soldier who has ever been wounded. *How will I be accepted back in the World?*

The next day, the doctors sewed me back together. After that, my body was about as sore as sore can be. I hated being operated on so many times. Each time I had to put my life in some other person's hands. I didn't care if they were doctors, it was unnerving. While I was in the recovery room, other soldiers were wheeled in and out. Their wounds were too terrible to describe.

Wednesday, 26 March 69 249ᵗʰ Army Hospital, Osaka, Japan

Later, back in my bed, a medic came by and told me that I would be leaving in the next day or two. I was to be transferred to Walter Reed Hospital in Washington, D.C. I asked him the date. I had been in Japan a full week. That was long enough!

As I lay there feeling more hopeful, I tried to dream of home and my future, but it was hard to focus. I tried to work out a plan in my mind for going to college, but it was too difficult.

A few times I was caught off guard. The 12 March battle reappeared and replayed itself in my mind, leaving me feeling anxious and depressed. I knew that these episodes couldn't be good for healing, so I tried to stop them, but they crept in anyway. Over and over I experienced the firing, the yelling, charging the bunker, the explosion, the noise, the confusion, the helicopter under fire—and more yelling when Revis got hit.

I realized I would have to start over. Nam was the price I had paid to get to go to college. My life would never be the same. I had used my

360

skills to become a Shake 'n Bake sergeant in the Vietnam War. I had done my best. The little boy who had loved to play with his plastic toy soldiers and to draw pictures of warriors had become one. Now this boy couldn't stand war. The thought of it made him sick to his stomach.

Silently, I cried in my hospital bed. I didn't want anyone to hear me. Soldiers weren't supposed to cry.

Epilogue

Alone in the jungle, the three Tracers had a whispered, but heated, discussion on how to locate the company. They did not have a radio, so they would have to hump out of trouble. Rocky wanted them to work their way north up the trail, but the other two men decided to seek cover in the thick brush for the time being. So the group split up. Rocky started down an elephant trail. Then he must have seen something that the rest of the group did not see, because he opened fire to his right flank. Then he ran out of sight down the trail. That was the last time anyone definitely saw Rocky Robinson.

For two weeks after his disappearance, company-sized operations were conducted in the area in which Rocky Robinson had last been seen without anyone turning up a sign of him. At this time Rocky was officially classified as Missing in Action.

The last possible sighting of Rocky Robinson was reported by an LOH pilot who saw a guy standing in a bomb crater, waving his shirt at the pilot, hoping for a rescue. The pilot was on a medical emergency and could not descend, so he radioed the soldier's location to his HQ. The description he radioed back to Robinson's unit matched that of Sgt. Robinson. But while the soldier was waving his shirt, the pilot saw an NVA appear out of the forest and shoot him. The soldier fell, and the chopper disappeared over the horizon. The body was never recovered. Was that Rocky?

Pee Wee and Jocko both made it back to the company. It took them two full days. Then they walked into the perimeter like a couple of ghosts from the past. The men in A-1-8 were astonished that they were alive.

Charles Revis, James Fullerton, Floyd Robinson, James Franklin, Frank Runge, and Sergeant Major Gilbert died on March 12th as a result of the NVA ambush.

In late March of 1969, soldiers from the 3rd and 4th Platoons held a memorial service for our comrades who had died on 12 March and to remember the ones who had been wounded. The Battalion Chaplain flew out on a helicopter to hold the service at a lonely firebase near Cambodia. It was a time to reflect on the battles that had been fought and to pay homage to the missing comrades. I wish I could have been there, standing tall and proud as a 4th Platoon sergeant. Many who attended knew that they could have easily been counted among the dead or missing.

The Battalion Surgeon declared both A Company and C Company physically and mentally unfit for further action, they were soon to be assigned to An Khe for duty guarding a bridge. For most of these men, their fighting days were over.

When my company left the Plei Trap Valley, it numbered only thirty-eight men. Only 2nd Platoon had survived without suffering any losses. The other three platoons, including mine, had lost over half their men either killed or wounded. Pappy was right. The Plei Trap was truly "the Valley of Tears."

Once I returned from Vietnam, I never heard the words Shake 'n Bake for thirty years until the day I read the book *The Teams* with Jesse Ventura's words. Thirty years ago it seemed the world had the same negative opinion of us Shake 'n Bakes.

It turned out that the last Shake 'N Bake Sergeant graduated from Fort Benning on March 18, 1972. The Army concluded that the program was a success. Because of it the Army implemented two new, similar programs. These programs gave new opportunities for advancement to career soldiers returning from Vietnam. The new schools established at Fort Benning were BNCOC (Basic NCOC) and ANCOC (Advanced NCOC). Our Shake 'n Bake program is the basis for all training of NCO's in today's Army.

Some Shake 'n Bakes's are still in the service today, but many have since retired as Senior NCOs and Officers. A number of NCOCs completed their career in the Army and at least two of them attained the rank of Sergeant Major.

The Shake'n Bake Sergeants served with distinction as leaders in infantry units, and they suffered high causalities in combat and many were highly decorated. We were assigned to units that experienced heavy fighting and we were invented for only one purpose—to lead men in combat. And that we did. There were three Medal of Honor recipients graduated as NCOCs.

Thirty years later, the general consensus among many of the graduates was that NCOC School was the best experience they ever had in the service. The training was the best of its kind at the time. Many graduates reported that it was instrumental in their survival and the survival of their men in combat.

363

I had graduated on June 7, 1968, in the twenty-fifth class of NCOCs, with 133 graduates. I was promoted to Sergeant E-5 as an 11B40 Light Weapons infantryman. Eight members of my graduating class lost their lives during the Vietnam War.

On November 9, 2000, I stood with six other comrades, who had served with me in the fiery battle in the Plei Trap Valley, as honored veterans in a Fort Carson Veteran's Day celebration. Thirty years after we had been wounded in the line of duty on March 12, 1969 we received recognition from the United States Army for our acts of gallantry and bravery in one of the worst battles of the 1969 Tet Offensive in Vietnam.

Dr. Jerry S. Horton
The Shake 'n Bake Sergeant

I was awarded two Silver Stars—the third highest award for valor in combat—on a star-spangled parade field, with a mounted color guard, music from the 4th Infantry Band, and to the singing of "I'm Proud to Be an American," by a young sergeant. It was a heart-warming and gratifying moment in my life, and a deeply satisfying finish to my journey of discovery. It was a moment that gave me the peace I had sought, after Ventura's statement had spurred me into reclaiming a long-forgotten part of my past. I am proud to say that I was a Shake 'N Bake sergeant in the United States Army.

My journey of discovery has taken me thousands of miles, and many years into my past. I found it to be a good journey, a worthwhile journey. At the end of it now, I feel at peace. Perhaps I should have made this journey a long time ago, but, until now, I was not ready. Like many veterans, I have never talked about my past involvement in the war. For many years I simply blocked these memories out of my mind. I went on with life's business.

The few times I was asked about Vietnam, my explanation left people wide-eyed, as though they hadn't heard what I said. I am sure that many of them didn't believe me. How could such a plain guy like Jerry Horton have been there and done that? I am sure what I said did not register on them.

My journey back in time was initiated by a negative comment that made me mad, and it also made me curious. But now, I see that I have done my job. I really do not have anything else to prove. I never did.

My journey is, of course, not complete, but I have many old friends with me now. Friends I share a special bond with, friends who almost died with me, and for me. No matter what happens now in our lives, nothing can erase what we went through together. We have experienced life's most cruel, brutal, and intense emotional experience together, and somehow we lived through it.

And yes, we did perform with honor. We were combat infantryman who stared at death, face to face, not ten yards away, and we did it with honor. I am proud to have been an infantryman with these men and, most of all, I am honored to have served with the guys of Alpha Company, 1st Battalion, 8th Infantry of the 4th Division. You are all my heroes.

From left to right: Greg Rollinger, Spider, Tom Porter, Frank Novotny, Jerry Loucks, Don White, Snook, Ken McCormack

On August 14 and 15, 1999, our comrades up in Heaven, those who had died in Vietnam, must have been smiling. They would have been watching us and thinking, *Down there are our buddies, together again after thirty years. They are relaxed and at peace now, part of the family again, just as though thirty years had not passed by. They are relaxing in the beautiful and peaceful Minnesota wilderness, far away from war.*

And they would be right. There we were at our first reunion, the guys from the A-1-8, singing, happy, remembering the good times and the bad times, united again. For two days we talked about events so long ago in Vietnam, and about how our time had been so short but so intense together, and now how incredible our experiences were.

Our reunion was just what you would hope for. When we met, after so many years, everyone had "the look." No one glanced away; everyone peered straight into the other man's eyes. We all had a wisdom you could see and feel: *Been there and done that, and it was with you, buddy.* Our wisdom and understanding, borne of so much experience, was deep. We had formed an unbreakable bond. We could all feel it, without words.

The men from the A-1-8 did well that day. Now each man took the time to remember and to share. Our reunion could have not been better. That day we were happy. At last we have found peace.

367

March 1969 Recollections

Many parts of this book were written from recollections of events in Vietnam by either me or others who were there with me. All were incorporated in this story. The following sections contain individual recollections written after the final draft of the book and include events up to the end of March 1969.

These recollections are from events that occurred almost 50 years ago and are presented from memories and not from written notes. Therefore, there are some differences in timing and individual's recollection of the events.

March 12 1969 Recollections

Marc Lawrence

I recall that in the days leading up to March 12 we were humping with Company A 1st of the 8th Battalion in the Plei Trap Valley near the Cambodian Border. This was after Combat Assault Helicopters inserted us in a location near the Dak Ho'drai River March 3rd. My artillery battery (A/6/29 Arty) occupied Firebase 20 and there was a battery of 155's at Landing Zone (LZ) Swinger. There was a couple of 175 artillery pieces at LZ Mary Lou. All of this artillery was my Artillery support while I was located with the A-1-8.

It was my responsibility to keep accurate track of our position at all times in case of enemy contact and I could call in immediate Artillery fire safely if necessary. As a Forward Observer (FO) I had my recon sergeant and Radio Operator (RTO) with me as we moved with Company A. We all three moved and stayed with the Company Headquarters (HQ) group and for this reason we had a different perspective than the other infantrymen in the Company.

On the day of March 11 we entered an open area bordering a stream. The clearing was at least 100 meters wide. To the north of the clearing we began receiving artillery fire not mortars as normal. I immediately called all the batteries within range of our location ordering cease fire only to discover that none of them were firing. That was our "oh shit" moment when we realized that the NVA also had artillery (105mm) and they knew where we were.

Our mission was to perform a BDA (bomb damage assessment) on an Arclight B-52 strike that was due to come in later that night of March 11. We had to be located at least 3 km from the bombing to be safe. The problem was that the enemy knew where we were and our location was

369

not a position we could defend. So we moved to a small hill inside the buffer zone and we lied to our battalion headquarters about our true position so they wouldn't order us move. We weren't taking any chances.

The Arclight bombing occurred that night on schedule. It was terrifying as it crept towards us. The ground was shaking and the noise was so loud you could not hear yourself think. The next day of March 12, 1969 Capt. Hockett flew our intended patrol route in a LOH helicopter in order to recon ahead. Upon his return, the company started out on our BDA mission in the direction of the Arclight bombing. Within a few hours we came upon large bomb craters thirty-five feet in diameter. We noticed bits of commo wire scattered about the craters but at that time paid no attention to them. The commo wire did not register as being very sinister at that time but it should have. We also noticed unoccupied bunkers on the edges of some of the craters.

We traveled as a company slowly through the jungle with two platoons ahead of us and two behind us. I with my men humped with the HQ group located in the middle of the platoons. Company A was under strength with only 72 soldiers including me and my two men.

All hell broke loose. The two lead platoons came under heavy enemy contact. In just a few minutes the whole company was surrounded and under fire from well-equipped enemy in bunkers and snipers in the trees.

The first thing I remembered was the NOISE! It was deafening. I could not hear verbal orders so I had to rely on hand signals with others to communicate. Radio communication was near impossible. I had to shout into the handset. The noise of the firefight was so loud and so close I could not even hear myself talk or think and I could barely hear the transmission on the other end of the radio.

The forward two platoons were cut off from the rest of the company and we were all surrounded on all sides by the enemy. A number of their men were wounded. I was not sure of the location of the forward platoons so I could not call in Artillery on the enemy. I did not know exactly where they were.

We had two other problems. The forward platoons were located down a spine or saddle from us and our location was on the gun target line which is the imaginary straight line from the gun to the target. Artillery fire would have to come right over our location with the Headquarters in order to drop on the NVA engaged with forward platoons. Calling in

370

Artillery was not feasible since it was too dangerous. We were taking enough casualties from enemy fire. We did not need casualties from friendly fire making the situation worse.

At some point in the fire fight word spreads along the perimeter to keep watch for the two leading platoons. They were fighting their way back up the spine or saddle to join us. I remember being in a prone firing position and ordering my recon sergeant to call in Artillery fire to our west while I crawled forward watching for the forward two platoons.

My M-16 suddenly kicked back. I wondered what the hell was going on. Did I squeeze off a round accidently? It was a crazy feeling. I wondered what the hell was going on and was dazed for a moment. I looked down to see there was a hole torn through the sling of my M16 and then I saw a hole in the stock of the weapon too. A bullet had passed under my right hand between my right arm and chest and out through the stock of my rifle. At that time, I thought nothing of it since bullets were flying everywhere. Before that moment too much was going on to think about it. For the first time in the fire fight, I realized that it wasn't a stray round, but someone had me in their sights and was just a lousy marksman......thank God! My mind and body was filled with adrenaline and the noise was deafening.

I remember kneeling holding my M-16 in my right hand when all of a sudden the rifle flew backwards again. I looked down to see a large hole was in the hand guard. The NVA had missed me twice but hit my rifle twice. I still thought nothing about it. No time to think about it just react and survive.

I remember seeing one of the HQ RTO's named Rip kneeling a few feet away from me. Then all of a sudden I saw a large chunk of tree disappear from beside his head. I recalled laughing and yelling at him, "damn, Rip that one almost got you!" Everything happened so fast, we battled for our lives and there were so many close calls.

Word spread that the forward platoons were getting close to join us. I crawled out to find them and guide them back into our perimeter. As I was crawling I saw a large man backing up towards me. I started yelling "over here, over here." In the cacophony of the firefight he couldn't hear me. Being talented as an extremely loud whistler, I let out several shrill whistles. Still no reaction.

Then everything seemed to go into slow motion. The big man still had his back to me and I noticed he had on a large rucksack. When finally, he

371

heard my whistle he turned to his left and as he turned in my direction and I saw his weapon and noticed his weapon had a round drum under it. It crossed my mind that we didn't have any guns like that. Then he looked at me and I looked straight at him. I realized "oh shit he's NVA!" and I was in deep shit. I was out of ammo and didn't have a grenade ready and was staring directly at the NVA.

I could do nothing as he fired his machine gun at me. His bullets seemed to go in slow motion and were kicking up the leaves on the jungle floor reaching out toward me. I buried my face in the ground. I was suddenly crushed into the dirt as one of the rounds tore into my helmet jamming my face deeper into the ground. I grabbed my Russian pistol but by now the NVA had disappeared. Then someone threw me a bandolier of ammo and I was back in business. The NVA was gone from sight.

The forward platoons rejoined us slowly and we reformed the perimeter around the wounded.

Now I knew where everyone was located so I started bringing artillery in earnest. The before mentioned gun target line bringing in fire on the north and south made bringing in the artillery still difficult. The NVA believed that if they could get within 50 meters of our position they were safe from our artillery. WRONG! I asked the artillery battery to put the Executive Officer (XO) on directly supervising the outgoing fire since I was bringing it in dangerously close to our location. The artillery fire was so accurate and close that its shrapnel was singing over us. The XO ensured accurate settings on each howitzer before it was fired.

I also employed the 155mm howitzer from LZ Swinger but their range was longer and slightly less accurate so I wasn't comfortable bringing them as close as the 105's.

At that time the forward platoons joined us but we were running dangerously low on ammo. We also had no landing zone (LZ) to extract wounded. Several birds flew over us trying to drop out ammo cases but all received heavy fire and failed. We had to cut down trees so the birds could get closer to the ground even though we were still fighting the enemy. We had some badly wounded that needed evacuation so we had no other choice.

Finally, ammo was successfully dropped into our makeshift LZ. Once we had the ammo we layed down fire in a mad minute toward the enemy positions so the Dustoff helicopter could get down as low as possible

372

without getting fired upon. Once a Dustoff came in I remember helping lift guys up on our fingertips to get them into the helicopters. The artillery fire ceased during this time so the helicopters would not be endangered by friendly fire.

We loaded as many of the wounded as we could on the Dustoff and they were evacuated. There were some wounded that did not get evacuated until the next day. We then tightened our perimeter and dug in for the night.

I kept artillery firing until Puff the Magic Dragon (this was a Douglas AC-47 Spooky plane loaded with firepower) arrived and fired their mini guns around our position at night. We deployed strobes so the aircraft could see our position. At this time, we were not concerned about the enemy because they already knew exactly where we were anyway! Puff put on quite a light show from heaven! The mini guns hummed and rained down fire from the sky. It looked like lasers until the bullets hit and ricocheted all around. This kept the enemy at bay all night.

The next morning, we were ordered to head west to hook up with Charlie Company. We planned to recon by fire (fire artillery in front of us as we progressed along), but then I was informed in code that because of the previous day's activity there was not enough artillery ammo to do this. They only had enough ammo for contact missions.

"Stand by", I told them. And sure enough within a few minutes we were in contact and remained in contact for quite some time.

I recall moving into a location where we stayed about three days. We took mortar fire every morning at the same time. By now I had a good idea where the mortars were located. I called for a TOT (Time On Target) mission. I had three batteries fire so that all the rounds landed at the same time on the same place. We never heard from those mortars again.

Recollection of Receiving Charlie Company 1st of the 8th Infantry Battalion

David Hockett

Right around the 10th of March Charlie Company walked into an ambush close to the Cambodian border and needed assistance. My company A, was ordered to move to an LZ, we had been in and out of since insertion into the Plei Trap Valley.

The LZ was just east of a stream and had two hills just east of it with a trail running between the hills going east and west. We had in the past few days established fighting positions on both hills. I had my company secure the area with a large perimeter and started receiving C company. They were flown in Huey Helicopters and all day long we received replacements of personnel, equipment, clothing, ammunition, rations and my executive officer out to pay the troops, it being past payday.

As the day wore on I got the feeling we were being watched. I decided to move everyone out of that location before nightfall.

Captain DeHart, the Charlie company commander, wanted to stay in the area of the LZ because it was peaceful, had water to bath and he felt safe with 2 companies in defense. I told him that I felt we were going to be attacked by the enemy infantry or artillery before nightfall.

With that in mind I had C company occupy the hill to our north, coordinates **YB 825034**, with two platoons and his CP and the remaining two platoons spread further north in ambush positions. I then ordered A company to occupy the southern hill, coordinates **YB 824028**, with 2 platoons and the CP and the remaining 2 platoons spread south in ambush positions.

At this point I informed the battalion HQ what my plan was and where each element of both companies would be located with coordinates for each location. I further stated that I would confirm each position if they were within 100 meters. All day long I confirmed each position with battalion.

With all units in position I moved my CP to the southern hill and awaited the last helicopter to take the back haul and my executive officer back to the brigade base camp. Suddenly two big guns went off and two high explosive rounds landed approximately 1600 meters to the west. I knew this was the NVA because the American Army always fires first round smoke to prevent friendly fire casualties.

At that point I had the forward observer request a fire mission and called all units to give me an azimuth to the sound of the guns. I started giving these compass readings for each location and the battalion informed me they did not have locations on my units.

I threw off all metal equipment took my map and compass and jumped into my foxhole and oriented the map and drew lines on the map from three locations giving polar coordinates to the enemy guns. I had the FO give the artillery the coordinates as well as coordinates to the location on a ridge 2500 meters to the west where I felt the FO for the NVA was observing and directing the artillery against us.

The enemy got off the spotting rounds and adjusted the next two rounds close to the creek. The next explosions were a full battery of 6 in our old LZ. By this time our own artillery fired the enemy gun positions and the enemy FO position and that stopped the enemy fire.

My XO came flying up the hill in a hurry leaving the rest of the payroll back on the landing zone with the backhaul. Needless to say, he stayed the night in primitive conditions, for he had not come prepared to spend the night here with the company.

All was quiet that night and the 4th Division Aviation battalion had an L-19 Birddog flying over our position all night long, which prevented any further attack from succeeding. The following morning a recon plane found that our artillery had destroyed a 100 mm gun and a truck similar to our 21/2 Ton vehicle. Nothing was reported on the enemy forward observer, but I think we might have given him a one hell of a headache.

We were ordered to proceed east south east to make contact with elements of the 66th NVA regiment. Captain DeHart and I went on a recon of our route of march. We loaded up in the back seats of a Hughes Hu-6 LOH and flew the route for about 5 minutes until we started receiving fire from a 51 Caliber machine gun.

The pilot turned the helicopter to the right and the door gunner spotted the gun position out in a field. He immediately engaged the gun with the M60 machine gun and walked his bullets right into the hole where the gun was mounted on a pedestal of earth so that it could fire in 360 degrees. The enemy soldier flew out of the hole seeking cover and we continued on. It was felt that this was intentional trying to lure a helicopter down to ambush it trying to retrieve the weapon, looking back this was a precursor to the events that happened on March 12th.

Into the Valley of Death rode the Six Hundred. In this case it was two understrength companies Alfa company with 72 able bodied men and Charlie company with even less. Being the senior commander of Alfa company I assigned one squad of the recon platoon in advance of our line of march. We headed south from our night location of the 11th for about 11and 1/2 kilometers and then headed east south-east.

At about coordinates **YB 842013**. The 4th platoon, Lt. Andrew Lepeilbet platoon spotted what appeared to be an NVA soldier at or about coordinates **YB 844009** headed into the woods and turned south to intercept.

The whole company proceeded to approximately coordinates **YB 847005**, which I estimated to be near Hill 387 at elevation 365. The action started when the 4th platoon went downhill on a slight ridge headed east. The 3rd platoon under command of Sergeant Don White followed and when the action started everyone surged forward till the CO and the Artillery forward observer were at the top of **Hill 387**. Fire from rifles and grenades. kept building until it was a continuous roar.

I was receiving fire and kept rolling from side to side to avoid being hit. I was in a small depression and realized that the enemy was in the trees. I yelled to everyone "They are in the trees.: The men around me reacted and killed the snipers located in the trees. When I was able to move I noticed a dead squirrel where I had been rolling back and forth with bullets hitting the ground all around me.

I immediately gave the Forward Observer (FO) the coordinates for our location for the artillery to fire on the enemy. I contacted the Battalion CO and made him aware of the situation and requested any assets that could be spared.

About this time, it was learned the NVA had slipped in between 3rd platoon and the rest of the company. If the company moved forward to help the 3rd and 4th platoons, we would have to use plunging fire down the saddle to kill the enemy located between us and the 3rd platoon but that would undoubtedly kill or wound men in the two platoons that were in contact with the enemy. I elected to have the 3rd and 4th platoons retreat to our location and to clear the enemy infiltrators in the process.

The battle started around 1200 hrs. and continued until about 1800.

Recollections of March 12, 1969

John Andrews

I remember that I was ordered to set up a perimeter around Company CP and I turned to see Frank Runge coming down the trail behind and above me. We had just started to take fire from our left and from down the finger off to the left but not from the top of the hill when Jim Olson and Charles Revis were both hit by enemy fire . I told Frank to take his squad and secure the top of the hill. The 2nd platoon was not in position at that point because of the accordion effect of moving the whole company.

At the time it was my thought and my intention that we would move the company to the high ground once the 3rd platoon and the 4th platoon could break contact and get back to 1st and 2nd platoons.

Frank was killed as he moved his squad toward the hilltop into the thickly wooded area. The NVA already held the hill but had not fired at us as we and the 1st platoon had moved in front of them and down the finger. The enemy must have been waiting for the right time to attack.

Eventually the 3rd and 4th platoons broke contact and were able to move back up the finger. The enemy contact started at about 11:30 AM and I remember it taking at least an hour before the 3rd and 4th platoons rejoined the rest of the Company. That was probably about 1:30 or 2 PM. The 1st platoon did go down the finger a short distance to assist the 3rd and 4th platoon with wounded and to provide security.

It took a while to get organized once the 3rd and 4th platoons rejoined the Company. The wounded were moved to the middle of the perimeter and the remainder of the 3rd and 4th were combined into one platoon.

The 2nd platoon was in contact with the NVA at the top of the hill. We were not receiving much fire from down the finger or much from our left flank or our right flank where the landing zone (LZ) eventually was cut at that point.

With 3rd and 4th platoons rejoining the rest of the company, Captain Hockett ordered me to take six of my men and go down the finger to try to rescue the two Recon guys. That was around 3 PM or a little earlier. When I left on this mission, the LZ for the Dustoff Helicopters had not been cut and no wounded had been evacuated.

On the mission to rescue the Recon guys we went down the center of the finger for what seemed like a long way but really it was not. We were moving very cautiously moving from tree to tree and moved to a location in a small clearing. The clearing contained a bomb crater.

As we started across the clearing the NVA opened up on us and our point man was hit in the thigh. We were being shot at from our immediate front and also from what appeared to be bunkers to our right just off the finger in a flat lower area.

Helicopter gunships had been called in and made multiple runs across the finger and in the bunker area. They laid down intense fire on the bunkers during the firefight that ensued.

After we made multiple attempts to cross the open area to rescue the trapped recon soldiers, we were ordered to return back to the Company's current location. The Company perimeter was about 500 meters from our location.

We took a slightly different route on our return to the company. We traveled off to the right side of the finger. We feared that the NVA were set up waiting for us on our return back up the middle of the finger.

About half way back we came across rucks with water and ammo that the 3rd and 4th platoon had dropped. We took as much as we could since we had no water and little ammo. We did not return to the Company perimeter until just after sunset or around 6 PM.

379

Recollections of March 12, 1969

John Seim

I remember us moving down on the right side of a long flat finger. We received some fire from snipers tied in trees that were located to our left.

We moved down finger and Dave Muck had us take cover. I was watching to the front and right. I saw three NVA come from behind a large tree to my front about 100 feet away. I shot two and the 3rd ducked back behind the tree. I threw a frag by the tree and there wasn't any more movement.

Don White got hit by an explosion to my left front. It was like a grenade or RPG. I thought his leg was hit pretty bad.

I stayed at my same location for a while and then my squad leader Dave Muck or Jerry Loucks got us to tighten up our perimeter.

Then we started slowly moving back up the finger. Our perimeter was circular about 20 feet across as I remember. We had our wounded in the middle with our rucks around them to protect them.

As a group we crawled and dragged ourselves up the finger while the enemy was firing at us. Most of the fire came from our right flank.

I can remember one round clipped Jerry Loucks's ear and I remember he was wearing my sunglasses.

We crawled and dragged up to an area where we joined the rest of Company. They were engaging the enemy and were firing to our right. That was northeast of us. We moved our wounded to an open area with other wounded from the 1st and 2nd platoons and waited for the Dustoff helicopters to arrive. Later we formed a defensive line off to the West.

The helicopters came in and dropped resupply of ammunition. We got new magazines for our M16's that were sealed in Mylar. And I remember that I got three bandoliers of ammo in stripper clips. We also sorted through the rucks to find ammo and then dug holes and filled sand bags.

I remember dragging a tree to put across the front of the sand bags.

Someone came around and told us that they were firing an NVA AK rifle. They told us not to shoot them if we heard it.

That night I remember seeing strobe lights as we watched the fire from the plane (Puff) that circled above. You could see the leading edge of the intense stream of bullets from the plane , you could see the burst of fire starting and its trailing edge when it stopped.

The next morning, Dave Muck, Chris Krukow and Jerry Loucks, maybe others and I crawled around to our South and threw grenades in bunkers that were right by our perimeter. I remember Dave saying "4 seconds right" as he got ready to drop one in a bunker. He released the spoon and counted 1 to 2 before he dropped it in. Someone fired a M72 into one of the bunkers and the whole mound kind of lifted up.

Later we humped over to another hill and met up with Charlie Company. I don't remember taking fire on the way. I remember the mortar rounds and someone saying it was a 4 duce.

Frenchy looked at what turned out to be a bullet fragment in my left thigh and I flew to an aid station the next morning on a supply slick. There they jabbed a large needle in the bullet hole and squirted in some stuff that really stung. They put in a stitch and a dressing on it and said I would be fine. I was gone for two days and flew back on a resupply Huey with Jerry Loucks and a bunch of canned hams he had requisitioned". My leg didn't bother me.

The company had moved and was dug in on a hilltop with heavy tree cover and jungle as I remember it. Captain Hockett was gone and we had a Sargent Phifer as platoon leader. I think we had a mortar platoon there and they had an injury caused by powder bags igniting.

Recollections of March 20, 1969

John Seim

We spent the night of the March 19th, listening on the radio about an engineer that had been ambushed and killed attempting to detonate a charge on a road not far from us. The next morning we saddled up to go get the engineer and help recover the body.

I had been walking point as Jerry Louck's apprentice for a while and got to take point on the hump to the engineer's location. I liked walking point; I got to read a map.

We humped through a lot of trees and bushes and finally broke out of the trees on a hill overlooking a road. There was a pile of what I assumed were explosives in the middle of a curve of the road.

One squad of our patrol went to the where the engineer was located and our squad was told to do a "clover leaf" sweep on the opposite side of the road.

We descended the hill carefully as there was minimum cover and we were all exposed. We got to the road and Dave Muck had the M60 machine gunner cover the road to our left.

We crossed the road and went up the bank and into the trees. I think I was about 50 feet in front of our patrol when I saw movement to my left. I saw several spider holes to my left and a guy with black hair looking around. I don't think he saw me. I instantly realized he was the enemy.

I dropped to a crouch and shot at the NVA. I don't know if I hit him but the next thing I knew the whole tree line lit up with the NVA firing at me. I never yelled "ambush 9 o'clock" like I was trained to do as a point man.

I was hit in the leg from enemy fire. One round went through my left calf just below the knee and knocked me down. I crawled behind a tree and a grenade went off just off to my left. I thought my leg was gone but when the dust cleared it was still there but broken with a baseball size chunk missing. It didn't hurt, it was just numb.

I started tossing grenades in the direction of the spider holes. I remember I had nine hand grenades in my gas mask case. I threw them all. I had a tough time getting the safety wires (C rat wire) out of them. I had heard stories of guys forgetting to take the safety wires out and only pulling the main pin. Of course the grenades didn't go off if you did that. I had a White Phosphorous grenade also but didn't dare to throw it with all the trees.

Our new "platoon leader" Sergeant Phifer had insisted that we take gas masks when we headed out that morning. He even looked to see if we were carrying them as I recall. He didn't check inside the gas mask case, however. He also would not let everyone bring ponchos so we had nothing to make stretchers out of. I used my gas mask case to store my grenades.

When my grenades were gone there was a lull in the shooting. I heard Dave Muck yelling at me asking if I was ok. I yelled that I was hit and he yelled back that I should crawl back toward his position.

I started crawling. It seems like it took a long time to crawl back and there was a lot of shooting and grenades going off.

I finally got close and Dave had crawled out to meet me. He dragged me back behind a log. Someone wrapped my leg with a dressing. I also remember someone draped over me to protect me when a grenade went off real close to us. The situation we found ourselves in is depicted below.

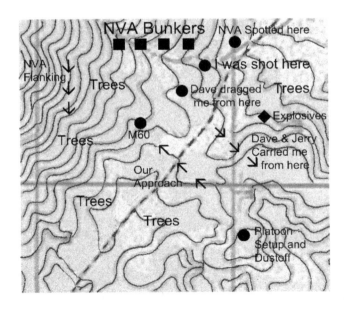

Soon we started to pull back as the M60 machine gunner on the road was firing steadily. Dave picked me up on his shoulder and ran across the road and started up the hill we had come down earlier. I still had my M16 and tried to shoot back at the wood line but Dave yelled at me to stop. I gave my M16 to someone that was helping us.

I realized that in the melee I had been also hit in the right leg. It must have clipped an artery; the blood was squirting everywhere as people helped Dave carry me up the hill. I remember how much Dave's shoulder hurt in my stomach as he carried me.

Jerry Loucks helped me and told me that he should have been walking point. Both Dave and Jerry seemed to have felt responsible for me getting hurt since Jerry usually walked point. I thought I had done an ok job on point. At least I saw the NVA first before he saw me.

The fighting continued for quite a while. Artillery shells were landing across the road. Eventually a Dustoff helicopter came and hovered over the trees. I was loaded into a Stokes basket and winched up into the helicopter. I remember rounds pinging on the skids as I was going up. The enemy was trying to shoot down the Dustoff.

They lifted me out of the basket and sent it back down. The basket came back up with our new "platoon leader". He had been hit in the forearm I think. I remember the medic reaching back for his M16 which my leg was laying on. I yelled when he wrenched it out from under my leg.

I flew to an aid station, Polei Klang. I remember being really thirsty. I pleaded for some water and watched a nurse dip a sponge in a basin and wring it out with forceps.

She placed the now dry sponge between my lips and it didn't help at all.

I was put on a Huey for the hospital at Pleiku. I had been given a shot of morphine and I remember the ride was something special.

At Pleiku I remember being in a triage area for a long time. Finally I went to surgery and woke up in a ward.

They put your home state on a note on your bed and a nurse brought me a can of cold Coke and asked where I was from in Minnesota. I told her Alexandria and turned out she was from Buffalo. She had gone to nursing school at St Barnabas hospital. She knew Carol, my wife. (Fiancée then). Her name was Diane Carlson and she was one of the people involved with the Women's Vietnam Memorial. We had "in-

384

coming" one night and she came and dumped me out of bed and covered me with a mattress.

Several days later I flew to Cameron Bay, where they took away my Puma knife, and on to Japan. I was taken to the 249th general hospital just North of Tokyo.

I had more surgery there and was told I was going back to "the world " (home). When I had been there for several days I got an orderly to wheel me down to the hospital PX. I bought five small blue transistor radios. I mailed four of them back to Dave Muck and still have the 5th. I think Dave said he never got them, however. I know that I was still in Japan on March 28 as that is the day Dwight Eisenhower died. The civilian workers at the hospital were crying and I asked why. They told me Ike died.

I flew from Japan to Travis Air Base in CA arriving about April 2 or 3. Some family friends from Palo Alto visited me and I had the obligatory steak dinner welcome. A couple days and I flew to Denver and Fitzsimons Army Hospital. I arrived at 2:00 AM on Easter morning April 6th. At about noon, after the obligatory steak dinner, the Bunnies from the Denver Playboy Club showed up. They pushed us around in wheelchairs, wrote letters for those that couldn't, and sat and talked to us. A few days later the lovely and amiable Carol Martinson showed up (fiancée/wife). It was so good to be "back in the world". I was discharged on July 31st.

Recollections of March 20, 1969

Greg Rollinger

On March 20, 1969 third Platoon was sent to the previous day's contact site to retrieve the SSG Avery's body. He was an engineer who had been killed in an ambush the previous day. We were under command of Sergeant E7 Pfeifer.

Posey was Squad Leader for 2nd Squad that day. I'm not sure where Woodall was; he was the normal squad leader.

When we got to the site of the contact, the Engineer, SSG Harvey C. Avery, was still laying in the road near the shape charge that he was going to use to blow up the road.

I remember the road as being quite wide. The NVA used the road to drive trucks for supplies and men. There was a big crater on the side of the road and that is where I set up my M60 to cover the retrieval of SSG Avery's body.

Lieutenant Porter was the Officer in Charge from the previous day. SSG Avery's body was recovered without any contact.

I thought we were going to get out of there without further casualties. But then somebody decided to run a patrol sweep across the road to pick up demolition materials.

I'm not sure how the patrol participants were decided, but half of the 3rd Squad went and half including Jerry Loucks didn't.

John Seim led the patrol walking point. An NVA opened up on John Seim with a 51 caliber machine gun almost immediately. I heard Pfeifer yell "guns up" so I got up with Harold Proctor , my assistant gunner, and ran across the road.

I saw Harry James and Jerry Jensen had set up with their M60. I then ran past Pfeifer and Joe Doucette, (his RTO), and found a depression next to a big tree right past where Pfeifer and Joe were laying.

I hit the ground. I couldn't see John Seim but I knew he was off to my right. The first thing I noticed was a bunch of C4 hanging on the tree. I was next to with detonation cord wrapped around it and heading off in two directions.

I decided that was a little dangerous so I got up and yanked the C4 off the tree and tossed it away from Proctor and me.

At first it looked like Pfeifer and Doucette were laying in a small clearing. It turned out to be an NVA sleeping bunker. There was no opening in the front but it had an opening in the back. The NVA started throwing grenades out the back of the bunker at us from the opening.

An arm would appear and then grenades flew through the air – one after another.

One grenade flew out and landed right in front of Pfeifer and Doucette. Both of them took shrapnel in the face. Pfeifer got up and ran past me yelling and screaming back across the road with an eyeball hanging out.

Doucette was blinded by the shrapnel and was laying there saying he could not see.

Another grenade rolled under Harry James and Jerry Jensen's M60 destroying their machine gun and M16.

I'm not sure how Doucette got out of there but somebody must have taken him back across the road.

Proctor and I were the only ones still in action and I couldn't really do much because I didn't know exactly where Seim was. The NVA kept throwing grenades at us but we were in this small depression where the shrapnel just went over us.

It was weird watching the arm appear and the grenades fly through the air coming right at us. We just tried crawling under our helmets.

Shortly thereafter, Dave Muck came up to me and asked where Seim was. I told him he was off to my right but I didn't know how far.

So Dave crawled away and came back pulling Seim with him and headed back towards the road.

Now that I had a clear field of fire, I opened up with the M60 to cover Dave's withdrawal. There was one NVA who appeared in our front who was using small trees for cover. I opened up with the M60 and could see

387

the rounds go right through about 8 inch trees and the bark fly off the other side.

I don't know how many rounds I fired but the jungle in front of me started on fire from my tracers.

Finally I heard someone yell for me to come back across the road. So Proctor and I turned directly around and low crawled to the road and then across. I set my gun back up on the crater. Jensen came up and was on my right side. I opened fire again and the shell casings from gun went right into Jensen's shirt. So he jumps up and is doing a little dance to get the hot casing out of his shirt.

The whole firefight lasted about three hours. And since we had not brought more than our fighting gear, everyone was out of water. I was exhausted.

By the time we pulled out, we had two KIAs to carry and 11 WIAs. We went back up the hill before calling in the Dustoff to get John Seim and SSG Pfeifer using the jungle penetrator.

The rest of the wounded were carried back to the Task Force Alpha area. I went over and talked to Doucette where he was lying next to the LZ waiting for the Dustoff. His eyesight had come back but his whole face looked like somebody had sprinkled pepper on it.

Also the kid I came into the company with and ended up in Novotny's squad was wounded. His name was Paul Woodsey and he had a 51 caliber machine gun hole in his calve muscle. I was amazed because it wasn't bleeding but you could look right through his leg and see the grass. He was happy because he figured he had a million dollar wound. We never saw him again.

After Action Report says we lost 3 M16A1 rifles, and one M60 machine Gun.

Recollections March 19-20. 1969

Jerry Aldous

On March 19, 1969 Sergeant Avery an engineer and demolitions expert who was supporting our company was killed. He was with our squad as we were blowing up trees across a road near the Cambodian border. This portion of the Pleui Trap Valley had many roads that the NVA used to transport men and supplies. Our job was to destroy the roads the best we could.

We got ambushed by the NVA in the process of blowing up several trees. The demolition wire was strung and the explosives were ready to go off. Just then the NVA attacked us.

The NVA were not far off the road. They were only about 80 feet from us when it happened.

The firefight started when an NVA threw a grenade. I heard the NVA in the bush as the grenade was being thrown so I hit the ground right away. The grenade went off close to me to my right and all hell then broke loose once it exploded.

I remember that I was hit by a small piece of shrapnel in my right arm. The shrapnel was small and at the time didn't even know I was hit. My arm did burn a bit. I thought I'd been bitten by a bug or something like that.

Ron Stone was close and he was carrying the radio. The blast from the grenade tore into his arm but most the shrapnel hit his radio. That day the radio saved his life.

During the firefight that ensued I laid flat on the ground. The bullets were whizzing by just inches over my head.

At some point my fear turned to anger. I really got pissed. I started to get up on one knee and return fire at the NVA. Before I could rise, Sergeant Avery came over and leaned on my back so I couldn't get up.

He asked where my platoon sergeant was. I told him that he was somewhere to my left.

The engineer then turned to stand and moved to my left and then fell back on top of me. I rolled him to side and asked if he was hit. I could not see any wounds.

He laid there gasping for air.

Then I rolled him over on his back. That is when I saw the wound in the center in his back.

He died within a couple minutes after that. The bullet hit his heart and lungs.

I have always been haunted knowing that he saved my life when he stopped me from getting up to fire at the enemy. He saved my life but he never got to know it.

As the firefight continued we then had to pull back off the road and retreated up the hill. At that time we thought that we were going to be overrun. We stayed at our location on the hill until the next day. We were not attacked at that location.

The next day another platoon showed up to help us retrieve SSG Avery. We told them where his body was located. When they got down there they also came under fire just as we did the day before. The NVA were still there. Another firefight ensued and they returned to our location on the hill. They could not locate the body.

After that I returned with my squad to recover that body since I knew exactly where SSG Avery was located. He died right on top of me.

When we got to the location we also came under intense fire. But we still were able to recover the body even with the NVA firing at us. We took turns carrying the engineer back up the hill.

That day March 20 was a terrible experience. Mortars were coming in from our company base camp located on Hill 467. The mortars were called in on the NVA and were landing very close to where we were. I remember a mortar round coming right over the top of the engineer's body and exploding just to our front while we were retrieving the body.

It was not a good day in Vietnam.

Recollection of March 19-20, 1969

Jerry Jensen

On the 19th March we did not hear much about the mission that was occurring on a road near the Cambodian border. We knew that part of our company was blowing up the roads and we had heard that an engineer got killed. On the morning of the March 20th we were told that the 3rd platoon was going to retrieve the engineer's body.

A-1-8 had joined up and combined with C-1-8 on March 13. On March 19 – 20 was Task Force Alpha (TFA) was formed.

The location Hill 467 of the TFA was quite a way from the battle location of March 12th. The location was almost a day's hump from where the engineer got killed.

When we arrived at the location of the firefight on March 20th we met 2nd platoon and 4th platoon led by Tom Porter. They were set up on the side of the hill. They were to provide security while engineer's body was being recovered. They also were provided security the previous day when the engineer was killed. The purpose of the overall mission was to blow up trees across the road to make it unusable by the NVA.

I was in third squad of 3rd platoon. My squad consisted of John Seim, Dave Muck, Harry James and Bill Moran and myself. Our new platoon sergeant SFC Pfeifer and his RTO Joe Doucette was also there with us.

My squad was led by David Muck. The 1st squad was there and was led by Frank Novtny. The 2nd squad led by Posey and 3rd squad was led by

Dave Muck. Novotny's squad was actually led by one of his men since Novotny was acting platoon sergeant that day.

We got to the area where the engineer's body was located. We set up on the hill overlooking the road. There were no incidents of any type traveling to this location.

Part of patrol went down to retrieve the engineer's body. As we retrieved the body we made no contact with the enemy.

After the body was retrieved then our squad was ordered to make a sweep of the area. We were ordered to recon the area and retrieve detonation (det) cord and explosives that might have been left.

We set out on the recon mission with SFC Pfeifer and Joe Doucette behind us.

Only part of our squad was sent on the sweep recon patrol. This group consisted of John Seim, Dave Muck, Harry James, Bill Moran, and mef. Harry was an M60 machine gunner who he inherited from Chris Krukow. Krukow was wounded on March 13 and had left the field. I was assigned assistant machine gunner to Harry.

John Seim walked point followed by Muck then me , Harry and Moran. Pfeifer and Doucette were walking between Muck and Harry.

The rest of the platoon was set up on the side of the hill overlooking the road. That group included Greg Rollinger (Rollie) and Harold Proctor and further to the top was Ken McCormack and Jerry Loucks. Rollie and Proctor were near the road but on the hill and were set up one step off of the road.

Our recon patrol left our equipment on the hill to travel lighter on the sweep. We did not have ruck sacks just web gear and our weapons and ammunition. We had been ordered by Pfeifer to travel lightly that morning and as a result, we were out of water and thirsty by the time the day ended.

Wey went down the hill and crossed the road. When we crossed we were six to eight feet off the road traveling on a slight incline.

Immediately John Siem got shot. We opened up on the enemy firing our weapons in the direction of the shooting but couldn't really see the enemy at first. All this happened just as we were crossing the road and on the slight incline. We kept returning fire in the direction of the NVA but couldn't see them. We knew they were very close perhaps 60 feet in front of us.

392

Seim lay wounded hit by a NVA machine gunner. The enemy machine gunner was directly in front of him firing continuously at him and the guys across the road located on the hill. Those guys started firing back at the machine gunner but really could not see him either.

Rollie was back on the side of the hill and had not moved across the road. He then left the side of the hill with Proctor and moved across the road to fire at the enemy on the orders of Sergeant Pfeifer.

Rollie and Proctor ran past Harry, Pfeifer, Dousette and me. Seim was laying wounded somewhere to Rollie's right and was out in front of us laying in the open.Muck was pinned down by a sniper unable to crawl to Seim.

About that time Rollie opened up with his M60 machine gun. That intense fire kept the enemy's heads down.

Dave Muck was then able to crawl forward and drag Seim all the way back across the road to the rest of the platoon.

At the same time this was going on Harry also was firing the M60 at the enemy and Moran and I were firing our M16's. We were in the middle of an intense firefight.

Suddenly we saw three NVA running in front of us. The three NVA were attempting to flank us and get us into a crossfire. They were running parallel to us and were not that far away.

We fired directly at them. The last NVA of the three then turned and started running back to where he came from.

I shot him and he went down almost immediately. He was within 60 feet of our location.

Harry's M60 jammed and he was trying his best to clear it. I kept shooting with my M16.

I looked up and I saw a grenade in the air coming to us. It was coming from the NVA I had shot. I hollered as loud as I could the words "grenade" and then it went off. It went off just to my right and slightly behind me where Pfeifer and Doucette were laying.

More enemy grenades kept coming at us. The wounded NVA I shot was kept throwing them at us.

I was lying to Harry's right and Muck was to my right. When the grenades went off I rolled left and accidently laid my arm on Harry's M60 barrel burning my arm. That hurt like hell but I kept firing my weapon at the enemy.

393

The exploding grenades had done some damage. I got shrapnel in my leg but didn't realize it at the time. It must have been the adrenaline since I could not feel a thing.

Sergeant Pfeiper and Joe Doucette got the brunt of one of the explosions directly in their faces. They were both lying on the road and both were yelling and they were located right in front of the enemy bunkers.

The enemy kept throwing grenades at Rollie and Proctor even after Pfeifer and Doucette we hit.

The NVA threw many grenades during this short time period and were located extremely close to us.

Finally, Harry and I rolled off the incline. We had enough. The explosions were too close and we had no other choice. We rolled back down the incline on our backs and bellies until we were directly on the road. Rollie and Harold Proctor were already there on the road. They were providing cover with the M60.

In the melee and confusion that transpired somehow we lost the M60 machine gun and my M16. Looking back on the matter we were pretty sure our M16 and M60 were destroyed by the explosions.

When we rolled onto the road, we saw Pfeifer's M16 and Doucette's M16 so grabbed them. At least we had weapons to defend ourselves now.

Pfeifer was wounded badly and had got up and ran across the road. Doucette laid there yelling. He could not see and was blinded by the shrapnel of the explosions. Someone crawled up to Doucette and helped him back across the road.

I remembered tossing a grenade back over the incline toward the NVA. I am not sure whether it hit the enemy or not.

Then Harry, Moran and I stayed next to Rollie and Proctor for a while. Everyone continued firing. We also were throwing hand grenades back to where we thought the enemy was located.

After some time, we were called to come back up the hill. So we moved cautiously as we could back up the hill to our original locations and joined with the rest of the platoon. That was when I first noticed my leg was bleeding. The medic then put a wrap on it.

We all continued firing and throwing grenades from our location on the hill. Many grenades were thrown. It sounded like artillery coming down from our location. But artillery came in later after we all had pulled back further and Dustoff was gone. A Dustoff helicopter used baskets to lift out Pfeifer and Seim and Paul Woodley.

Paul Woodley was in Novotny's squad. His squad was spread out along the road providing security. He got hit by a sniper in the calf muscle as a clean shot and the bullet went straight through the calf.

At some time during the battle Harold Johnson got hit and killed. He was set up on the hill and had not moved down on the road and got hit by stray enemy bullet.

We humped back to Hill 467 that day and carried Harold Johnson and the Sgt. Avery's bodies. We had to take turns carrying them. It was rough terrain moving through the mountainous jungle so we had to keep switching men as we carried the litters.

I was told by the medic to go to the rear to have my leg looked at, so I left on the same chopper that Dave Muck was on. Dave Muck and I both flew back to the rear together to have our wounds looked after at the aid station.

The rest of our platoon then went back to the company perimeter.

I came back to the field a couple of days later and to join our company. Our company was now on Firebase 20. We pulled security for the artillery. Company B Company took our place on patrol searching for the NVA near Cambodia.

The A-1-8 in March 1969

Operation Wayne Grey was planned as a spoiling attack to disrupt the enemy post-Tet offensive against Kontum by severing the enemy's line of communication into his Cambodian sanctuary. This purpose was accomplished as evidenced by the lack of major enemy offensive action in the vicinity of Kontum City. The initial combat assaults into the Plei Trap surprised the enemy and caused him to deal with an unexpected threat to his rear.

In Operation Wayne Grey 1st Brigade conducted offensive operations in Plei Trap area to destroy enemy forces, prevent reinforcement and supply of the 66th and 24th NVA Regiments from Cambodia, and prevent their withdrawal into Cambodia.

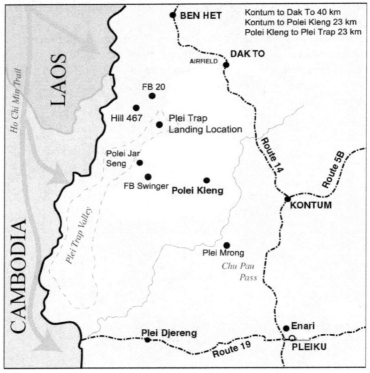

396

The 1st Brigade moved forces to Polie Kleng and launched helicopter assaults early March into various locations in the Plei Trap Valley. The area of operation was relatively small geographical area. The Plei Trap was only 23 Km or 20 minutes by helicopter.

On 27 February, 1st Brigade deployed to Polei Kleng for staging an assault into the northern Plei Trap area. At least a couple of thousand hard core NVA troops were located in and around the mountains surrounding this valley include over 1200 of the 66th NVA Regiment, one of the toughest enemy soldiers of the Vietnam war.

The Ho Chi Minh trail had many branches, one of which was call the Plei Trap Road. The road entered Vietnam in the northern Central Highlands and ran through the Plei Trap Valley south of Ben Het close to the tri-border of Vietnam, Laos and Cambodia.

Polei Kleng Camp (also known as Camp Le Vanh, Firebase Bass, Landing Zone Bass or Polei Kleng Special Forces Camp) is a former U.S. Army and Army of the Republic of Vietnam (ARVN) base west of Kontum in the Central Highlands of Vietnam.

The Polei Kleng base was established in June 1966 approximately 16 km west of Kontum by the 5th Special Forces Group.

Organization of the 1st Brigade

The 1st Brigade was organized into three Battalions. These were 1/8th Infantry called the Bullets, 3/8th Infantry called Draggons and 3/12th Infantry called Braves. In terms of Artillery the 6/29 FA (field artillery) battalion supported the 1st Brigade.

Battalions were then organized into companies that range from typically from 70 to 120 men at full capacity. The 3/8th Infantry consisted of Companies A, B, C and D and the 3/12th Infantry was organized into Companies A, B, C and D. The 1/8th Infantry Battalion was organized into four companies A, B, C and D and there was a Company E which consisted of Long Range Reconnaissance. Company E was known as Tracers that was assigned in the 1/8th Infantry Battalion.

Launching of Operation Wayne Grey

On March 1 Company A/3-12th Infantry combat assaulted into
Firebase (FB) Swinger from Plei Mrong. The firebase was occupied by
enemy troops who had prepared positions and anti-helicopter mines on
the LZ.

Combat assaults were then conducted by B/1-8th Infantry into FB 20
an C/3-8th Infantry into Firebase Pause followed by artillery support
A/6-29th Artillery and C/6-29th Artillery respectively.

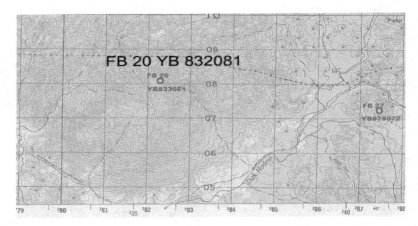

On 2 March, simultaneous combat assaults were conducted by the 1-8th
Infantry and the 3-8th Infantry. D/1-8th and C/1-8th assaulted into LZ
Susan and began reconnaissance by force operations along the enemy
roads in the area. The locations that units launch to are shown on the
following page.

Unit	Plei Trap Location	Landing Zone
A/1/8	YB 822 031	Near LZ Turkey
B/1/8	YB 832 081	FB 20
C/3/8	YA 868 889	FB Pause
D/1/8	YB 742 032	LZ Susan
C/1/8	YB 742 032	LZ Susan
A/3/8	YB 784 916	LZ Mary
B/3/8	YB 784 916	LZ Mary
D/3/8	YB 784 916	LZ Mary
C/3/12	YA 734 953	
B/3/12	YA 743974	
D/3/12	YA 747923	
A/3/12	YA 837 965	FB Swinger

Geographic locations for the launch are shown below. Company A of the 1-8th Infantry combat assaulted into a location near LZ Turkey to establish a blocking position and conduct ambush operations along routes of egress.

Companies A/3-8th, B/3-8th, and D/3-8th Infantry combat assaulted to LZ Mary to establish a firebase. C/3/12th and B/3/12th combat assaulted to YA734953 and YA743974 respectively to reconnaissance by force east. The initial positioning was completed on 3 March with the combat assault of D/3-12th to YA 747923.

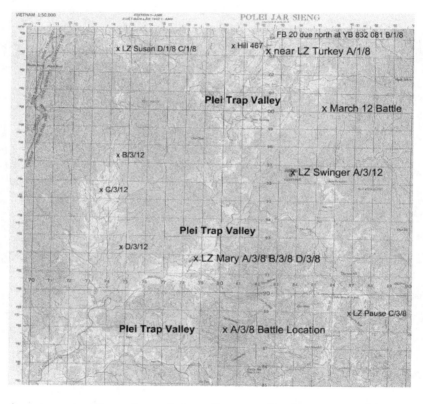

As one can see from the map the valley extends a large geographic distance and is surrounded by mountains of thick vegetation. The 1st Brigade launched their units all along the valley based on the best intelligence available at the time with the objective of finding the enemy and eliminating their bases within the area and their means of supply and routes to Vietnam major cities such as Kontum and Pleiku.

Leadership of Operation Wayne Grey

Operation Wayne Grey was assigned to 1st Brigade 4th Infantry Division and at the time the 4th Division was headed by Major General Donn R. Pepke.

The 1st Brigade was led by Col Hale H. Knight who was an accomplished jungle fighter early on in his career in the China-Burma-India Theater of World War II.

Company A was part of the 1/8th Infantry. LTC Allen M. Buckner was the battalion commander during March 1969.

During March 1969 there were three Infantry Commanders for Company A - Captain David Hockett,1LT Bill Leuing, John Andrews, Major Donald W. Androsky. On March 15 Company A and Company C were merged during March into a combined unit called Task Force Alpha commanded by Major Donald Androsky.

Organization and Strength of the Enemy

POWs and documents identified the 66th NVA Regiment with the K7, K8, and K9 Battalions, the K25B Engineer Battalion and elements of the 40th NVA Artillery Regiment. This was about 2000 NVA and most were infantry.

66th NVA Infantry Regiment

- 7th Battalion, 66th NVA Infantry Regiment
- 8th Battalion, 66th NVA Infantry Regiment
- 9th Battalion, 66th NVA Infantry Regiment

The typical NVA division had a strength of approximately 10,000 men grouped into three infantry regiments, with a supporting artillery regiment or battalion, and signals, engineers, medical and logistic formations. The artillery units were generally armed with mortars although they might use heavier weapons in an extended set-piece operation. The regiments were generally broken down into 3 foot-soldier

401

battalions of 500–600 men each, along with the supporting units. Each battalion in turn was subdivided into companies and platoons, with heavy weapons units augmenting the small arms of the line troops.

Both the VC and NVA formations operated under a "system of three" – three cells to a squad, three squads to a platoon, 3 companies to a battalion etc. This could vary depending on operational circumstances. Small-arms dominated the armament of typical infantry battalions, which deployed the standard infantry companies, logistical support, and heavy weapons sub-units of modern formations. Heavier weapons like 82 mm mortars or recoilless rifles and machine guns were at the battalion's combat support company. Members of the combat support unit were also responsible for placing mines and booby traps. Special detachments or platoons included sappers, recon, signals, etc. and were directly responsible to the battalion commander.

The Plei Trap and its Geography

The Plei Trap Valley was located in map grid zones YA and YB running roughly from YA 63-47 in the south (Pleiku province) to YB 88-15 in the north (Kontum province), II Corps.

The upper portion of the Plei Trap Valley is on map name Polei Jar Sieng. Map sheet name Phum Hay shows the lower portion of the Plei Trap Valley.

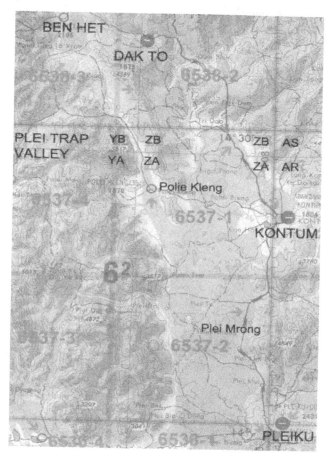

The Plei Trap Valley ran parallel to the Cambodian border following the Nam Sathay river. A more detailed view of the geography of the valley is shown below.

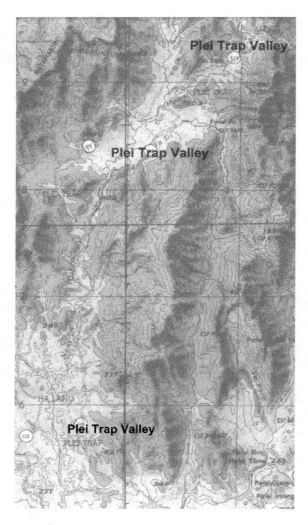

There were numerous 4th Infantry Division operations in this valley since the early days of the war. Operation Wayne Grey would be one of the largest ever conceived.

In the past the Plei Trap Valley was thoroughly dominated by the NVA. They operated from large, secure bases just across the border in Cambodia. If U.S. forces engaged them and had the upper hand, the NVA would simply disengage and would slip back across the Cambodian border since U.S. Forces were prohibited from pursuing them or even firing artillery across the border.

The valley was rugged and desolate and at the extreme range of artillery support from firebases. The dense jungle greatly reduced observation from the air and ground and prevented long range observation of likely avenues of enemy movement.

The dense jungle severely restricted employment of flat trajectory weapons except at very close ranges or with extensive clearing of firing lanes.

The steep hill masses, deep ravines and dense vegetation provided good cover throughout the area of operations, except along the Plei Trap Valley floor and in the relatively flat terrain leading from the Northern Plei Trap to the east and the north of Chu Mom Ray, (Hill 1773). Even in these areas, the cover was fair.

Throughout the area, dense jungle and broken terrain provided excellent concealment against ground and air observation, often completely hiding hardened positions and trail networks that were later found when artillery, air strikes or chemical defoliation destroyed the canopy.

The steep slopes and dense jungle were obstacles to any type vehicular movement and hinder foot movement in the steepest areas. Steep banks make most streams obstacles unless extensive work was done to provide a fording site.

Routes of movement generally follow the valley areas and cross the hill masses in the saddles. Major avenues in the area extended from the Cambodian Border (Northern Plei Trap to the south along the Plei Trap Valley and to the east along the valley floor south of FSB 20 (YB8208) and north of Chu Mom Ray).

Overall Map and Locations of Company A: The map shown on the following page is a combination of two of the maps used in Vietnam and shows Polei Kleng where the Wayne Grey operation was launched from to the locations where Company A operated. There was one location Fire Support Base (FB) 20 that is not shown on the map but is at location **YB 832081**. Only Company A locations are shown on this map. However,

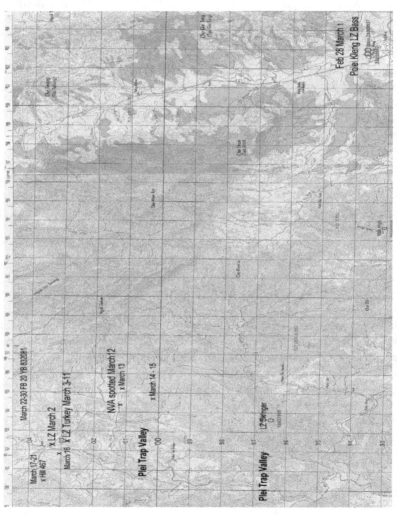

the Brigade sent troops to numerous locations in the northern part of the Plei Trap Valley as part of Wayne Grey.

The sequence of events of the A-1-8 are discussed on the following pages followed by a tabular summary of the highlights of March 1969.

1 March, 1969: 1st Battalion, 8th Infantry began its first Combat Assault (CA) by moving Company B from Fire Support Base 34 to Fire Support Base 20. The Headquarters minus (a portion of the Headquarters) and A Battery, 6th of the 29th Artillery (Direct Support Battery) were moved from LZ Bass at Polei Kleng to Fire Support Base 20. The battalion mortar section minus (a portion of a section) was moved from LZ Bass to Fire Support Base 20 along with Headquarters minus.

Companies C, D and A along with Headquarters minus remained at LZ Bass. This was in preparation for Companies C and D's move to LZ Susan and Company A's Combat Assault to LZ Turkey.

The reconnaissance platoon Company E remained at LZ Bass to work in liaison with Company A. Artillery at Fire Support Base 20 employed 45 rounds of 175 mm support fires from Ben Het.

2 March, 1969 1st Battalion, 8th Infantry continued combat assault operations from LZ Bass to LZ Susan with Companies C and D. Company A made a Combat Assault to vicinity **YB 822031** near LZ Turkey within 450 meters. After Combat Assault, Company A walked to LZ Turkey.

Company D proceeded along the northern axis of advance and established night location at YB **740047**.

At LZ Turkey Company A was to establish a blocking force for Company C sweeping on the southern axis and Company D sweeping on the North. These axes are centered on trails vicinity **YB 762032** and **765055** running from East to West respectively.

Company A reported light contact with an ambush by the 81 platoon and some sniper fire in route to the night location. The 4th platoon reported contact with an enemy force in bunkers in the vicinity **YB 820025**. They pulled back and called in 81-mm mortars. Enemy casualties were unknown. One U.S. soldier was wounded in action.

The reconnaissance platoon from Company E was employed in liaison with Company A. The mortar platoon minus (a portion of the platoon)

407

supported Company A's activities at LZ Turkey, and the remainder supported battalion operations from Fire Support Base 20.

Air Support: The 7th of the 17th Cavalry encountered heavy fire from vicinity **YB 765030**. This fire encountered was on the combat assault into LZ Susan. The Cavalry also reported two 2-½ ton trucks destroyed by airstrike, vicinity **YB 760033**. Three NVA soldiers were confirmed killed by an airstrike by the Airforce. The airstrike was at **YB 765034** on an enemy vehicle in the open.

Artillery: LZ Susan had 200 HE 105-mm howitzer rounds fired from Fire Support Base 20. LZ Susan had 25 HE rounds of 155-mm fired in their support from LZ Swinger. LZ Turkey had 125 HE 105-mm rounds fired from Fire Support Base 20. LZ Turkey had 25 rounds HE 155-mm fired from LZ Swinger. Company A's 84C upon contact fired 105-mm from Fire Support Base 20 at grid **8002**.

3 March, 1969: 1st Battalion, 8th Infantry continued reconnaissance in force operations with Companies C and D sweeping from West to East and Company A blocking at vicinity LZ Turkey.

Company B continued to secure Fire Support Base 20 with local security, patrols and two platoon sized ambushes. Company B ambushes were located at vicinity **YB 808068** and **YB 824066**.

Company A reported contact vicinity **YB 819029** with enemy in bunkers. Mortars and artillery were employed with unknown results. Elements were drawn back to night location so airstrike could be employed. One U.S. WIA in initial contact and 2 NVA were found in a sweep after the airstrike and artillery were employed. At vicinity **YB 815023** Company A's 1st and 4th platoons found 1 NVA who had been killed in action and 2 AK-47s.

Reconnaissance platoon Trace 5 operation in liaison with Company A sighted 4 or 5 NVA near their night location at **YB 846024**. Mortar platoon minus supported battalion operations from Fire Support Base 20. One 81 section supported Company A operations at LZ Turkey.

Air Support: The 7th of the 17th Cavalry supported Company C when they heard vehicle movement near their captured truck. They drew ground fire vicinity **YB 761034**. Gunships employed rockets and Cavalry reported 2 NVA killed. Gunships were employed at **YB 819029** in support of Company A. Gunships also sighted and engaged bunkers at

408

grid **YB 815023** and **YB 814026**. Cider 10 (Forward Air Controller) emplaced air strikes on **YB 819029** in support of Company A.

Artillery: Grid **762033**. Company C's 4th platoon employed 105-mm rounds from Fire Support Base 20 on enemy truck's location. Contact mission for 155-mm from LZ Swinger and 105-mm from Fire Support Base 20 on grids **YB 810023** and **YB 814025** for Company A with 105-mm from Fire Support Base 20 at grid **YB 816023**.

4 March, 1969: 1st Battalion, 8th Infantry continued its reconnaissance in force mission. Company A moved from **YB 822032** to **YB 825042** to reestablish a new patrol base. Company A's 83B (ambush) location at **819019** observed 15 NVA approximately 45 meters from their position but took no action. They also sighted 10 flashlights moving toward their position. Artillery was employed with negative results.

The reconnaissance platoon Tracer 5 continued to work in liaison with Company A. Mortar platoon minus supported battalion operations from Fire Support Base 20. One 81 section supported Company A's activities for A's location.

Air Support: None

Artillery: Reconnaissance by fire by 105-mm at Fire Support Base 20 for Company D. 105-mm emplaced at grid **YB 777018** fired on suspected enemy artillery position. Fifty rounds for this area added to night firing program. 105-mm and 155-mm fired at grid **YB 777016** against suspected enemy artillery position.

5 March, 1969: 1st Battalion, 8th Infantry continued reconnaissance in force with Companies C and D. Company A's 83B at grid **YB 819016** initiated ambush resulting in 2 NVA killed. Two AK-47 and one 9mm pistol were recovered. The same element moving back to Company A's night location observed 2 NVA. The NVA were taken under fire. One NVA was wounded and captured. He was extracted and flown to Polei Kleng.

Ambush 83C at **YB 813022** initiated an ambush at 2005 hours resulting in one NVA killed and two U.S. WIA. Fire from ambush's rear resulted in the two U.S. WIA. This contact was believed to be with the flank element of a large unit. Artillery was employed in same area with unknown results. Company A also secured LZ for Company C's extraction. Companies C and A moved to co-location at **YB 822032** and established a patrol base employing maximum platoon-sized ambush elements.

One section of mortars operated in support of Companies C and A at **YB 822032**. A combat skyspot (ground-directed bombing operation) called for at 2400 hours on enemy artillery location **YB 777016** from information received from Battalion Commanding Officer, liaison (Artillery) Officer Company C, and gunship observations.

Air Support: The 7th of the 17th Cavalry supported Company C's move with slicks and flew cover for them as they moved. They also assisted Company C in breaking contact by firing close in fire with their gunships. Gunships also fired suppressive fires on suspected artillery location grid **YB 777016**.

Artillery: From Fire Support Base 20 105-mm fired reconnaissance by fire on grid **YB 819016** for Company A at 0905 hours. At 1030 hours 105-mm and 155-mm fired 92 and 50 HE respectively on suspected enemy battery position. At 1300 hours 155-mm fired reconnaissance for Company D. Reconnaissance by fire was initiated at 1315 hours by 105-mm for Company C at grid **YB 790021**. Reconnaissance by fire was called in by Company D grid **YB 777047**(155-mm). Reconnaissance by fire was called in at 1355 hours for Company C at grid **YB 790022** (30 HE, 105-mm). At 1450, 155-mm and 105-mm counter fire was directed against **YB 776016**. At 1845 hours at grid **YB 777016** 105-mm emplaced to silence enemy being placed on Company C.

6 March, 1969: 1st Battalion, 8th Infantry continued reconnaissance in force with Companies A, C and D. Company A's emplaced platoon-sized ambushes at grids **YB 819027** and **YB 818027** at 1814 hours. Company A experienced incoming from a 105-mm howitzer. This was countered by a battery from Fire Support Base 20 at grid locations **YB 810020** and **YB 811039**.

Reconnaissance platoon Tracer 5 worked in liaison with Company A. Part of a mortar platoon supported battalion operations from Fire Support Base 20. One mortar section supported Companies A and C operations.

Air Support: HH47 adjusted 105-mm's from Fire Support Base onto grid **YB 806032** (possible bunker complex) HH46 adjusted 3 Firecracker rounds, vicinity **YB 806032**, onto suspected enemy positions.

Artillery: At 0750 reconnaissance by fire for Company A at grid **YB 807021**, 105-mm. At 1055 4.2 inch and 105-mm for Company D at grid **YB 797054**, enemy in open. At 1820 hours Company A received incoming. Counter battery was directed on grid **YB 810020**. At 1825 hours counter mortar on grid **YB 811039**. Night Firing Program (NFP) was initiated at location YB **805040** 100 rounds of 4.2 inch and location **YB 777016** 150 rounds 105-mm.

7 March, 1969:1ˢᵗ Battalion, 8ᵗʰ Infantry continued reconnaissance in force with Companies A and C in the A.O. Company A continued security of night location, vicinity **YB 825027**, utilizing OP, LP, patrols. Their platoon-sized ambushes at **YB 819024** and **YB 818027** kept up their surveillance. Two NVA were sighted near Company A's CP location. They were taken under fire with negative results.

Reconnaissance platoon Tracer 5 worked in liaison with Company A at **YB 826030**. Part of the mortar platoon continued to support battalion operations from Fire Support Base 20 with one section at Company A and C's location.

Air Support: The 7ᵗʰ of the 17ᵗʰ Cavalry operated in the A.O. At 1635 Comic 31 reported sighting 2 artillery pieces at grid **YB 779028**. Gunships were employed and they reported destroying one piece and damaging the second.

Artillery: At 1300 hours 155-mm fired a firecracker round on suspected enemy artillery position. At 1610 105-mm fired in support of Company A receiving small arms fire. Night fire program: 75 rounds 4.2-inch mortar on grid **793058**.

8 March, 1969: 1ˢᵗ Battalion, 8ᵗʰ Infantry continued its reconnaissance in force mission with Company A and C.

Reconnaissance platoon Tracer 5 continued to operate in liaison with Company A. Mortar platoon continued in support of battalion operations from Fire Support Base 20. Generally, the Battalion's operations had negative results.

Air Support: Cider 10 (Forward Air Controller) employed an airstrike at grid vicinity **YB 778018**. The 7ᵗʰ of the 17ᵗʰ Cavalry's red birds reported destroying 1 NVA truck (2 ½ ton) and killing 1 NVA soldier in the vicinity of 105-mm howitzer position. They also reported sighting another truck at the same general grid. Comic 31 also sighted another

411

truck, vicinity YB **780022**. Dust off was utilized at Fire Support Base 20 to remove one injured engineer.

Artillery: Vicinity **773026** the Battalion Liaison Officer employed 110 HE rounds of 105-mm howitzer and 15 firecracker rounds of 155-mm on enemy in open vicinity **YB 847007**. Results were three confirmed NVA KBA (Artillery). Vicinity **773026** the 7th of the 17th Cavalry employed 155-mm on suspected enemy location. Vicinity **77017** Cavalry employed 105-mm against an enemy artillery position with unknown results. Vicinity **834074** Company D employed mortars from Fire Support Base 20 in a reconnaissance by fire program. Night firing program: 110 rounds of 105-mm against suspected enemy artillery positions and areas of enemy sightings that day.

9 March, 1969: 1st Battalion, 8th Infantry continued its mission to interdict the enemy's movement within the area of operations. Company A conducted a bomb damage assessment (BDA) from their night location at **YB 853025** and returned to the night location **YB 826028** due to airstrikes being employed in the vicinity of their BDA mission's area of operation. Company A also employed 2 platoon-sized ambushes vicinity **817022** and at **824014**.

Air Support: Comic Blue 6 reported enemy trucks vicinity **777018** and **780024**. These trucks had been previously destroyed by an airstrike but they had been covered with foliage during the night. Artillery emplaced with unknown results.

Artillery Night firing program. 167 rounds of 105-mm howitzer were employed on routes of regress to the Southwest. An arclight area where enemy were sighted in the open near a suspected mortar position was also fired upon.

10 March, 1969: 1st Battalion, 8th Infantry continued its reconnaissance in force mission with two companies operating from patrol bases utilizing maximum platoon-sized forces and local patrols.

11 March, 1969: 1st Battalion, 8th Infantry continued its reconnaissance in force mission with Company B securing Fire Support Base 20 utilizing local patrols and security, and platoon-sized ambushes to the Southwest, South and Southeast of Fire Support Base 20.

Companies A and C received mission to conduct BDA vicinity **YB 870984**. These two companies moved overland toward that location with negative results. Reconnaissance platoon Tracer 5 continued to operate in liaison with Company A. Mortar platoon continued to support battalion operations at Fire Support Base 20 employing 7 81-mm mortars and 4 4.2 inch mortars. Four additional mortars are located at LZ Mary Lou. Artillery from A Battery 1st of the 29th Artillery was employed against enemy anti-aircraft gun position vicinity **YB 827021** by Headhunter 46. Previously these guns had fired on Hummingbird 1 assisting in Company A and Company C BDA.

Air Support: Forward Air Controllers Cider 10 and Cider 15 worked area vicinity **YB 827011** and employed airstrikes. This was the area that enemy 105-mm artillery guns were extracted the previous day.

12 March, 1969: 1st Battalion, 8th Infantry continued operating in assigned area of operations (A.O.) with Companies A and C conducting Bomb Damage Assessment(BDA) near the Cambodian border.

A map showing the Company A locations leading up to and including March 12 is shown on below.

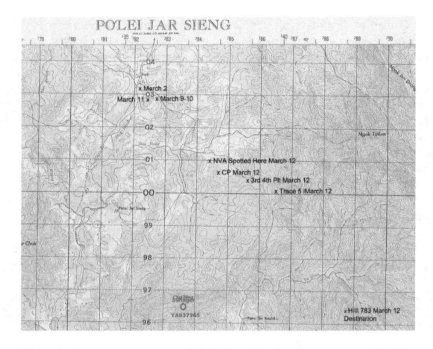

The mission was to move to Hill 783 and make assessments of B-52 strikes there. Company A was 6 or 7 km from the desired location of the Bomb Strike when they encountered enemy contact.

Company A was traveling with Trace 5 recon unit and the unit was maintaining about 300 meters in front of their movement.

At about 1130H an NVA trail watcher was spotted by the lead platoon of Company A at location **YB844009**. The company moved forward following the NVA and ran into a large complex of bunkers. The NVA had let the Tracer 5 recon unit through waiting for the larger unit in the movement. Tracer 5 had reported the bunker complex to the CP (Command Post) but were not attacked by the enemy.

Heavy contact was then encountered in the vicinity **YB847005** with enemy company dug in. The enemy force was dug-in in bunkers and had part of A Company pinned down.

The company was unable to maneuver against the enemy force since the lead platoons not pinned down were extracting wounded personnel and providing security for them. Company A had their forces separated

414

with the 1st and 2nd platoons on high ground and the 3rd and 4th platoons on the low ground down a finger. Company A was surrounded from all sides by NVA. The diagram below depicts the situation. The CP with the 1st and 2nd platoons were on high ground and the 3rd and 4th platoons were separated down the finger separated from the CP.

After a long extended firefight lasting hours and the interjection of Cobra Helicopters the 3rd and 4th platoons fought their way back up to join with the CP dragging their wounded up the hill. Tracer 5 was ahead of the CP within the NVA bunker area trapped in the middle of the enemy. After about an estimated 4 to 5 hours of fighting the 3rd and 4th platoons completely joined the rest of the company at the top of the hill.

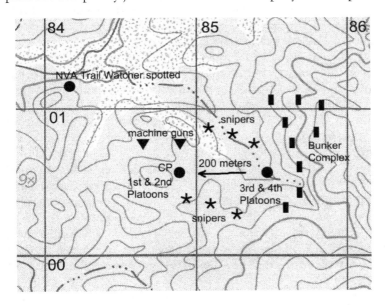

Results of action were 22 NVA KIA, U.S. casualties 2 KIA, 15 WIA and 3 MIA (from Tracer 5).

Company A withdrew to night location vicinity **YB 852011** to regroup and reorganize. This was approximately 800 meters or one half mile from the initial contact that day. They conducted local security in vicinity of night location.

Company C continued BDA mission in conjunction with Company A moving on a parallel axis with Company A.

Company C encountered light contact vicinity **YB 85199**9 with possible enemy squad dug in. After that action Company C maneuvered to vicinity night location **YB 847006**, to regroup and reorganize. Results of action were 1 NVA KIA and 1 U.S. WIA.

Company C conducted local security vicinity night location.

Company D was on standby to combat assault into Company A's location and to reinforce or relieve in place and continue BDA mission, with Company C.

The Reconnaissance Platoon Tracer 5 (Company E) continued to work in conjunction with Company A on the BDA mission. Tracer 5 apparently was used as flank security for Company A.

When contact was initiated Tracer 5 was cut off resulting in three MIA. Two men (one WIA) trying to escape and evade back to Company A's night location were detected by radio contact.

A mortar platoon continued support of battalion operations on Fire Support Base 20 with 7 81-mm mortars and 4 4.2-inch mortars. Mortar platoon fired support fires for all the Companies that were in contact and continued to support both Companies A and C throughout the night.

Air Support: Hummingbird 5 medevaced one U.S. WIA from Company C contact. Medevac was employed vicinity Company A's location for 5 WIA and vicinity Fire Support Base 20 for 1 WIA. Comic 47 with the 7th of the 17th Cavalry supported both Companies A and C and Tracer 5 along with Blue 6 (7th of the 17th Cavalry) during days' contact. Spooky 21 supported Companies A and C in contact throughout the night.

Artillery: Artillery support from A Battery 6th of the 29th Artillery was fired in support of Company A contact throughout the day. A total of 405 rounds were expended in night fire program in support of Companies A and C.

Combat Losses: Green memo book containing call signs and frequencies of Company A and Battalion net; SOI (compromised with appropriate action taken); total of 7 M16A1 rifles; one starlight scope; one An/PRC-25 radio; 58 rucksacks; ten D-handle shovels; 16 machetes.

Total NVA KIA for 12 March 1969 was 33. Total U.S. casualties were 13 WIA, 4 KIA and 2 MIA.

13 March, 1969: 1st Battalion, 8th Infantry continued operations in assigned A.O. with Company A regrouping and evacuating WIA and KIA and receiving light contact while moving from previous position to link up with Company C.

Company A remained at the previous night location vicinity **YB 852011.**

Prior to the move Company A employed patrols to retrieve missing and killed personnel absent from company. All WIAs and KIAs that were found were evacuated from nearby LZ.

Also resupply was accomplished during this action.

During the move to the site to link with Company C, Company A experienced light contact resulting in 3 NVA KIA and 4 NVA possible wounded.

Also Company A received incoming mortar attack during move with no casualties. Company A employed artillery extensively to cover their advance on the flanks and front formation. Air strike was employed against possible enemy mortar position with unknown results.

Company B remained on standby to reinforce and/or assist Company C in their operations. Company C was located in vicinity **YB 847003** and remained in position throughout the day awaiting arrival of Company A. Company C sent element to link with Company A and guide them to Company C position.

Company C maintained local security and two platoon-sized ambushes near their vicinity throughout the day.

Company D along with Company B continued security mission Fire Support Base 20 employing local security, local patrols and Company D supplying one platoon-sized ambush.

The reconnaissance platoon Tracer 5 (Company E) continued to work in liaison with Company A with mission to retrieve KIA and WIA. They moved with Company A to new location and established patrol base. At that time reconnaissance platoon had one KIA, one died of wounds and 3 MIA from previous day's action. One MIA walked into Company A's previous night location and informed element that the other MIA was dead.

Mortar platoon supported battalion operations on Fire Support Base 20, firing no missions on that day.

Air Support: The 7th of the 17th Cavalry's Cider 12 and 15 employed air strike on possible enemy mortar position firing on Company A and C

417

position vicinity YB 850005. Headhunter 46 supplied surveillance and employment of artillery in support of battalion operations. The 7th of the 17th Cavalry supported Company A's operations, which consisted of extraction of WIA and KIA. Medevac also employed in vicinity Company A's previous night location.

Artillery: Artillery support for Company A was fired by Battery A, 6th of the 29th Artillery. Supported retrieve of Company A WIAs and KIAs. Artillery also covered Company A flanks and frontal portion of formation while moving to link with Company C. Artillery was employed on possible enemy bunker complex vicinity Company A's previous day's contact.

14 March, 1969: 1st Battalion, 8th Infantry continued operations in assigned A.O. with Company A and C operating from vicinity **YB 847003** employing one platoon-sized reconnaissance patrol each. This new location was 943 meters (.585 miles) from Company A's previous location.

Fifteen rounds assorted 82-mm and 60-mm mortars were received in location of Companies A and C from enemy positions on three occasions throughout the day. Each time artillery was used in response from Fire Support Base 20 resulting in suppression of enemy fire.

Throughout the night Companies A and C employed squad-sized ambushes for local security.

Company C employed two platoon-sized patrols who encountered, vicinity **YB 856992** to **YB 852995** to **YB 859994** what appeared to be a large U-shaped enemy bunker complex. They also observed approximately 20 individuals in vicinity of this area and heard voices and what appeared to be large artillery pieces firing vicinity **YB 842000**. Artillery was employed with negative results.

Companies B and D continued Fire Support Base 20 security employing local security patrols, and Company B employed one platoon-sized ambush vicinity **YB 820043** with negative results.

Reconnaissance platoon Tracer 5 (Company E) continued working in conjunction with Company A at their night location.

Mortar platoon continued supporting battalion operations at Fire Support Base 20.

Air Support: Spooky 22 supported Companies A and C vicinity YB 847003. Headhunter 46 and 6 reported heavy enemy activity at vicinity YB 8697 to YB 8797. It was checked extensively and revealed heavy trail network with extremely recent use.

Artillery: Artillery support from Battery A, 6th of the 29th Artillery was fired on grids YB 852005 CB, YB 854010 adjusted onto enemy bunker, YB 854002, support of Company C platoons, YB 849008, enemy in open for Company A, YB 862997 Company C reconnaissance by fire, YB 856996 Company C reconnaissance by fire, YB 835995 Company A CB, and YB 855000 CNF. Night Firing Program (CFP) Night fires at Fire Support Base Swinger, 500 rounds HE grids YB 853995, YB 859994, YB 857992, YB 850998, YB 838996, YB 838992, YB 838989 and YB 820006; 105-mm howitzer from Fire Support Base 20. Five roadrunners general grids, YB 8300, YB 8599, YB 8699 and YB 8698 – 100 rounds HE.

15 March, 1969: 1st Battalion, 8th Infantry continued operations in assigned A.O. with Company A and C operating from patrol base employing ambushes and patrols.

Company A and C were mortared two times in their patrol base location vicinity **YB 847003**. A total of 12 rounds were received resulting in 7 U.S. WIA.

Companies C and D continued security mission of Fire Support Base 20 employing local patrols, local security, and three platoon-sized ambushes with negative results.

Reconnaissance platoon continued to operate in liaison with Company A.

Mortar platoon continued support of battalion operations on Fire Support Base 20.

There was a change of command for Company A. Captain Hockett was sent to Firebase 20 and Major Androsky took command of both Companies A and C operating as a Task Force.

Lieutenant Colonel C. Buckner who was the 1-8 Bn. Co. and was located at FB 20. He ordered Major Androsky consolidate two companies into a Task Force, Alpha and Charlie, who had been conducting bomb damage assessment (BDA) operations in the valley and

419

to take them to Hill #467 and establish a perimeter. The combination would be called Task Force Alpha (TFA).

At the time TFA was formed, Company A had significant losses in personnel and weapons reducing their strength to significantly fewer than 100 men. Company C was slightly better off with personnel and had no significant weapons loss.

TFA was therefore comprised of two under strength rifle companies. Company A was officially listed as A company (-).

The new location of TFA was situated on a vulnerable piece of terrain, like Hill #467. It was located in a well trafficked valley area cordoned by roads that the enemy was actively using. It straddled the area of operations of the 66th N.V.A. Regiment with a strength of 1,265 including other active NVA units.

TFA was to remain at Hill #467 and it was their mission to interdict and suppress enemy movement in the valley.

Air Support: Forward Air Observers Cider 13 and 14 operated in the A.O. employing an air strike at vicinity **YB 862997** for support of the 7th of the 17th Cavalry sighting of possible U.S. MIA in that vicinity. The 7th of the 17th Cavalry operated in A.O. and sighted enemy in open. They employed ordinance with results unknown. Also in same vicinity they sighted U.S. MIA in bomb crater. Extraction was attempted with negative results due to enemy ambush.

U.S. individual was sighted vicinity **850998**. Medevac was utilized at Company A and C location vicinity **847003** for 7 WIA. Headhunter 46 worked A.O. with negative results.

Two MIA, John Pizarski and Wayne Joslin, lost in action of 12 March 1969, walked into Company A's position unharmed. This accounted for 3 MIAs of T-5 element. One KIA, one individual still MIA, Floyd Robinson, at this time.

Artillery: Artillery from Battery A, 6th of the 29th Artillery fired on grid **YB 855002** which was suspected enemy in open with fire coming close to friendly element at 2020 hours. Artillery also fired a night firing program of 150 rounds 105-mm from Fire Support Base 20, and 100 rounds 155-mm from Fire Support Base Swinger. The purpose of these fires was dual. First to supply support for Companies A and C at vicinity **YB 847003** against close in concentrations and also H and I.

16 March, 1969: The following morning, with Charlie company in the lead, the Task Force headed to Hill #467.

During the move the Task Force encountered two NVA trucks, destroying one by air and killing the occupants.

TFA arrived at Hill #467 with no casualties, established a perimeter and reported completion of the mission.

The first concern of TFA was establishing a defensive perimeter. The two companies began digging bunkers and gathering overhead for protection from the inevitable weapons attacks we could expect.

Battalion began helicoptering in sand bags and defensive material, claymores, etc. to support the efforts. Included in the first lifts of supplies was an x-mode radio and operator for communicating directly with the Battalion commander. It enabled TFA to talk in the clear with Battalion while monitoring the company and battalion nets.

In the first day, Alpha sent patrols out to bomb crater and surrounding area near a ford southwest of the patrol base and Charlie conducted platoon sized patrols in the area.

All of the patrol and interdiction missions were sent directly to the companies from the Battalion Commander.

The TFA requested additional support to establish a blocking position (strong point) on the southern approach to the patrol base as it was a likely avenue of approach for an attacking force. An element of the recon platoon reinforced the perimeter there.

Elements of recon platoon also performed security patrols in TFA immediate vicinity throughout the occupation of Hill #467. On 18 March a mortar section was also attached to TFA, giving TFA immediate response to requests for fire support in and around the perimeter.

From the day TFA established our perimeter, air strikes were called in with increasing regularity as TFA continued to occupy Hill #467. The air assets, not organic to the 4th Infantry Division consisted of Fastpacers, like F-4 Phantoms,F-100 Super Sabre, F-105 Thunderchief and the ever reliable and deadly Sky-raider. Almost all of the Fastpacers were return flights from up north with a variety of ordinance and varying amounts of time on stations.

Most strikes were ten minutes or less due to fuel considerations. Ordinance varied from 500 pound bombs with stand offs, rockets, napalm, or strafe.

In the case of one F-4 Phantom, TFA conducted a strike with no ordinance, just noise! In effect, TFA got what wasn't expended up north. Using the Skyraiders TFA were fortunate to have an array of weapons: rockets, bombs, and strafe. They stayed on station for about 45 minutes expending all amunition they had.

"Spooky" was also used at night to good effect. In one of their many airstrikes, one pilot's response to being fired at by enemy forces was in his transmission after completing his gun run was "Fiveniner: Those little bastards are shooting at me. Over!" My R.T.O was grinning at me when TFA replied, "Yeah, they do that a lot here."

1st Battalion, 8th Infantry continued operating in assigned A.O. with Companies A and C operating as a Task Force named Task Force Alpha (TFA) moving from previous night location to vicinity **YB 817030**. The new location was 4037 meters (2.5 miles) from the previous location.

During move 2 NVA were sighted, taken under fire, with negative results, vicinity **YB 838068**. Also in same area another NVA was sighted and killed.

Companies A and C employed local ambushes in vicinity of their night location.

Artillery: Artillery from Battery A 6th of the 29th Artillery fired 15 Roadrunners to support Task Force A with 150 HE rounds from Fire Support Base 20 and 75 rounds 155-mm HE from Fire Support Base Swinger. Task Force A movement was assisted with reconnaissance by fire by artillery throughout the day.

17 March, 1969: 1st Battalion, 8th Infantry continued operating in assigned A.O. with TFA mission to interdict and suppress enemy movement vicinity of roads near their location.

TFA moved from previous location to **YB 804034** and established patrol base. This was 1360 meters (.85 miles from their previous location). This new location was Hill #467.

Company A sent two platoons to vicinity **YB 788023** mission to crater and abertee ford that vicinity. This mission was successfully accomplished.

Ambush actions for TFA were concentrated on roads to the east, north and south.

Company C ambush vicinity **YB 815022** observed three NVA moving northeast. These individuals were taken under fire at approximately 50-75 meters with negative results.

Air Support: Cider 10 drew ground fire vicinity **YB 731055** while working in A.O. Redlegs employed Firecracker bombs at grid **YB 724055** with one large secondary explosion. They fired on grid **YB 731055** intelligence from higher with negative surveillance. Cider 13 performed an airstrike vicinity **YB 739055**. Headhunter 46 worked A.O. employing Artillery and adjusting it on suspected enemy location.

Artillery: Artillery fired the Night Fire Program on vicinity **YB 735046** on suspected enemy location expending 108 HE 105-mm.

18 March, 1969: 1st Battalion, 8th Infantry continued operating in assigned A.O. with TFA mission to interdict and suppress enemy movement vicinity of roads near their location.

The TFA remained on Hill #467 at **YB 804034**.

The battalion furnished patrols and local security of areas occupied by companies. Company A continued security of Task Force A.

Company C employing 3 platoon-sized ambushes.

Company C minus conducted road cratering and abertee from coordinates **YB 768031** to **YB 771029**. Craters were blown at grids **YB 790030**, **YB 789030** and **YB 797031**. One platoon ambushed vicinity **YB 797034**.

A bunker complex was found by Company C vicinity **YB 779035** to **YB 781035** to **YB 779032**.

Approximately 75 bunkers with commo wire running between them, 2-man size camouflaged well, showing no signs of recent use.

Air Support: Cider 22 employed air strike vicinity **YB 720053** to **YB 730049** for purpose of cutting road that vicinity. One Medevac was employed with Company B for two WIA.

Artillery: Artillery shot 5 Roadrunners of 105-mm, 150 rounds HE in support of Task Force A. Also fired 5 rounds of 155-mm, 75 rounds of HE in support of TFA from Fire Base Swinger.

19 March, 1969: 1st Battalion, 8th Infantry continued road interdiction, ambushes and patrols in the A.O.

The TFA remained on Hill #467 at **YB 804034**.

Company A had 2 platoon-sized ambushes operating in vicinity of TFA. These were the 4th Platoon led by E7 Platoon Leader Holland and 2nd Platoon led by LT. Porter.

An abertee was successfully constructed grid **YB 805053** by one of the 4th platoon and they moved on. This location was approximate 1903 meters (1.2 miles) from the location of the TFA on Hill #467.

At location **YB 801043** they came under intense ground fire. They received one U.S. KIA SSG Harvey Charles Avery and one wounded.

The other ambush, 2nd platoon led by LT. Porter, linked up with the 4th platoon in contact vicinity **YB 801043**. The objective was to go back into area and retrieve SSG Avery's body. This location was approximate 949 meters (.60 miles) from the location of the TFA on Hill #467.

They were unable to move back due to intense enemy fire.

They pulled back and set up on a hill overlooking the ambush site and employed mortar fire from TFA location.

Mortar accident occurred TFA's location Hill #467 resulting in 12 WIA. Medevac was employed.

Air Support: The 7th of the 17th Cavalry made a bomb damage assessment (BDA) of area location **7179**. They received small arms fire during BDA vicinity **YB 863987** by approximate squad sized element. Also rocket fire and small arms fire were received by Cavalry White Birds in the vicinity of **YB 849991**. Cider 14 employed air strike vicinity **YB 876003**. A total of 3 Dustoffs were called to Task Force A's location.

Eight Helocib AN/GSO-128 Censors were employed by elements from Fire Base 20 with support from the 7th of the 17th Cavalry in vicinity **YB 779026, YB 784023, YB 782025, YB 776026, YB 813019, YB 810023, YB 805022** and **YB 815021**. These censors were to be used by our battalion as a test to estimate their value in a combat situation. A crew from Division was assigned to the battalion to monitor the portascope after the drop. When the Censors were dropped they were supposedly correctly activated. However, no indications were observed on the portascope to confirm activation right after one was dropped. Late the next day Artillery fired on these grids confirming negative activation of the Censors. A preliminary conclusion was that the Battery assembly was not correctly set in the Censors before they were sent to Fire Base 20.

Artillery: Artillery fired Night Fire Program with normal H & I accomplished.

20 March, 1969: 1ˢᵗ Battalion, 8ᵗʰ Infantry continued ambush patrols and interdiction of roads in assigned A.O.

Company A minus (part of the Company) consisting of the 3ʳᵈ Platoon led be E7 Sgt. Pfeifer moved from the TFA Hill #467 to vicinity of previous day's contact and swept area and recovered 1 U.S. KIA.

Company A minus (3ʳᵈ Platoon) made contact again at grid **YB 801052** resulting in one U.S. KIA (Harold Johnson), 11 U.S. WIA and 4 NVA KIA. This location was 412 meters (.25 miles) from the location the engineer got killed the previous day and 1825 meters or 1.13 miles from the TFA located at Hill #467. Company A employed ambush vicinity **YB 792021**.

Air Support: One Medevac was utilized vicinity of Company A's contact with one being utilized at TFA location. The rest of wounded in contact

Air Support: One Medevac was utilized vicinity of Company A's contact with one being utilized at Task Force A location. The rest of wounded in contact.

Artillery: Artillery fired on censor location grids to test their operation. Fired HE rounds 105-mm from Fire Base 20 in support of A Company in contact. Regular Night Fire Program was accomplished (both 105-mm and 155-mm were fired).

21 March, 1969: 1ˢᵗ Battalion, 8ᵗʰ Infantry continued ambush patrols and road interdiction in assigned A.O.

Company A conducted airlift from TFA to **Fire Support Base 20** located at **YB 832081 (5070 meters or 3.15 miles from Hill #467)** assuming security mission and employing ambushes vicinity **YB 814082** and **YB 819082**.

Each day, the task force occupied Hill #467 the N.V.A. increased their presence by attacks on the patrol base accompanied by probes of the perimeter. The enemy was patiently preparing the patrol base for ultimate destruction

Alpha Company left TFA on the 21st of March and was replaced by Bravo Company. Alpha incurred additional casualties and loss of weapons on 19 – 20 March as a result of an enemy ambush during an interdiction mission on the 19th. This reduced their under-strength status and was the deciding factor in their replacement.

Alpha Company's performance from 15 March until 21 March as a part of the TFA was noteworthy considering their strength handicap.

Company B minus conducted airlift from Fire Support Base 20 to TFA with one platoon closing TFA by ground prior to airlift.

Company B minus moved overland to area of Company A's previous day's contact with mission to interdict road in that vicinity. However, this mission could not be accomplished. Therefore, a secondary mission of destroying 11 enemy bunkers vicinity **YB 812048** was accomplished.

Company B employed one platoon-sized ambush vicinity **YB 816048**.

Artillery: Artillery fired for a combat mission for **5321** element at grid **815024**. Negative surveillance for support of Task Force A. Night Fire Program: two Roadrunners expended, 50 HE 155-mm, 100 rounds HE 105-mm, 36 rounds HE 4.2 inch mortar, 20 rounds HE 81-mm mortars all in support of TFA.

22 March, 1969: 1st Battalion, 8th Infantry continued operations with patrols, ambushes and road interdiction missions in A.O.

Company A continued security of Fire Base 20, with local security, patrols and two platoon-sized elements used as ambushes vicinity **YB 818088** and **YB 814082**.

Air Support: Cider 24 and Cider 15 and Cider 10 employed two air strikes vicinity **761042** and **755044**. Resupply helicopter supplying Task Force A received ground fire resulting in a disabled air craft. One R/S bird was received Task Force A location, with no ground fire prior to this. This helicopter was utilized to Medevac Company C WIA. Gunships were employed vicinity of where helicopter was receiving enemy ground fire, with unknown results. The gunships also received a heavy volume of fire vicinity Task Force A.

Artillery: Approximately 2250 hours Artillery was employed on truck movement, vicinity **796-19**. Also employed mortars from Task Force A location with negative surveillance. Artillery was employed for reconnaissance by fire for moving elements of the battalion throughout the day. Also employed 150 rounds HE 105-mm in support of Task Force A and 60 HE 81-mm mortars in Night Fire Program.

23 March, 1969: 1st Battalion, 8th Infantry continued ambush patrols, and road interdiction missions in A.O.

Company A continued security of Fire Support Base 20 with local security, patrols and ambushes vicinity **YB 819066, YB 819078, YB 820084**, and **YB 825083**.

During the time Company A occupied Hill #467 patrols that were sent out to interdict roads and communication junctions were at first somewhat effective, but quickly became a nuisance to the enemy rather than impeding their lines of supply and communication. An occasional abati across the road or crater was never going to deter a determined enemy who had occupied the valley for years, unopposed and enjoyed sanctuary approximately five kilometers away in Cambodia.

Our primary task at TFA after the 23rd of March quickly morphed from interdiction of roads and lines of communication to increasing the perimeter defense. TFA attempted to identify and break up enemy troop concentrations that could comprise an attacking force. An unintended result of TFA was that effectively, the TFA was bait for the NVA. All of the patrol activity was to interdict and disrupt his lines of communication became secondary to luring his units towards Hill #467.

Air Support: The 7th of the 17th Cavalry worked in A.O. with unknown results. R/S birds conducted support of Task Force A, receiving sporadic ground fire. Cider 15 and Headhunter 40 and Headhunter 48 assisted in location of enemy artillery positions and adjusted artillery on to these with unknown results. Spooky 21 was employed in support of Company B 24 element contact.

Artillery: Arc light 7183 was employed at 2115 hours 3000 meters southwest of Task Force A. Artillery was in support all day for the battalion. When incoming started 175-mm from Ben Het were employed on grid **750092** with negative results. Artillery was in support of Task Force A. Also on suspected enemy artillery positions. Mortars were also employed from Fire Support Base 20 in support of Task Force A.

24 March, 1969: 1st Battalion, 8th Infantry continued ambush patrols and road interdictions in the A.O. Company A continued security of Fire Base 20, local security and patrols.

They employed platoon-sized reconnaissance patrols to **YB 818054** with night location vicinity **YB 819066**.

They employed short range patrols to vicinity **YB 818078** to **YB 820038**.

Fire Support Base 20 received incoming artillery and indirect fire weapons. Number of rounds received unknown.

Air Support: Cider 10, 12, 13 and 14 employed air strikes in vicinity Task Force A's location. Daisy Cutter's vicinity **YB 877044**. Medevac was called to Task Force A location. It received heavy ground fire and was unable to land. Artillery was employed to Task Force A to extract two most seriously wounded. Resupply was conducted by one slick receiving heavy ground fire and also removing rest of wounded. The 7th of the 17th Cavalry operated in A.O. sighting NVA in open vicinity **849982**. Gunships were employed by Company B 23 element contact with results unknown. There was one U.S. WIA. A1E Skyraiders were also utilized in this vicinity after contact had terminated with unknown results. The Cavalry also conducted BDA vicinity Arc light 7183. Air strikes were employed Task Force A vicinity **YB 807033** with two secondary explosions resulting from air strikes and strafing runs. Arc light 7186P was employed at 2120 hours southwest of Task Force A.

Artillery: Artillery was fired with two roadrunners in support of Task Force A. 100 HE 105-mm rounds were fired on suspected enemy artillery location, 50 HE 155-mm rounds were fired in support of Task Force A. Reconnaissance by fire was employed to support battalion operations throughout the day.

25 March 1969: 1st Battalion, 8th Infantry continued ambush patrols and interdiction of roads in assigned A.O.

Company A continued security of Fire Support Base 20 with local security and patrols. They employed platoon-sized ambush vicinity **YB 855074**.

This platoon's additional mission was to form outpost for Fire Support Base 27. Short range patrols were employed to vicinity **YB 824085, YB 775055, YB 772028, YB 819084, YB 817077, YB 825082** and **YB 855074**.

TFA came under attack at 0700 receiving B-40 rockets and small arms fire. Gunships, airstrikes and mortar fire were employed against enemy in open with results unknown. Results of ground action: 13 U.S. WIA, 1

U.S. KIA, 2 NVA KIA, possible 3 additional NVA KIA and 1 AK-47 CIA.

At approximately 0700 hours LP on west side of perimeter of TFA 3 individuals were observed to the west. The LP returned back to the perimeter and 81-mm mortar was fired. A reconnaissance squad was sent out to check the area. Three to five NVA took the element under fire approximately 25 meters outside the perimeter. The point man was wounded. The patrol could not recover the U.S. WIA so they employed fire and maneuver and withdrew to perimeter. A reaction force was hastily organized and sent to recover wounded man. This element came under mortar fire and small arms fire. They returned with their wounded to perimeter. The area of contact was fired on by automatic weapons, M-79 and M-16 fire. One small maneuver element was sent along north side of saddle and recovered wounded man. The element received B-40 rocket and small arms fire from three locations of the saddle while getting the wounded man.

When all elements had returned to the perimeter of Task Force A, gunships were employed in area of contact and positions of enemy fire. The gunships drew ground fire from four positions, northwest, west, southwest and south of the perimeter. Two sets of gunships were employed. Two sets of A1E fighters and eight sets of fast pacers were employed to the west, south and east of the perimeter. The results were that 2 enemy firing positions silenced and 2 NVA were KIA.

Air Support: Gunships, A1E Skyraiders, fast pacers fighters were employed vicinity Task Force A. Cider 13 and Cider 12 were utilized to adjust air strikes. A CS drop was employed vicinity road west to east **YB 775055** and **YB 772026**. Medevac was employed to Company B minus vicinity to extract wounded taking ground fire and hits. Resupply was accomplished to Company B minus resulting in one helicopter being hit. Resupply bird vicinity Fire Base 20 drew small arms fire. Spooky gunship was on station to assist Company B minus throughout the night.

Artillery: Artillery fired three roadrunners, two times that night utilizing 105-mm and 155-mm. One roadrunner of 50 HE 155-mm was utilized in support of Task Force A. Reconnaissance by fire was utilized throughout the operation during the day. All artillery support available was used.

26 March, 1969: 1st Battalion, 8th Infantry continued operations in assigned A.O. Company A conducting patrols, local security and road interdiction.

Company A continued Fire Support Base 20 mission employing local security and patrols. One Company A platoon moved from their previous night location to Fire Base 27 to secure this area for Company D who was to move from TFA location to this new location.

Fire Support Base 20 began receiving incoming artillery and mortar rounds from enemy positions approximately 1320 hours. A total of 13 rounds of 105-mm, 7 impacted inside the perimeter, were received. At 1400 hours this barrage ended.

At 1535 hours Fire Support Base 20 again receiving incoming artillery which ended at 1600 hours. A total of 19 rounds were received with 18 impacting inside the perimeter. Counter artillery and mortar fire was employed during both instances resulting in stopping the enemy fire. Results of the artillery and mortar attacks were: 1 U.S. KIA, and 2 U.S. WIA, Battery A 6th of the 29th Artillery suffered 2 U.S. KIA and 7 U.S. WIA as a result of the enemy attack. Daniel Hinkel of the A/1/8 was killed this day.

One more round of incoming artillery was received at 1800 hours with negative injuries and damage.

Air Support: Air support was prominent throughout the battalion A.O. Air strikes were employed vicinity **YB 730030, 770029** and vicinity Task Force A and enemy artillery positions **746095** by Cider 12. Armed helicopters were employed throughout the day to assist resupply of Task Force A. Resupply ships were able to resupply Task Force A on 2 occasions both times receiving enemy fire with one being hit. Medevac was accomplished 2 times, once at Fire Base 20 and once vicinity Company B minus location. Medevac was attempted vicinity Task Force A unsuccessfully. Headhunter 44 worked area vicinity Task Force A supporting Company D move to Company B minus location and assisting in locating enemy position in that area. One CS drop was accomplished by Gulf 25A vicinity **775055**.

Artillery: Battery A, 6th of the 29th artillery (Direct Support) supported battalion operations from Fire Support Base 20 firing in support of ground movement, counter artillery and harassment and interdiction. Two roadrunners and one point target were engaged by 155-mm expending 80 rounds HE in support of Task Force A. Three roadrunners and 2 point targets were fired upon by 105-mm from Fire Support Base 20 expending 200 rounds of HE. This was also in support of Task Force A.

27 March, 1969: 1ˢᵗ Battalion, 8ᵗʰ Infantry continued operations in assigned A.O. employing reconnaissance patrols, short range patrols and local security.

Company A minus located vicinity of Fire Base 20 continued security of Fire Support Base 20 with local OPs and LPs.

Their 21 and 24 platoons were located on Fire Support Base 27 where they established an outpost.

Company A employed 3 short range patrols vicinity Fire Support Base 20 and 2 short range patrols vicinity Fire Support Base 27.

Fire Support Base 20 received incoming 105-mm at approximately 1047 hours.

A total of 19 rounds received with 12 impacting inside the perimeter.

The enemy artillery barrage ended at 1127 hours. Results were 2 U.S. WIA.

Air Support: Air support in battalion A.O. was prominent with air lift of Company D accomplished from Task Force A to Fire Base 27. A total of 14 slicks and 2 sets of gunships were employed in this action. One set of gunships was utilized in second contact of Company C, with one helicopter receiving damage to the aircraft by enemy ground fire. The 7ᵗʰ of the 17ᵗʰ Cavalry worked the A.O. briefly and short missions due to operational difficulties. Cider 12 was beneficial in adjusting artillery from Fire Support Base 20 on enemy gun emplacements firing on Company C. One medevac was conducted successfully from Fire Support Base 20. Headhunter 40 was employed throughout A.O. on possible enemy infiltration routes and positions. CS drop by Gulf 25A was completed at **YB 7603** east to west successfully at 1455 hours.

Artillery: Battery A, 6ᵗʰ of the 29ᵗʰ Artillery (Direct Support) fired reconnaissance by fire missions throughout the day for the battalion. Cider 12 sighted enemy artillery positions vicinity **725071** and employed counter artillery. K-14 and Cider 12 adjusted 105-mm from Fire Base 20 and 175-mm from Ben Het on these positions. K-14 spotted enemy in open running from these artillery positions and employed Firecracker resulting in 3 confirmed NVA KIA. Night Fire Program consisted of 50 155-mm HE employed against enemy artillery position, and in support of

Task Force A. A total of 200 HE 105-mm was employed on enemy artillery position and in vicinity of Task Force A for their support.

28 March, 1969: 1st Battalion, 8th Infantry continued to operate in assigned A.O. employing local security, reconnaissance patrols and short range patrols.

Company A minus continued security of Fire Support Base 20 with local Ops and LPs. The 21 and 24 platoons departed Fire Support Base 27 but did not close Company A minus location. Platoons 21 and 24 linked up at night location vicinity **YB 832089**.

Company A employed 4 short range patrols around Fire Support Base 20 for purposes of security.

Fire Support Base 20 received one round of incoming 105-mm.

Air Support: Air support in battalion A.O. was prominent. Headhunter 40 and 44 assisted in observing area vicinity Task Force A and area of enemy gun emplacement. Medevac was accomplished vicinity Task Force A without incident. Resupply at Task Force A was completed. Resupply for other elements were completed without incident. The 7th of the 17th Cavalry worked A.O. sighting enemy truck convoy vicinity **YB 817088**. Cavalry expended and Company D fired artillery on convoy. Results were one possible vehicle destroyed. Two Combat Sky Spot missions were employed in area of enemy artillery emplacements with unobserved results. Gulf 25 employed a CS drop vicinity 7404. Cider 10 assisted in locating and employing artillery and air strikes on enemy gun positions.

Artillery: Battery A, 6th of the 29th Artillery (Direct Support) fired in support of Task Force A receiving incoming. 175-mm and 105-mm was fired vicinity gun emplacements at **YB 727072**. Throughout the day artillery was employed against these positions with results unknown. Reconnaissance by fire was also employed in support of Task Force A with 105-mm.

29 March, 1969: 1st Battalion, 8th Infantry continued operations in assigned A.O. with local security and short range reconnaissance patrols.

Company A continued security of Fire Support Base 20 employing local security and short range reconnaissance patrols.

Two short-range patrols were employed vicinity **YB 819087** and **YB 814085**.

432

Fire Support Base 20 received a total of 16 rounds of 105-mm enemy artillery fire throughout the afternoon with 12 falling inside the perimeter.

Counter artillery was fired into suspected enemy locations vicinity **YB 716062, YB 731074** and **YB 729071** with results unknown.

Major Androsky commander of the TFA left Hill #467 on 29th of March. The results of T.F.A. in terms of U.S. casualties are a follows: 16 U.S. KIA; 66 U.S. WIA, 6 U.S. MIA.

Significant damage to enemy personnel, equipment, trucks, weapons, and artillery can be attributed to TFA in the total recorded in the 1st Brigade After Action Report. The mission of TFA to interdict and disrupt the enemy's lines of communication was accomplished, but not as planned. The overwhelming artillery and air support accomplished much of the "spoiling attack" mission while TFA at hill #467 acted as the bait causing the enemy to present vulnerable targets of destruction.

Air Support: Air support was prevalent throughout the battalion A.O. Spooky 22 was employed in vicinity of Task Force A during the early morning against suspected enemy concentrations preparing for a ground attack. Cider 12 assisted in visual observation of Task Force A and employing artillery fire on suspected enemy artillery emplacements. Nine Combat Sky Spots were employed vicinity enemy artillery emplacements vicinity **YB 716062, YB 731074** and **YB 729071**. Cider 13 Headhunter 44 and 40 were utilized throughout A.O. to adjust artillery on suspected enemy locations. Resupply of Task Force A was accomplished with 2 slicks and 3 WIA were evacuated on the first helicopter. A total of 6 slick sorties were employed from Fire Support Base 20 to Fire Support Base 27 to air lift Company D 24 element. Gulf 25 employed 2 CS drops on enemy infiltration routes vicinity 752038 to 758035 and 762041 to 756047. One light observation helicopter was employed vicinity Task Force A with Psychological Operations team aboard, resulting in light damage to the aircraft.

Artillery: Artillery support throughout the battalion A.O. was performed by Battery A, 6th of the 29th Artillery (Direct Support) vicinity Fire Support Base 20, 155-mm located LZ Swinger and 175-mm located Ben Het. Heavy radar and Infrared readings indicated heavy enemy troop movement toward Task Force A along southern road vicinity **YB 774008, YB 774023, YB 776024, YB 788022** and 774006. Headhunter

433

40 adjusted artillery from Swinger and Fire Base 20 onto the locations. K-12 air observer sighted 3 enemy artillery tubes vicinity **YB 716062, YB 731074** and **YB 729071**. 175-mm from Ben Het was adjusted onto these positions. Task Force A received support from 4.2 inch mortar vicinity Fire Support Base 20 with 150 HE and 50 White Phosphorus being employed on suspected enemy locations. 105-mm from Fire Support Base 20 was also employed with 800 rounds of HE being expended vicinity Task Force A on suspected enemy locations. 155-mm from LZ Swinger employed 65 rounds HE in support of Task Force A. Two secondary explosions resulted from these supporting fires. One to the southeast and one to the west was sighted at Task Force A.

30 March, 1969: 1st Battalion, 8th Infantry was in the process of moving all elements to Fire Base McNerny for stand down and regrouping.

Company A located on Fire Support Base 20 moved from that location to Polei Kleng and remained there during the night.

Enemy artillery harassed the movement from Fire Support Base 20 with a total of 40 rounds being received starting at 0100 hours and lasting until final extraction of all elements at 1830 hours.

One U.S. WIA was evacuated from Fire Support Base 20 by Medevac as a result of the enemy artillery.

Tactical Operations Center minus remained with Company A throughout the night at Polei Kleng.

Reconnaissance platoon was extracted along with Company A. Reconnaissance platoon remained with Company A at Polei Kleng. Mortar platoon was extracted along with Company A at Fire Support Base 20 with one section being extracted with Task Force A.

Air Support: Air support during the battalion operation was excellent. Chinooks were successful in extraction sorties from Fire Support Base 20. UH10 helicopters and gunships succeeded in extracting Companies C, D and B. An Air Force Spat was employed vicinity Fire Support Base 20 to cover the extraction. Cider 15 assisted the Spat operation and also assisted with air surveillance in the areas of extraction. Gulf 25A employed CS drops vicinity **YB 730060, YB 730030, YB 760060, YB 760030** and **YB 7401**.

434

Artillery: Battery A, 6th of the 29th Artillery (Direct Support) was extracted from Fire Support Base 20 with last extraction complete at 1730 hours. 175-mm from Ben Het and 155-mm from LZ Swinger was employed on enemy positions throughout the day's activities in support of the operation.

31 March, 1969: 1st Battalion, 8th Infantry assumed stand down status at Fire Base McNerny. Company D moved from LZ Mary Lou and closed Fire Base McNerny at 1100 hours. Company A, mortar platoon minus, reconnaissance platoon, and Tactical Operations Center minus closed Fire Base McNerny at 1500 hours.

An event summary for the A-1-8 is given below highlighting the major events experienced by the company in March 1969.

Event Summary for A-1-8 March 1969

Seq.	Date	Location	Comments
1	March 2 1969	**YB 822031**	Combat Assault **near** LZ Turkey within 450 meters
2	March 2 1969	**YB 822032**	4th platoon reported contact with an enemy force in bunkers
3	March 3 1969	**YB 822033**	A reported contact with enemy in bunkers
4	March 3 1969	**YB 822034**	Company A's 1st and 4th platoons found 1 NVA who had been killed in action and 2 AK-47s
5	March 3 1969	**YB 846024**	Reconnaissance platoon Trace 5 operation in liaison with Company A sighted 4 or 5 NVA near their night location
6	March 4 1969	**YB 825042**	Company A moved to new patrol base
7	March 5 1969	**YB 819016**	Company A's 83B initiated ambush resulting in 2 NVA killed.
8	March 5 1969	**YB 813022**	Ambush 83C initiated an ambush at 2005 hours resulting in one NVA killed and two U.S. WIA.
9	March 5 1969	**YB 819016**	Fire Support Base 20 105-mm fired reconnaissance by fire for Company A at 0905 hours
10	March 6 1969	**YB 819027**	Company A experienced incoming from a 105-mm howitzer
11	March 7 1969	**YB 819024**	Two NVA were sighted near Company A's CP location. They were taken under fire with negative results
12	March 8 1969	**YB 853025**	Company A operated out of this patrol base
13	March 9 1969	**YB 826028**	A conducted a bomb damage assessment (BDA) from their night location returned to the night location
14	March 10 1969	**YB 826028**	Operated from patrol bass utilizing maximum platoon-sized forces and local patrols
15	March 11 1969	**YB 824028**	Night Location then moving to this location to **YB 870984** for BDA
16	March 12 1969	**YB 852003**	Heavy contact was encountered by Company A Results of action were 22 NVA KIA, U.S. casualties 2 KIA, 15 WIA and 3 MIA. Location AAR and National Archives
16a	March 12 1969	**YB 844009**	NVA spotted headed into the woods
16b	March 12 1969	**YB 847005**	Company A moved near Hill 387 elevation 365
17	March 13 1969	**YB 852011**	Company A withdrew to night location to regroup and reorganize
18	March 14 1969	**YB 847003**	Company A and C operating employing one platoon-sized reconnaissance patrol each

436

Event Summary for A-1-8 March 1969

Seq.	Date	Location	Comments
19	March 15 1969	**YB 847003**	Consolidation of two Companies A&C into a Task Force
20	March 16 1969	**YB 817030**	Task Force Alpha (TFA) moving from previous night location to this location
21	March 17 1969	**YB 804034**	TFA moved to Hill #467 establishes patrol base
22	March 18 1969	**YB 804034**	TFA remained at new patrol base Hill #467
23	March 19 1969	**YB 801043**	Company A received one U.S. KIA SSG Harvey Charles Avery and one wounded
24	March 20 1969	**YB 801052**	Company A minus (3rd Platoon) made contact again one U.S. KIA (Harold Johnson), 11 U.S. WIA and 4 NVA KIA
25	March 21 1969	**YB 832081**	Company A conducted airlift from TFA to Fire Support Base 20
26	March 22 1969	**YB 818088**	Company A continued security of Fire Base 20, with local security, patrols and two platoon-sized elements
27	March 23 1969	**YB 819066**	Company A continued security of Fire Base 20, with local security, patrols and two platoon-sized elements
28	March 24 1969	**YB 819066**	Company A continued security of Fire Base 20, with local security, patrols and two platoon-sized elements
29	March 25 1969	**YB 855074**	Company A continued security of Fire Support Base 20 with local security and patrols. They employed platoon-sized ambush
30	March 26 1969	**YB 832081**	Company A lost Daniel Hinkel due to mortar attack on FB 20
31	March 27 1969	**YB 832081**	Company A continued security of Fire Support Base 20 with local security and patrols. They employed platoon-sized ambush
32	March 28 1969	**YB 832081**	Company A minus continued security of Fire Support Base 20
33	March 28 1969	**YB 832089**	The 21 and 24 platoons departed Fire Support Base 27 but did not close Company A minus location. Platoons 21 and 24 linked up at night location vicinity
34	March 29 1969	**YB 832081**	Company A continued security of Fire Support Base 20 with local security and patrols. They employed platoon-sized ambush
35	March 30 1969	**ZA 029937**	Company A moved to Polie Kleng
36	March 31 1969	**BR 023522**	1st Battalion 8th Infantry assumed stand down status

437

A map summary of location of the movements of the A-1-8 are shown below between March 2 to March 20 1969. The A-1-8 combat assaulted into the Plei Trap March 2 and for the first 11 days performed operations near where they landed. On March 12 Company A moved over land to perform a BDA assessment and engaged a large force of NVA at the location shown. On March 16 both Company A and C humped 3-4 km out of the area of the battle of March 12 to a new location YB804034 near Hill 467 which was their final destination. From March 17 to March 21 Company A operated as part of Task Force Alpha out of the FB established at Hill 467. On March 21 Company A was airlifted to FB 20 north of Hill 467 approximately 5-6 km.

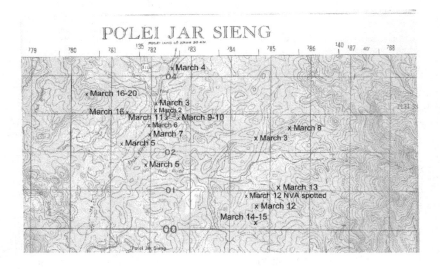

438

The locations of the A-1-8 from March 19 to March 31 are shown on the following map which includes the map area for FB 20. The cross reference number to the table of events is shown before the location.

From March 21 to March 30 Company performed security and platoon sized ambush as well as short range reconnaissance mission on and around FB 20 and FB 27.

On March 30 Company A was airlifted to Polei Kleng.

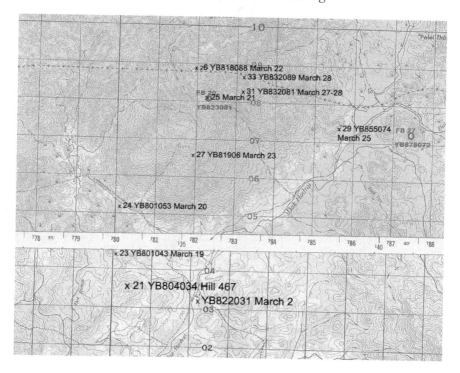

Lt. Andrew LePeilbet's Diary

2 March 69 – Combat Assault from into Plei Trap Valley to First Firefight 1700 hrs. Sgt. Machado wounded

3 March 69 – Contact in same area. PFC Cheek wounded by MG – killed 2 NVA for sure Sniper fire. 1st Platoon.

4 & 5 March 69 – 3rd Platoon – SFC White's contact – killed five NVA in 2 days.

6 March 69 – Finally we are resupplied – received Mortar and 105 mm Artillery incoming on LZ Turkey from NVA. Hot Day.

7 March 69 – Sgt. Lestock left today for his early out.

7 March 69 – PLT. Sgt. Horton, 1st SQ, SP/4 Stone, 2nd SQ SP/4 Selden, 3rd SQ. SP/4 Rawls – Chain of command.

Afternoon – 2 NVA approached Lima position – both got away. Two hours later – 2 more NVA came - were fired at and got away. All night Arc-Lights went in to our east.

8 March 69 – Resupply while we were humping – First day no one was fired upon in our unit.

9 March 69 – Bomb Assessment – 0845 Change of mission – move west fast. First clean socks I have had since 29 Jan 69 – Platoon size ambush

9 March – Received letter from Anne, 2 Mar 69. Beer & Soda. Arc lights to our east & west. No contact.

10 Sunday, March 69 – Still on Ambush – Very hot day – Wrote 4 letters Shaved 1st time in five days. It will break Anne's heart when I don't show up today.

11 March 69 – Returned from ambush 0715 hours – airstrikes going in to our southeast all morning humping east again – C Company one man wounded just ahead of us – Rostafin sent in because of injured knee. Moved 3 kilometers and set up for the night.

12 March 69 – My platoon is point for the Company. Just after passing checkpoint, four (4 KM from mornings start) at 1130 hours, we came onto enemy bunkers. The firefight started. 1200 Hours I was wounded by an enemy frag grenade. SFC White, SGT Horton, SP/4 Pearce, and PFC Summerlin wounded by recoilless rifle. We fought our way back to the company. Everyone evacuated but me and couple walking wounded. I still can't walk.

13 March 69 – 1000 hours (22 hours after I was wounded) They evacuated me and the remaining wounded. By afternoon I was in 71st EVAC Hospital in Pleiku.

14 March 69 –

18 March 69 – Released from Hospital.

20 March 69 – Having tailored suit made for $65.00
Reports of A Company in heavy contact – Stone, Petree, and Rostifin wounded in action from my platoon.

21 March 69 – 0530 Hours – Rocket and mortar attack on Camp ENARI. I am in Camp ENARI.

A Special Thanks to my Friend Mike Rinehart

Thanks Mike for saving my life 37 years ago.

Index

About the Author

Jerry Horton was born in Charleston, W.Va. September 6, 1947. As he grew up, his Dad encouraged him to become an engineer. In pursuit of this boyhood dream he attended one year of college and then ran out of money. He entered the Army October 1967 with the idea of later attending college under the G.I. Bill. While in the service he became an infantry squad leader and served in Vietnam in 1968 and was wounded March 12, 1969, and then spent six months assigned to Walter Reed Hospital. While at Walter Reed he received the Purple Heart for the wounds he suffered.

Joining the Army and going to war was a hard way to earn an education, but he made the most of it. Jerry was awarded an engineering degree in 1972 and has been a lifelong student earning a Ph.D. in Electrical Engineering, MBA and MSEE and BSEE. He has been a leader in his field in electrical engineering and President and Founder of Engineering Software Associates, a leader in Educational Classroom Software for colleges and universities.

In 1999 Jerry began a journey into his past, uncovering what happened 31 years ago. He began by connecting to soldiers he served with. It was a long tedious process contacting his comrades from 30 years ago but in time his efforts paid off. Now each year well over forty of his A-1-8 infantrymen comrades meet each year to celebrate life and remember the past. Many have become close friends and most have had similar life experiences in the world.

As part of his journey to the past, Jerry researched and wrote this book with the help of many of his A-1-8 friends. During his research he found that he and six other soldiers were awarded medals thirty years ago but never received them. On a parade field at Ft. Carson, Colorado in year 2000 and in front of 500 soldiers from the Army's 4th Division Jerry and his buddies were presented their medals in an official ceremony. Jerry received two Silver Stars. On that day, "it was a wonderful ceremony," said Horton. "The General of the Army's 4th Division pinned medals on the seven of us. It was a surreal event as we all remembered those times from so long ago."

Jerry now resides in Sarasota, Florida and is married. He has one son, one daughter, one step daughter and four grandchildren.

Where they are now

Mike Rinehart

Mike left active duty in 1971 and continued flying with the Tennessee National Guard. He now works as the Corporate Director of Safety and Risk Management for North American Midway Entertainment and lives together with Betty, his wife of 46 years and a schoolteacher, in Tallahassee, Florida. They had two children, Brandy and Sean and a granddaughter, Parker. Mike passed away February 2015.

Ken McCormack

Ken McCormack lives in Spring Valley California with his wife Patty, the same Patty that he married one month before being drafted and sent to Vietnam. High school sweethearts, married at 19. Ken became an Auctioneer and with his wife owns and operates McCormack Auction Co. in San Diego. They have two grown sons Jeremy and Josh.

Andrew Lepeilbet

Andy was a successful entrepreneur and owned his own company in Reno. Formally he was a senior executive of a large international company. Andy is now involved with Real Estate and Business Brokering and consulting. For his bravery 40 years ago Andrew was awarded the Distinguished Service Cross.

Don White

Don lives in Oklahoma City, Oklahoma and retired after twenty years in the Army. He and his wife Hope have three children and five grandchildren and they both are successful in real estate. Don is an avid outdoorsman and likes to both hunt and fish. Don was a decorated with a Silver Star and Purple Heart for his bravery in Vietnam. Don is the author of a great book called "No Body Armor" published in 2013.

Carey "The Flea" Pearce

Randy Pearce "The Flea" Randy lives in Dover Tennessee. He is married to Reba Mayall and has two children, Marvin and Cari, and three stepchildren, Deanna Joy, Michael Lee and Wayne Robert. Randy was decorated in Vietnam with a Silver Star and Purple Heart. Randy wrote my last letter home at my hospital bed - thank you Randy.

Paul "Airborne" Summerlin

He lived in Mulberry., Florida. .He was married to Gwendolyn, he had a daughter named Amber Crystal, son named Paul Jr. Paul worked for Florida Tile for 16 years. He was awarded the Silver Star for heroism for his actions on March 12, 1969. Paul passed away in 2007, his last battle was Leukemia thought to be from Agent Orange in Vietnam

John Andrews

John lives in Sewell New Jersey and is the vice president of a small spring manufacturing company. He is married to Claire and has two sons. John has been involved in youth ice hockey and is the president of the South Jersey High School Hockey League.

Dr. Charles T. Porter

Charles T. Porter, Jr. "Tom" The youngest Lieutenant in the Army since the Korean War. After release from active duty in 1971, he finished college under the GI Bill at the Citadel in Charleston, South Carolina. He served as a medical officer aboard the USS Kitty Hawk CV-63 and an Anesthesiologist in the Navy for 15 years, retiring in 1989 with the rank of Commander. He is married to Karen and they live in Galveston, Texas.

Greg Rollinger

Greg Rollinger "Rollie" Greg lives in Inver Grove Heights Minnesota. He was a software support manager for Honeywell and Groupe Bull of France. He is married to Dee and has three children; Greg, Amy and Chris; plus 4 grandchildren, Ashley, Tony, Jordan and Nicholas.

Robert "Pappy" Rawls

Robert Rawls "Pappy" Pappy lives in Jacksonville Arkansas and is married to April. He has three girls and two grandchildren children. Pappy retired from the Army.

John Campbell

John lives in Central Point Oregon and is married to Pamela. He worked as a logger. He likes to fish and hunt and is an outdoorsman.

Don Cheek

Don lives in Litchfield Arizona and has been a teacher for 30 years. He is now retired. In his years as a teacher he would also lecture his students on Vietnam on anniversary of the day he got shoot, March 3, 1969. He is also a musician having played in a band part time for many years.

Chris Krukow

Chris lived in Pine River, Minnesota. He passed away in 2013. He was a logger and an outdoorsman living on 300 acres of beautiful Minnesota north words. He was married to Sheila and has two children.

Randolph Chrietzberg "LRP"

Randolph T. Chrietzberg "LRP" Randy lives in Rescue, California with his wife Nancy. Randy has 3 children, Nancy has 2 and together they have 7 grandchildren. Randy was a line driver for Consolidated Freight lines. Randy is retired from the Teamsters Union.

Gary "Country" Feldman

Country owns a large farm in Illinois City Illinois and has spent the last 40 years as a farmer. He is married and has two sons.

George "Barry" Adornetto

Barry lives in New Jersey and is a retired roofing contractor. He has one grandchild and he and his wife, Maria, like to travel.

David Muck

David Muck lives in Sterling Heights Michigan where he is married to Sandy and has three kids and one grandchild. He is retired from a career as a Plant Manager.

Richard "Spider" Meli

Richard Meli "Spider" Spider lives in Staten Island New York. He was a licensed captain, and ran a tugboat and worked on the docks of New York. He is quite the entertainer and is good at playing and singing the old country western favorites – the really old ones.

David Hockett

David Hockett retired from US Army and currently resides in Fayetteville, Georgia with his 2nd wife Patricia Between them they have 6 children, 23 grandchildren and 12 great grandchildren.

Marc Lawrence

Marc Lawrence now lives in Houston, Texas with his wife of 34 years, Karen. After Vietnam, Marc received his BS and MS in Geology from the University of Florida and traveled the world in his chosen profession, even returning to Vietnam 5 times on business. Now semi-retired, they rescue Australian Cattle Dogs (Blue Heelers) which is a full time occupation in itself!

John Seim

John Seim lives in Alexandria, MN with his wife Carol with whom he has been going steady since 1964 and was engaged to when he was in RVN. Now retired, he was a mechanical engineer at Gresen Dana Corp for 7 yrs and taught Fluid Power/Automation at Alexandria Tech College for 30 yrs. He spends most of his time hunting and fishing.

Jerry T. Loucks

Jerry Horton and Jerry Loucks year 2000

March 12, 2000 we lost one of our true heroes, Jerry T. Loucks Jr. He passed away on a Sunday night 31 years after saving many lives in the Vietnam War. Jerry was with A/1/8 during 1968 - 1969. For his actions on 3/12/69, he was nominated for a Medal of Honor and was awarded a Distinguished Service Cross. As a then SP4, he took over the leadership of 3rd and 4th platoons after our officers and senior NCOs were wounded and unable to lead. With his leadership, we were able to fight our way out of an ambush sprung by a NVA Regiment in the Plei Trap Valley of Vietnam and link back up with the rest of the company, bringing all of our wounded with us. He was a brave soldier, a good friend and a true hero. We all will miss him very much.

Jerry T. Loucks Awarded the Distinguished Service Cross

From National Archives, Washington, D.C.

Specialist Fourth Class Jerry T. Loucks distinguished himself on 12 March, 1969, while serving as a rifleman with Alpha Company 1st Battalion, 8th Infantry, 4th Infantry Division in the Plei Trap Valley in the Central Highlands Republic of Vietnam.

The Fourth Platoon was the lead element for Alpha Company while on a bomb-assessment mission near the Cambodian border, west of the Polei Kleng Special Forces Camp, at approximately 1130 hours, the platoon encountered an enemy bunker complex. The complex was well-constructed and visual surveillance for entrances proved fruitless. The Platoon leader ordered one squad to maneuver left and search the complex and the remaining squads to cover their right and left flanks. Suddenly a devastating barrage of small arms, automatic weapons and M-79 grenade fire penetrated the friendly ranks, inflicting heavy casualties, disabling the command element and pinning the platoon in place. The Third Platoon was immediately dispatched to reinforce the stricken platoon. Upon arrival, fire and maneuver was employed to eliminate the bunkers which had the Fourth Platoon pinned, resulting in crippling injuries to the Third Platoon Leader. Specialist Loucks immediately assumed command, organized a fire team, and engaged the complex once again. An NVA soldier appeared from the bunker and assaulted the fire team, firing rapid bursts from his automatic weapon, wounding Specialist Loucks in the face. Despite the mortal danger and with complete disregard for his wounds, Specialist Loucks eliminated the insurgent and led the fire team on to destroy the fortifications, and then returned to the friendly perimeter under intense fire. The platoons were ordered to pull back to the Company's main element which was located approximately 100 meters from the point of contact. Specialist Loucks unhesitatingly began organizing the move by organizing the platoon as one and supervising the construction of litters for the wounded. Meter by meter the platoon began maneuvering down the slope, immediately encountering enemy resistance from all sides. Continually exposing himself, Specialist Loucks passed through the hail of fire from man to man directing their suppressive fire. While placing ruck-sacks around the wounded for protective cover. Specialist Loucks was again wounded. Suffering and exhausted, he refused medical aid for himself and continued to carry out his mission which resulted in temporarily silencing the enemy. Soon afterwards, the enemy force launched an all-out assault in an attempt to overrun the beleaguered platoon. Specialist Loucks persistently checked the makeshift perimeter, evacuated the wounded, and insured the perimeter was kept tight by physically re-positioning the platoon members. A long vicious fight ensued, resulting in numerous enemy casualties and abortion of the assault. The platoon was continually harassed by snipers and small-scale assaults throughout the remainder of the move. Specialist Loucks continued to display exceptional leadership, ingenuity and pure determination. Upon reaching the main element, he insured that correct tactical posture was maintained by placing his men in defensive positions, and then prepared the wounded for evacuation. He again refused medical attention for himself until a member of his platoon was aided. During the six hours of continuous combat, Specialist Loucks demonstrated numerous selfless acts of valor, instilling confidence and a willingness to fight within the platoon as he performed. His exemplary actions under hostile fire are in keeping with the highest and most cherished military traditions, and reflect great credit upon himself, his unit, and the UNITED STATES ARMY.

Eyewitness Lt. Andrew Lepeilbet

From National Archives, Washington, D.C.

On 12 March 1969, my platoon (4th Platoon) was walking point for our Company, (Alpha Company, 1st Bn, 8th Inf. 4th Inf Div.). We were on a bomb-damage assessment mission in the Plei Trap Valley near the Cambodian border, west of the Polei Kleng Special Forces Camp. At approximately 1130 hours that day, we discovered some enemy bunkers next to a large B-52 Bomb crater. The bunkers were well-constructed, and visual surveillance for entrances proved fruitless. As Platoon Leader for the 4th platoon I had one squad maneuver left to search the bunker complex, and my remaining squads cover their right and left flank. At this time, we started receiving periodic small arms fire from both the bunkers to our front and from areas to our flank. As we started to take the first bunker, both myself and PSGT White, Platoon Leader for the 3rd Platoon, were seriously wounded by grenade fragmentation's and B-40 fragmentation respectively. With the Platoon Leader of the 3rd Platoon badly wounded, I took charge of both platoons and integrated them as one. I then told Sergeant Woodall of the 3rd Platoon to keep trying to take the first bunker, while the medics were caring for the wounded. The Company Commander called me and said we would have to come back to his location to get the wounded out. There was 200 meters between us; and the enemy was also between us. I was quite able

to issue instructions, but was unable to supervise, so SP/4 Loucks of the 3rd Platoon did the supervising of both platoons. The enemy fire was increasing at this time. Many things SP/4 Loucks checked and did on his own, like constantly making sure the perimeter we had formed was secure and tight. We organized the moving of the wounded. While checking the forward line he received a wound in the face. He killed the enemy who fired the shot. Paying no attention to his wound, he continued to perform his duties. He was constantly on his feet running from man to man, placing each and every individual where he wanted him.

We moved the wounded to the rear of the perimeter and fought to push the perimeter to the company's location. We continued this moving the perimeter and then the wounded till we got within 50 yards of the Company, at which point the Company Commander sent one platoon to give us a hand. The move took about 2 hours, and SP/4 Loucks supervised the entire period. Once inside the perimeter, I placed my platoon and the 3rd Platoon into position, but not without the un-exhausting aid of SP/4 Loucks. SP/4 Loucks, under constant and sometimes heavy enemy fire, supervised and moved as an experienced and seasoned leader two infantry platoons for 200 meters to rejoin their Company, and did so with the enemy between the Company and us. His acts of valor and superb leadership inspired our men and instilled confidence and courage within the ranks. He performed his duty in a superior manner, and often, at the risk of his own life.

Andrew R. LePeilbet 1LT, Infantry   Commanding Officer

Eyewitness Ron Westbrook

From National Archives, Washington, D.C.

On this day (12 March 69) our company (Co. A, 1st Bn, 8th Inf, 4th Inf Div) came across an NVA bunker complex (in the Plei Trap Valley area, just west of Polei Kleng Special Forces Camp), and also an unknown size NVA force. All hell broke loose. Our point elements SP/4 Kaiser, PFC Summerlin, 1st LT LePeilbet, and SP/4 Pearce came under intense fire from these bunkers. 1LT LePeilbet got hit by grenade fragments. Then PSGT White and Sgt. Horton attempted to maneuver on the bunker with these men (PFC Summerlin, SP/4 Pearce). They almost reached the bunker, when a recoilless rifle went off wounding SP/4 Pearce, PSGT White, Sgt. Horton, and PFC Summerlin.

Since all our leaders were wounded, SP/4 Jerry Loucks took complete command. He and Sgt. Woodall maneuvered on the (same) bunker alone. SP/4 Loucks had received fragments before this, and refused medical aid. He moved up behind the bunker, and Sgt. Woodall came up on the (right) flank. A NVA started firing out of the rear of the bunker at SP/4 Loucks, wounding him in the face. While he (Loucks) sprayed the bunker (killing the NVA), Sgt. Woodall dropped a grenade down into it.

459

After all the bunkers were silenced, SP/4 Loucks took complete command, while still refusing medical aid. The NVA had split our forces from our main element, and SP/4 Loucks moved our two platoons to keep us from being wiped out. Whenever he would receive fire, SP/4 Loucks would immediately go to that area, and direct counter fire until the enemy was silenced. He directed the movement of the wounded, and also directed the movement of the two platoons back to the main force of our company. He continued to direct fire, distribute ammo, and help the wounded. He would run across open areas through intense machinegun fire to help people. Whenever some of our people were pinned down by the NVA, SP/4 Loucks would quickly silence the enemy.

When our two platoons rejoined the Company, SP/4 Loucks then had his wounds bandaged. When the dust-off came in, he refused to go. He had to stay and help the men. During the 6 hours of continuous fighting, SP/4 Loucks personally silenced one enemy bunker, and was wounded twice, and yet refused medical aid. He took command and saved our platoons, and I believe by his direction, the whole company. He took care of moving the wounded.

The man did an outstanding job. Without SP/4 Loucks the Company would have been overrun.

S/ Ron Westbrook   PFC   Infantry

Eyewitness John Seim

From National Archives, Washington, D.C.

Sergeant Woodall, Sergeant Muck, and SP/4 Loucks moved up on the same bunker PSGT White and several other men unsuccessfully had tried to take earlier. They started receiving fire from it, and SP/4 Loucks was hit in the face. He then killed the NVA, while Sergeant Woodall dropped a frag in the bunker and blew it up.

SP/4 Loucks organized the two platoons into a perimeter, had the wounded moved into the center, had litters made, and kept everyone calmed and reassured. He crawled out in front of the platoon (nearest the bunker complex) and directed these men to fall back towards the wounded, so that they wouldn't be hit by enemy fire, during the period when a sniper had us pinned down.

SP/4 Loucks would move the front of the perimeter closer to the rest of Alpha Company, then go to the rear of the element and bring them forward. Again he would move to the front of our perimeter, and advance us a little further. He directed our fire on the enemy, and kept the 3rd and 4th Platoons together during the withdrawal.

SP4 Loucks saved lots of lives at the risk of his own, and this day of 12 March 1969 will always be remembered by the men of our platoon and myself.

John K. Seim   PFC, Infantry

CPSIA information can be obtained
at www.ICGtesting.com
Printed in the USA
LVHW081430280419
615851LV00012B/419/P